SPICE & WOLF

Lawrence

A traveling merchant. He encountered Holo the wolf-girl in the village of Pasloe, and the two now travel together.

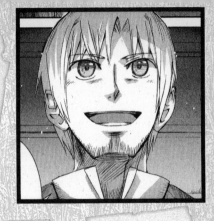

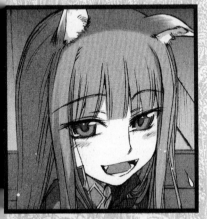

Holo

Once worshipped in the village of Pasloe as the wolf-god of the harvest, Holo hides centuries of wisdom behind her childlike face.

Zheren

A young merchant who brought a unique opportunity for profit to Lawrence's attention.

Yarei

A peasant of the village of Pasloe. He was the village's agent in the days when Lawrence traded wheat.

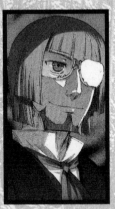

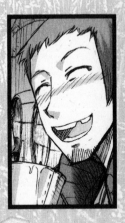

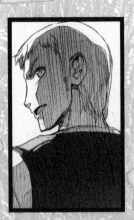

Marheit

The branch chief of the Milone Company's Pazzio office. He commands both significant respect and considerable resources.

Overview

It is an era of growth, with the expansion of new farming techniques that replace the old prayers to the gods.

Lawrence, a traveling merchant, has agreed to accompany Holo the wolf-girl north to her homelands—Holo, who claims to be Pasloe's harvest god.

On the way, the pair happen to seek refuge in a church, where a young merchant named Zheren tells them of an opportunity to profit from the changing purity of a particular silver coin—but Lawrence soon realizes that behind this opportunity lies a shocking plot...

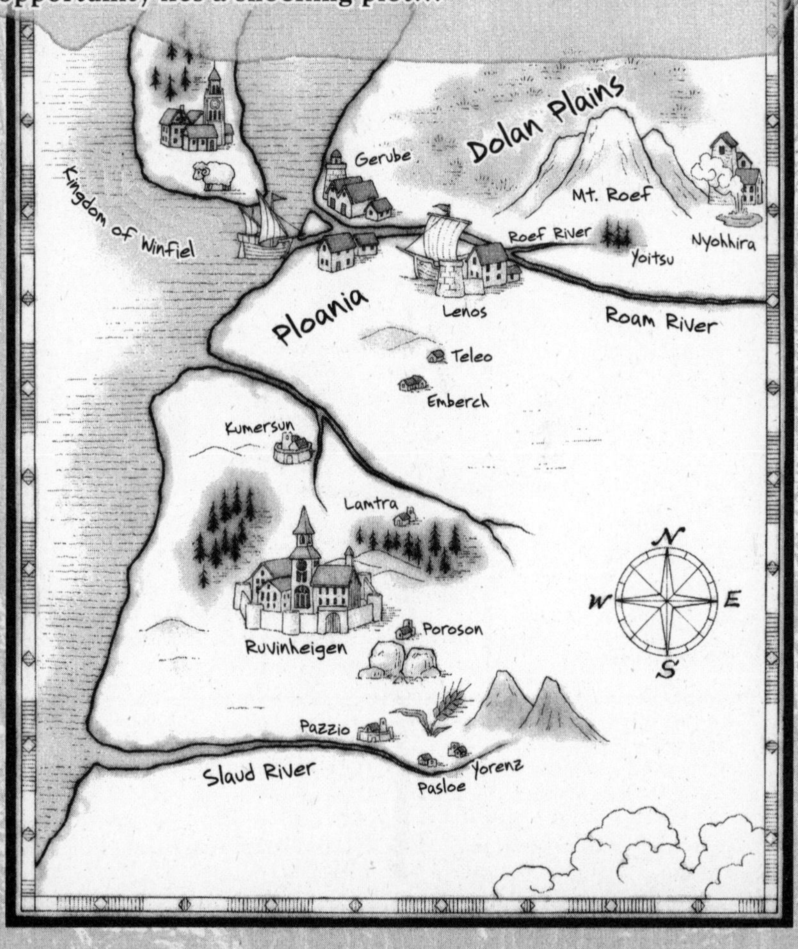

Dolan Plains
Gerube
Kingdom of Winfiel
Mt. Roef
Roef River
Yoitsu
Nyohhira
Ploania
Lenos
Roam River
Teleo
Emberch
Kumersun
Lamtra
N
W
E
S
Poroson
Ruvinheigen
Pazzio
Slaud River
Yorenz
Pasloe

Map Illustration: Hidetada Idemitsu

SPICE & WOLF

CONTENTS

Lumione Gold

One can live off a single piece of lumione gold for three months. It's generally worth between thirty-three and thirty-five pieces of trenni silver.

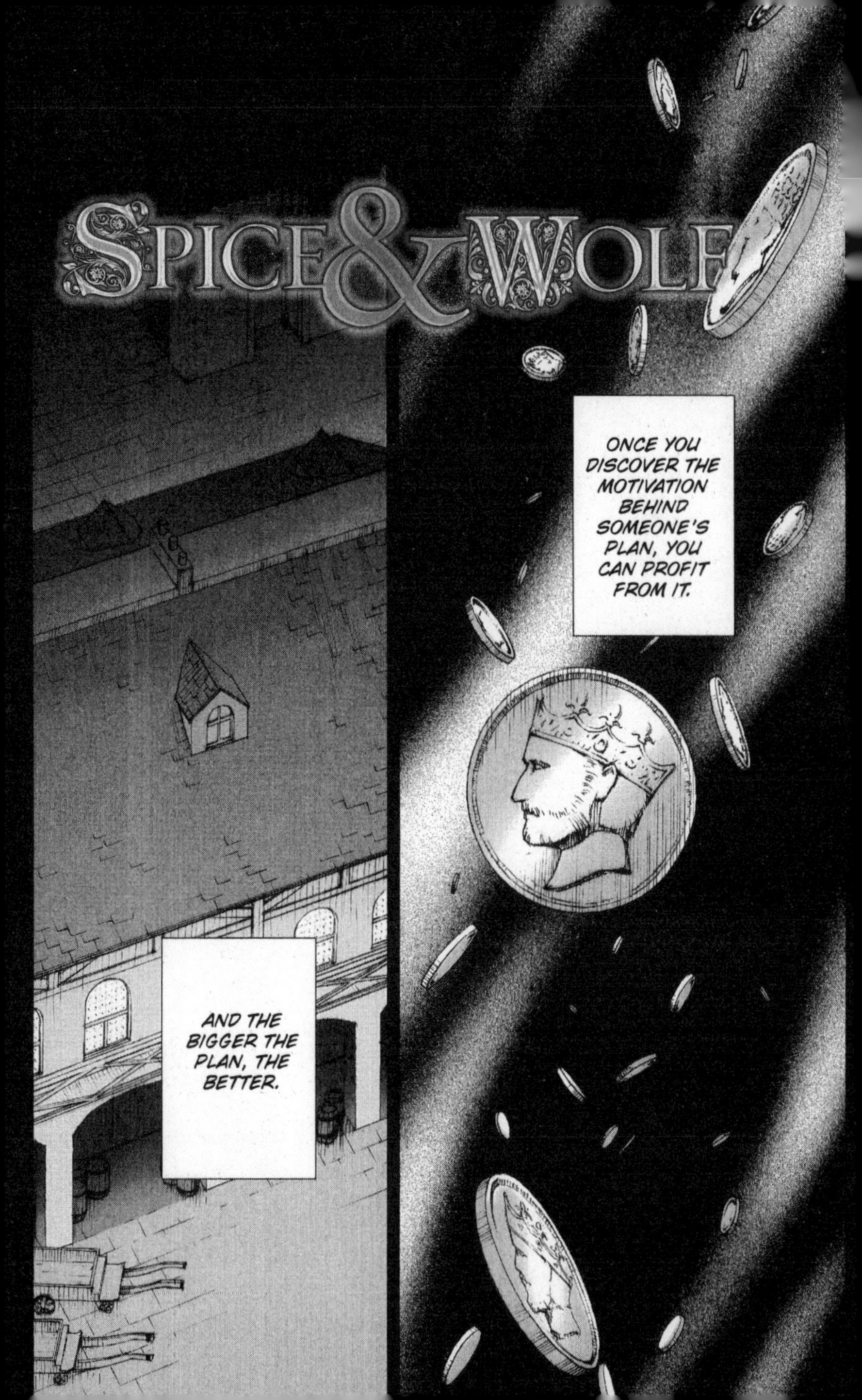
SPICE & WOLF
ONCE YOU DISCOVER THE MOTIVATION BEHIND SOMEONE'S PLAN, YOU CAN PROFIT FROM IT.
AND THE BIGGER THE PLAN, THE BETTER.

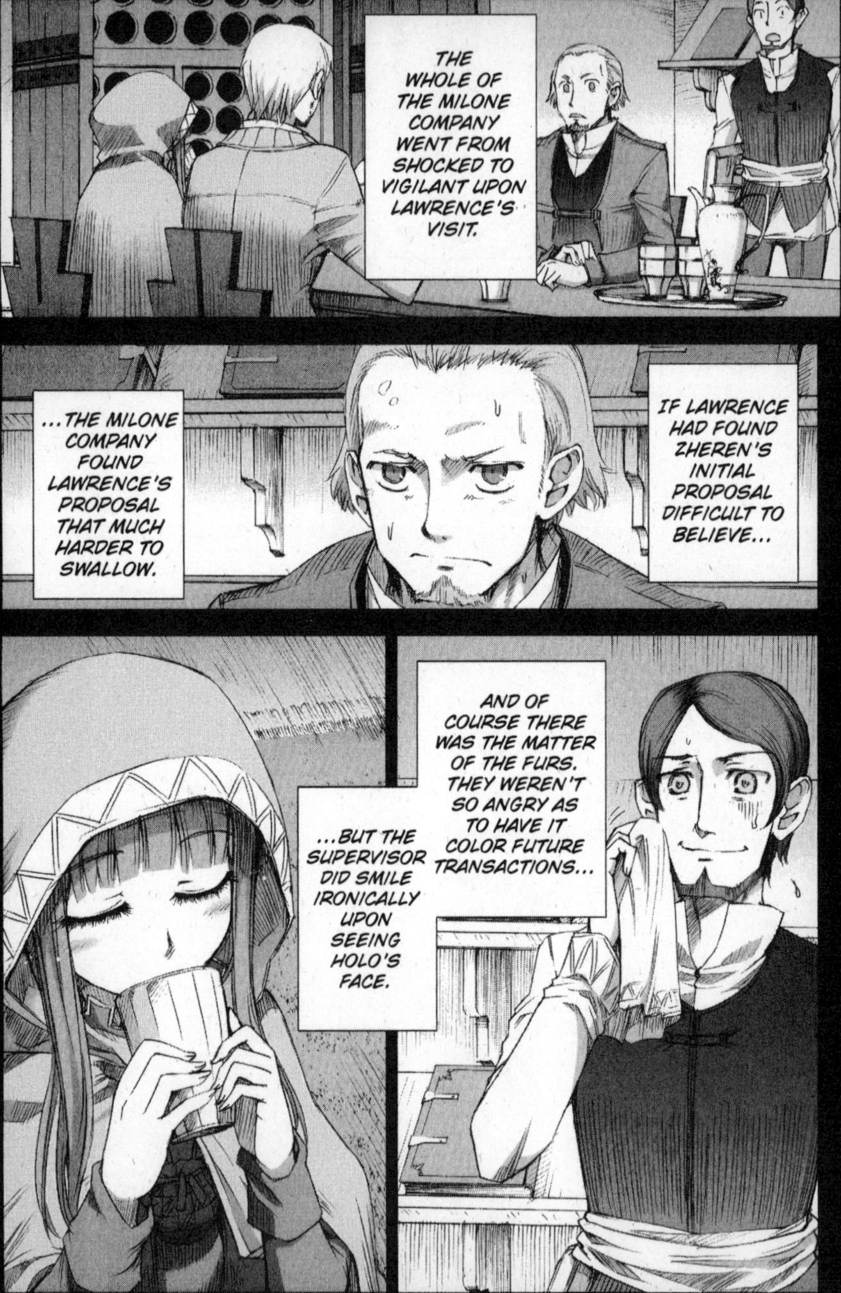
THE WHOLE OF THE MILONE COMPANY WENT FROM SHOCKED TO VIGILANT UPON LAWRENCE'S VISIT.
IF LAWRENCE HAD FOUND ZHEREN'S INITIAL PROPOSAL DIFFICULT TO BELIEVE...
...THE MILONE COMPANY FOUND LAWRENCE'S PROPOSAL THAT MUCH HARDER TO SWALLOW.
AND OF COURSE THERE WAS THE MATTER OF THE FURS. THEY WEREN'T SO ANGRY AS TO HAVE IT COLOR FUTURE TRANSACTIONS...
...BUT THE SUPERVISOR DID SMILE IRONICALLY UPON SEEING HOLO'S FACE.

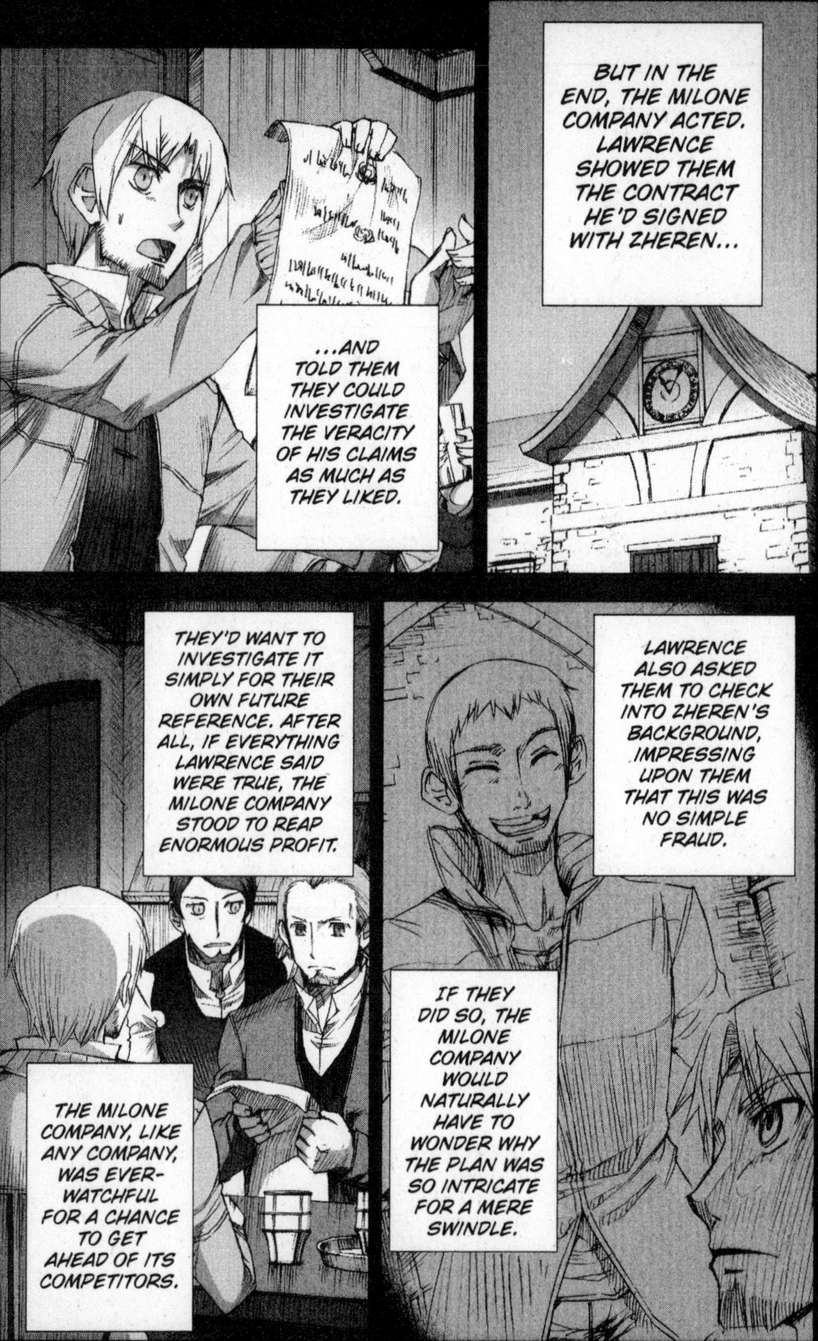
BUT IN THE END, THE MILONE COMPANY ACTED. LAWRENCE SHOWED THEM THE CONTRACT HE'D SIGNED WITH ZHEREN...
...AND TOLD THEM THEY COULD INVESTIGATE THE VERACITY OF HIS CLAIMS AS MUCH AS THEY LIKED.
LAWRENCE ALSO ASKED THEM TO CHECK INTO ZHEREN'S BACKGROUND, IMPRESSING UPON THEM THAT THIS WAS NO SIMPLE FRAUD.
IF THEY DID SO, THE MILONE COMPANY WOULD NATURALLY HAVE TO WONDER WHY THE PLAN WAS SO INTRICATE FOR A MERE SWINDLE.
THEY'D WANT TO INVESTIGATE IT SIMPLY FOR THEIR OWN FUTURE REFERENCE. AFTER ALL, IF EVERYTHING LAWRENCE SAID WERE TRUE, THE MILONE COMPANY STOOD TO REAP ENORMOUS PROFIT.
THE MILONE COMPANY, LIKE ANY COMPANY, WAS EVER-WATCHFUL FOR A CHANCE TO GET AHEAD OF ITS COMPETITORS.

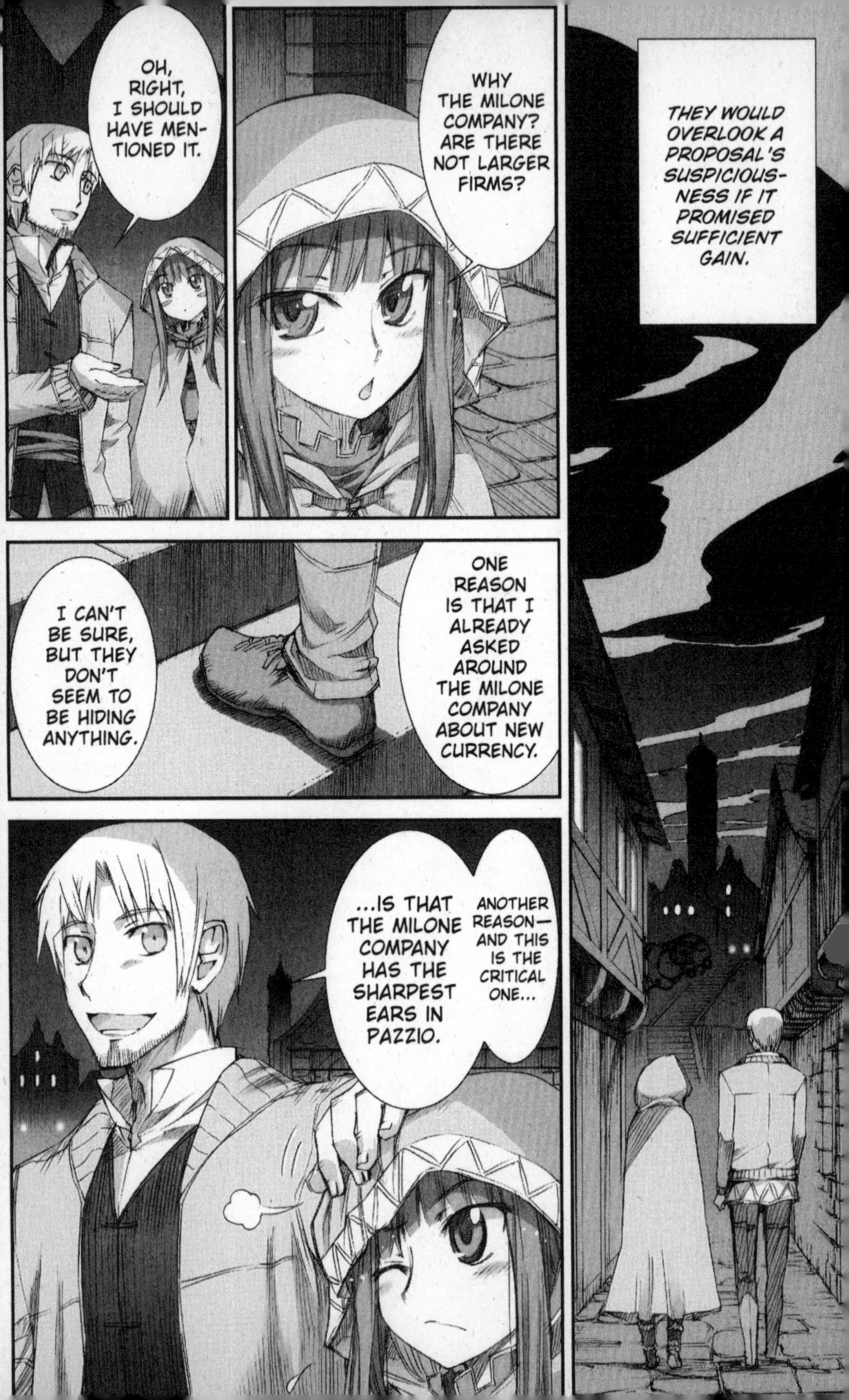
THEY WOULD OVERLOOK A PROPOSAL'S SUSPICIOUSNESS IF IT PROMISED SUFFICIENT GAIN.
WHY THE MILONE COMPANY? ARE THERE NOT LARGER FIRMS?
OH, RIGHT, I SHOULD HAVE MENTIONED IT.
ONE REASON IS THAT I ALREADY ASKED AROUND THE MILONE COMPANY ABOUT NEW CURRENCY.
I CAN'T BE SURE, BUT THEY DON'T SEEM TO BE HIDING ANYTHING.
ANOTHER REASON—AND THIS IS THE CRITICAL ONE...
...IS THAT THE MILONE COMPANY HAS THE SHARPEST EARS IN PAZZIO.

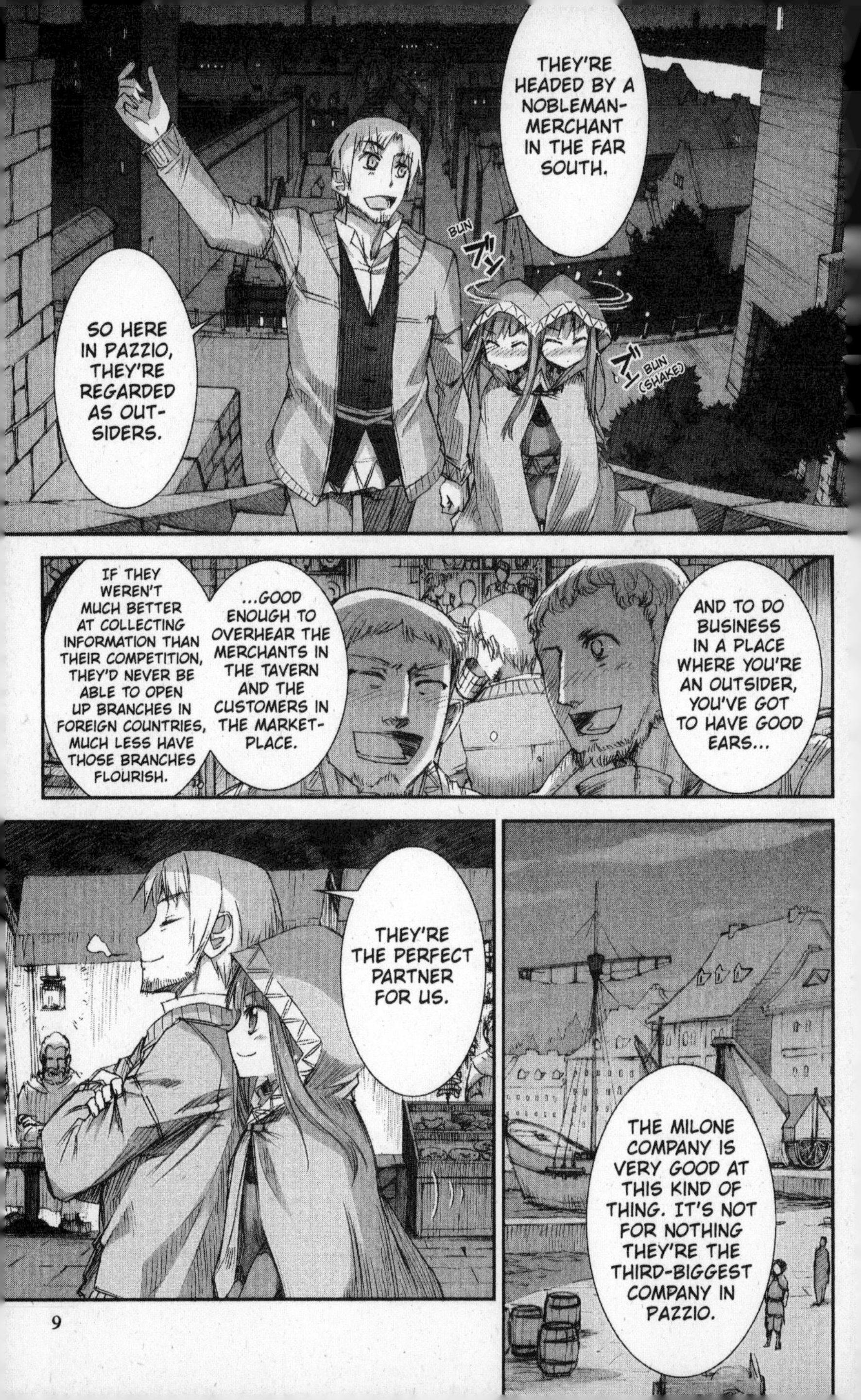
THEY'RE HEADED BY A NOBLEMAN-MERCHANT IN THE FAR SOUTH.
BUN
BUN (SHAKE)
SO HERE IN PAZZIO, THEY'RE REGARDED AS OUT-SIDERS.
AND TO DO BUSINESS IN A PLACE WHERE YOU'RE AN OUTSIDER, YOU'VE GOT TO HAVE GOOD EARS...
...GOOD ENOUGH TO OVERHEAR THE MERCHANTS IN THE TAVERN AND THE CUSTOMERS IN THE MARKET-PLACE.
IF THEY WEREN'T MUCH BETTER AT COLLECTING INFORMATION THAN THEIR COMPETITION, THEY'D NEVER BE ABLE TO OPEN UP BRANCHES IN FOREIGN COUNTRIES, MUCH LESS HAVE THOSE BRANCHES FLOURISH.
THE MILONE COMPANY IS VERY GOOD AT THIS KIND OF THING. IT'S NOT FOR NOTHING THEY'RE THE THIRD-BIGGEST COMPANY IN PAZZIO.
THEY'RE THE PERFECT PARTNER FOR US.

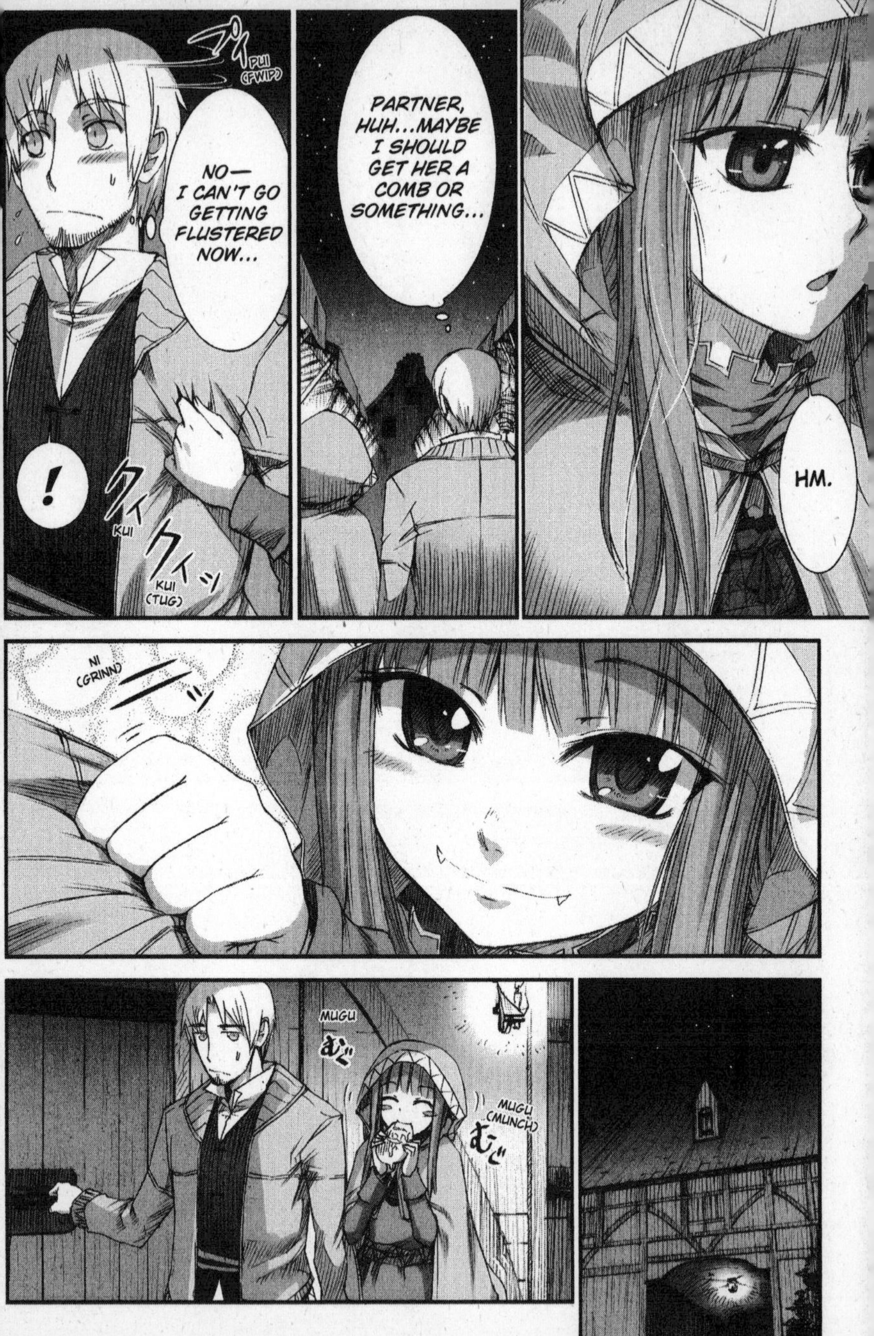
HM.
PARTNER, HUH...MAYBE I SHOULD GET HER A COMB OR SOMETHING...
プイ PUI (FWIP)
NO— I CAN'T GO GETTING FLUSTERED NOW...
!
クイ KUI
クイッ KUI (TUG)
ニッ NI (GRINN)
MUGU むぐ
MUGU (MUNCH) むぐ

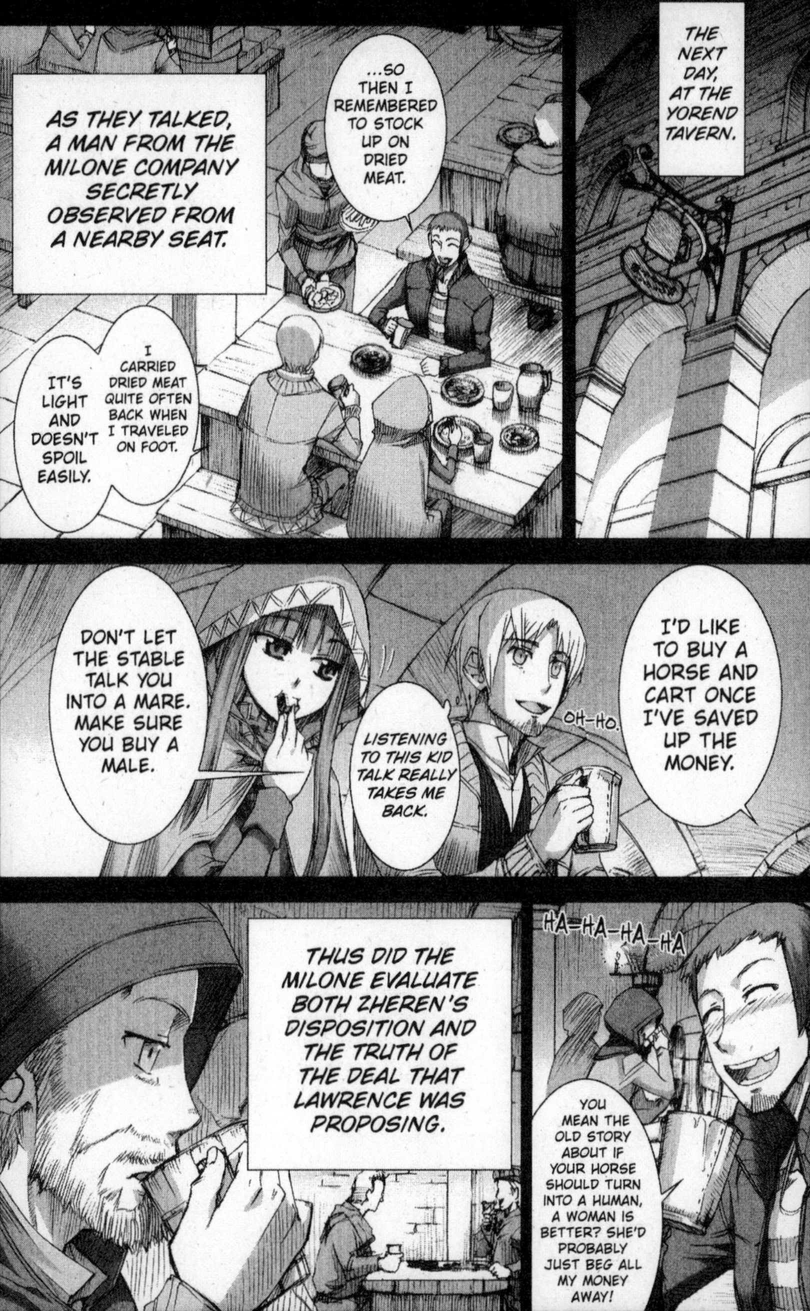
THE NEXT DAY, AT THE YOREND TAVERN.
...SO THEN I REMEMBERED TO STOCK UP ON DRIED MEAT.
AS THEY TALKED, A MAN FROM THE MILONE COMPANY SECRETLY OBSERVED FROM A NEARBY SEAT.
I CARRIED DRIED MEAT QUITE OFTEN BACK WHEN I TRAVELED ON FOOT.
IT'S LIGHT AND DOESN'T SPOIL EASILY.
I'D LIKE TO BUY A HORSE AND CART ONCE I'VE SAVED UP THE MONEY.
OH-HO.
LISTENING TO THIS KID TALK REALLY TAKES ME BACK.
DON'T LET THE STABLE TALK YOU INTO A MARE. MAKE SURE YOU BUY A MALE.
HA-HA-HA-HA
YOU MEAN THE OLD STORY ABOUT IF YOUR HORSE SHOULD TURN INTO A HUMAN, A WOMAN IS BETTER? SHE'D PROBABLY JUST BEG ALL MY MONEY AWAY!
THUS DID THE MILONE EVALUATE BOTH ZHEREN'S DISPOSITION AND THE TRUTH OF THE DEAL THAT LAWRENCE WAS PROPOSING.

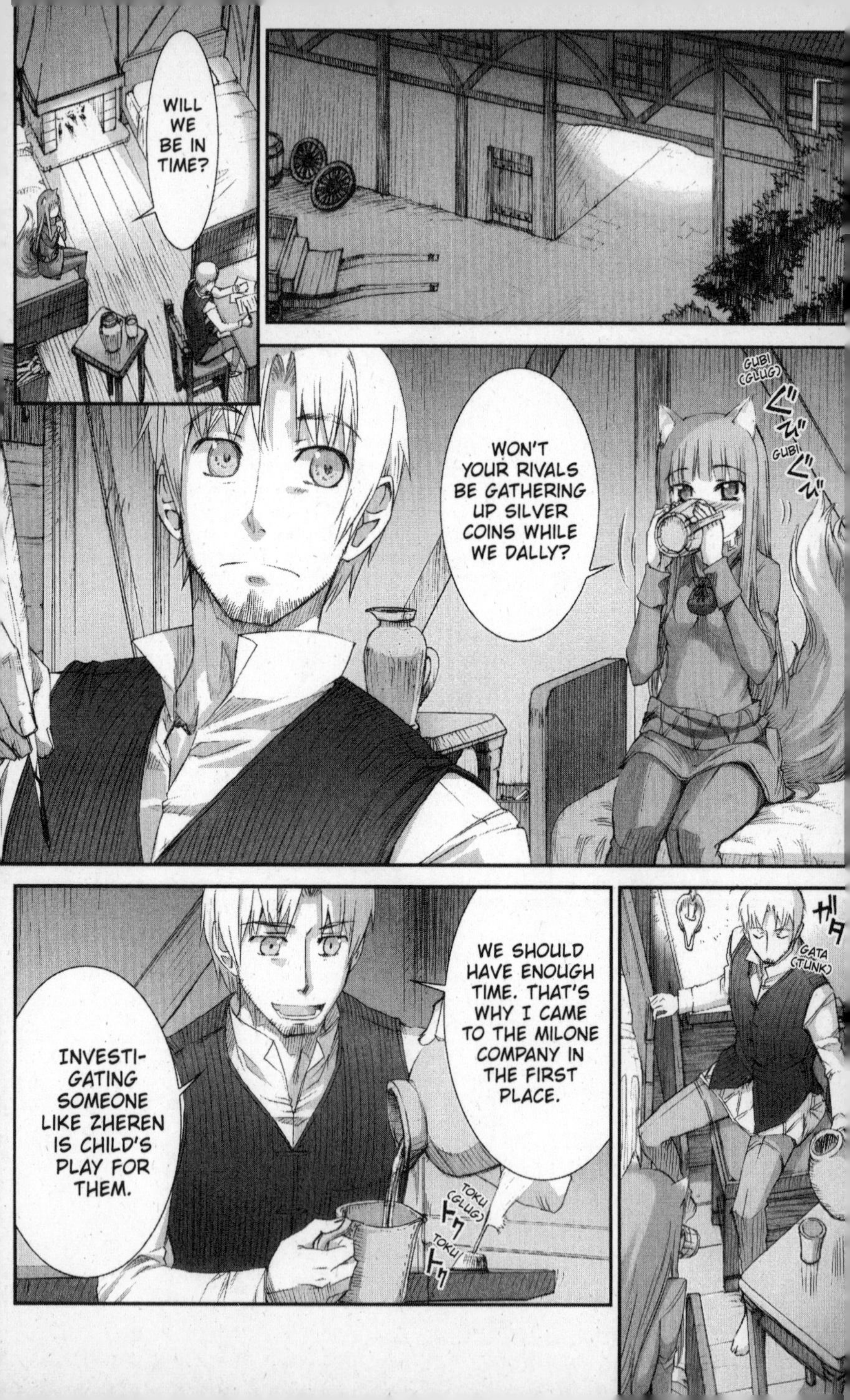
WILL WE BE IN TIME?
GUBI (GLUG) ぐび
GUBI ぐび
WON'T YOUR RIVALS BE GATHERING UP SILVER COINS WHILE WE DALLY?
ガタ GATA (TUNK)
WE SHOULD HAVE ENOUGH TIME. THAT'S WHY I CAME TO THE MILONE COMPANY IN THE FIRST PLACE.
INVESTI-GATING SOMEONE LIKE ZHEREN IS CHILD'S PLAY FOR THEM.
TOKU (GLUG) トク
TOKU トク

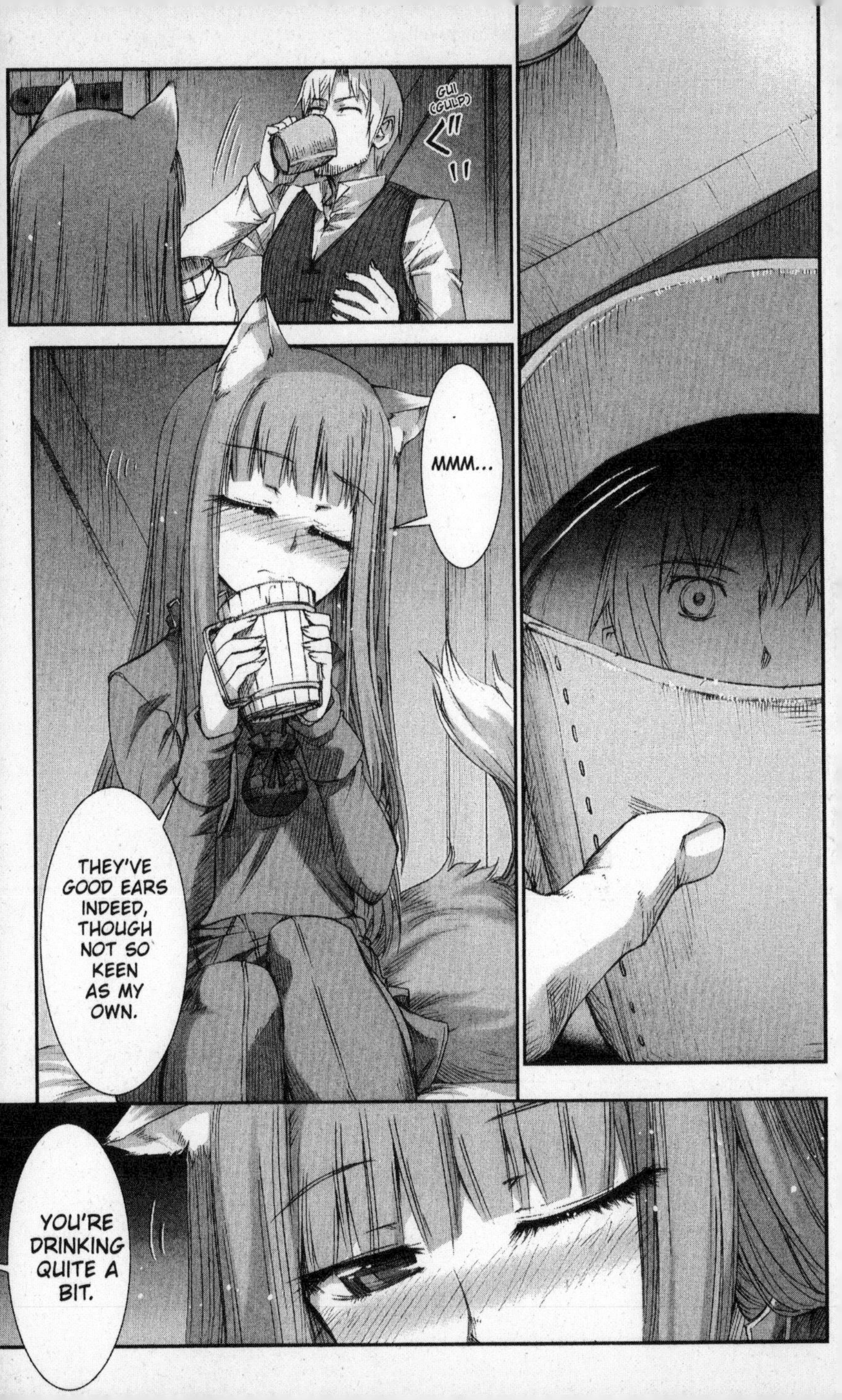
GUI (GULP)
ぐ''
MMM...
THEY'VE GOOD EARS INDEED, THOUGH NOT SO KEEN AS MY OWN.
YOU'RE DRINKING QUITE A BIT.

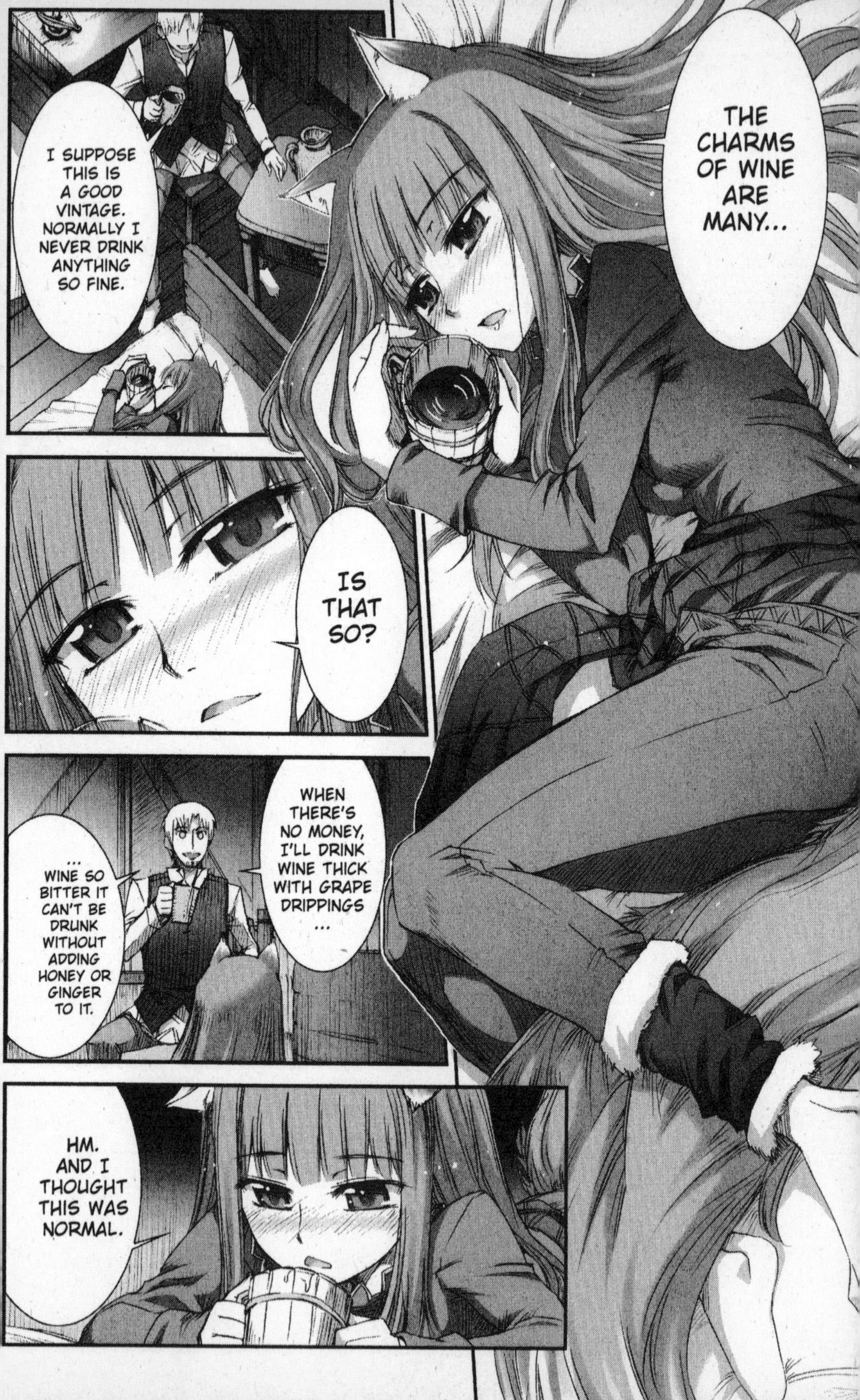
THE CHARMS OF WINE ARE MANY...
I SUPPOSE THIS IS A GOOD VINTAGE. NORMALLY I NEVER DRINK ANYTHING SO FINE.
IS THAT SO?
WHEN THERE'S NO MONEY, I'LL DRINK WINE THICK WITH GRAPE DRIPPINGS ...
... WINE SO BITTER IT CAN'T BE DRUNK WITHOUT ADDING HONEY OR GINGER TO IT.
HM. AND I THOUGHT THIS WAS NORMAL.

WELL, YOU'RE HIGHER AND MIGHTIER THAN I!

HA HA!

GOTO
(KA-TUNK)

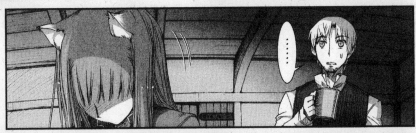

......

WHAT'S WRONG?

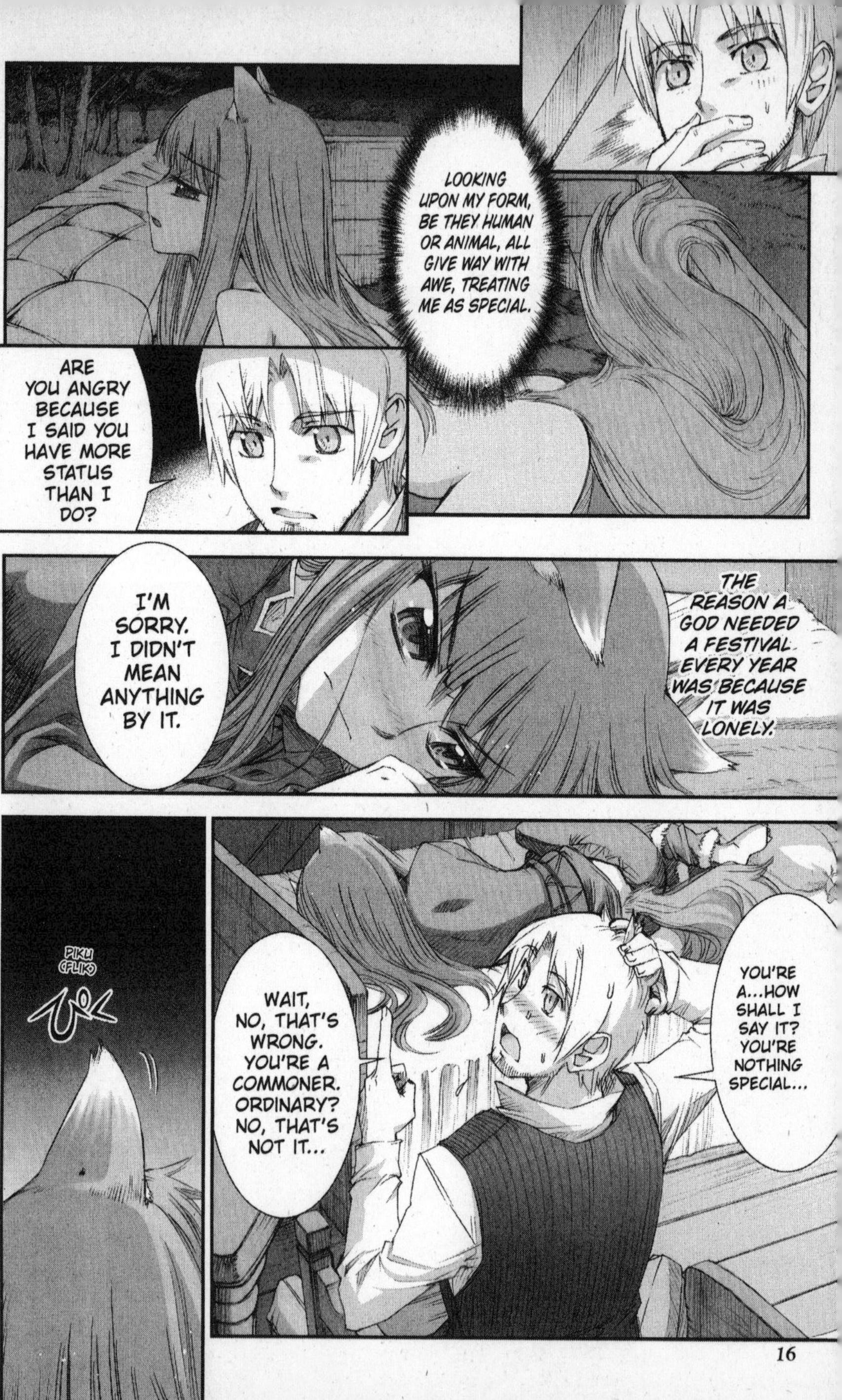
LOOKING UPON MY FORM, BE THEY HUMAN OR ANIMAL, ALL GIVE WAY WITH AWE, TREATING ME AS SPECIAL.
ARE YOU ANGRY BECAUSE I SAID YOU HAVE MORE STATUS THAN I DO?
THE REASON A GOD NEEDED A FESTIVAL EVERY YEAR WAS BECAUSE IT WAS LONELY.
I'M SORRY. I DIDN'T MEAN ANYTHING BY IT.
YOU'RE A...HOW SHALL I SAY IT? YOU'RE NOTHING SPECIAL...
WAIT, NO, THAT'S WRONG. YOU'RE A COMMONER. ORDINARY? NO, THAT'S NOT IT...
PIKU (FLIK)

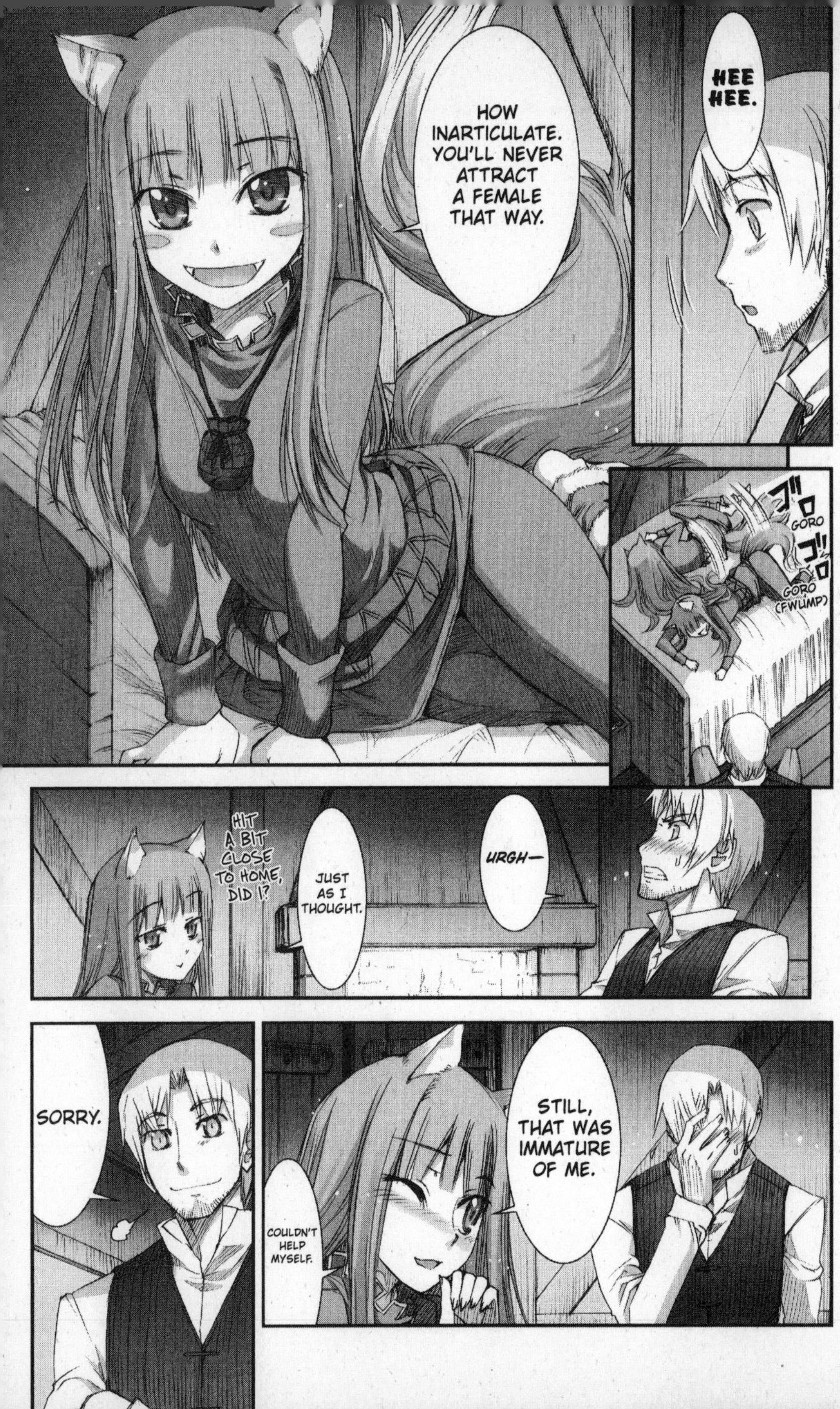
HEE HEE.
ゴロ
GORO
ゴロ
GORO
(FWUMP)
HOW INARTICULATE. YOU'LL NEVER ATTRACT A FEMALE THAT WAY.
URGH—
JUST AS I THOUGHT.
HIT A BIT CLOSE TO HOME, DID I?
STILL, THAT WAS IMMATURE OF ME.
COULDN'T HELP MYSELF.
SORRY.

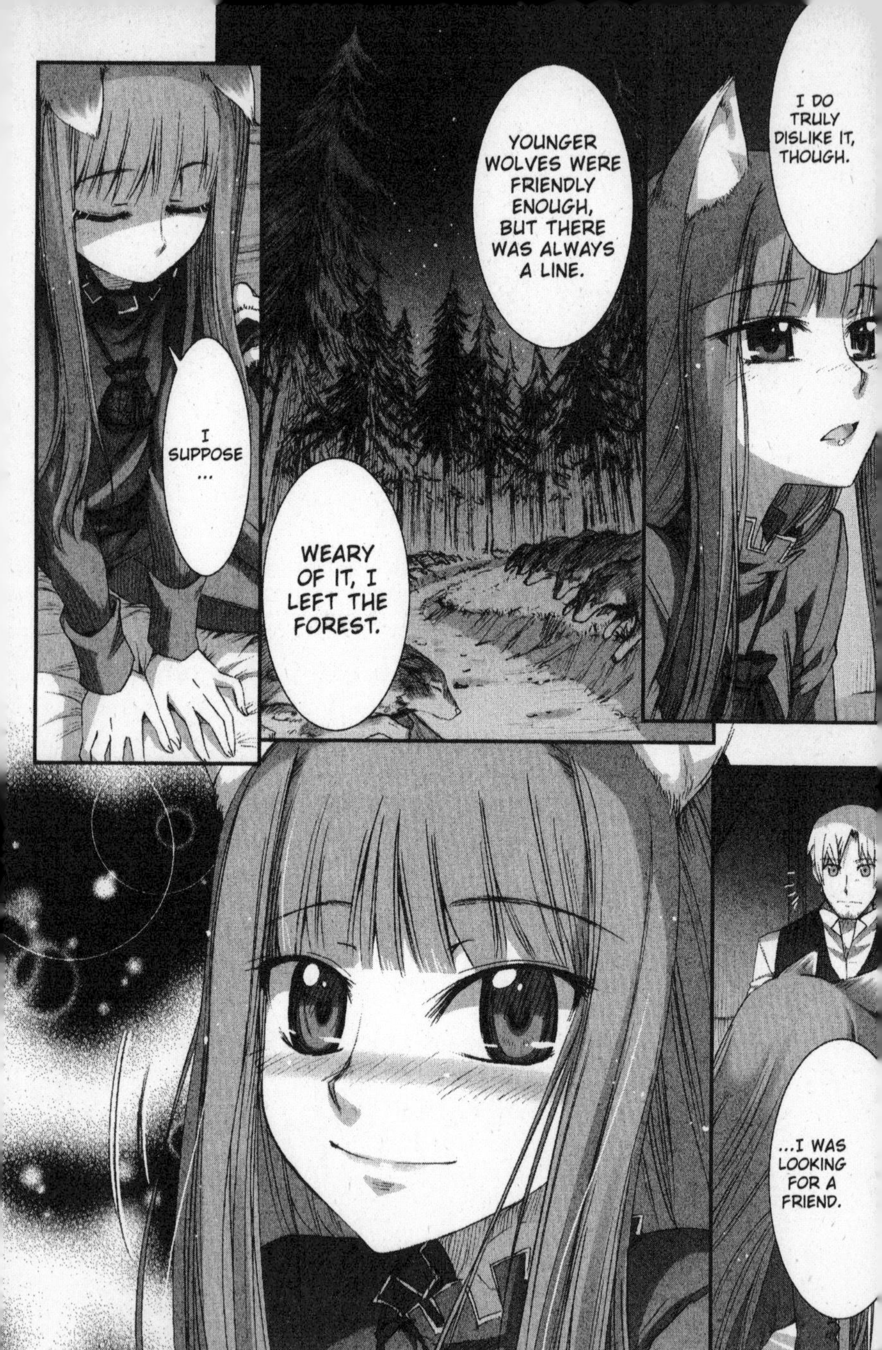
I DO TRULY DISLIKE IT, THOUGH.
YOUNGER WOLVES WERE FRIENDLY ENOUGH, BUT THERE WAS ALWAYS A LINE.
WEARY OF IT, I LEFT THE FOREST.
I SUPPOSE ...
...I WAS LOOKING FOR A FRIEND.

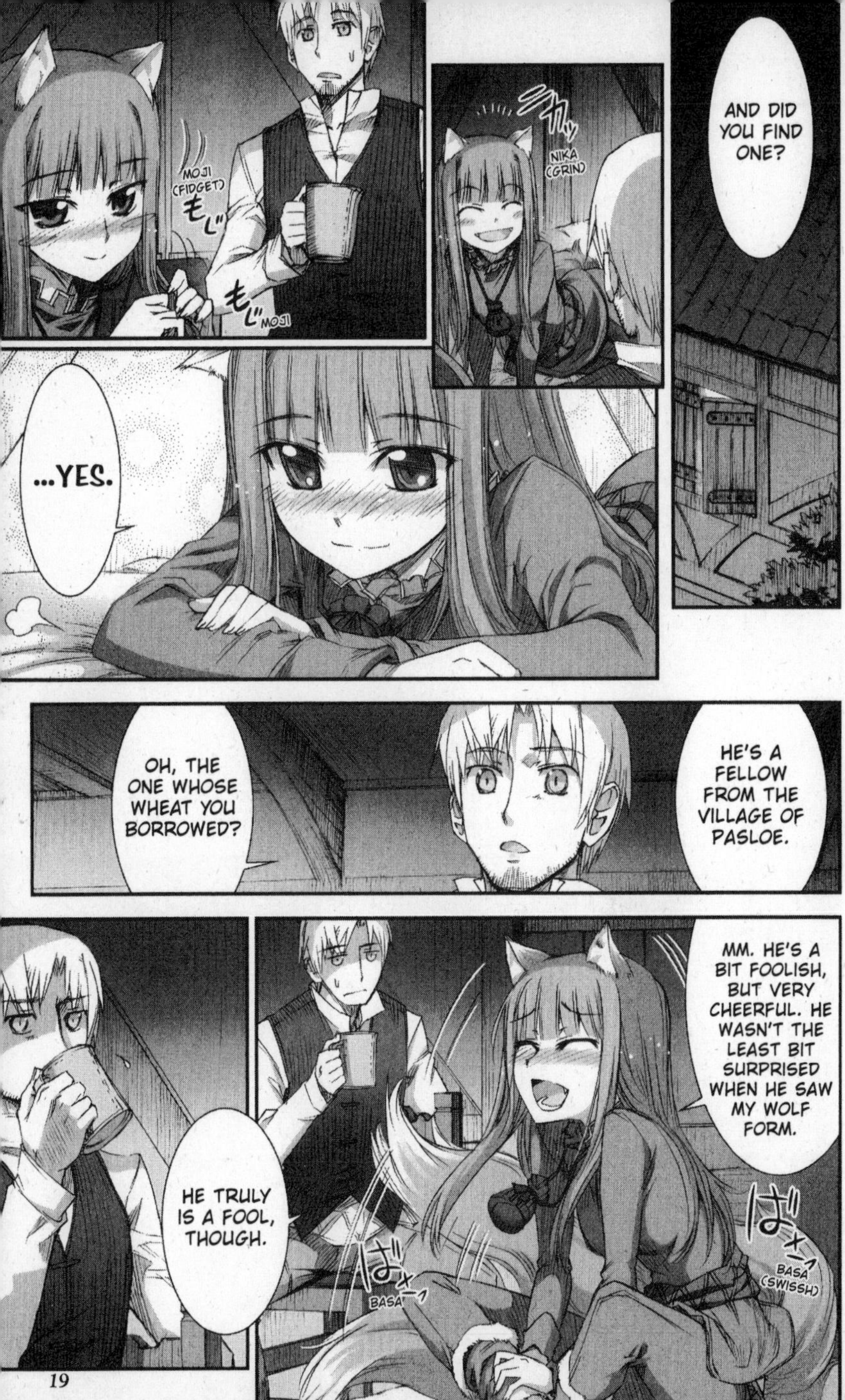

AND DID YOU FIND ONE?
NIKA (GRIN)
MOJI (FIDGET)
もじ
もじ MOJI
...YES.
HE'S A FELLOW FROM THE VILLAGE OF PASLOE.
OH, THE ONE WHOSE WHEAT YOU BORROWED?
MM. HE'S A BIT FOOLISH, BUT VERY CHEERFUL. HE WASN'T THE LEAST BIT SURPRISED WHEN HE SAW MY WOLF FORM.
ばさー
BASA (SWISSH)
ばさー
BASA
HE TRULY IS A FOOL, THOUGH.

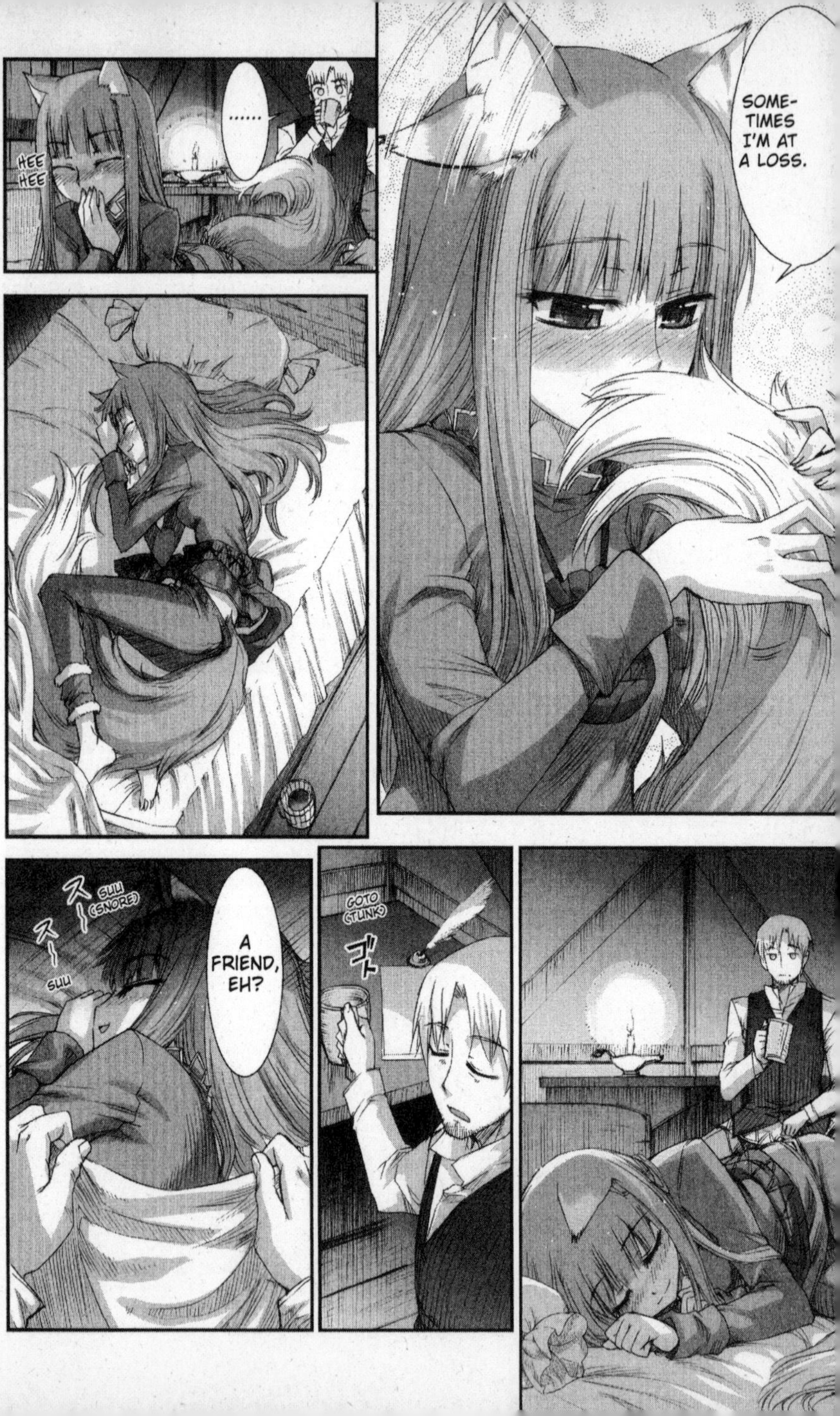
SOME-TIMES I'M AT A LOSS.
......
HEE HEE
ゴト
GOTO (STUNK)
A FRIEND, EH?
スー〜
SUU (SNORE)
スー〜
SUU

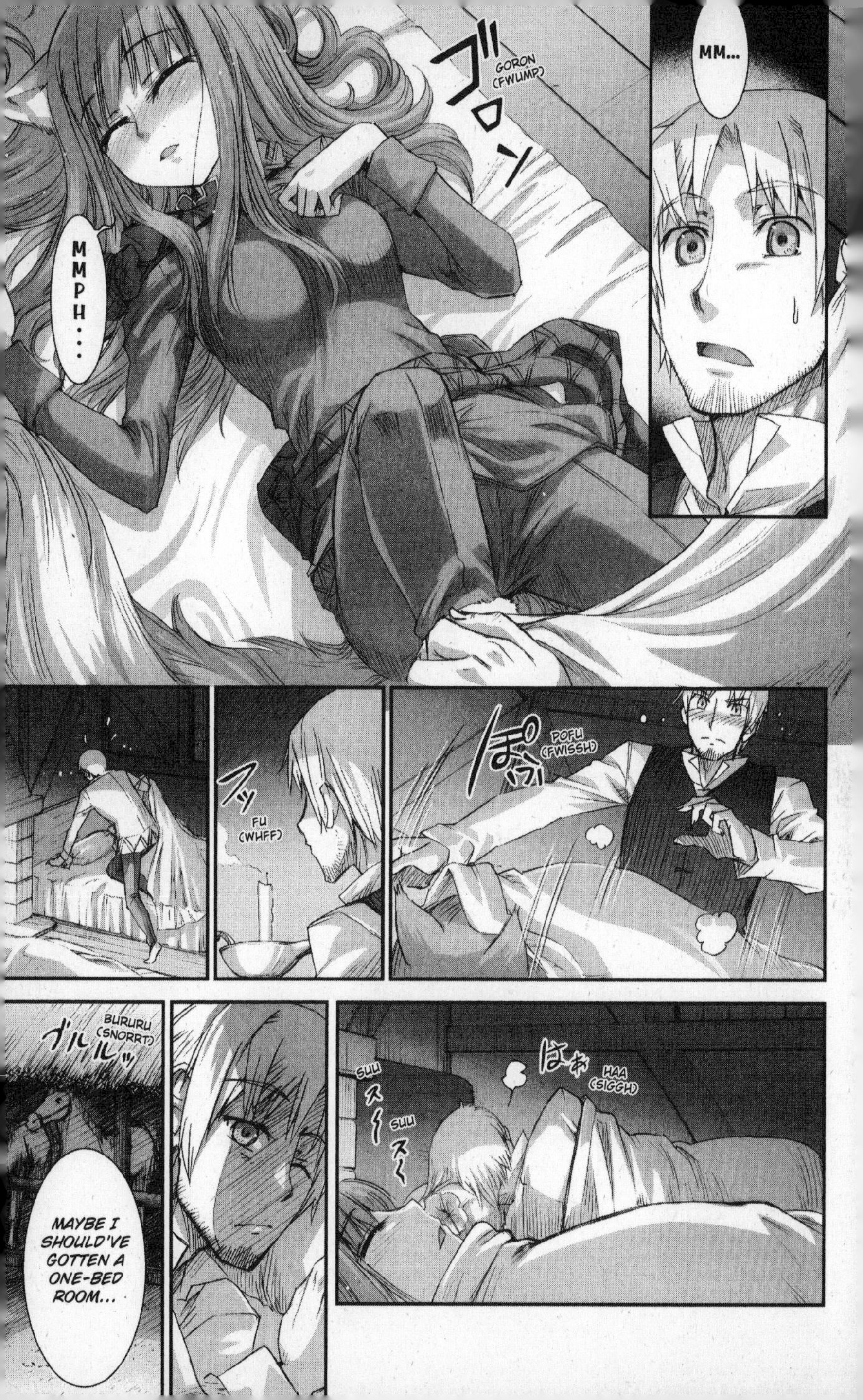
MM...
ゴロン
GORON (FWUMP)
MMPH...
ぽふ
POFU (FWISSH)
フッ
FU (WHFF)
はぁ
HAA (SIGGH)
SUU
スー
SUU
スー
ブルルッ
BURURU (SNORRT)
MAYBE I SHOULD'VE GOTTEN A ONE-BED ROOM...

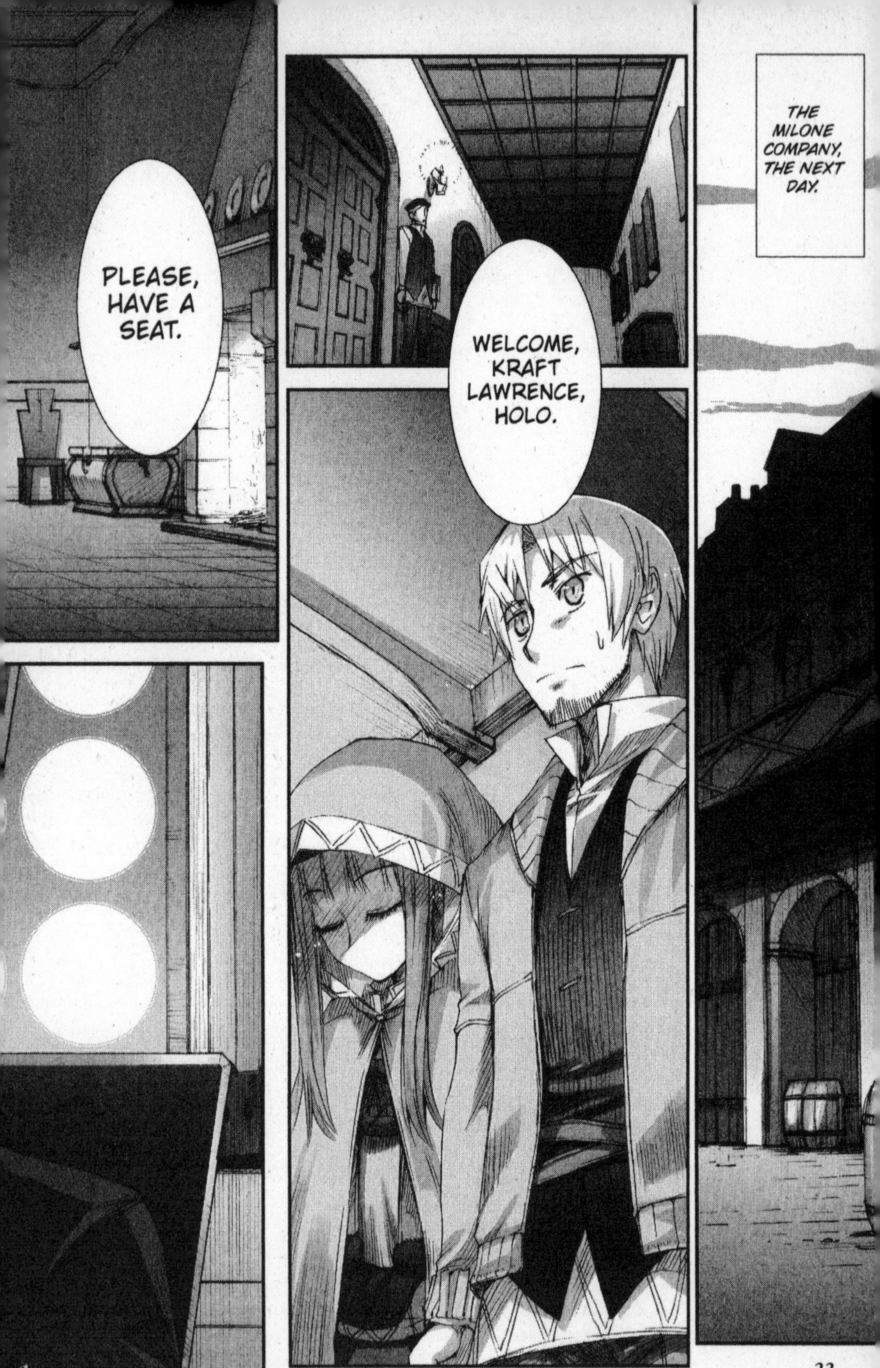
THE MILONE COMPANY, THE NEXT DAY.
WELCOME, KRAFT LAWRENCE, HOLO.
PLEASE, HAVE A SEAT.

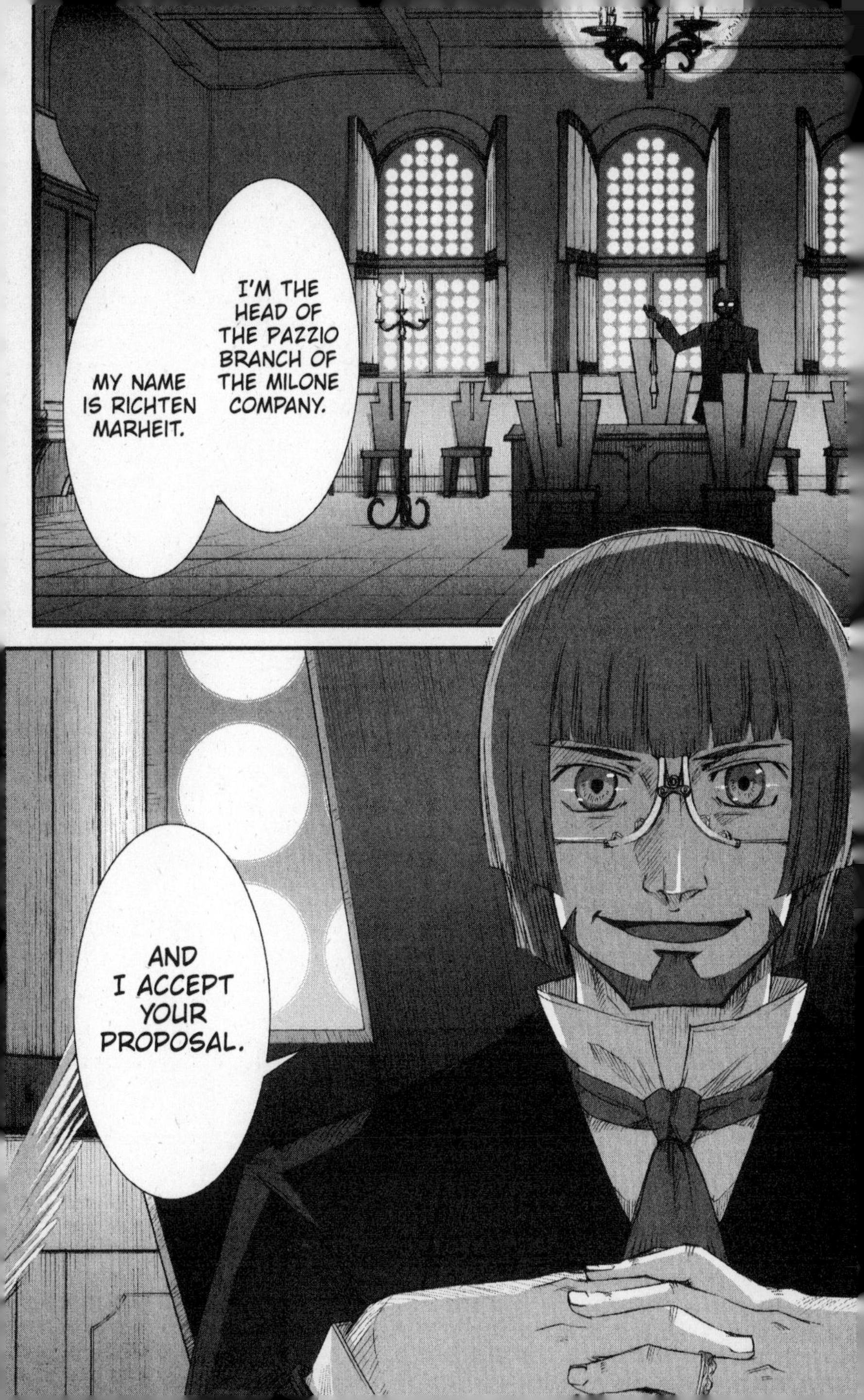
MY NAME IS RICHTEN MARHEIT.
I'M THE HEAD OF THE PAZZIO BRANCH OF THE MILONE COMPANY.
AND I ACCEPT YOUR PROPOSAL.

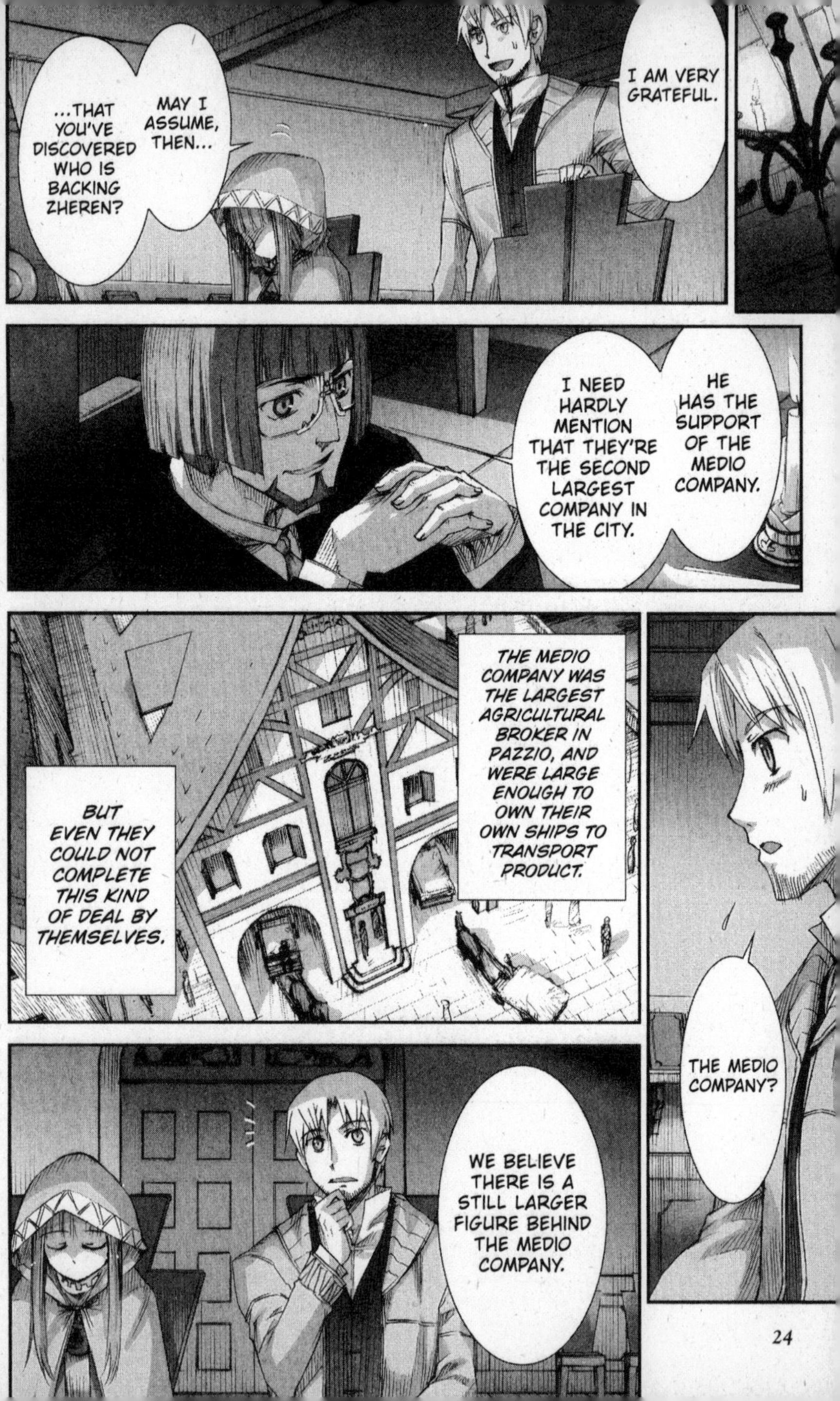
I AM VERY GRATEFUL.
MAY I ASSUME, THEN...
...THAT YOU'VE DISCOVERED WHO IS BACKING ZHEREN?
HE HAS THE SUPPORT OF THE MEDIO COMPANY.
I NEED HARDLY MENTION THAT THEY'RE THE SECOND LARGEST COMPANY IN THE CITY.
THE MEDIO COMPANY?
THE MEDIO COMPANY WAS THE LARGEST AGRICULTURAL BROKER IN PAZZIO, AND WERE LARGE ENOUGH TO OWN THEIR OWN SHIPS TO TRANSPORT PRODUCT.
BUT EVEN THEY COULD NOT COMPLETE THIS KIND OF DEAL BY THEMSELVES.
WE BELIEVE THERE IS A STILL LARGER FIGURE BEHIND THE MEDIO COMPANY.

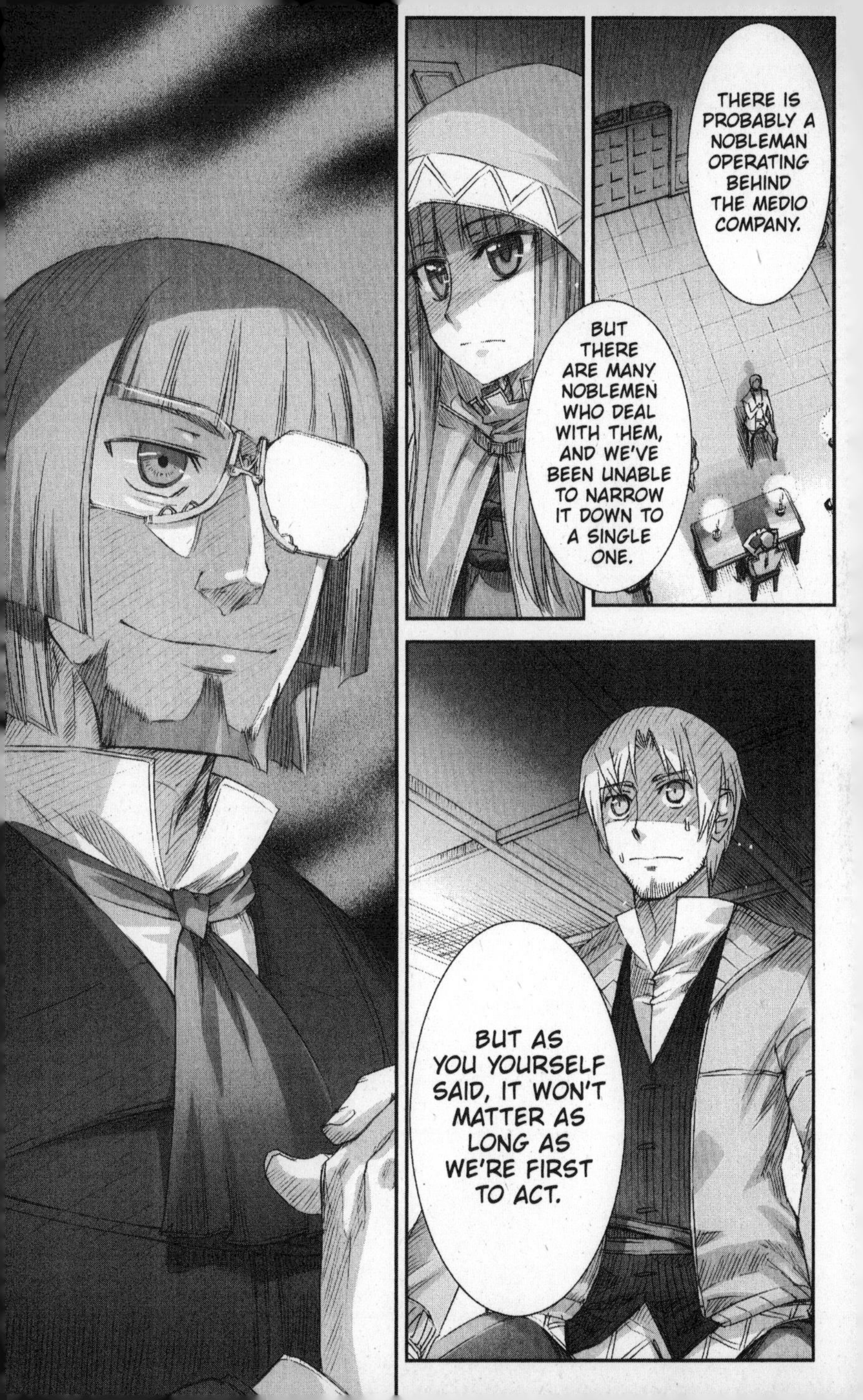
THERE IS PROBABLY A NOBLEMAN OPERATING BEHIND THE MEDIO COMPANY.
BUT THERE ARE MANY NOBLEMEN WHO DEAL WITH THEM, AND WE'VE BEEN UNABLE TO NARROW IT DOWN TO A SINGLE ONE.
BUT AS YOU YOURSELF SAID, IT WON'T MATTER AS LONG AS WE'RE FIRST TO ACT.

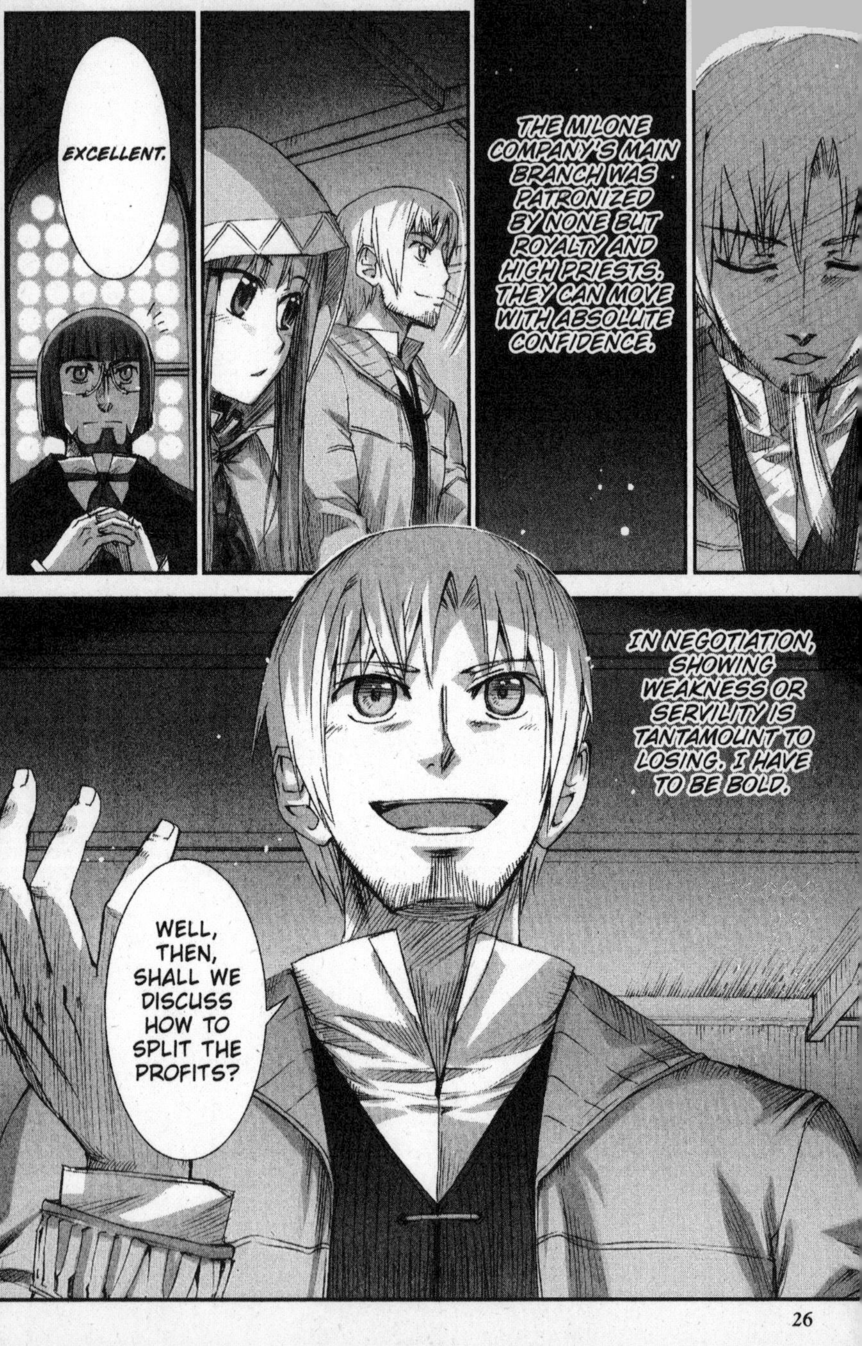
THE MILONE COMPANY'S MAIN BRANCH WAS PATRONIZED BY NONE BUT ROYALTY AND HIGH PRIESTS. THEY CAN MOVE WITH ABSOLUTE CONFIDENCE.
EXCELLENT.
IN NEGOTIATION, SHOWING WEAKNESS OR SERVILITY IS TANTAMOUNT TO LOSING. I HAVE TO BE BOLD.
WELL, THEN, SHALL WE DISCUSS HOW TO SPLIT THE PROFITS?

SPICE & WOLF

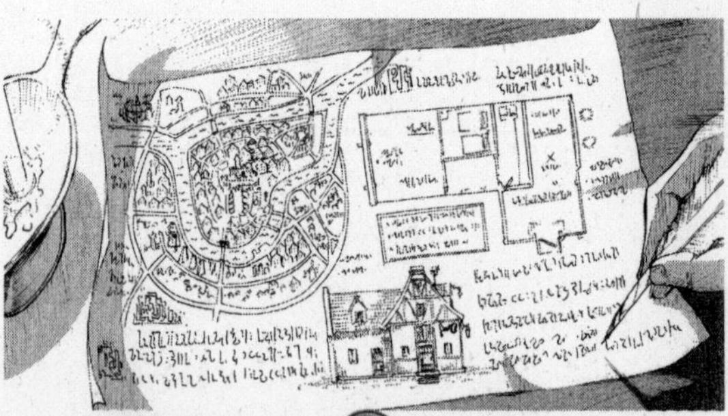

SPICE & WOLF

SPICE & WOLF

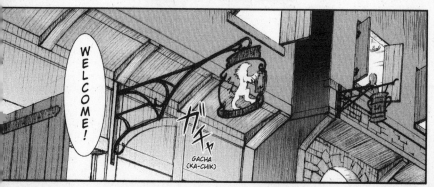

WELCOME!

GACHA
(KA-CHIK)

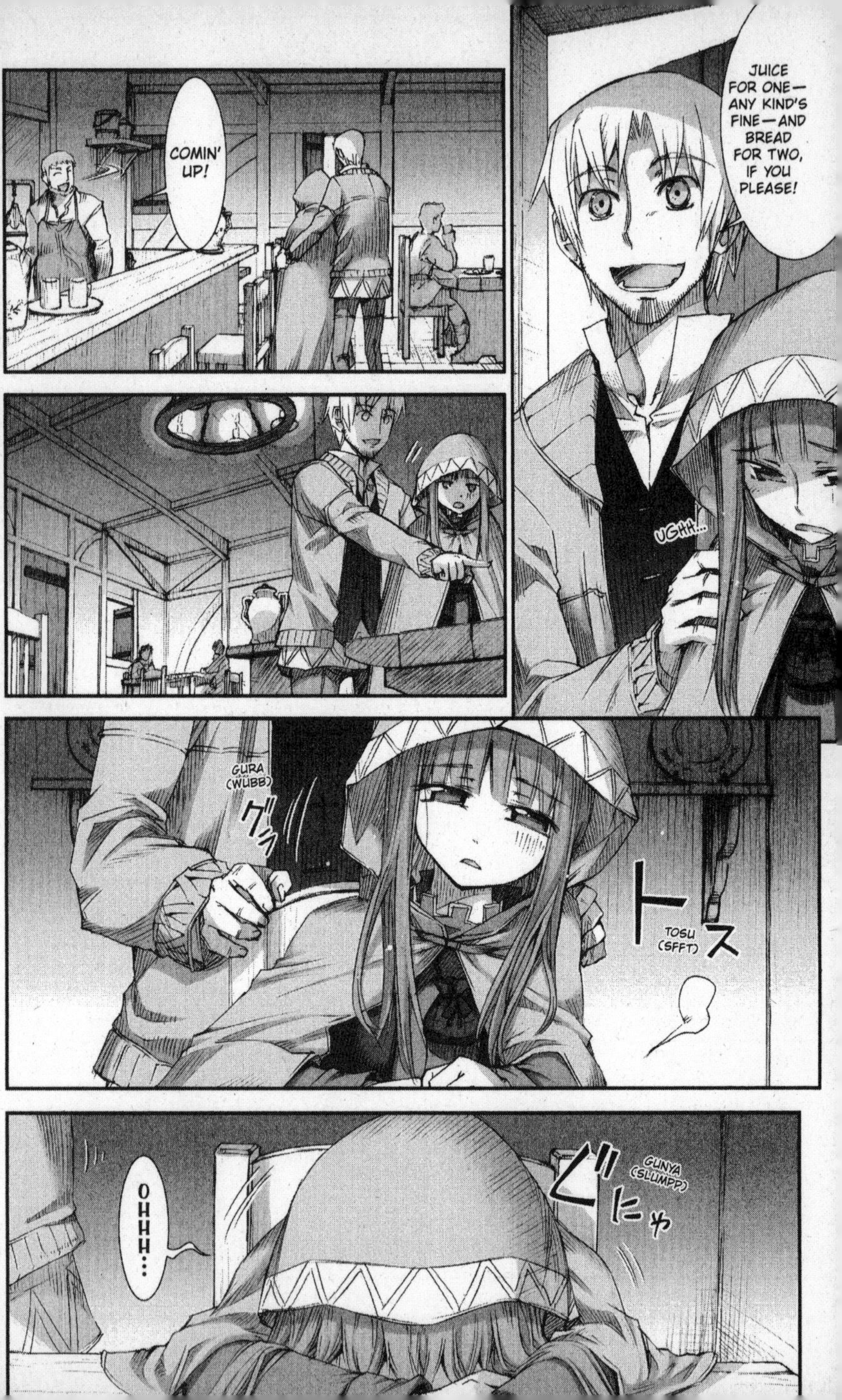
JUICE FOR ONE—ANY KIND'S FINE—AND BREAD FOR TWO, IF YOU PLEASE!
UGHH...
COMIN' UP!
GURA (WUBB)
TOSU (SFFT)
GUNYA (SLUMPP)
OHHH...

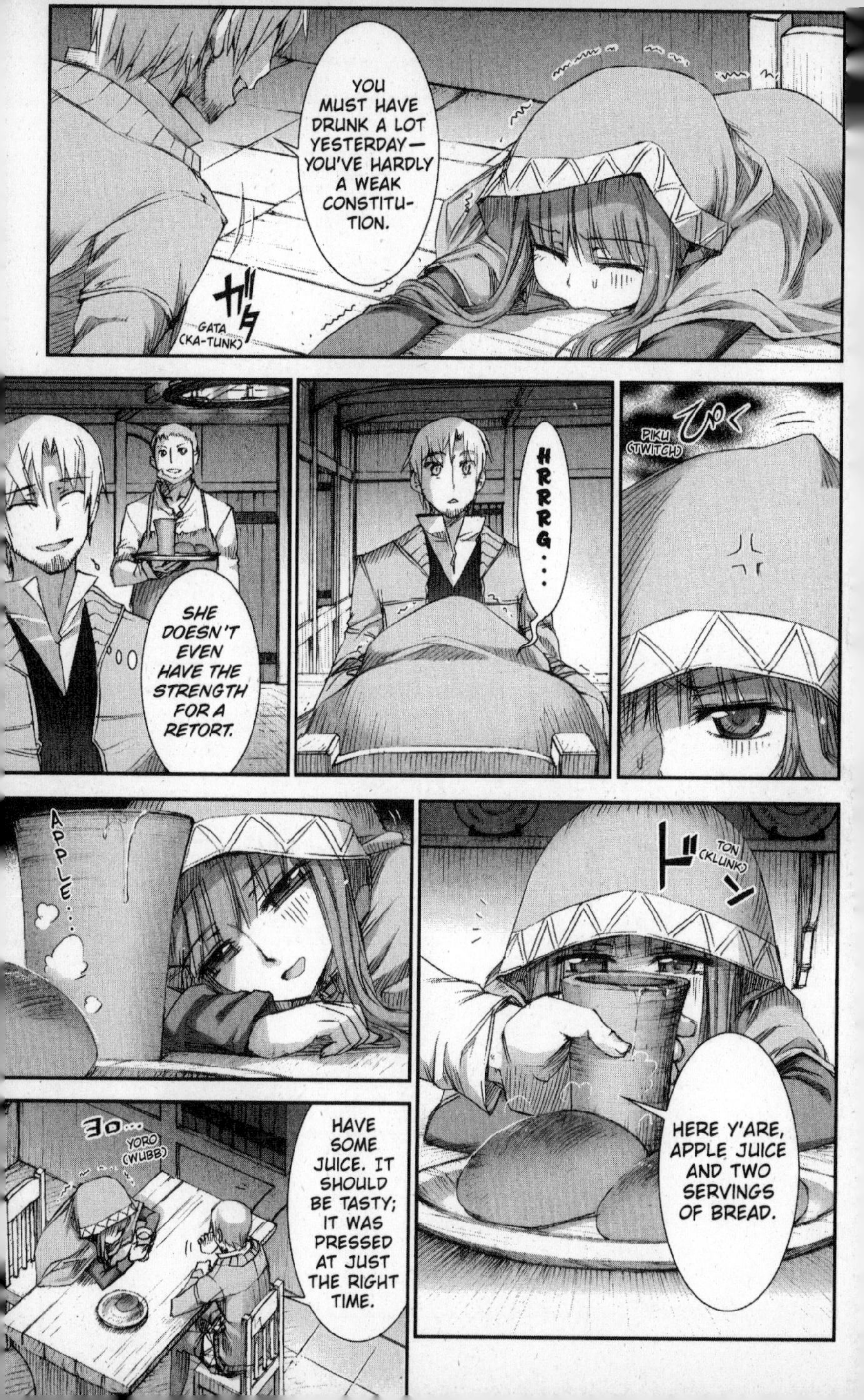
YOU MUST HAVE DRUNK A LOT YESTERDAY—YOU'VE HARDLY A WEAK CONSTITUTION.
GATA (KA-TUNK)
PIKU (TWITCH)
HRRRG...
SHE DOESN'T EVEN HAVE THE STRENGTH FOR A RETORT.
TON (KLUNK)
HERE Y'ARE, APPLE JUICE AND TWO SERVINGS OF BREAD.
APPLE...
YORO (WUBB)
HAVE SOME JUICE. IT SHOULD BE TASTY; IT WAS PRESSED AT JUST THE RIGHT TIME.

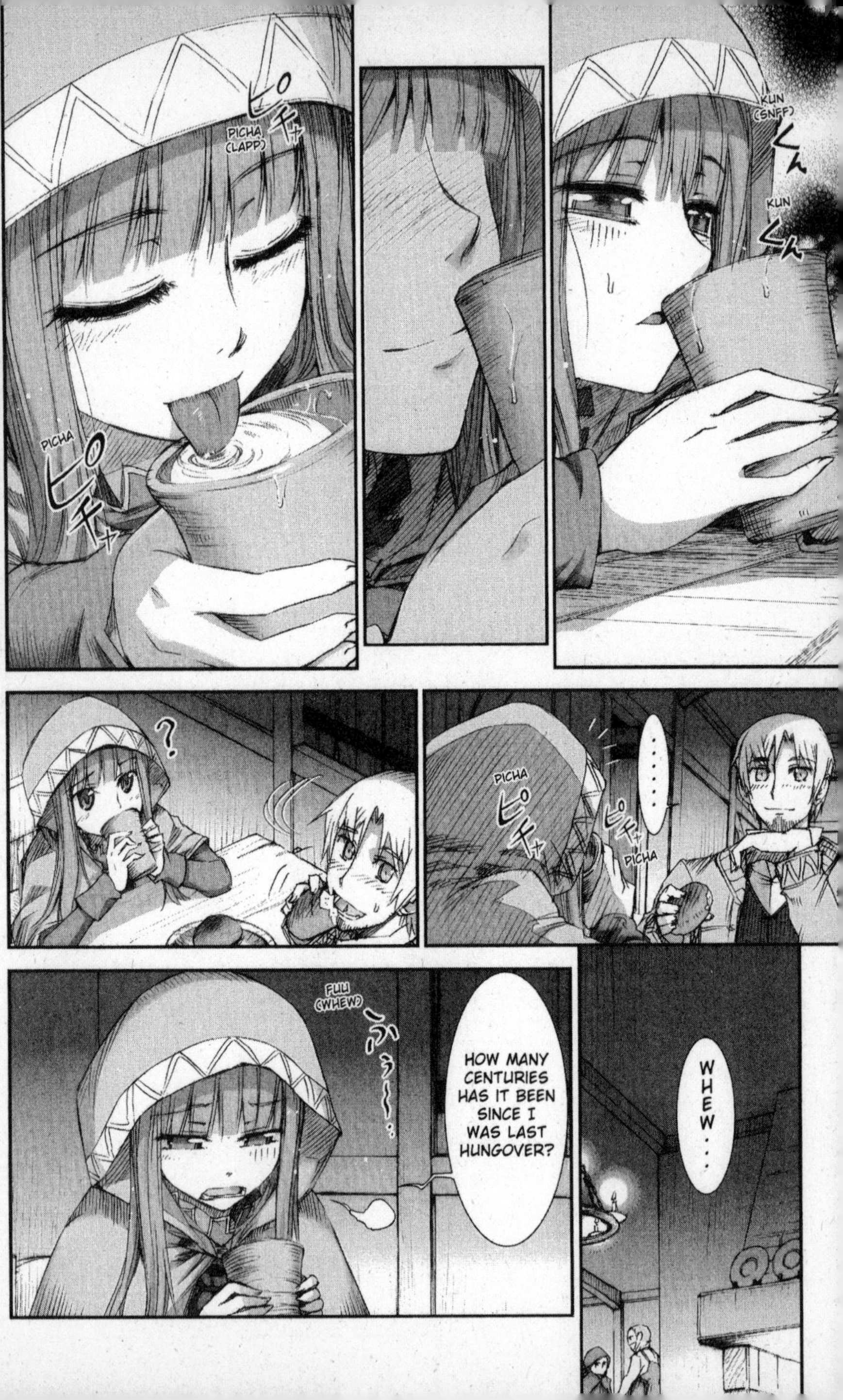

KUN (SNFF)
くん
KUN
くん
PICHA (LAPP)
ピチャ
PICHA
ピチャ
......
PICHA
ピチャ
ピチャ
PICHA
?
WHEW...
FUU (WHEW)
ふぅ~
HOW MANY CENTURIES HAS IT BEEN SINCE I WAS LAST HUNGOVER?

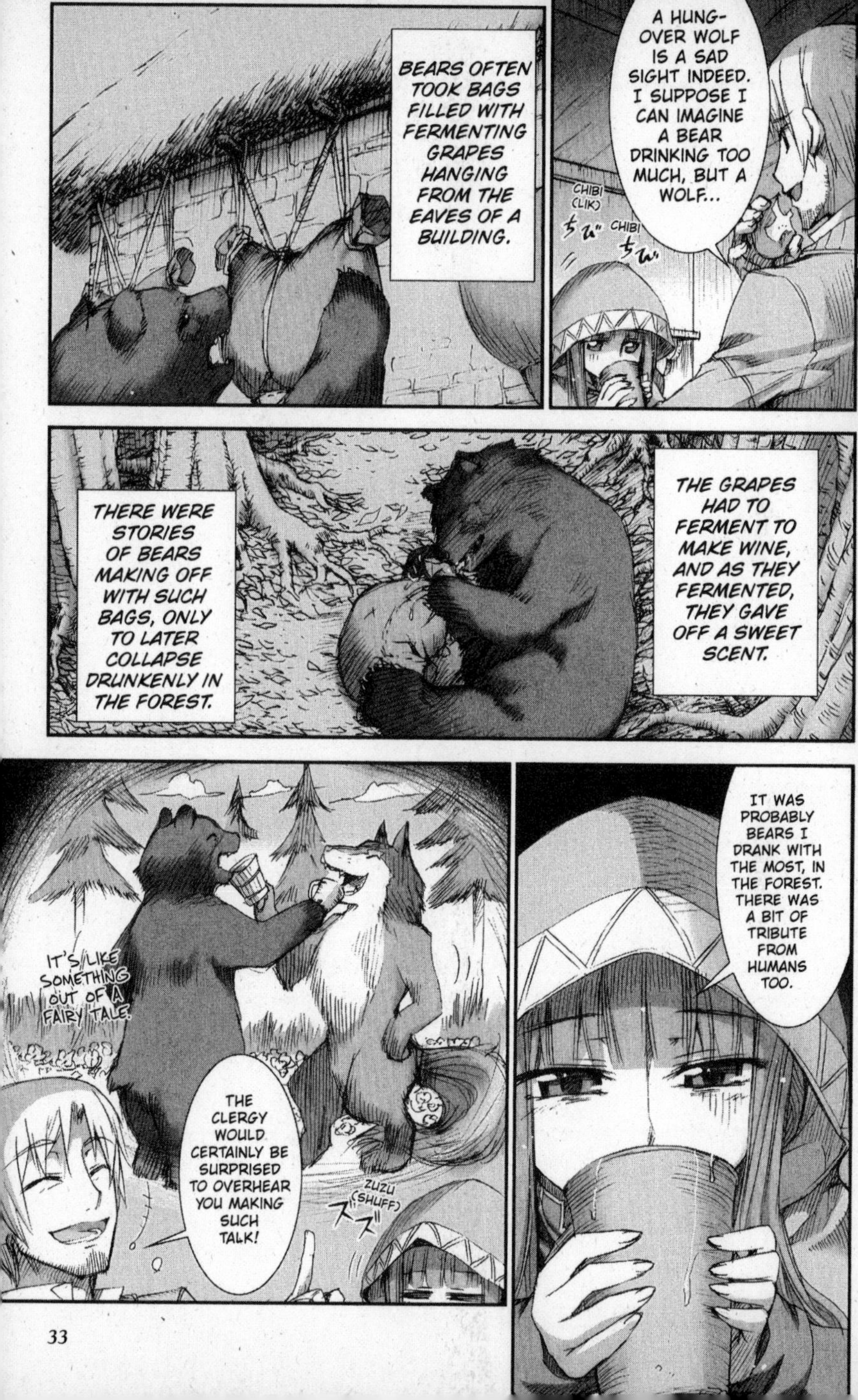
A HUNG-OVER WOLF IS A SAD SIGHT INDEED. I SUPPOSE I CAN IMAGINE A BEAR DRINKING TOO MUCH, BUT A WOLF...
CHIBI (LIK)
CHIBI
BEARS OFTEN TOOK BAGS FILLED WITH FERMENTING GRAPES HANGING FROM THE EAVES OF A BUILDING.
THE GRAPES HAD TO FERMENT TO MAKE WINE, AND AS THEY FERMENTED, THEY GAVE OFF A SWEET SCENT.
THERE WERE STORIES OF BEARS MAKING OFF WITH SUCH BAGS, ONLY TO LATER COLLAPSE DRUNKENLY IN THE FOREST.
IT WAS PROBABLY BEARS I DRANK WITH THE MOST, IN THE FOREST. THERE WAS A BIT OF TRIBUTE FROM HUMANS TOO.
IT'S LIKE SOMETHING OUT OF A FAIRY TALE.
THE CLERGY WOULD CERTAINLY BE SURPRISED TO OVERHEAR YOU MAKING SUCH TALK!
ZUZU (SHUFF)

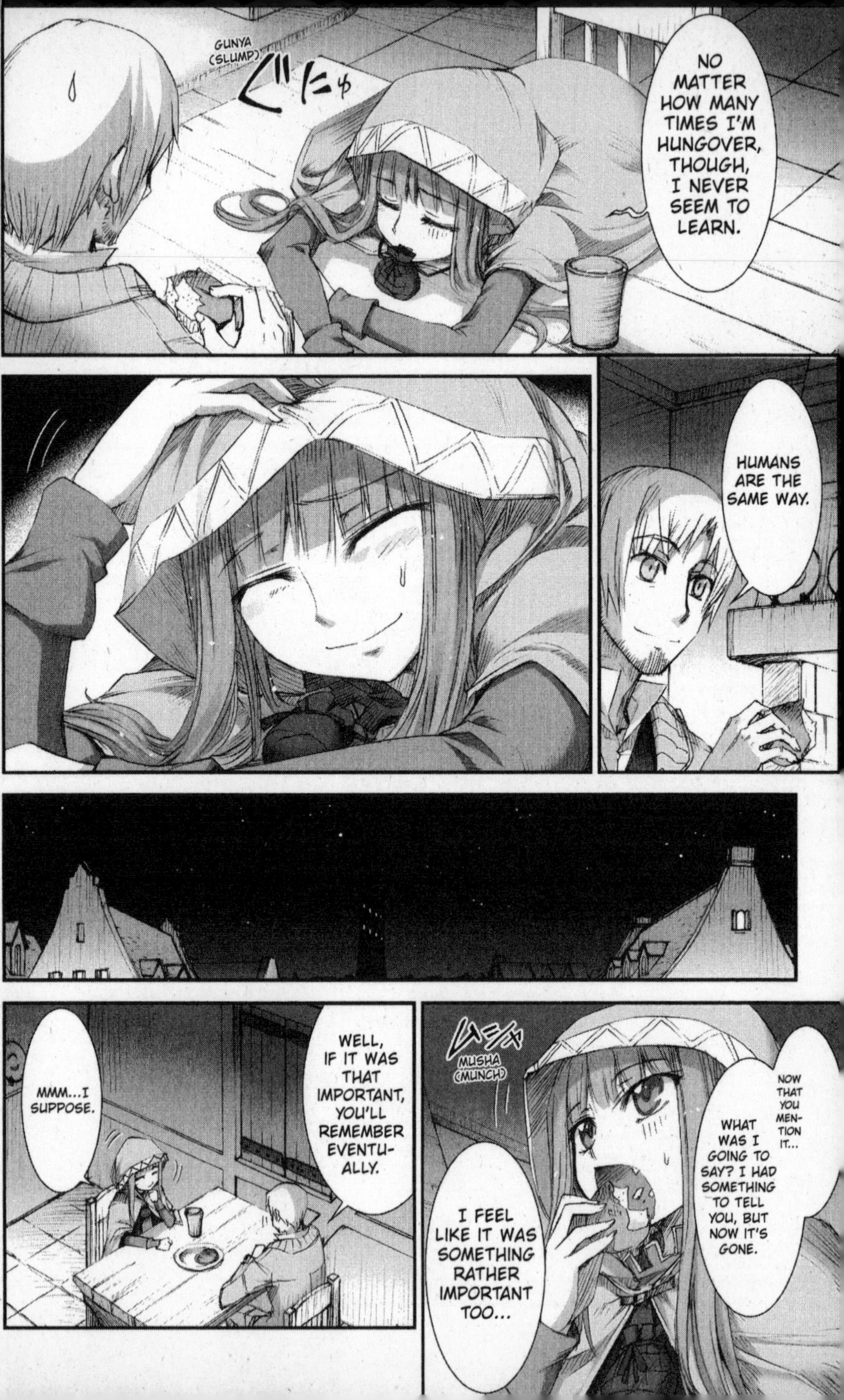
NO MATTER HOW MANY TIMES I'M HUNGOVER, THOUGH, I NEVER SEEM TO LEARN.
ぐにゅ
GUNYA (SLUMP)
HUMANS ARE THE SAME WAY.
NOW THAT YOU MENTION IT...
WHAT WAS I GOING TO SAY? I HAD SOMETHING TO TELL YOU, BUT NOW IT'S GONE.
ムシャ
MUSHA (MUNCH)
I FEEL LIKE IT WAS SOMETHING RATHER IMPORTANT TOO...
WELL, IF IT WAS THAT IMPORTANT, YOU'LL REMEMBER EVENTU-ALLY.
MMM...I SUPPOSE.

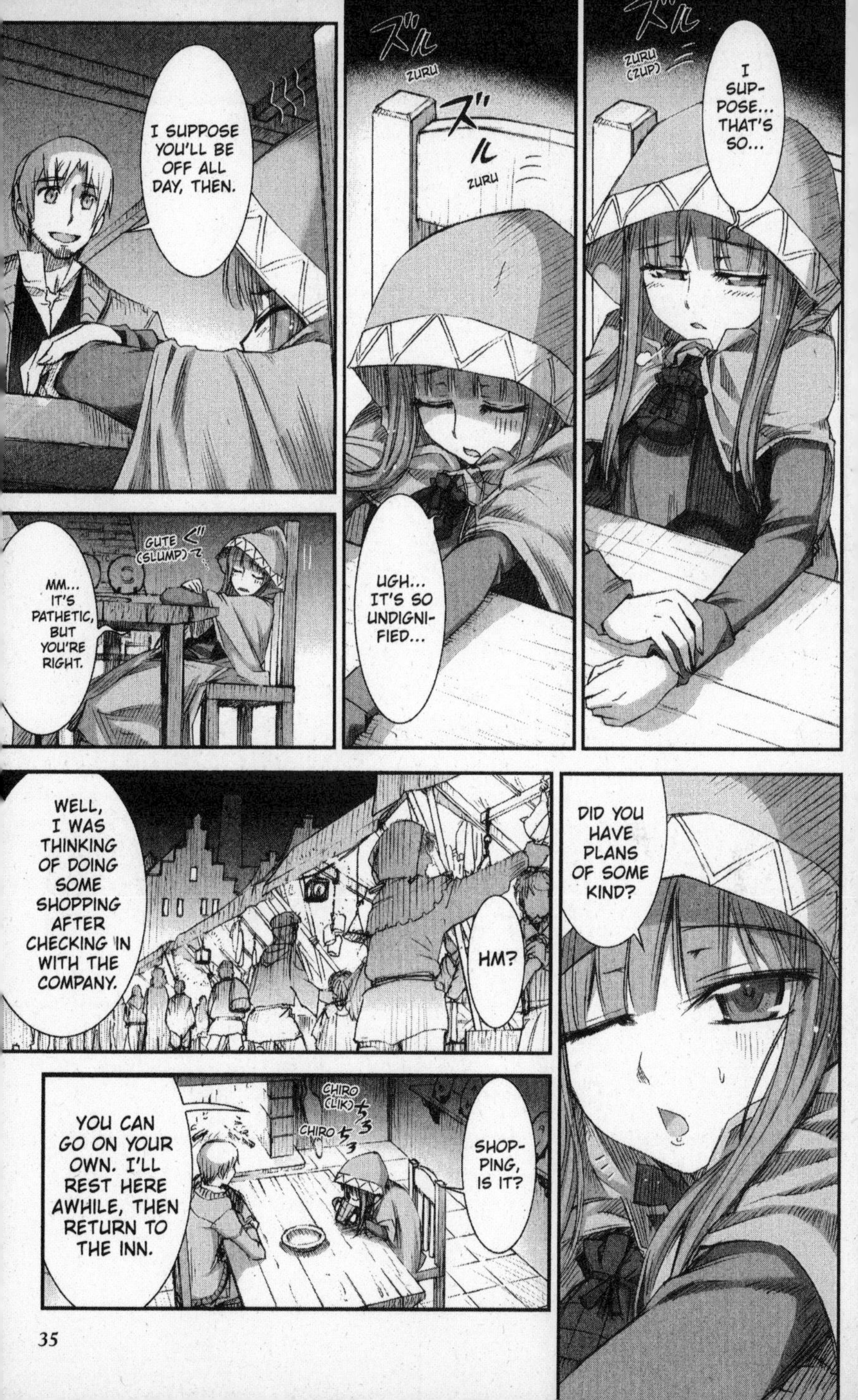
ズル
ZURU (ZUP)
I SUPPOSE... THAT'S SO...
ズル
ZURU
ズル
ZURU
UGH... IT'S SO UNDIGNIFIED...
I SUPPOSE YOU'LL BE OFF ALL DAY, THEN.
GUTE (SLUMP)
MM... IT'S PATHETIC, BUT YOU'RE RIGHT.
DID YOU HAVE PLANS OF SOME KIND?
HM?
WELL, I WAS THINKING OF DOING SOME SHOPPING AFTER CHECKING IN WITH THE COMPANY.
CHIRO (CLIK)
CHIRO
SHOPPING, IS IT?
YOU CAN GO ON YOUR OWN. I'LL REST HERE AWHILE, THEN RETURN TO THE INN.

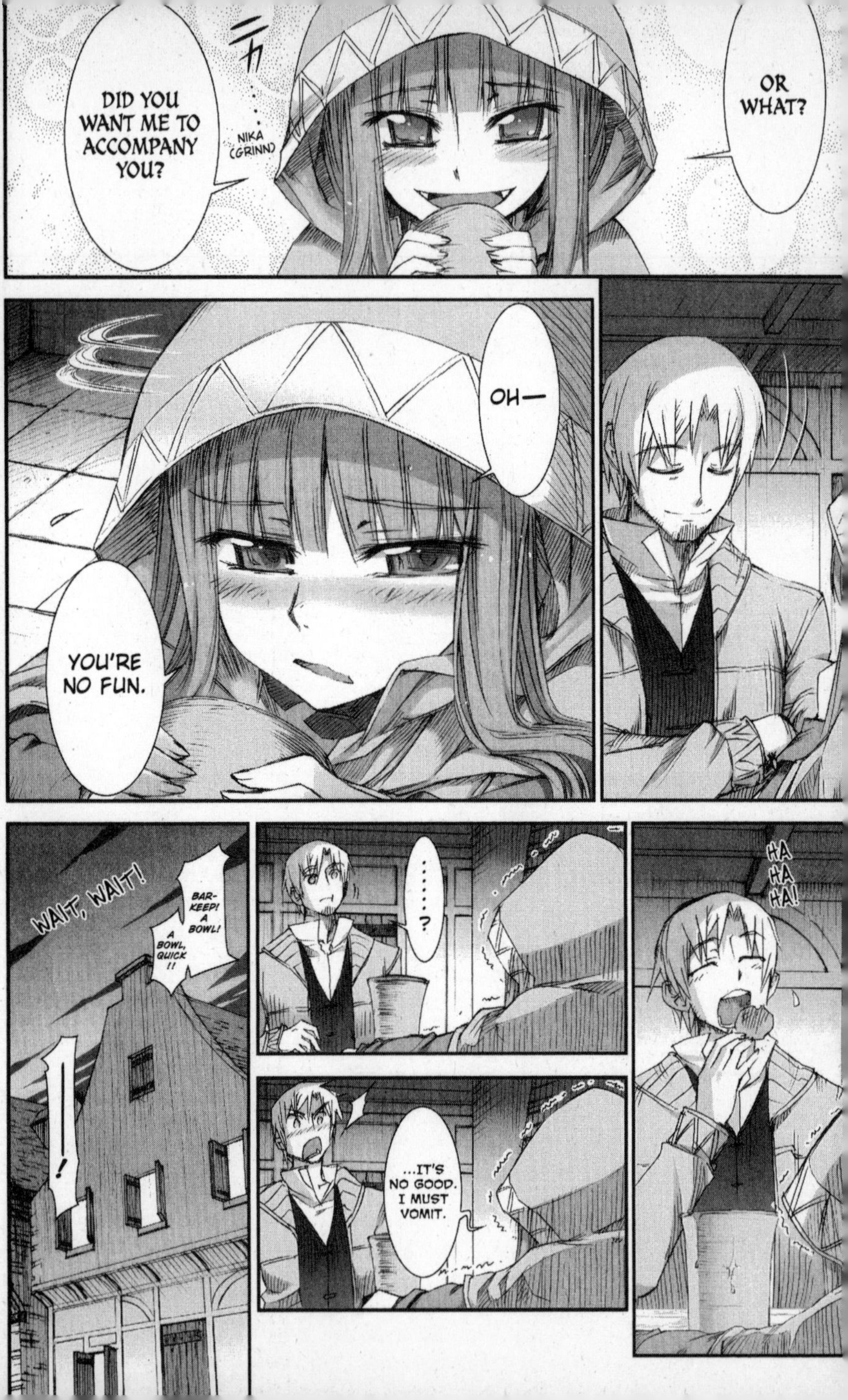
DID YOU WANT ME TO ACCOMPANY YOU?
NIKA (GRINN)
OR WHAT?
OH—
YOU'RE NO FUN.
HA HA HA!
......?
...IT'S NO GOOD. I MUST VOMIT.
!
WAIT, WAIT!
BARKEEP! A BOWL!
A BOWL, QUICK!!

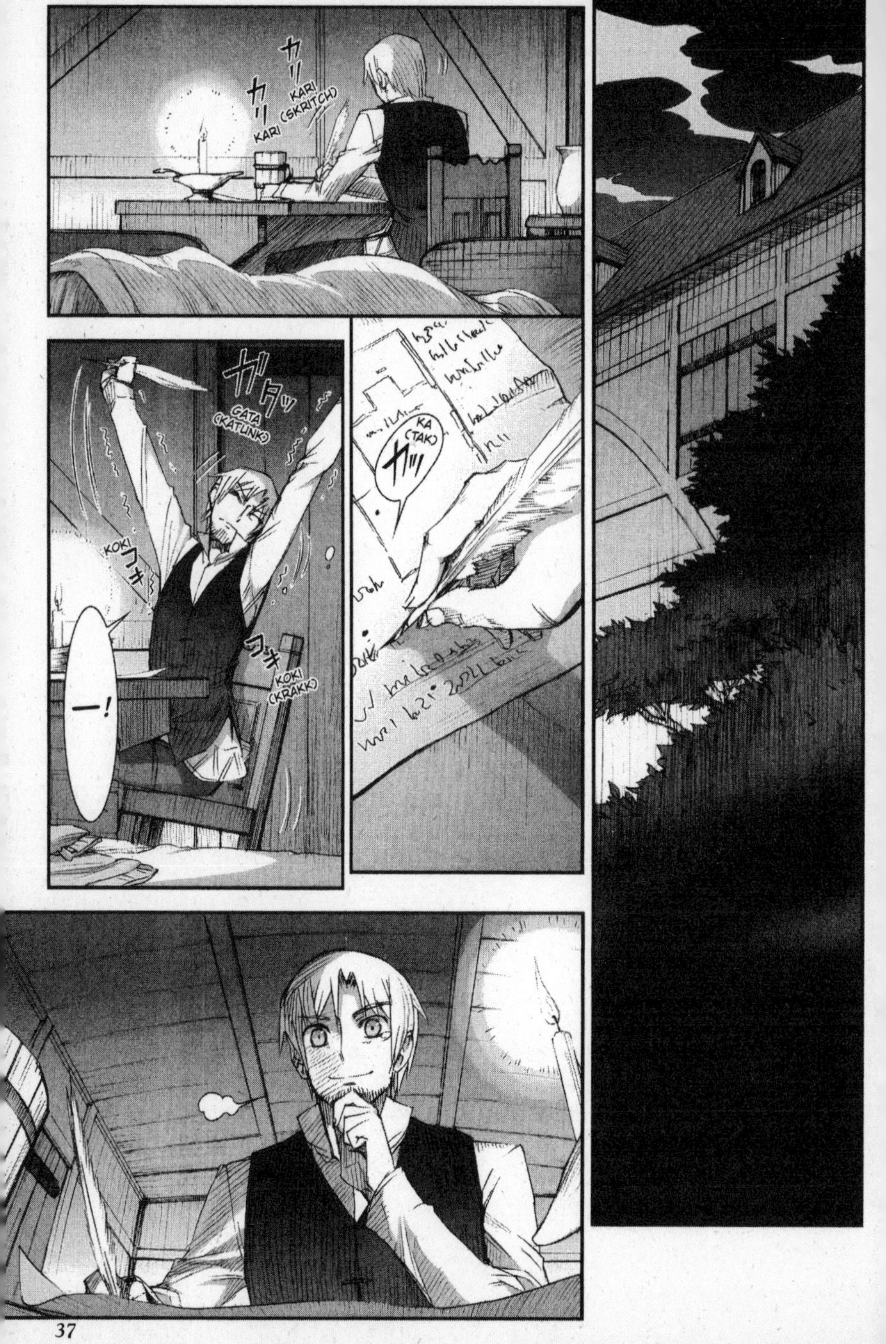
カリ KARI (SKRITCH)
カリ KARI
カッ KA (TAK)
ガタッ GATA (KATUNK)
KOKI コキ
コキ KOKI (KRAKK)
—!

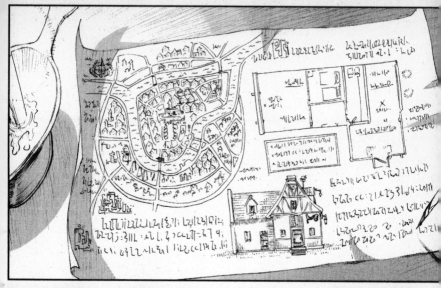

EVEN A WEEK AGO, MY DREAM WAS SO DISTANT, BUT NOW...

"LAWRENCE THE TOWN MERCHANT," EH?

WHAT'S THAT SOUND...?

GOSO
(RUSTL)

GOSO

MMPH...

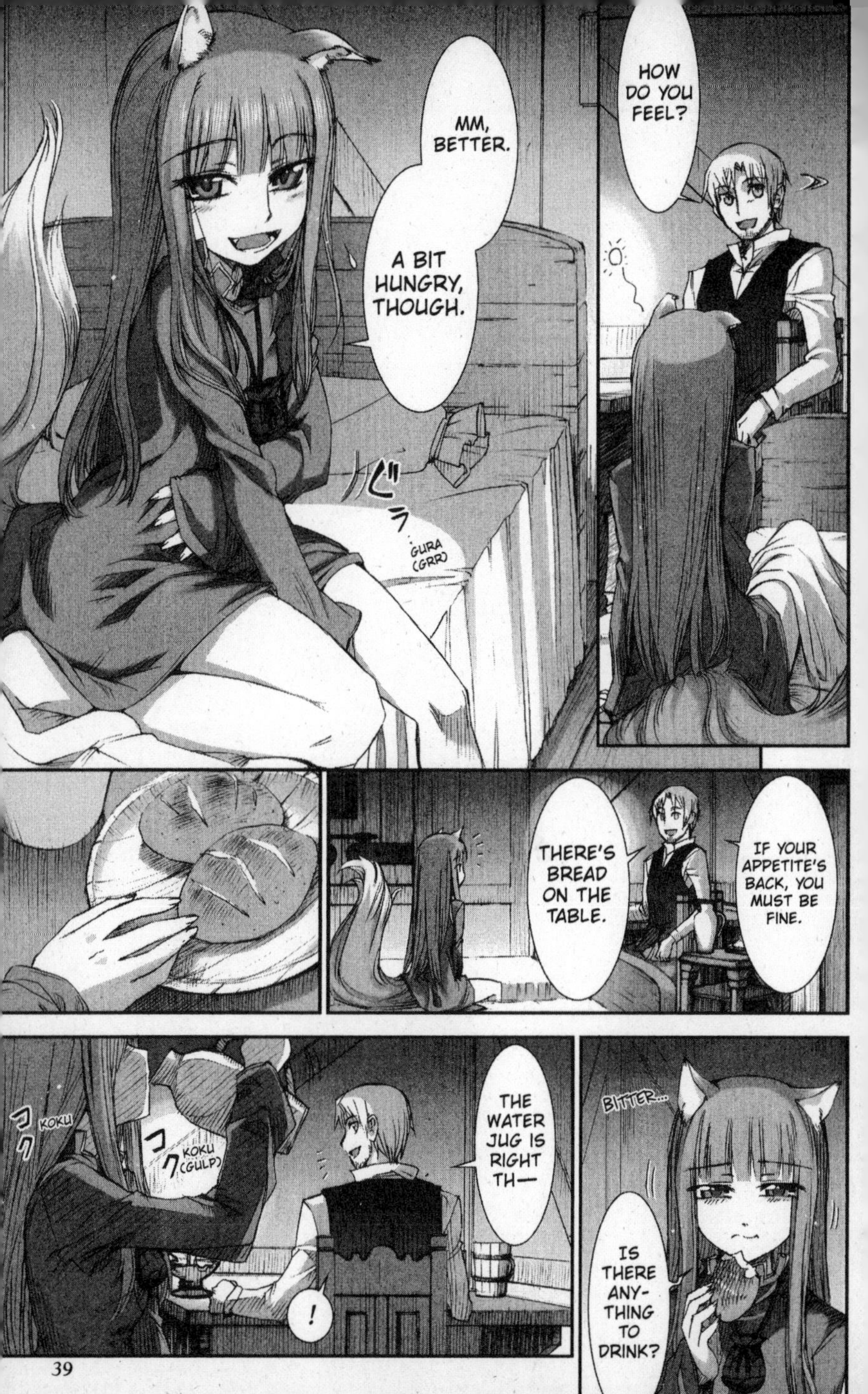
HOW DO YOU FEEL?
MM, BETTER.
A BIT HUNGRY, THOUGH.
グラ
GURA (GRR)
IF YOUR APPETITE'S BACK, YOU MUST BE FINE.
THERE'S BREAD ON THE TABLE.
BITTER...
IS THERE ANY-THING TO DRINK?
THE WATER JUG IS RIGHT TH—
コク
KOKU (GULP)
コク
KOKU
!

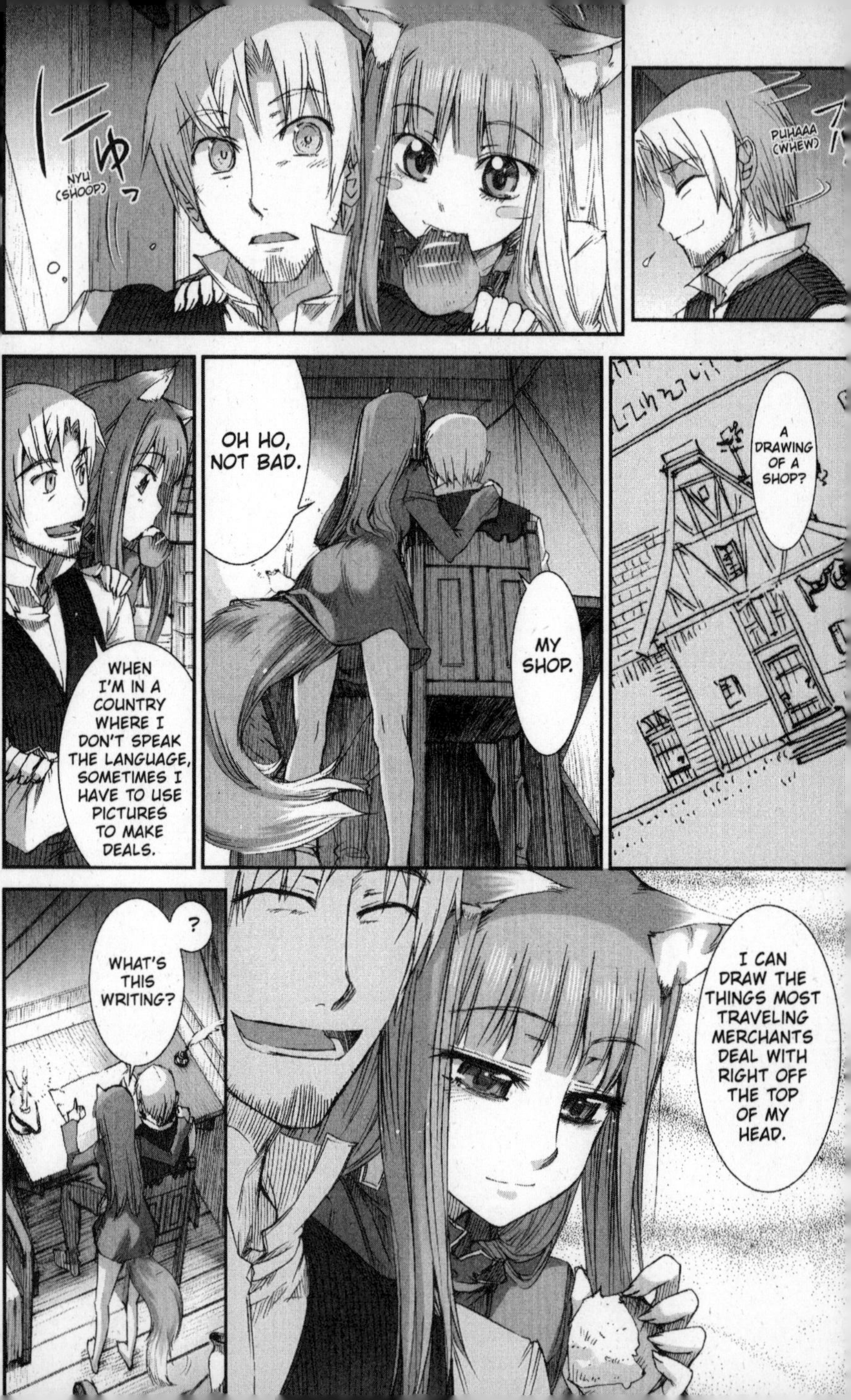
PUHAAA (WHEW)
NYU (SHOOP)
A DRAWING OF A SHOP?
MY SHOP.
OH HO, NOT BAD.
WHEN I'M IN A COUNTRY WHERE I DON'T SPEAK THE LANGUAGE, SOMETIMES I HAVE TO USE PICTURES TO MAKE DEALS.
I CAN DRAW THE THINGS MOST TRAVELING MERCHANTS DEAL WITH RIGHT OFF THE TOP OF MY HEAD.
?
WHAT'S THIS WRITING?

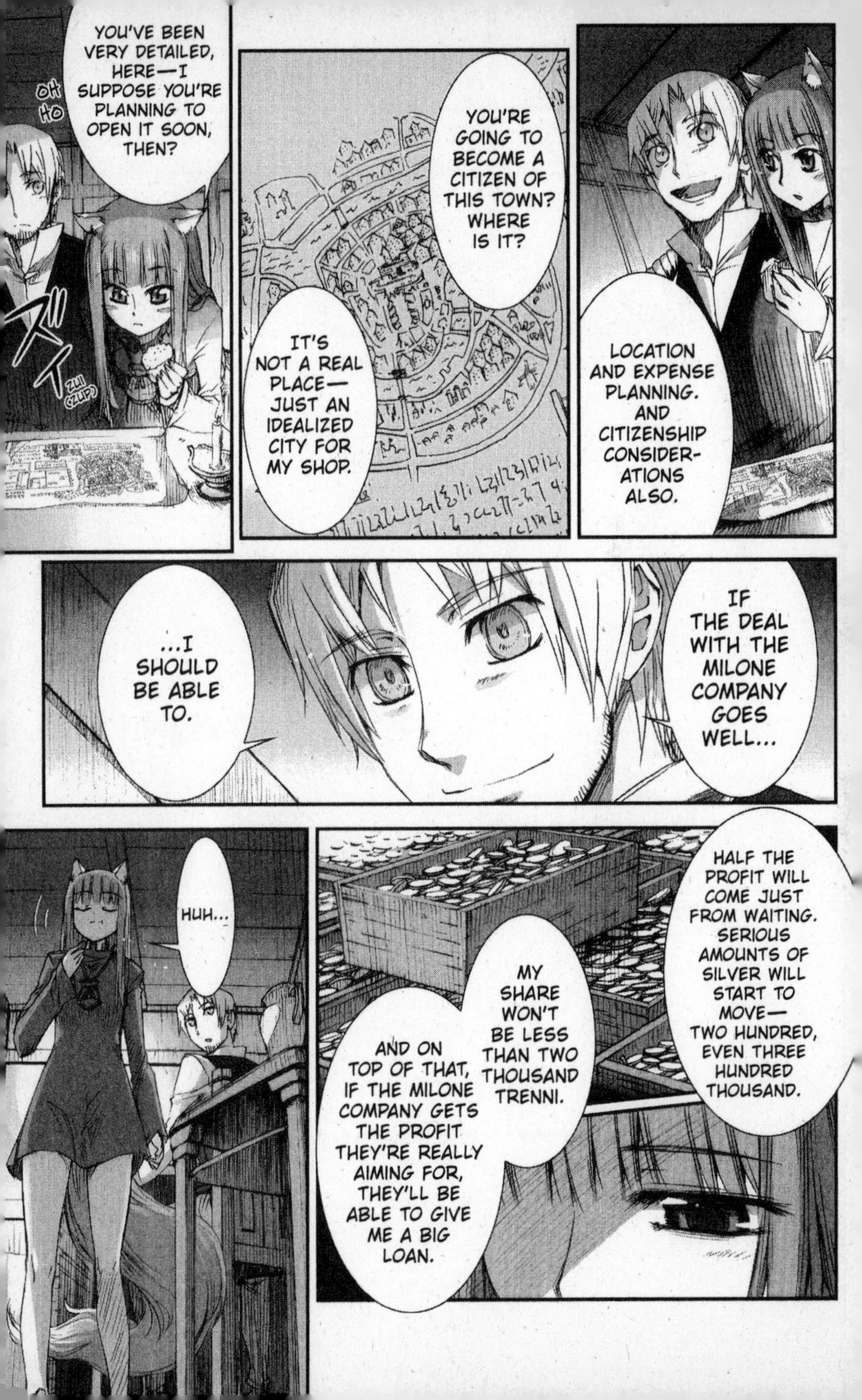
LOCATION AND EXPENSE PLANNING. AND CITIZENSHIP CONSIDERATIONS ALSO.
YOU'RE GOING TO BECOME A CITIZEN OF THIS TOWN? WHERE IS IT?
IT'S NOT A REAL PLACE—JUST AN IDEALIZED CITY FOR MY SHOP.
OH HO
YOU'VE BEEN VERY DETAILED, HERE—I SUPPOSE YOU'RE PLANNING TO OPEN IT SOON, THEN?
ズイ
ZUI (ZUP)
IF THE DEAL WITH THE MILONE COMPANY GOES WELL...
...I SHOULD BE ABLE TO.
HALF THE PROFIT WILL COME JUST FROM WAITING. SERIOUS AMOUNTS OF SILVER WILL START TO MOVE—TWO HUNDRED, EVEN THREE HUNDRED THOUSAND.
MY SHARE WON'T BE LESS THAN TWO THOUSAND TRENNI.
AND ON TOP OF THAT, IF THE MILONE COMPANY GETS THE PROFIT THEY'RE REALLY AIMING FOR, THEY'LL BE ABLE TO GIVE ME A BIG LOAN.
HUH...

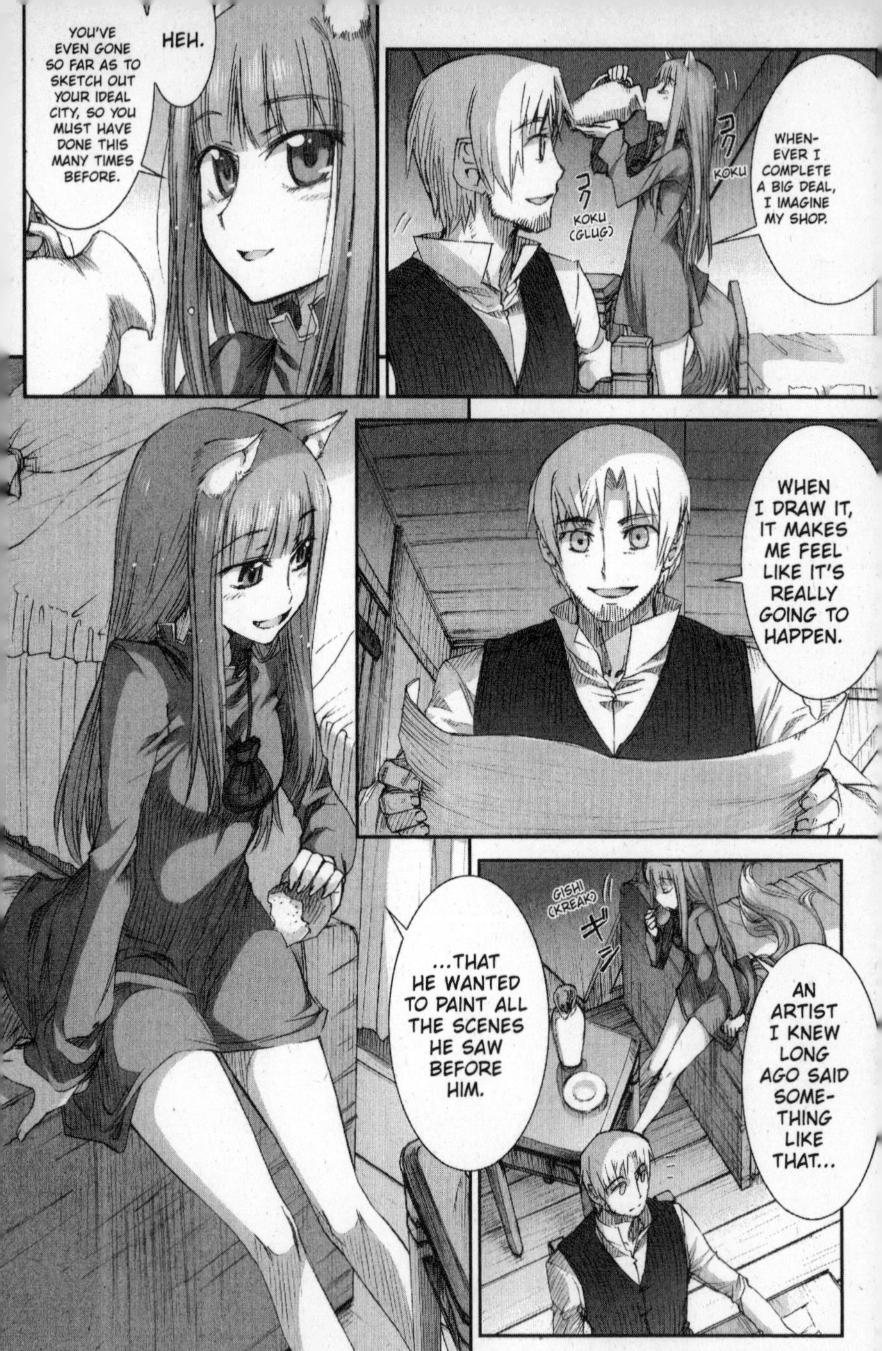
WHEN-EVER I COMPLETE A BIG DEAL, I IMAGINE MY SHOP.
コク KOKU
コク KOKU (GLUG)
HEH.
YOU'VE EVEN GONE SO FAR AS TO SKETCH OUT YOUR IDEAL CITY, SO YOU MUST HAVE DONE THIS MANY TIMES BEFORE.
WHEN I DRAW IT, IT MAKES ME FEEL LIKE IT'S REALLY GOING TO HAPPEN.
ギシ GISHI (KREAK)
AN ARTIST I KNEW LONG AGO SAID SOME-THING LIKE THAT...
...THAT HE WANTED TO PAINT ALL THE SCENES HE SAW BEFORE HIM.

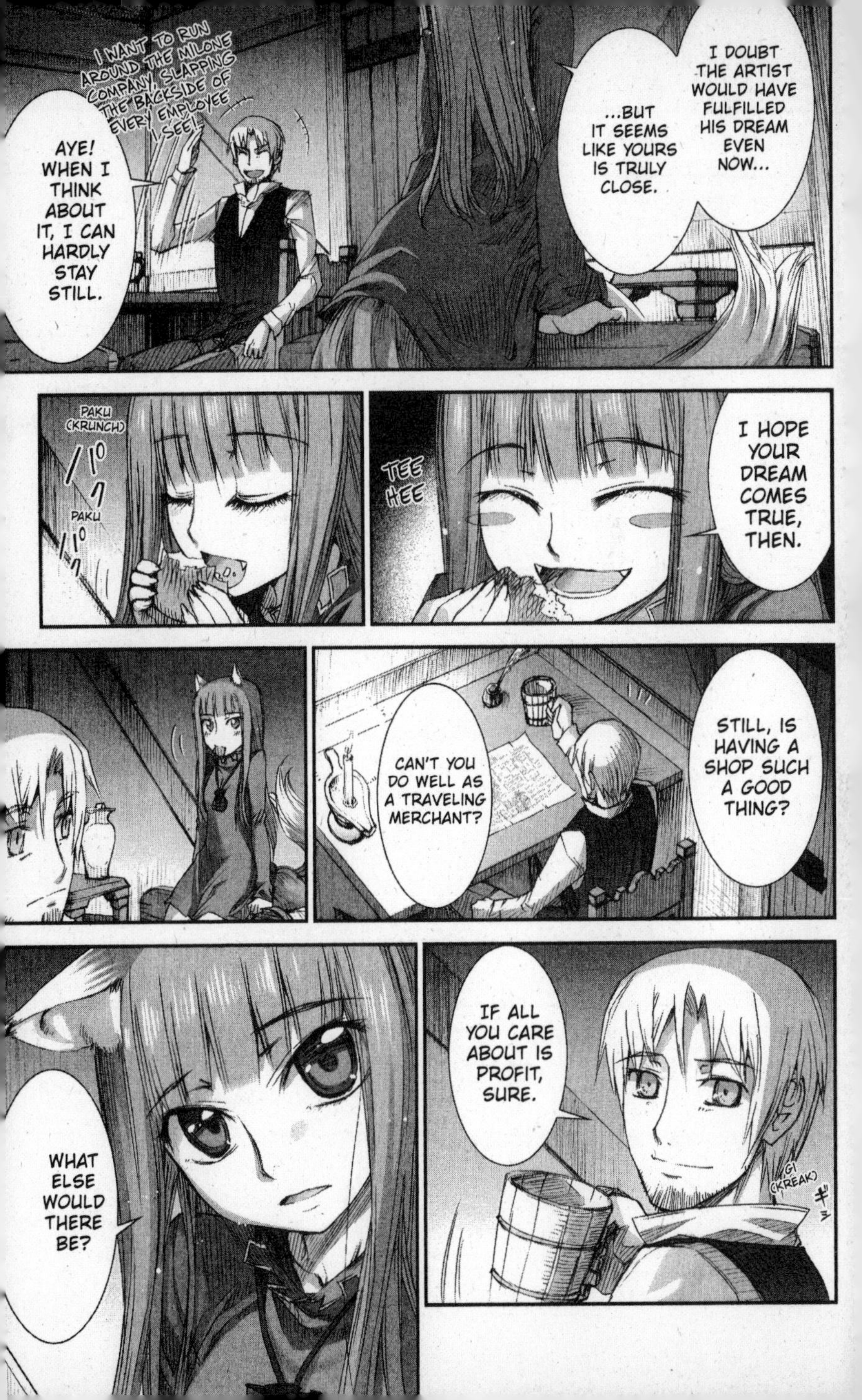
I DOUBT THE ARTIST WOULD HAVE FULFILLED HIS DREAM EVEN NOW...
...BUT IT SEEMS LIKE YOURS IS TRULY CLOSE.
AYE! WHEN I THINK ABOUT IT, I CAN HARDLY STAY STILL.
I WANT TO RUN AROUND THE MILONE COMPANY, SLAPPING THE BACKSIDE OF EVERY EMPLOYEE I SEE!
I HOPE YOUR DREAM COMES TRUE, THEN.
TEE HEE
PAKU (KRUNCH)
PAKU
STILL, IS HAVING A SHOP SUCH A GOOD THING?
CAN'T YOU DO WELL AS A TRAVELING MERCHANT?
IF ALL YOU CARE ABOUT IS PROFIT, SURE.
GI (KREAK)
WHAT ELSE WOULD THERE BE?

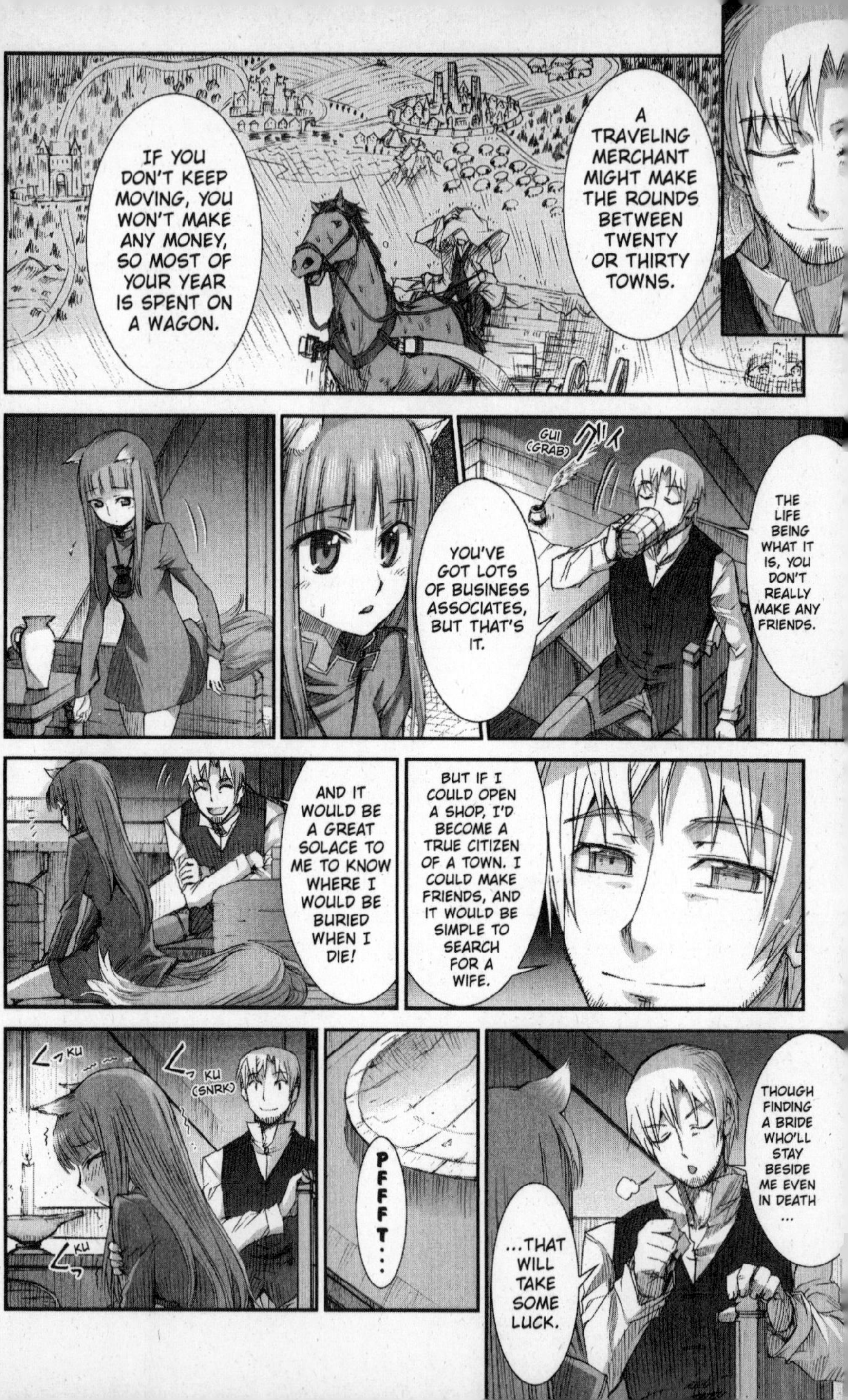
A TRAVELING MERCHANT MIGHT MAKE THE ROUNDS BETWEEN TWENTY OR THIRTY TOWNS.
IF YOU DON'T KEEP MOVING, YOU WON'T MAKE ANY MONEY, SO MOST OF YOUR YEAR IS SPENT ON A WAGON.
GUI (GRAB)
THE LIFE BEING WHAT IT IS, YOU DON'T REALLY MAKE ANY FRIENDS.
YOU'VE GOT LOTS OF BUSINESS ASSOCIATES, BUT THAT'S IT.
BUT IF I COULD OPEN A SHOP, I'D BECOME A TRUE CITIZEN OF A TOWN. I COULD MAKE FRIENDS, AND IT WOULD BE SIMPLE TO SEARCH FOR A WIFE.
AND IT WOULD BE A GREAT SOLACE TO ME TO KNOW WHERE I WOULD BE BURIED WHEN I DIE!
THOUGH FINDING A BRIDE WHO'LL STAY BESIDE ME EVEN IN DEATH...
...THAT WILL TAKE SOME LUCK.
PFFFT...
KU
KU (SNRK)
KU

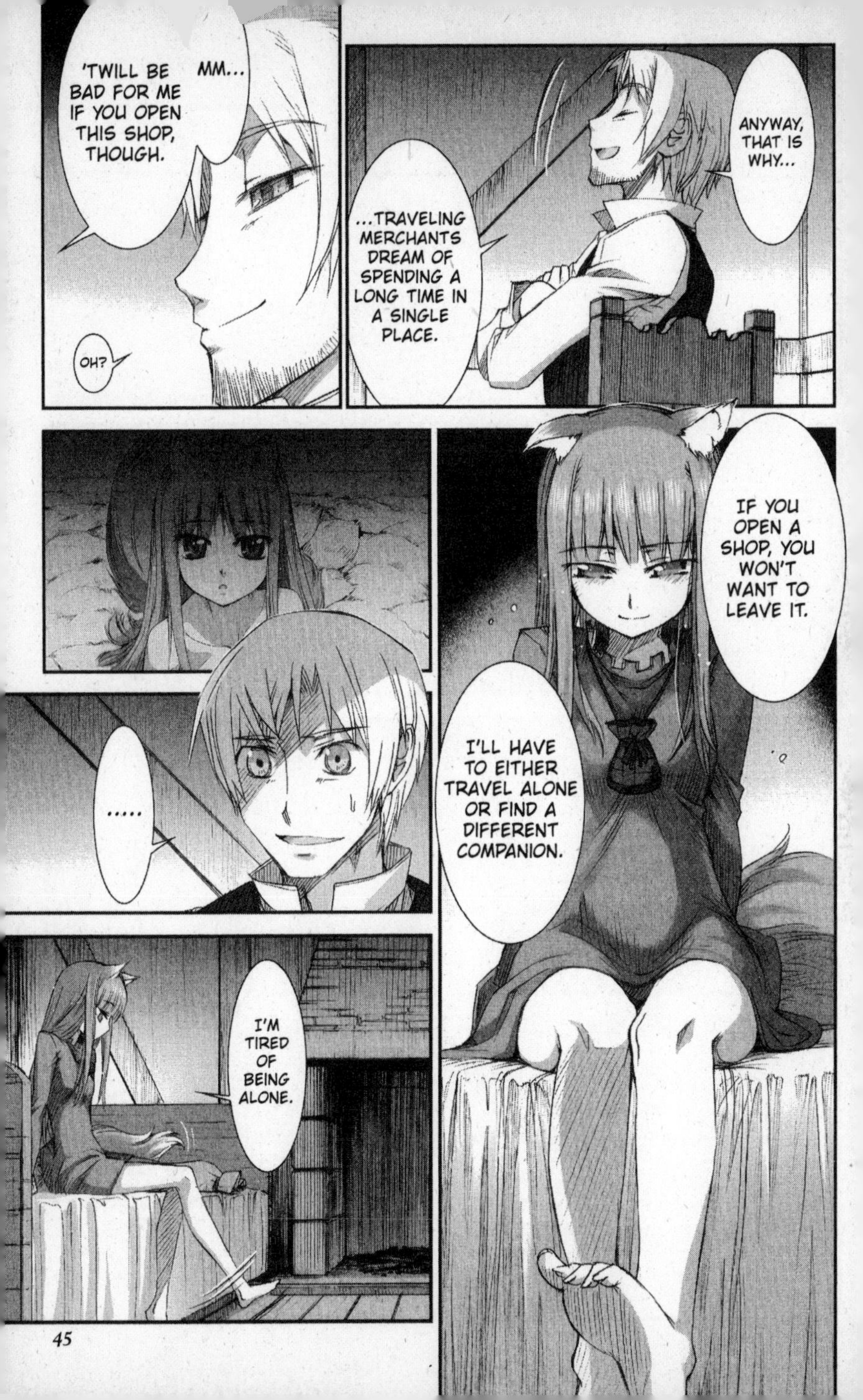
ANYWAY, THAT IS WHY...
...TRAVELING MERCHANTS DREAM OF SPENDING A LONG TIME IN A SINGLE PLACE.
MM...
'TWILL BE BAD FOR ME IF YOU OPEN THIS SHOP, THOUGH.
OH?
IF YOU OPEN A SHOP, YOU WON'T WANT TO LEAVE IT.
I'LL HAVE TO EITHER TRAVEL ALONE OR FIND A DIFFERENT COMPANION.
.....
I'M TIRED OF BEING ALONE.

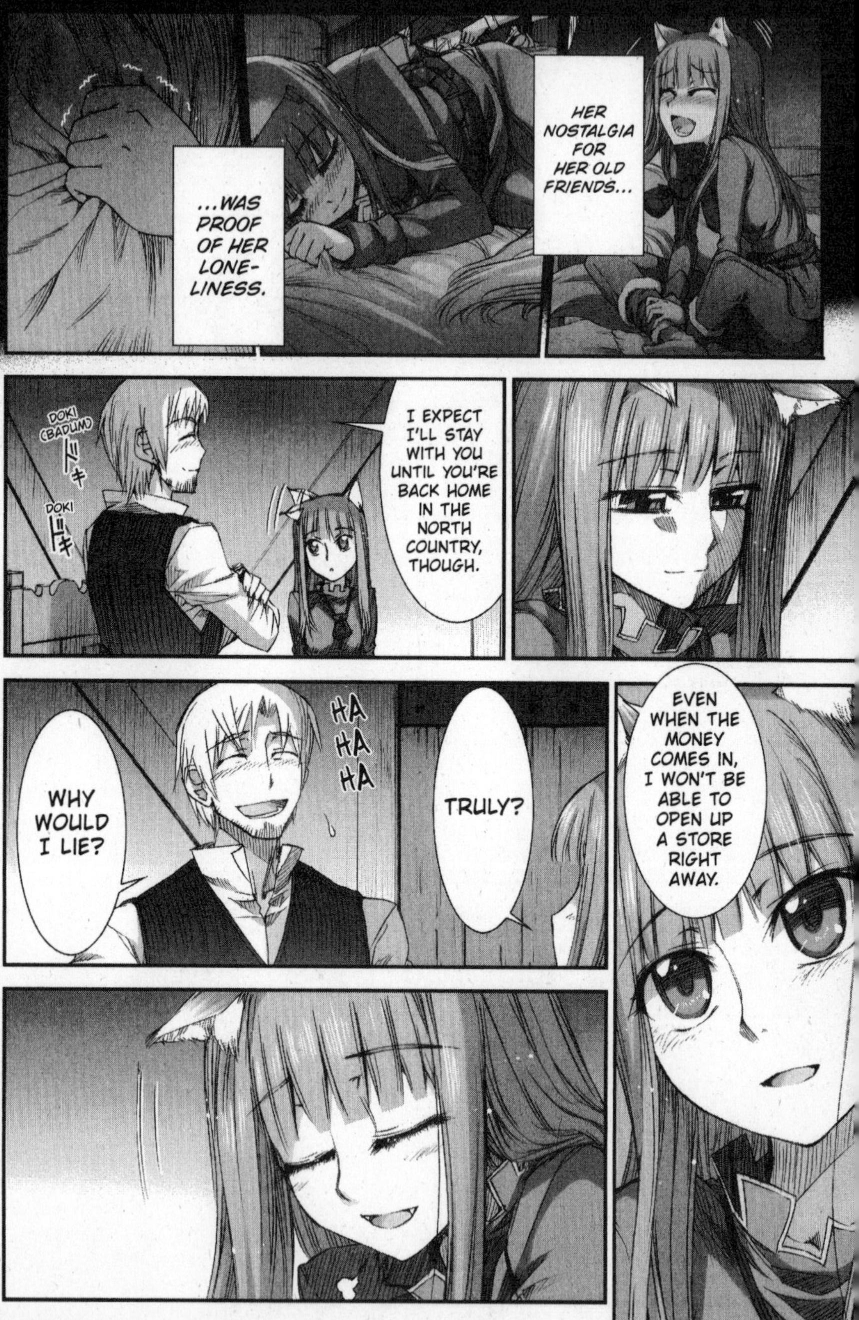
HER NOSTALGIA FOR HER OLD FRIENDS...
...WAS PROOF OF HER LONE-LINESS.
I EXPECT I'LL STAY WITH YOU UNTIL YOU'RE BACK HOME IN THE NORTH COUNTRY, THOUGH.
DOKI (BADUM) ドキ
DOKI ドキ
EVEN WHEN THE MONEY COMES IN, I WON'T BE ABLE TO OPEN UP A STORE RIGHT AWAY.
TRULY?
HA HA HA
WHY WOULD I LIE?

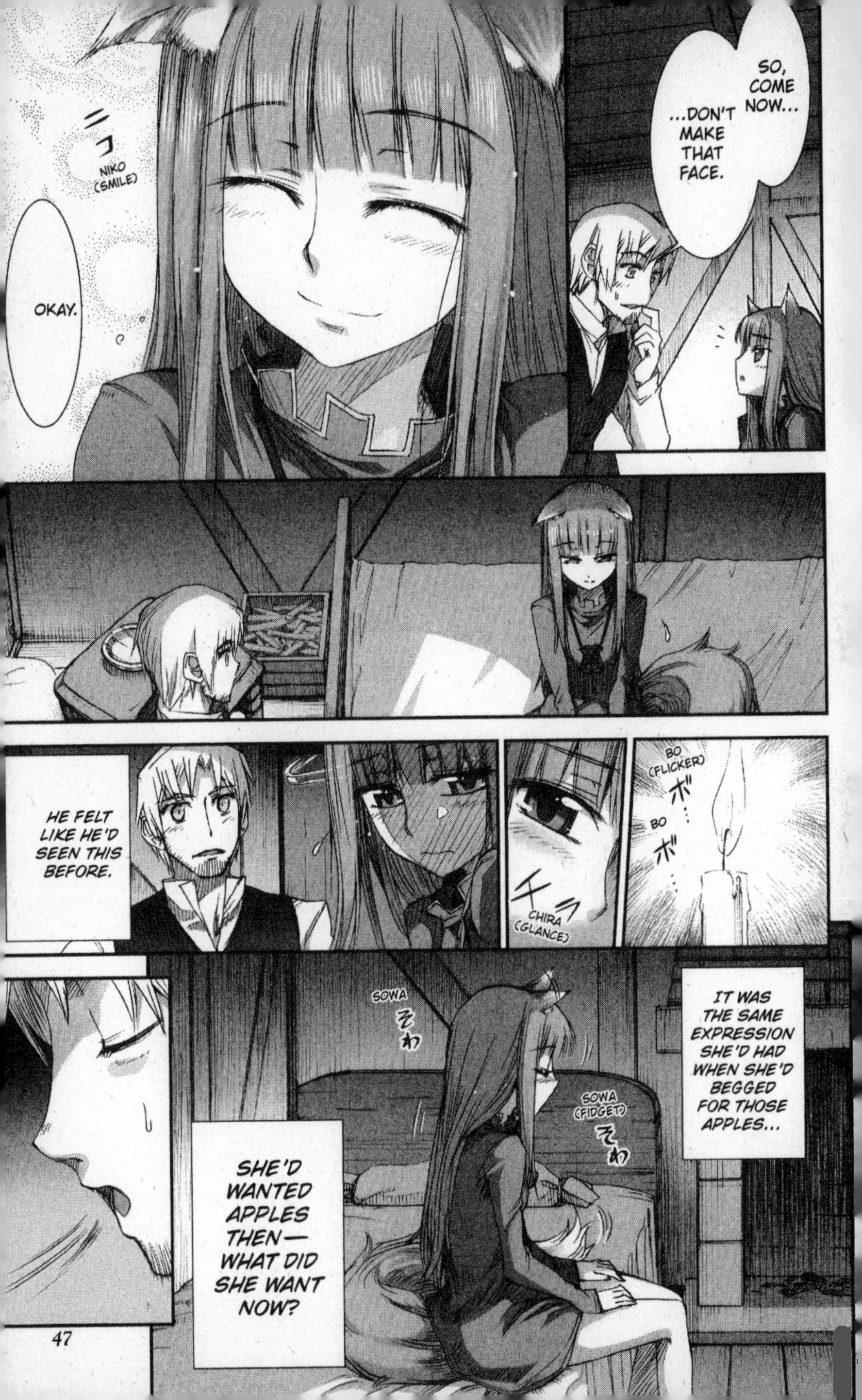
SO, COME NOW...
...DON'T MAKE THAT FACE.
ニコ
NIKO (SMILE)
OKAY.
BO (FLICKER)
ボ…
BO
ボ…
チラ
CHIRA (GLANCE)
HE FELT LIKE HE'D SEEN THIS BEFORE.
IT WAS THE SAME EXPRESSION SHE'D HAD WHEN SHE'D BEGGED FOR THOSE APPLES...
SOWA
そわ
SOWA (FIDGET)
そわ
SHE'D WANTED APPLES THEN—WHAT DID SHE WANT NOW?

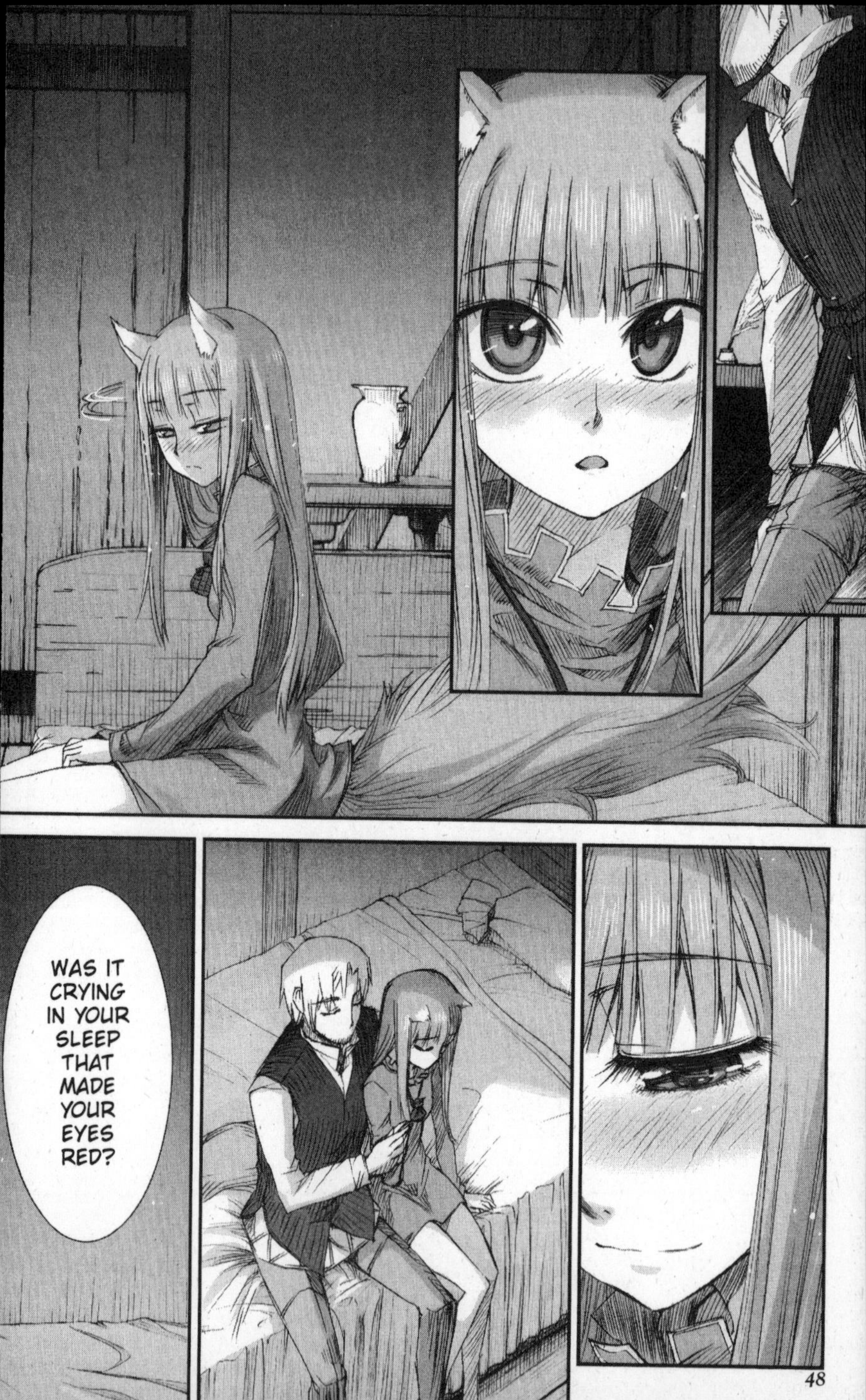
WAS IT CRYING IN YOUR SLEEP THAT MADE YOUR EYES RED?

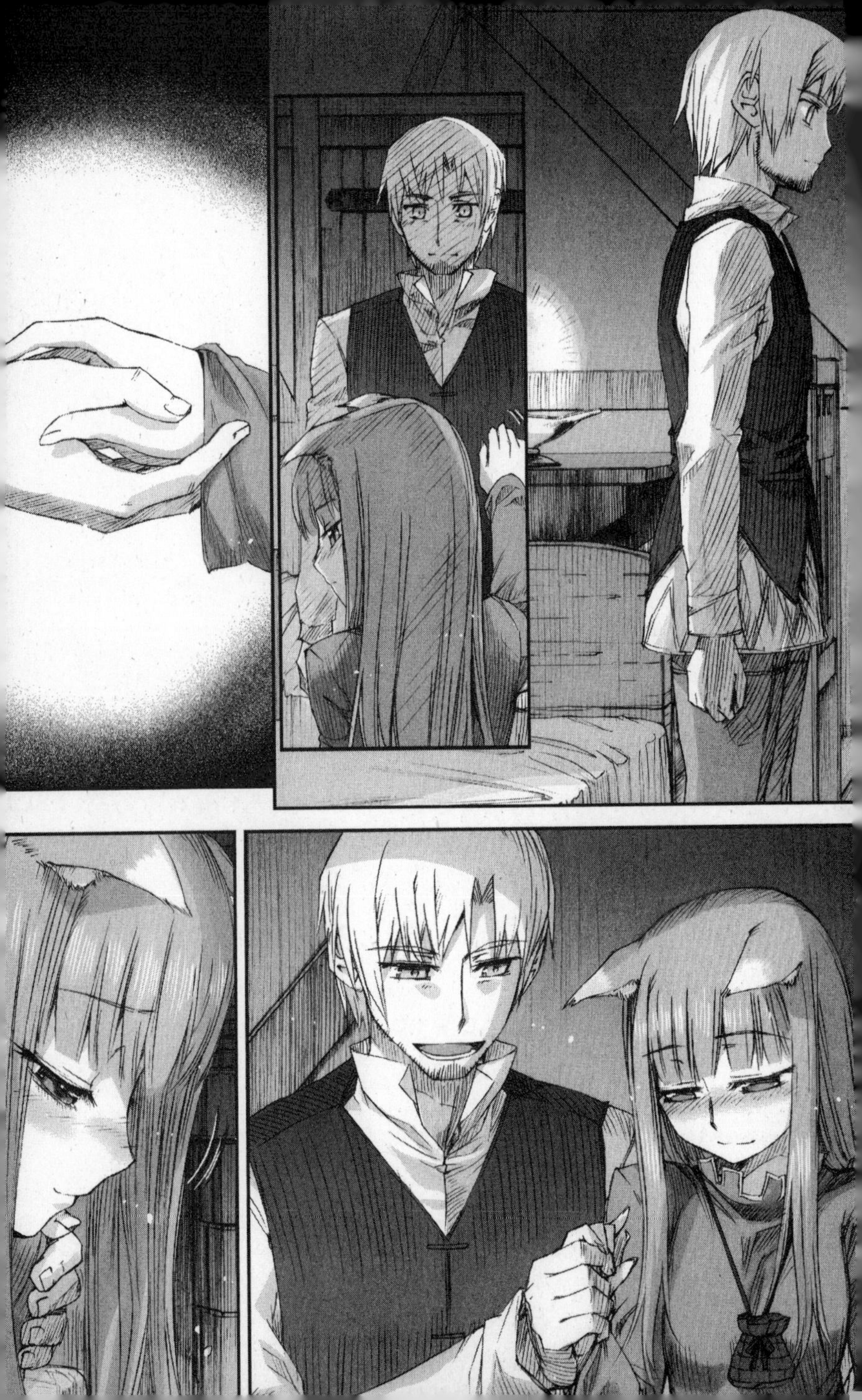

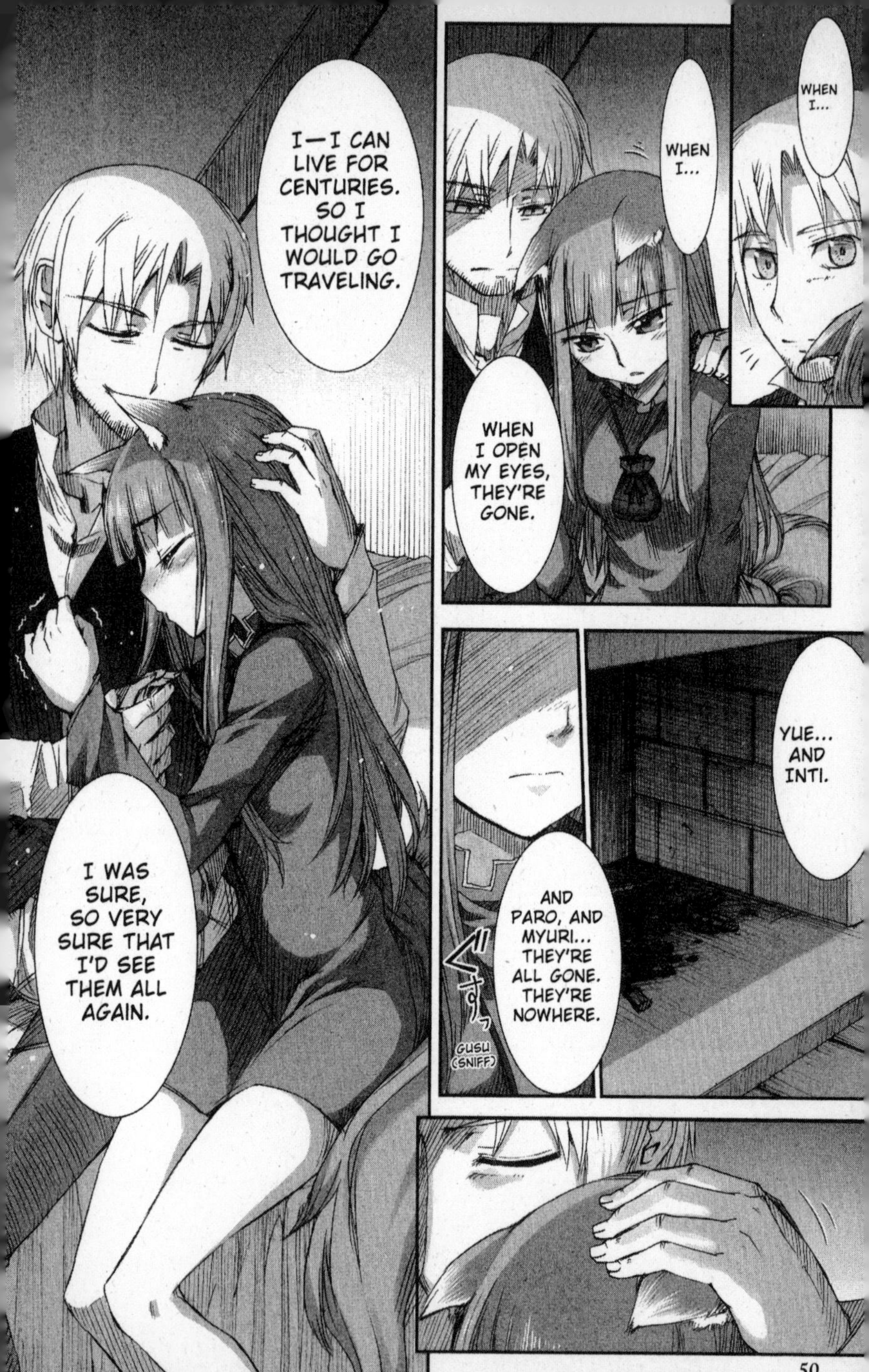
WHEN I...
WHEN I...
WHEN I OPEN MY EYES, THEY'RE GONE.
YUE... AND INTI.
AND PARO, AND MYURI... THEY'RE ALL GONE. THEY'RE NOWHERE.
GUSU (SNIFF)
I—I CAN LIVE FOR CENTURIES. SO I THOUGHT I WOULD GO TRAVELING.
I WAS SURE, SO VERY SURE THAT I'D SEE THEM ALL AGAIN.

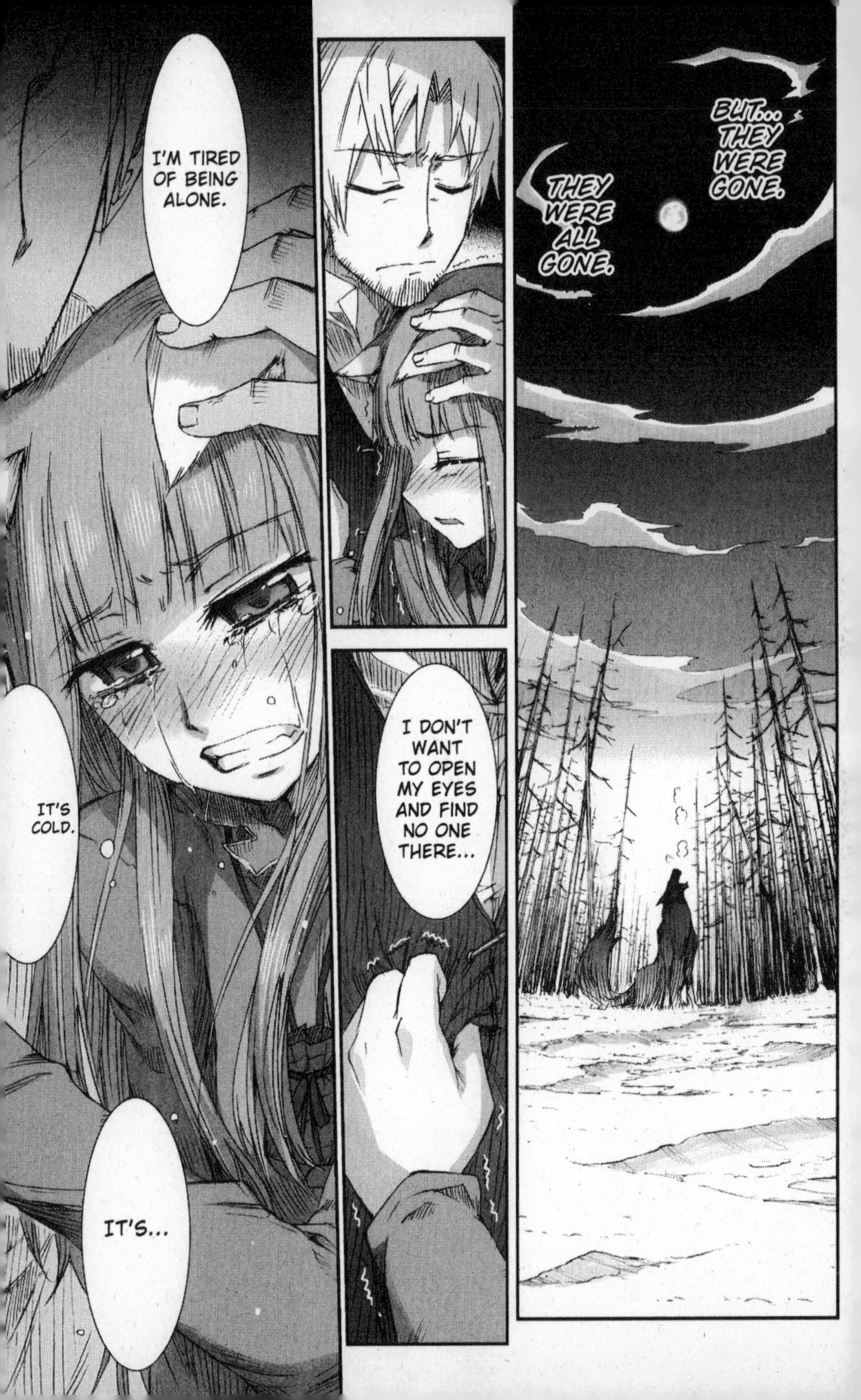
BUT... THEY WERE GONE.
THEY WERE ALL GONE.
I DON'T WANT TO OPEN MY EYES AND FIND NO ONE THERE...
I'M TIRED OF BEING ALONE.
IT'S COLD.
IT'S...

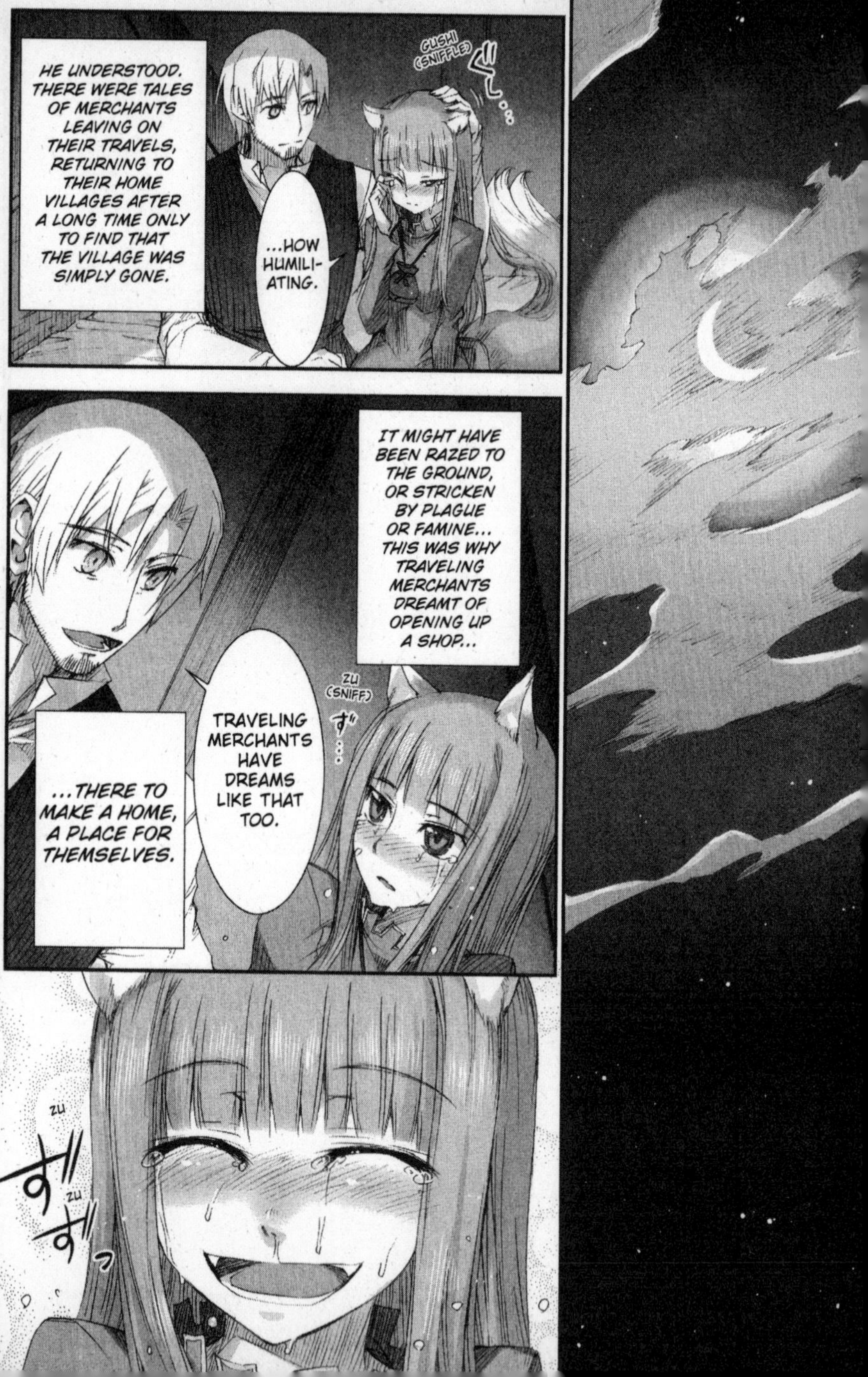
GUSHI (SNIFFLE)
ぐし…
...HOW HUMILIATING.
HE UNDERSTOOD. THERE WERE TALES OF MERCHANTS LEAVING ON THEIR TRAVELS, RETURNING TO THEIR HOME VILLAGES AFTER A LONG TIME ONLY TO FIND THAT THE VILLAGE WAS SIMPLY GONE.
IT MIGHT HAVE BEEN RAZED TO THE GROUND, OR STRICKEN BY PLAGUE OR FAMINE... THIS WAS WHY TRAVELING MERCHANTS DREAMT OF OPENING UP A SHOP...
ZU (SNIFF)
ず…
TRAVELING MERCHANTS HAVE DREAMS LIKE THAT TOO.
...THERE TO MAKE A HOME, A PLACE FOR THEMSELVES.
ZU
ず
ZU
ず

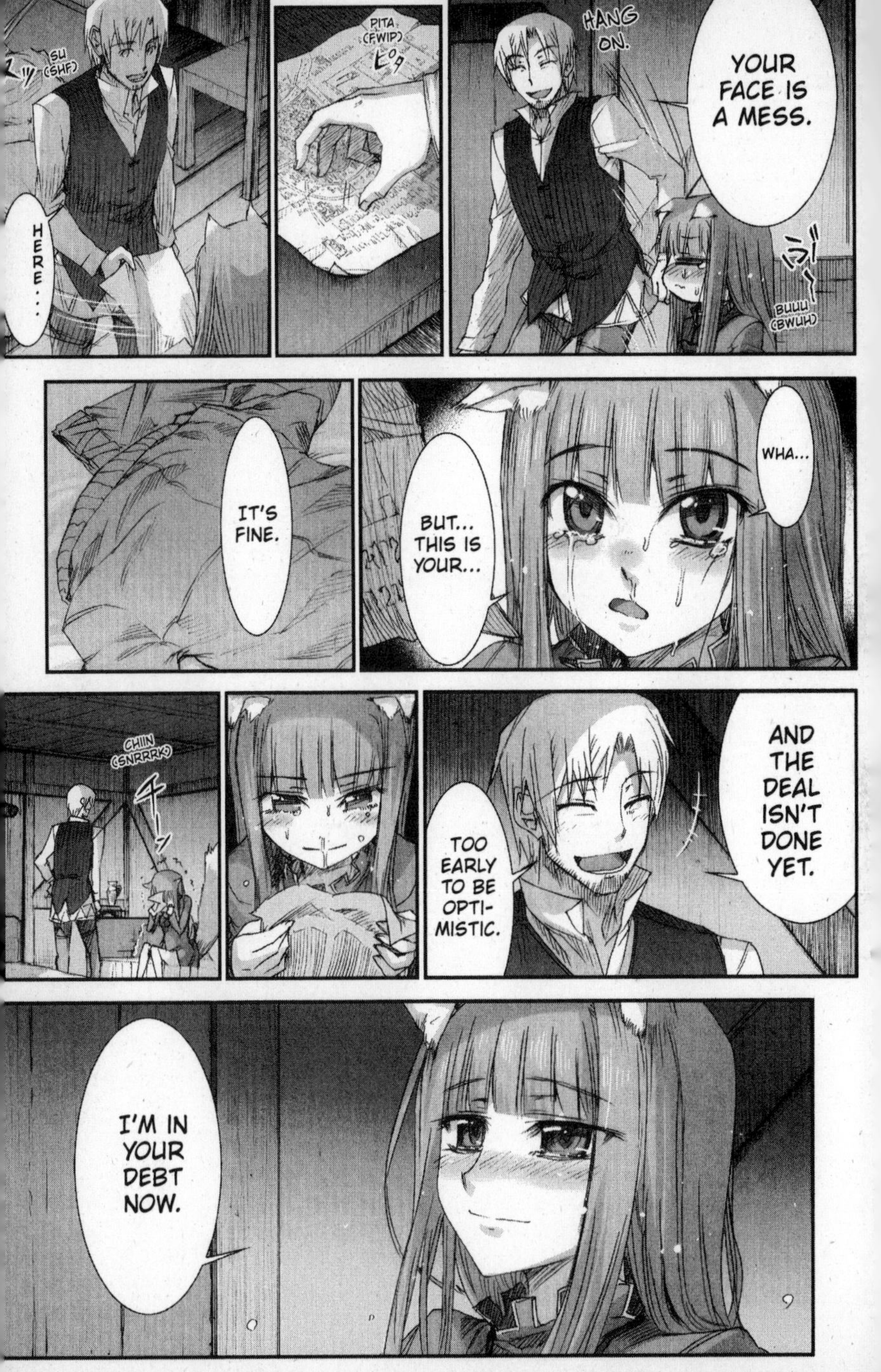
YOUR FACE IS A MESS.
HANG ON.
BUUU (BWUH)
PITA (FWIP)
SU (SHF)
HERE...
WHA...
BUT... THIS IS YOUR...
IT'S FINE.
AND THE DEAL ISN'T DONE YET.
TOO EARLY TO BE OPTI-MISTIC.
CHIIN (SNRRRK)
I'M IN YOUR DEBT NOW.

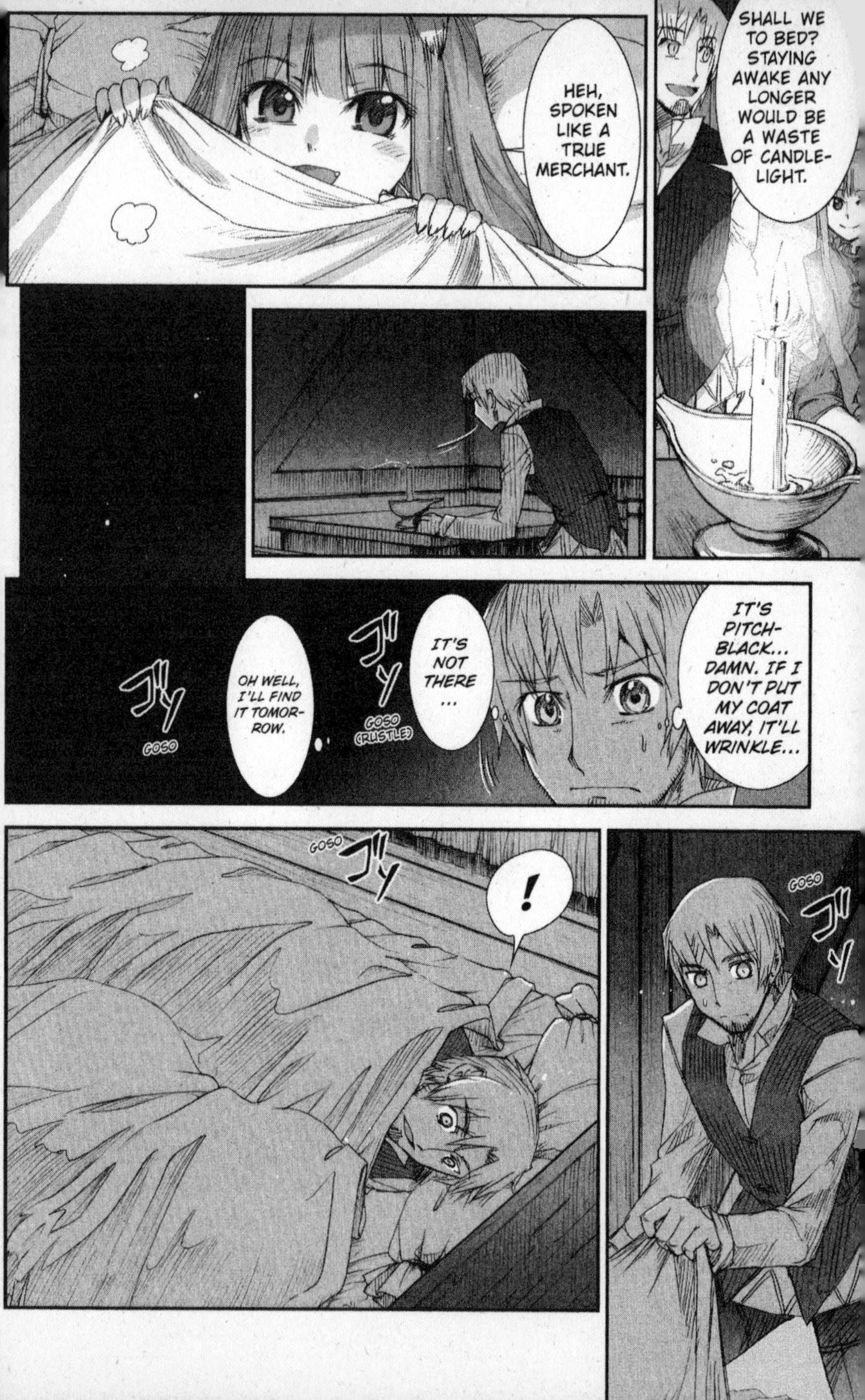
SHALL WE TO BED? STAYING AWAKE ANY LONGER WOULD BE A WASTE OF CANDLE-LIGHT.
HEH, SPOKEN LIKE A TRUE MERCHANT.
IT'S PITCH-BLACK... DAMN. IF I DON'T PUT MY COAT AWAY, IT'LL WRINKLE...
IT'S NOT THERE ...
GOSO (RUSTLE)
OH WELL, I'LL FIND IT TOMORROW.
GOSO
GOSO
GOSO
!

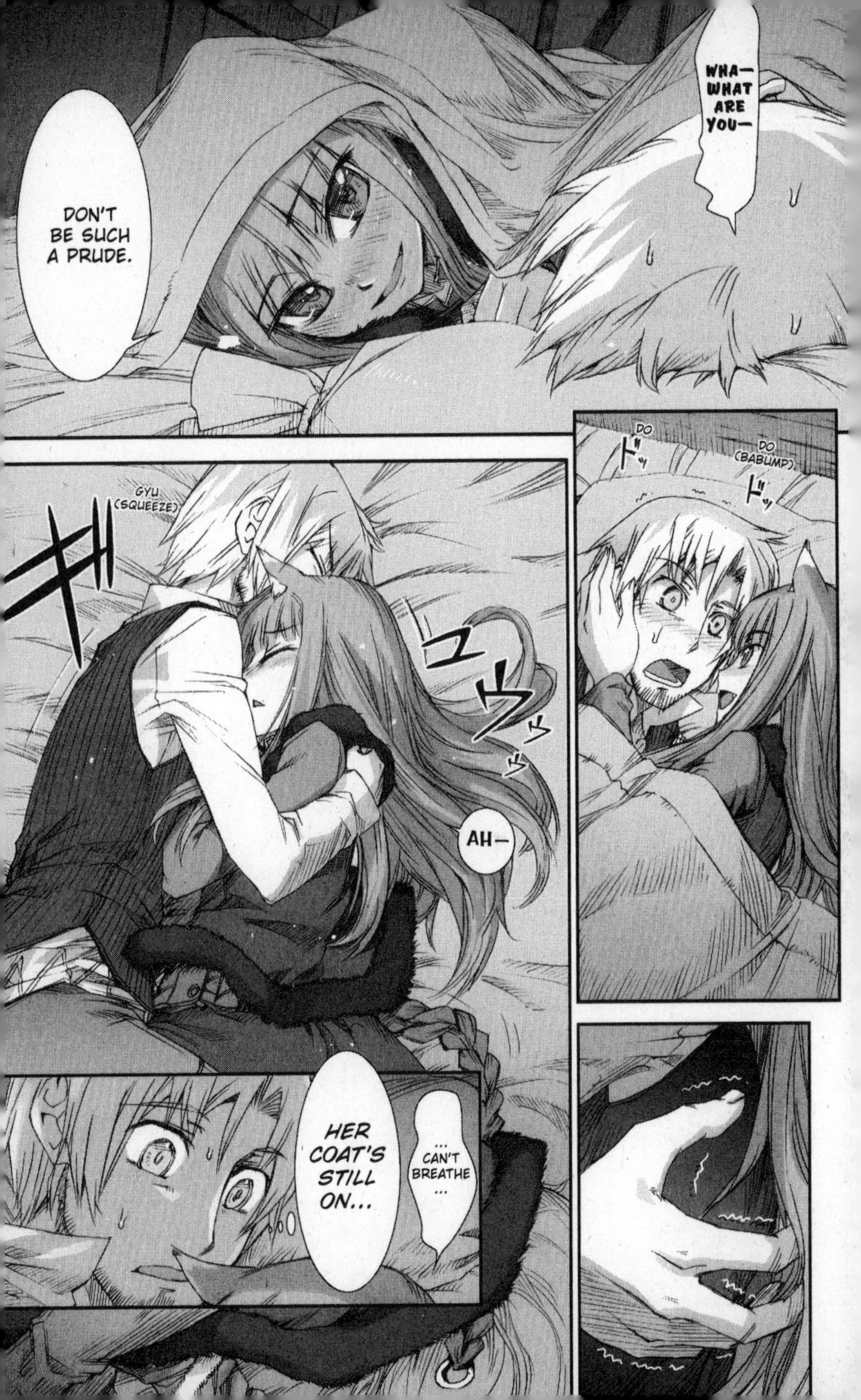
WHA— WHAT ARE YOU—
DON'T BE SUCH A PRUDE.
DO
DO (BABUMP)
GYU (SQUEEZE)
AH—
... CAN'T BREATHE ...
HER COAT'S STILL ON...

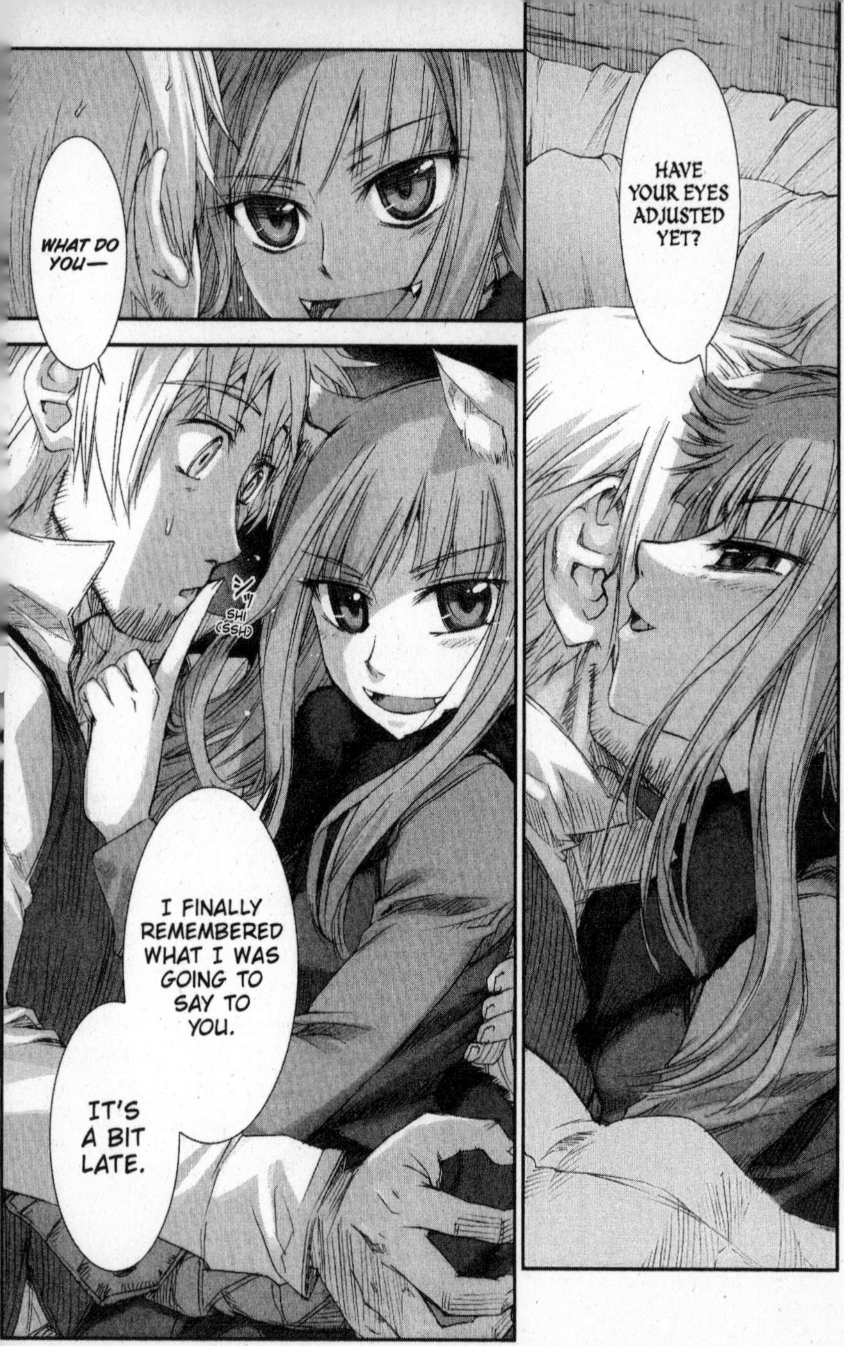
HAVE YOUR EYES ADJUSTED YET?
WHAT DO YOU—
SHI (SSH)
I FINALLY REMEMBERED WHAT I WAS GOING TO SAY TO YOU.
IT'S A BIT LATE.

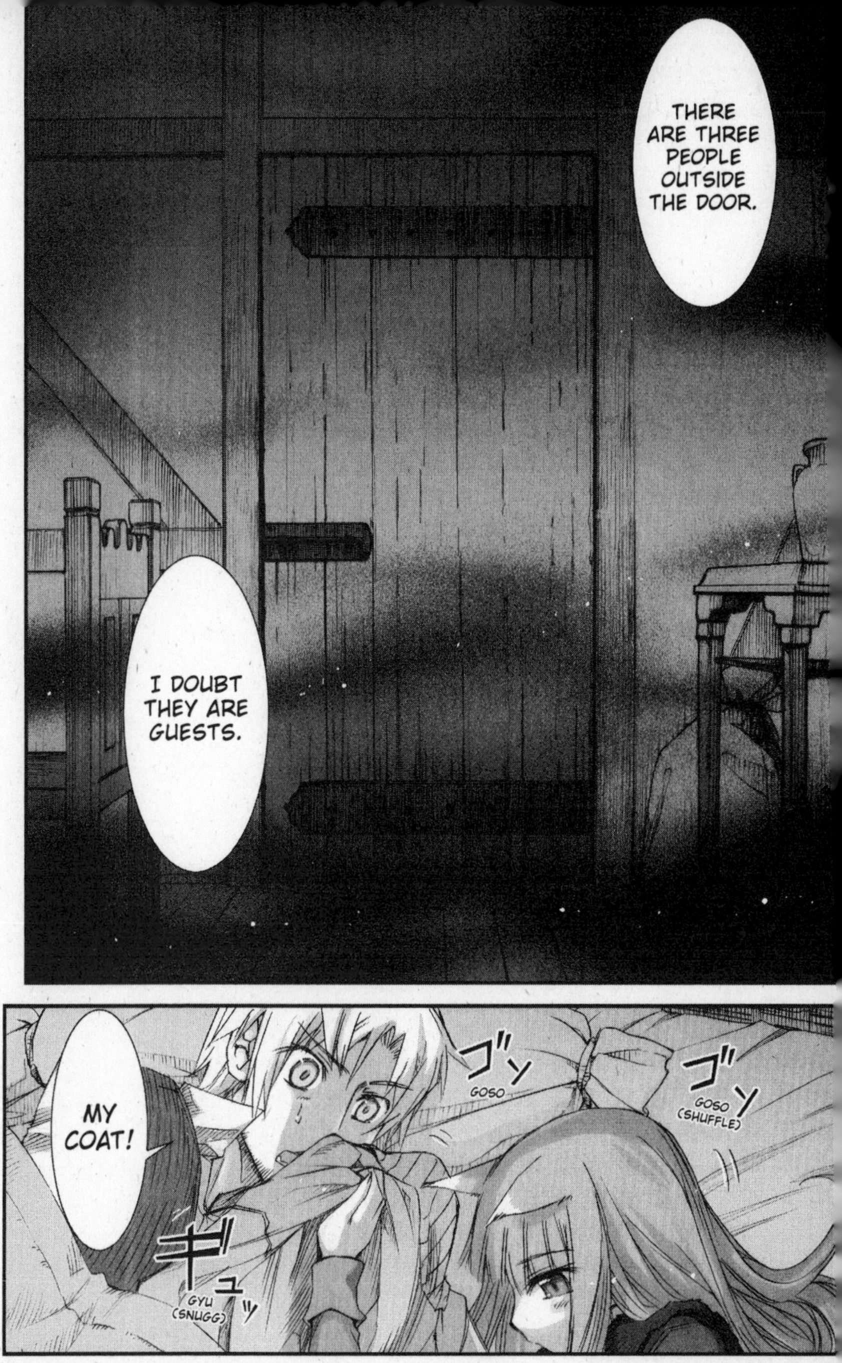
THERE ARE THREE PEOPLE OUTSIDE THE DOOR.
I DOUBT THEY ARE GUESTS.
ゴソ
GOSO (SHUFFLE)
ゴソ
GOSO
MY COAT!
ギュッ
GYU (SNUGG)

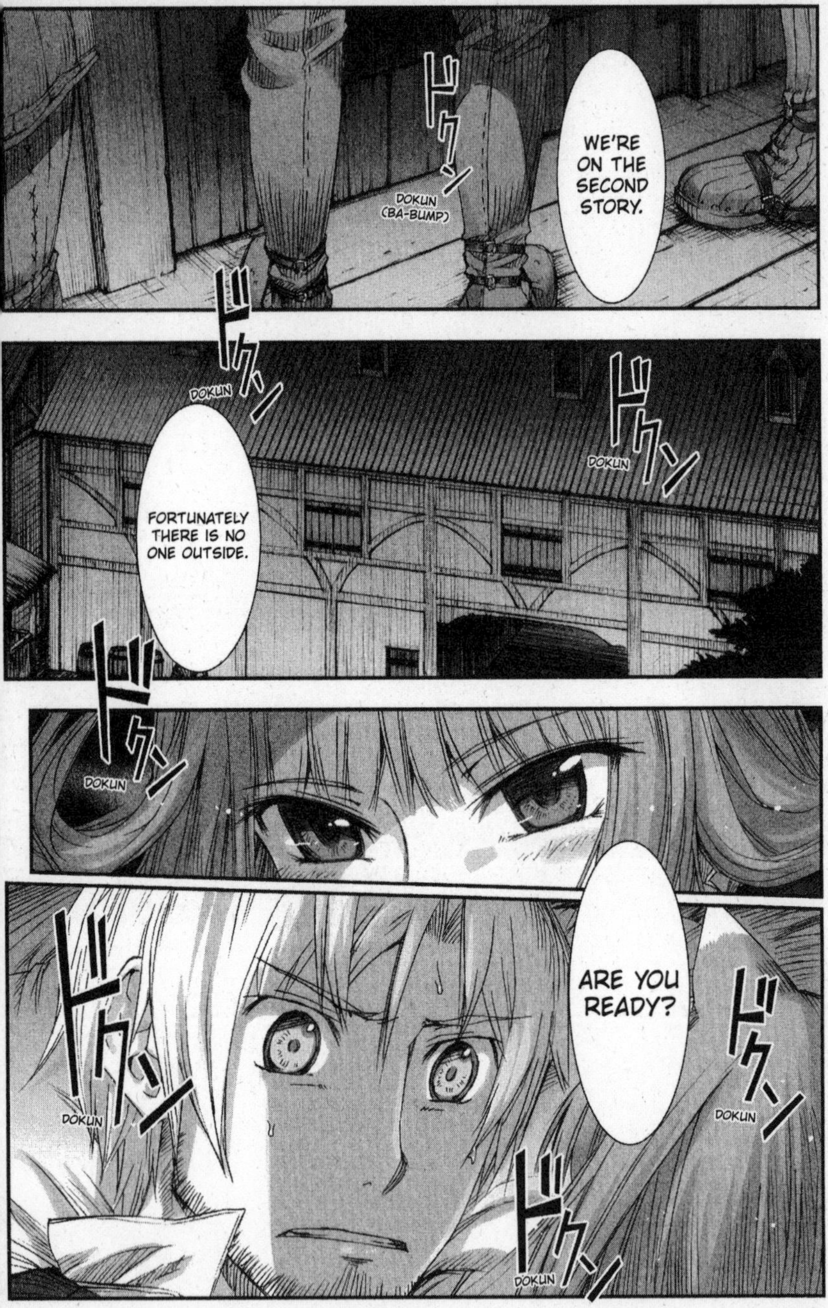
WE'RE ON THE SECOND STORY.
ドクン
DOKUN (BA-BUMP)
ドクン
DOKUN
ドクン
DOKUN
FORTUNATELY THERE IS NO ONE OUTSIDE.
ドクン
DOKUN
ARE YOU READY?
ドクン
DOKUN
ドクン
DOKUN
ドクン
DOKUN

SPICE & WOLF

SPICE & WOLF

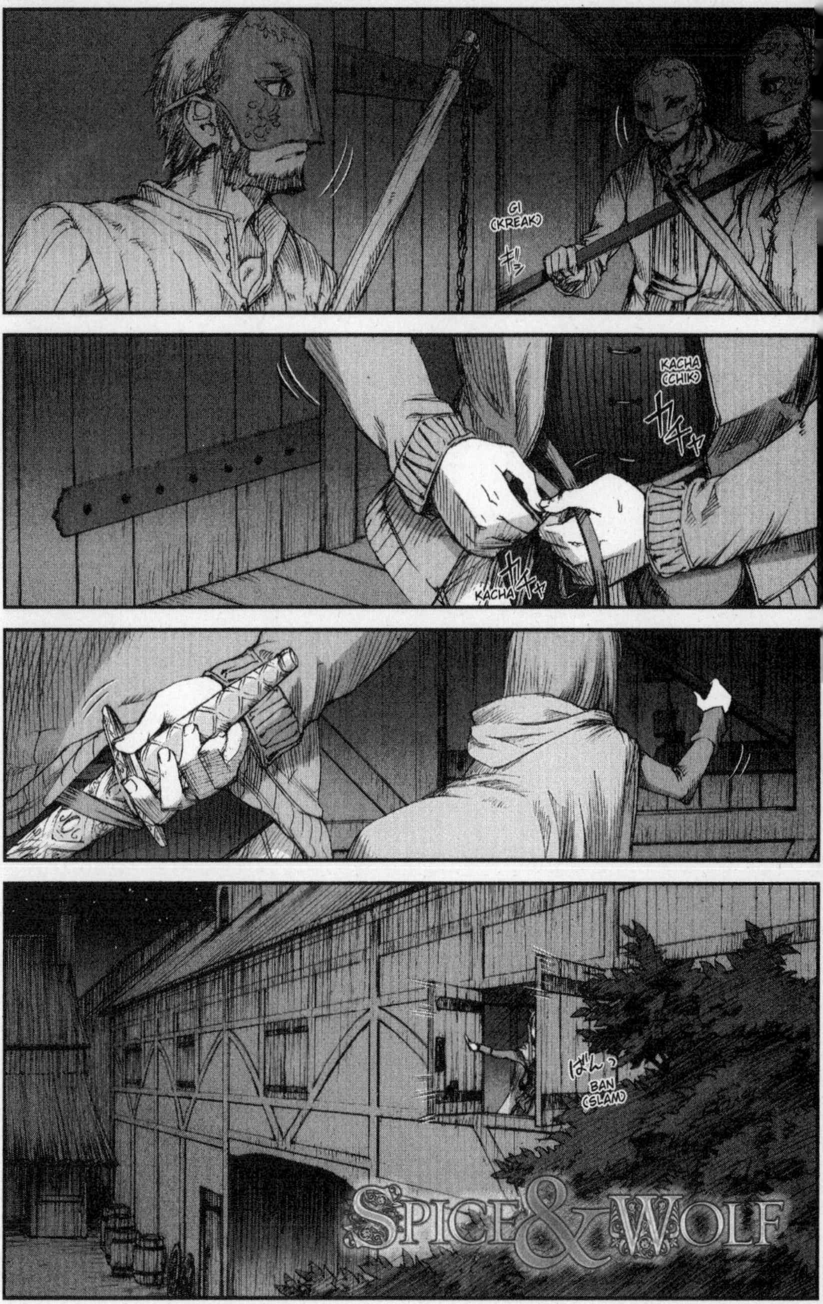
GI
(KREAK)
ギッ
KACHA
(CHIK)
カチャ
カチャ
KACHA
ばんっ
BAN
(SLAM)
SPICE & WOLF

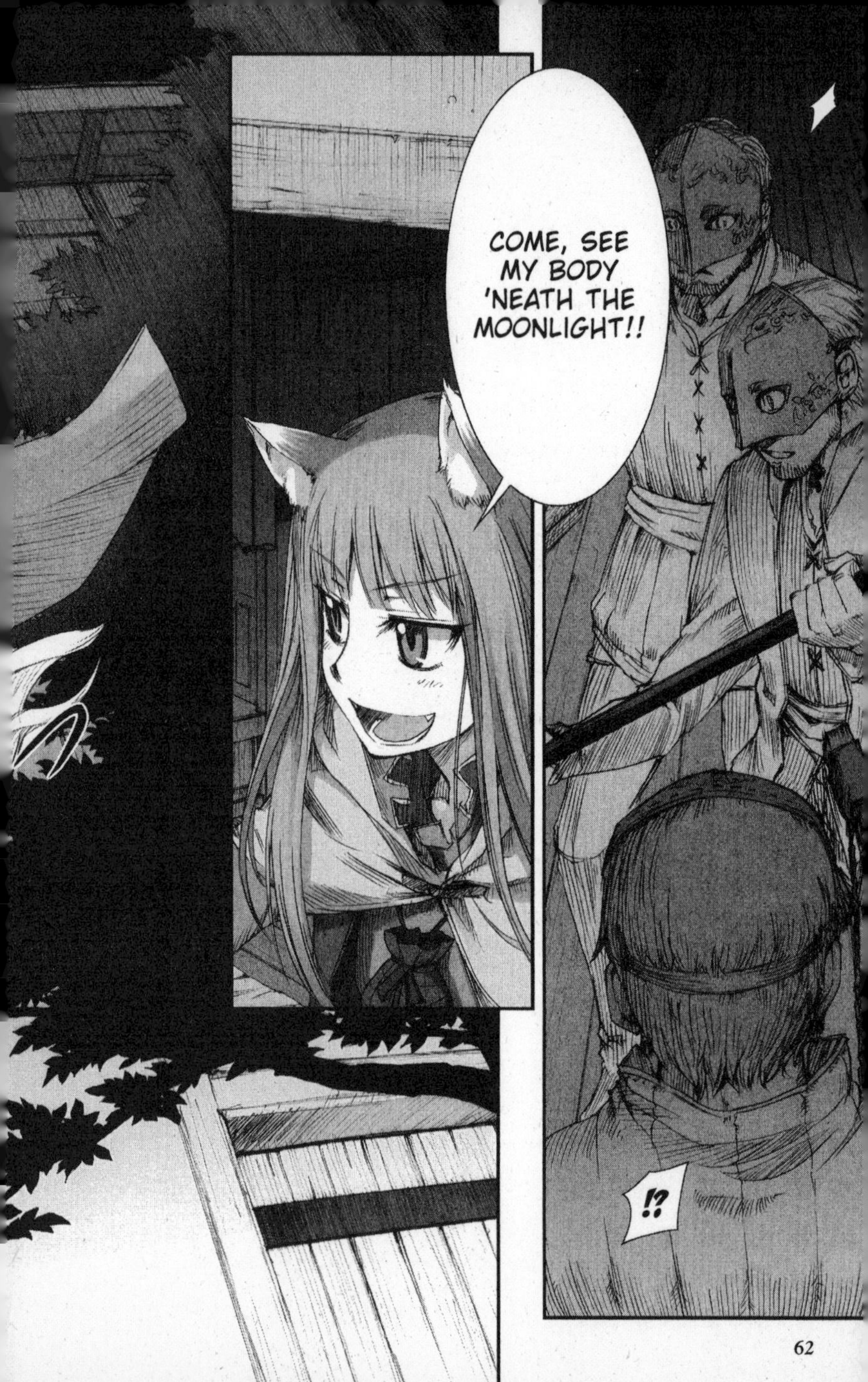
COME, SEE MY BODY 'NEATH THE MOONLIGHT!!
!?

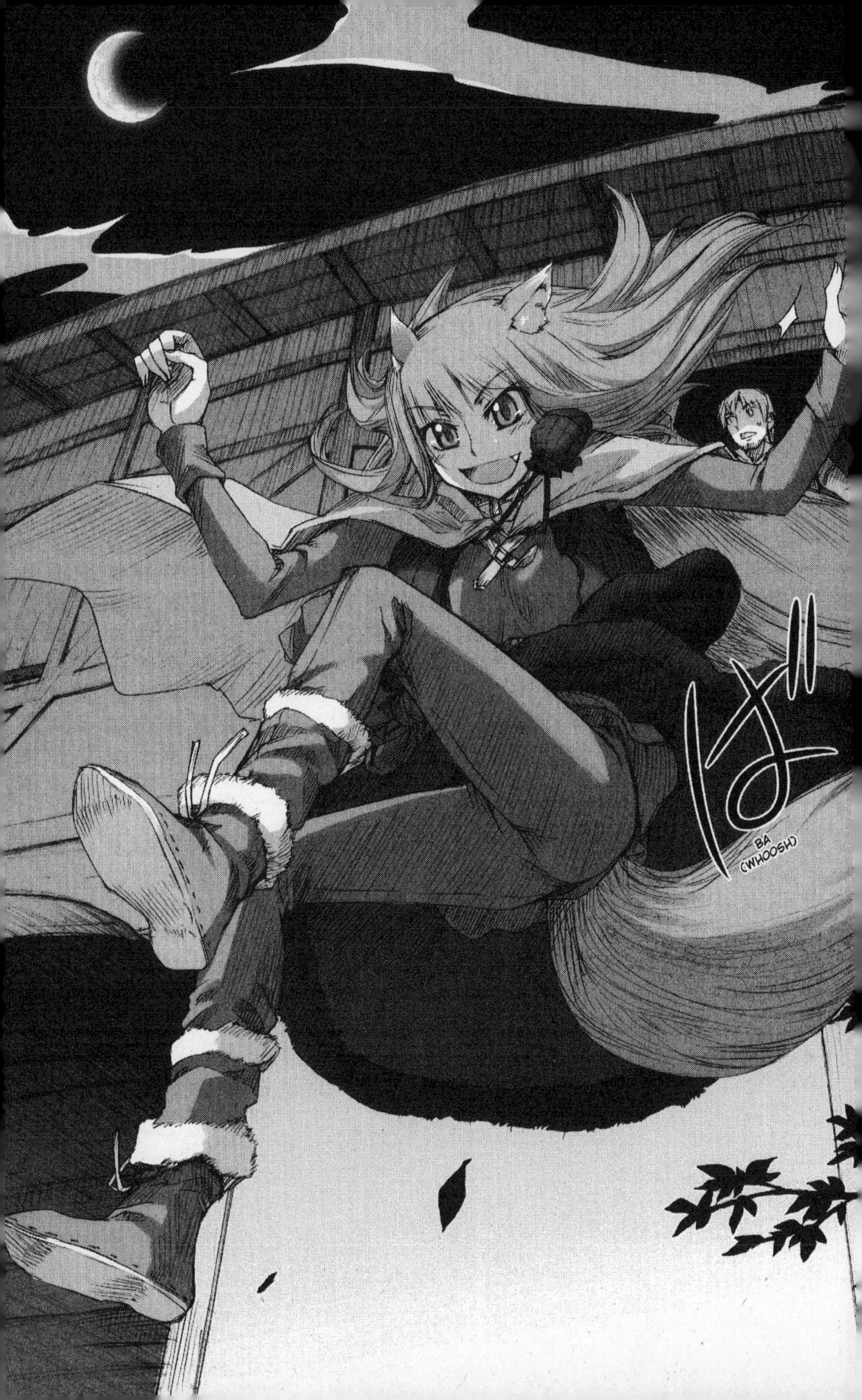
ば
BA (WHOOSH)

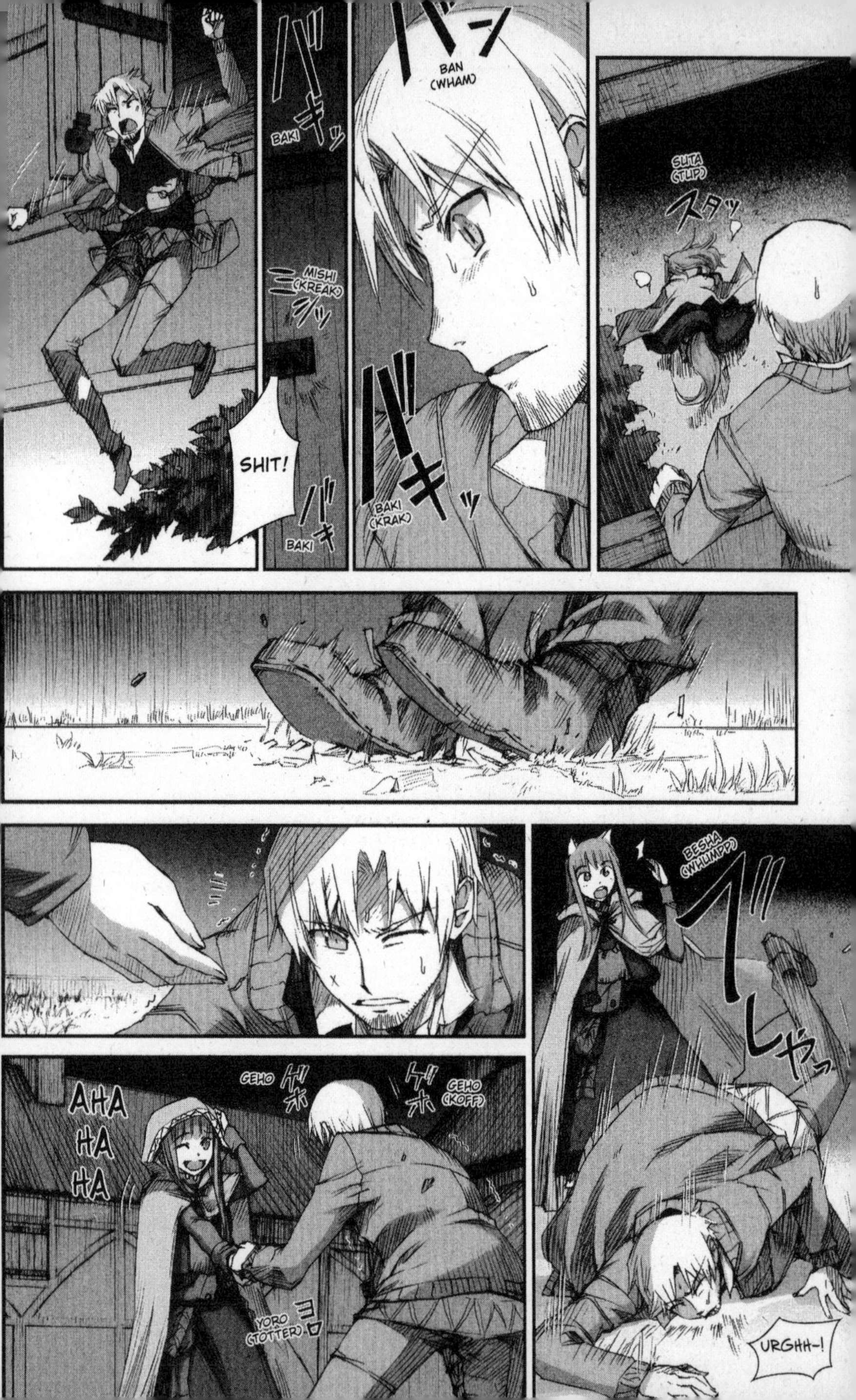
SUTA (TUP)
スタッ
BAN (WHAM)
バンッ
BAKI (KRAK)
バキッ
BAKI
バキッ
MISHI (KREAK)
ミシッ
BAKI
バキ
SHIT!
BESHA (WHUMPF)
べしゃっ
URGHH-!
GEHO (KOFF)
ゲホ
GEHO
ゲホ
AHA HA HA
YORO (TOTTER)
ヨロ

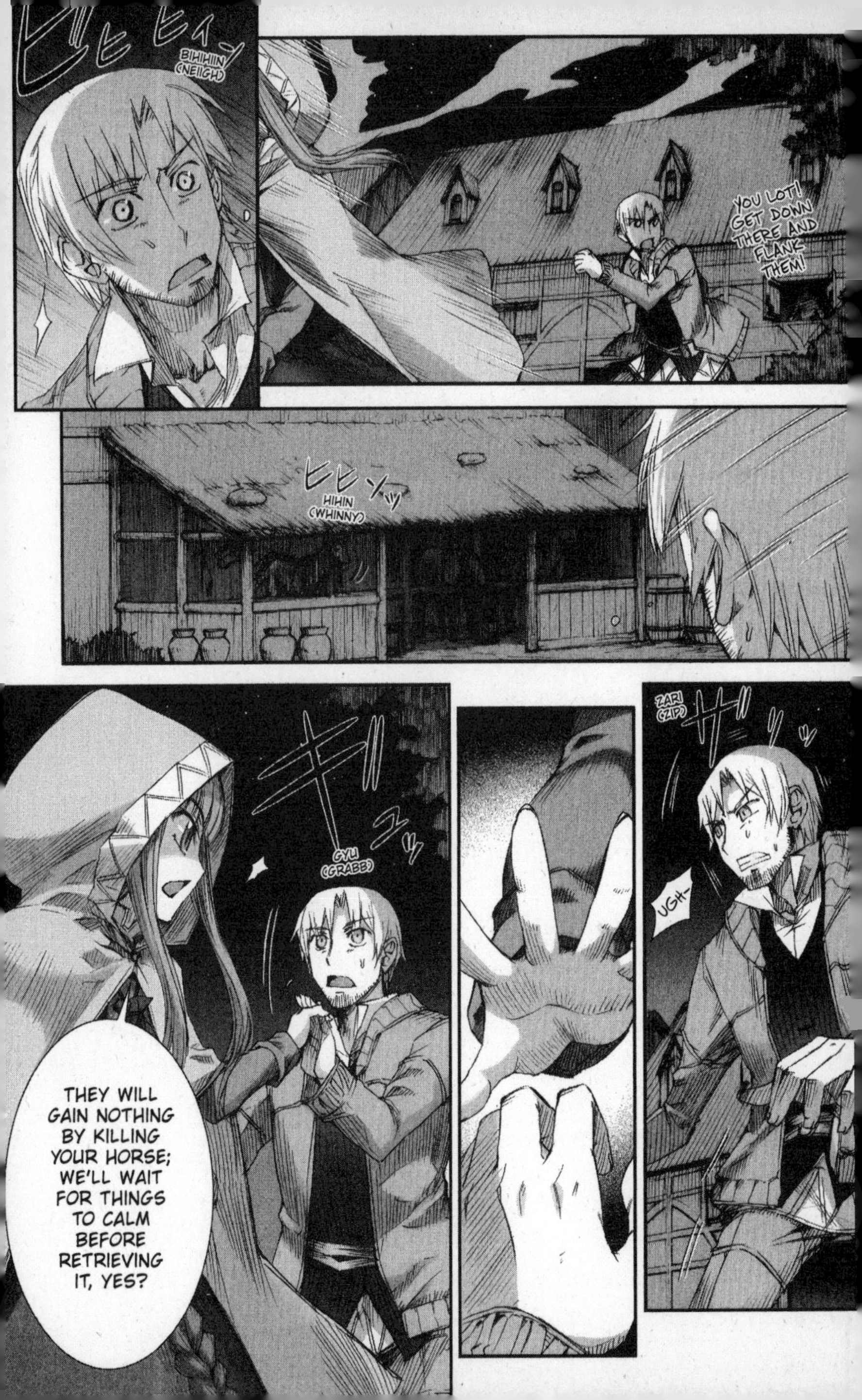
YOU LOT! GET DOWN THERE AND FLANK THEM!
BIHIHIIN (NEIIGH)
HIHIN (WHINNY)
ZARI (ZIP)
UGH-
GYU (GRABB)
THEY WILL GAIN NOTHING BY KILLING YOUR HORSE; WE'LL WAIT FOR THINGS TO CALM BEFORE RETRIEVING IT, YES?

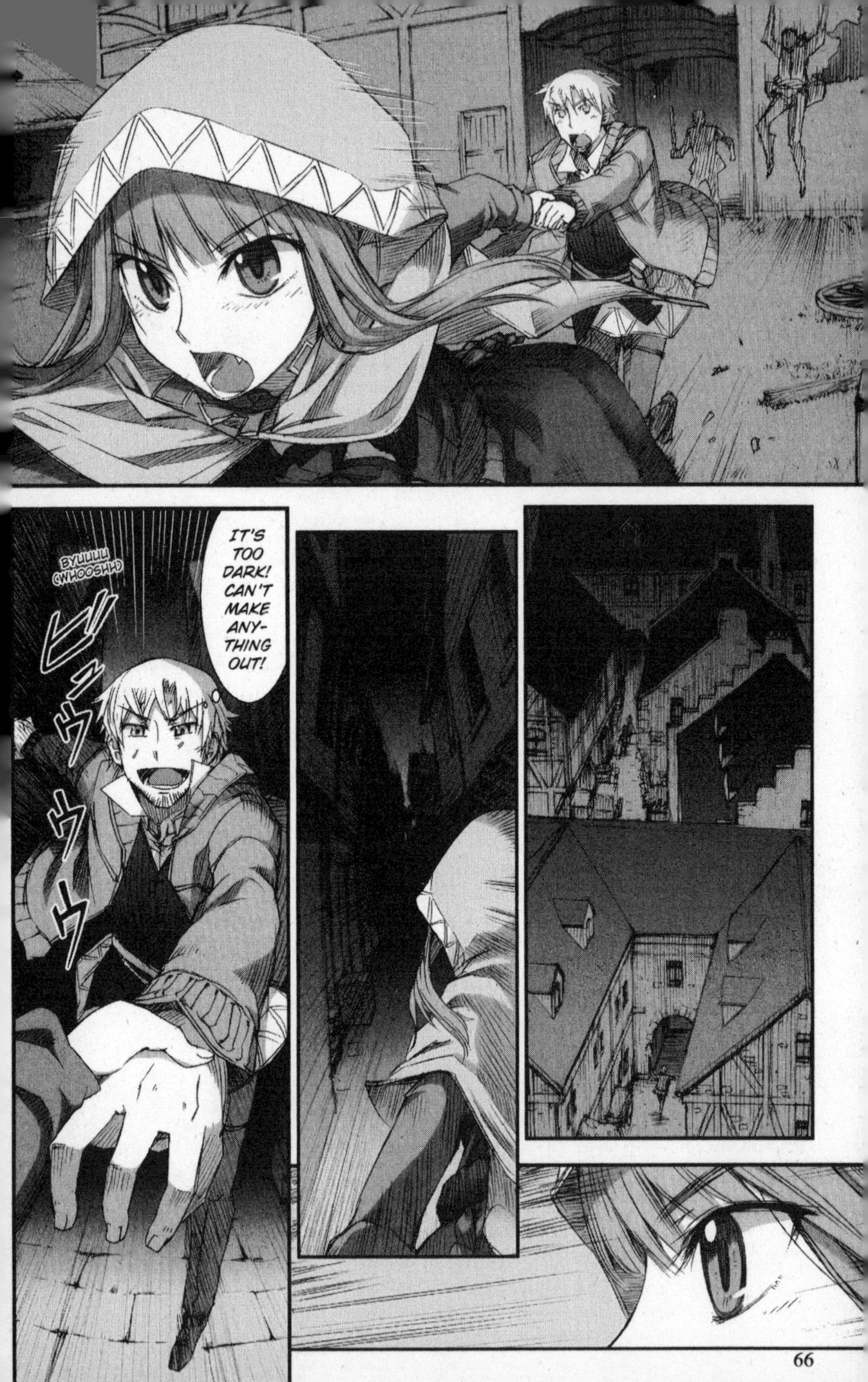
IT'S TOO DARK! CAN'T MAKE ANY-THING OUT!
BYUUUU (WHOOSH)

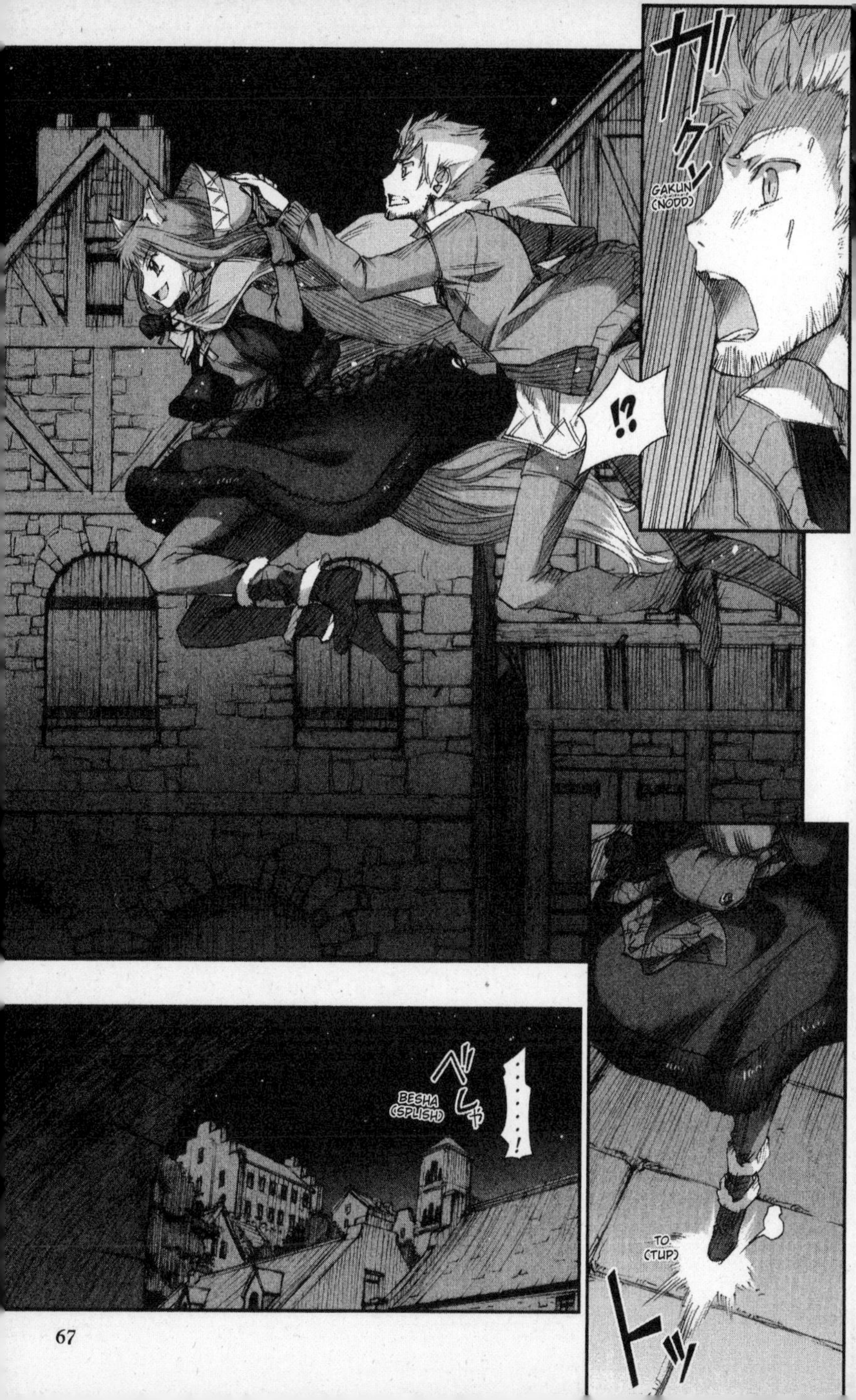

ガクン
GAKUN (NODD)
!?
トッ
TO (TUP)
べしゃ
BESHA (SPLISH)
......!

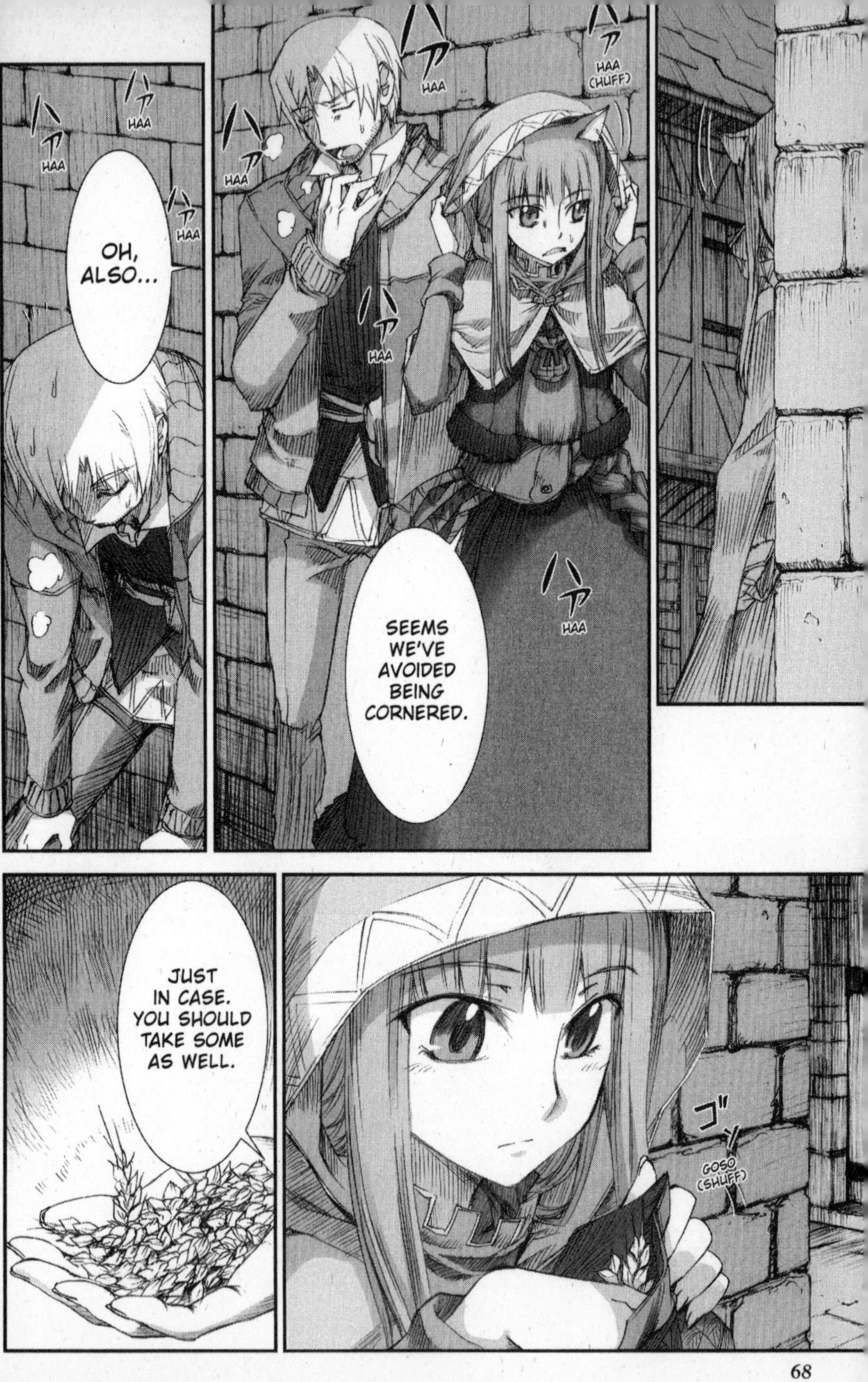
HAA (HUFF)
HAA
HAA
HAA
SEEMS WE'VE AVOIDED BEING CORNERED.
HAA
HAA
HAA
HAA
OH, ALSO...
GOSO (SHUFF)
JUST IN CASE. YOU SHOULD TAKE SOME AS WELL.

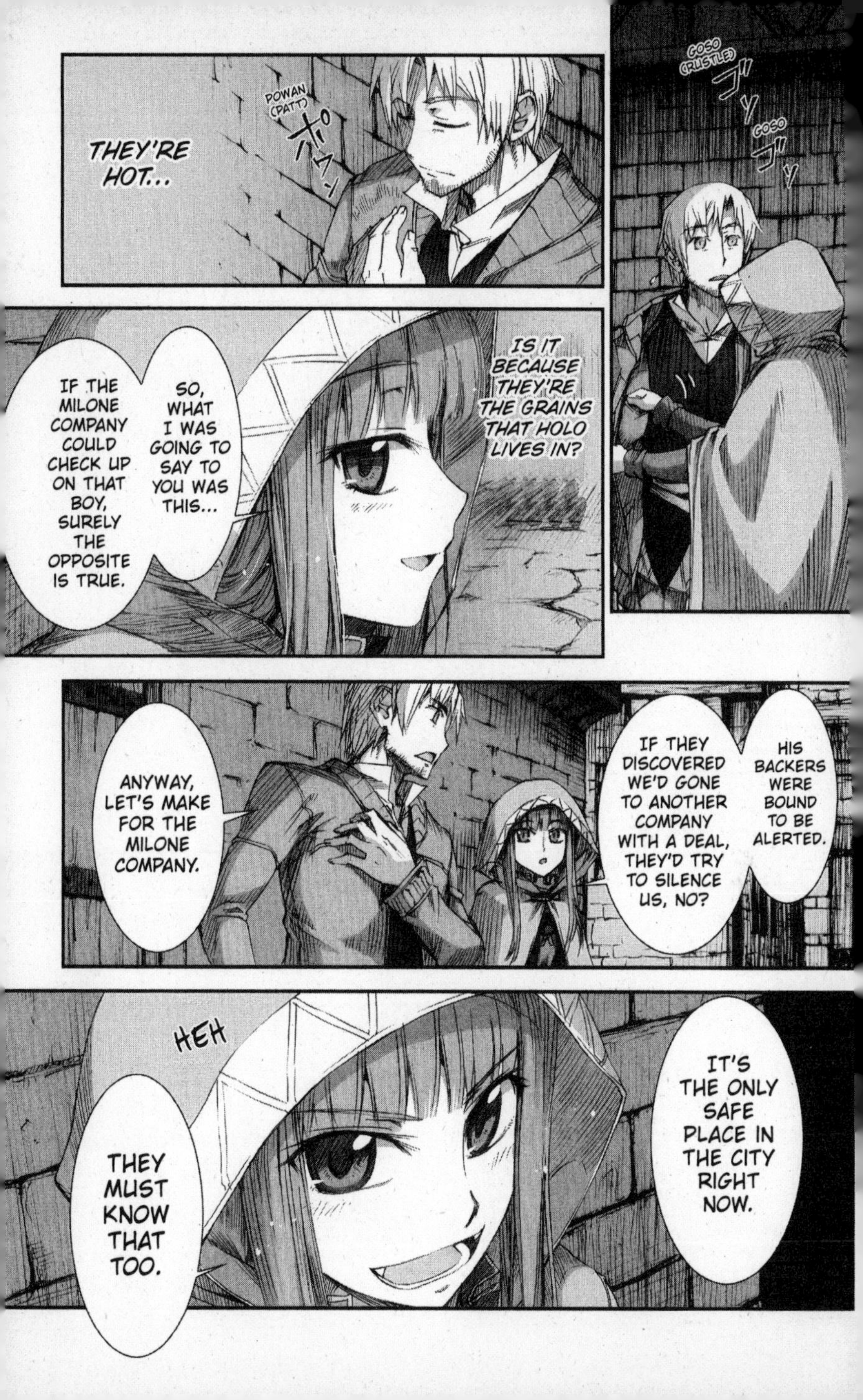
GOSO (RUSTLE)
ゴソ
GOSO
ゴソ
THEY'RE HOT...
POWAN (PATT)
ポワン
IS IT BECAUSE THEY'RE THE GRAINS THAT HOLO LIVES IN?
SO, WHAT I WAS GOING TO SAY TO YOU WAS THIS...
IF THE MILONE COMPANY COULD CHECK UP ON THAT BOY, SURELY THE OPPOSITE IS TRUE.
HIS BACKERS WERE BOUND TO BE ALERTED.
IF THEY DISCOVERED WE'D GONE TO ANOTHER COMPANY WITH A DEAL, THEY'D TRY TO SILENCE US, NO?
ANYWAY, LET'S MAKE FOR THE MILONE COMPANY.
IT'S THE ONLY SAFE PLACE IN THE CITY RIGHT NOW.
HEH
THEY MUST KNOW THAT TOO.

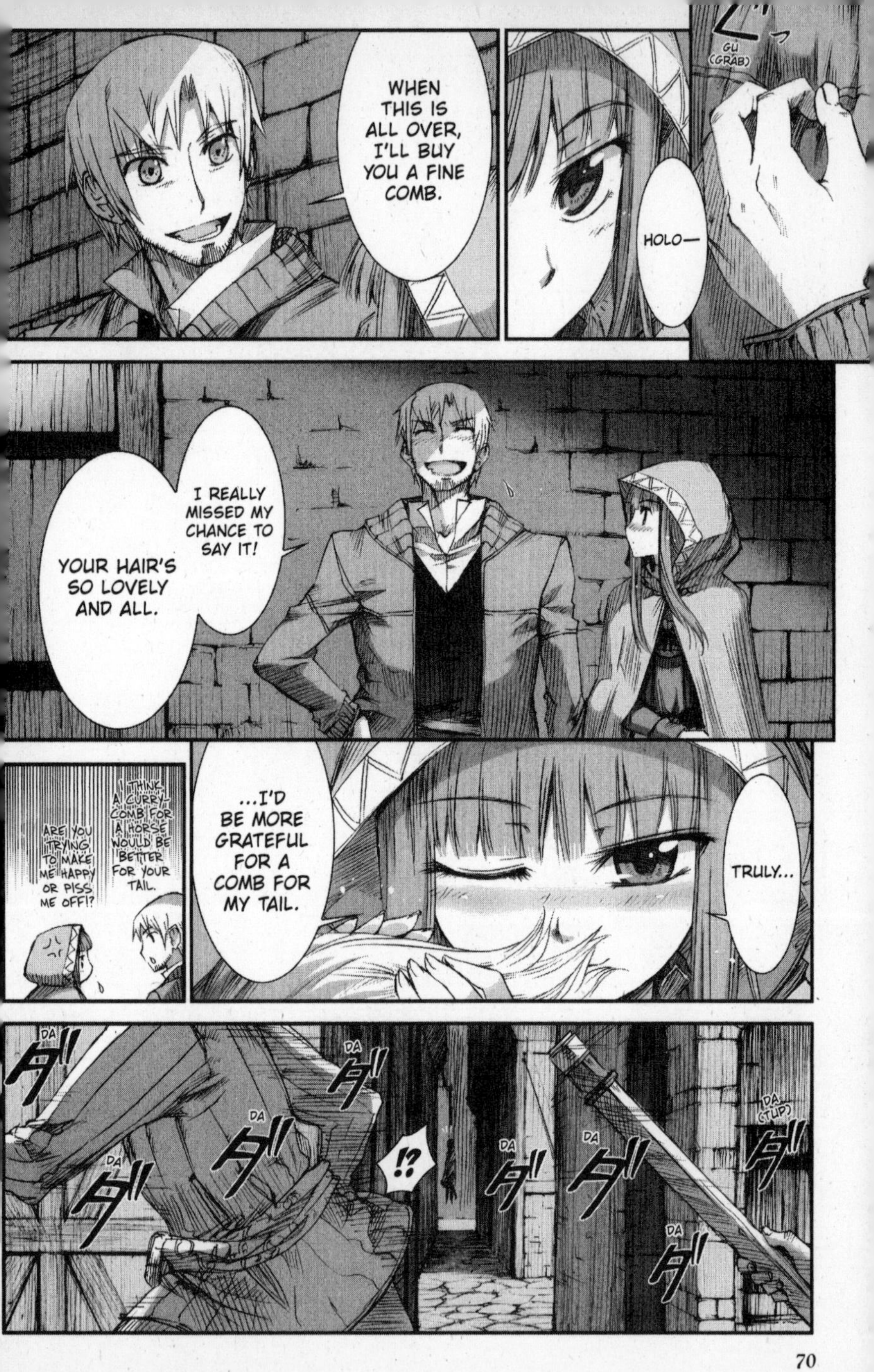
GU (GRAB)
HOLO—
WHEN THIS IS ALL OVER, I'LL BUY YOU A FINE COMB.
I REALLY MISSED MY CHANCE TO SAY IT!
YOUR HAIR'S SO LOVELY AND ALL.
TRULY...
...I'D BE MORE GRATEFUL FOR A COMB FOR MY TAIL.
I THINK A CURRY-COMB FOR A HORSE WOULD BE BETTER FOR YOUR TAIL.
ARE YOU TRYING TO MAKE ME HAPPY OR PISS ME OFF!?
DA (TUP)
DA
DA
DA
DA
DA
!?
DA
DA

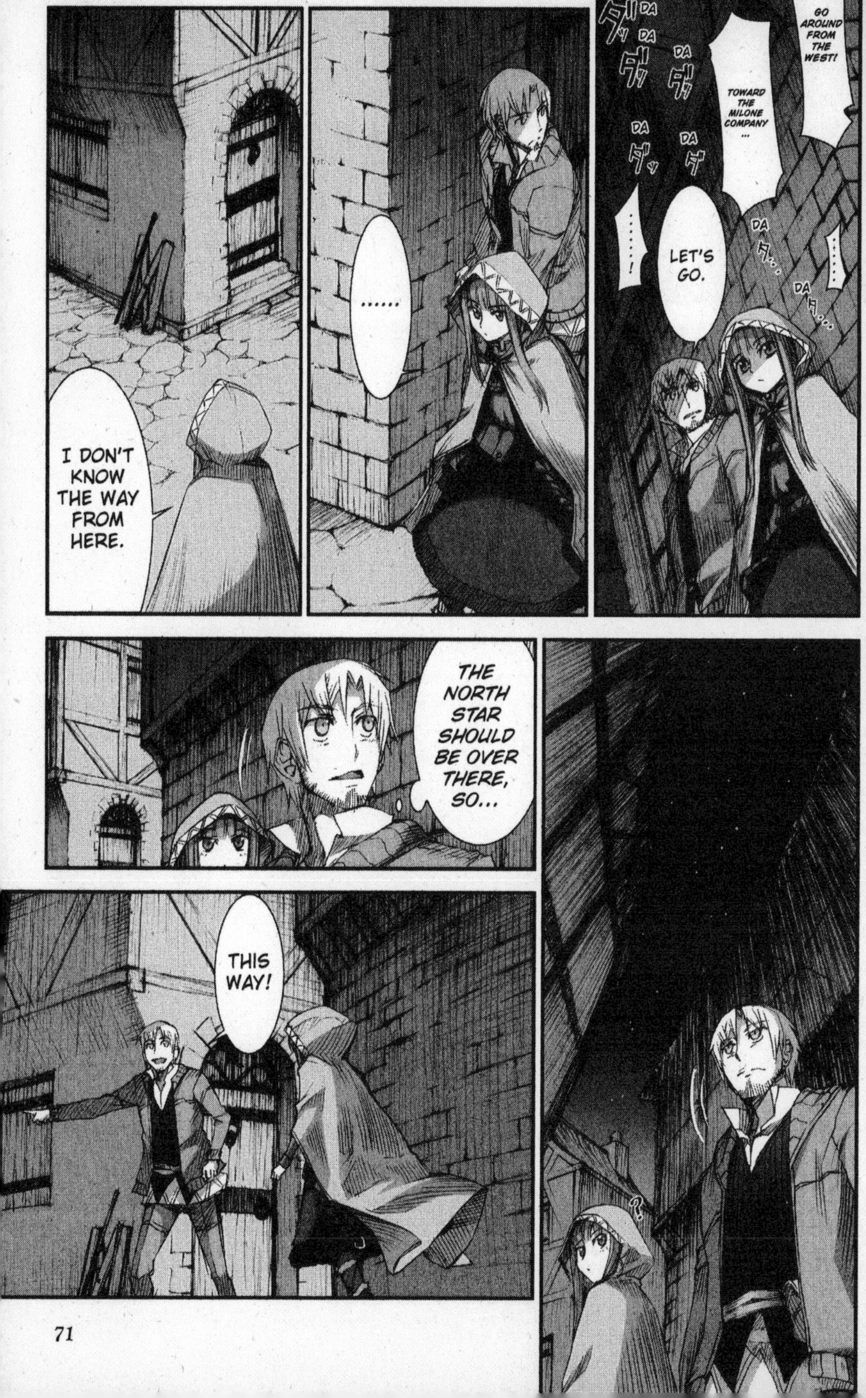
GO AROUND FROM THE WEST!
TOWARD THE MILONE COMPANY ...
DA DA DA DA DA
......!
LET'S GO.
DA... DA...
......
......
I DON'T KNOW THE WAY FROM HERE.
?
THE NORTH STAR SHOULD BE OVER THERE, SO...
THIS WAY!

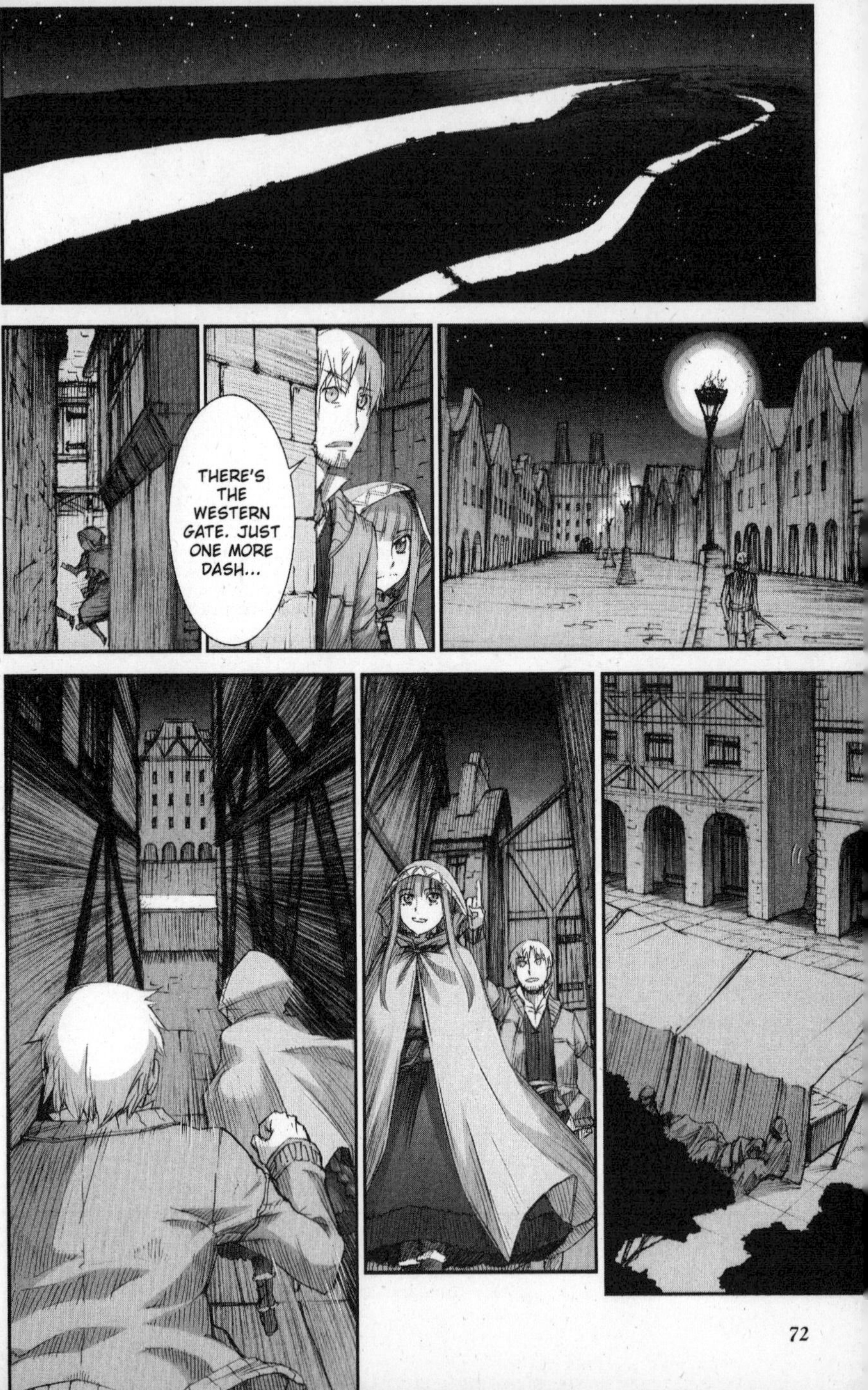
THERE'S THE WESTERN GATE. JUST ONE MORE DASH...

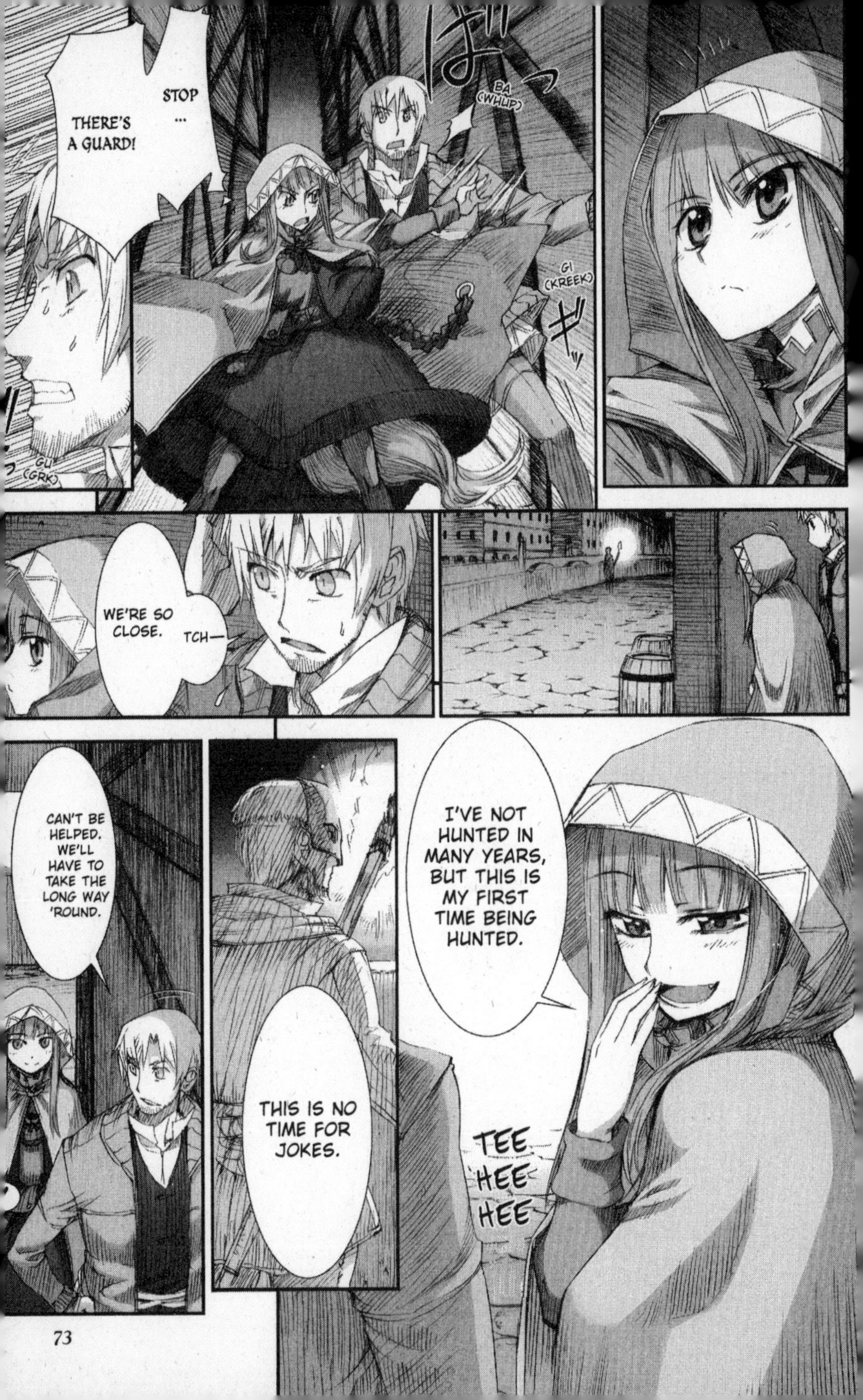

BA (WHLIP)
GI (KREEK)
STOP ...
THERE'S A GUARD!
GU (GRK)
TCH—
WE'RE SO CLOSE.
I'VE NOT HUNTED IN MANY YEARS, BUT THIS IS MY FIRST TIME BEING HUNTED.
TEE HEE HEE
THIS IS NO TIME FOR JOKES.
CAN'T BE HELPED. WE'LL HAVE TO TAKE THE LONG WAY 'ROUND.

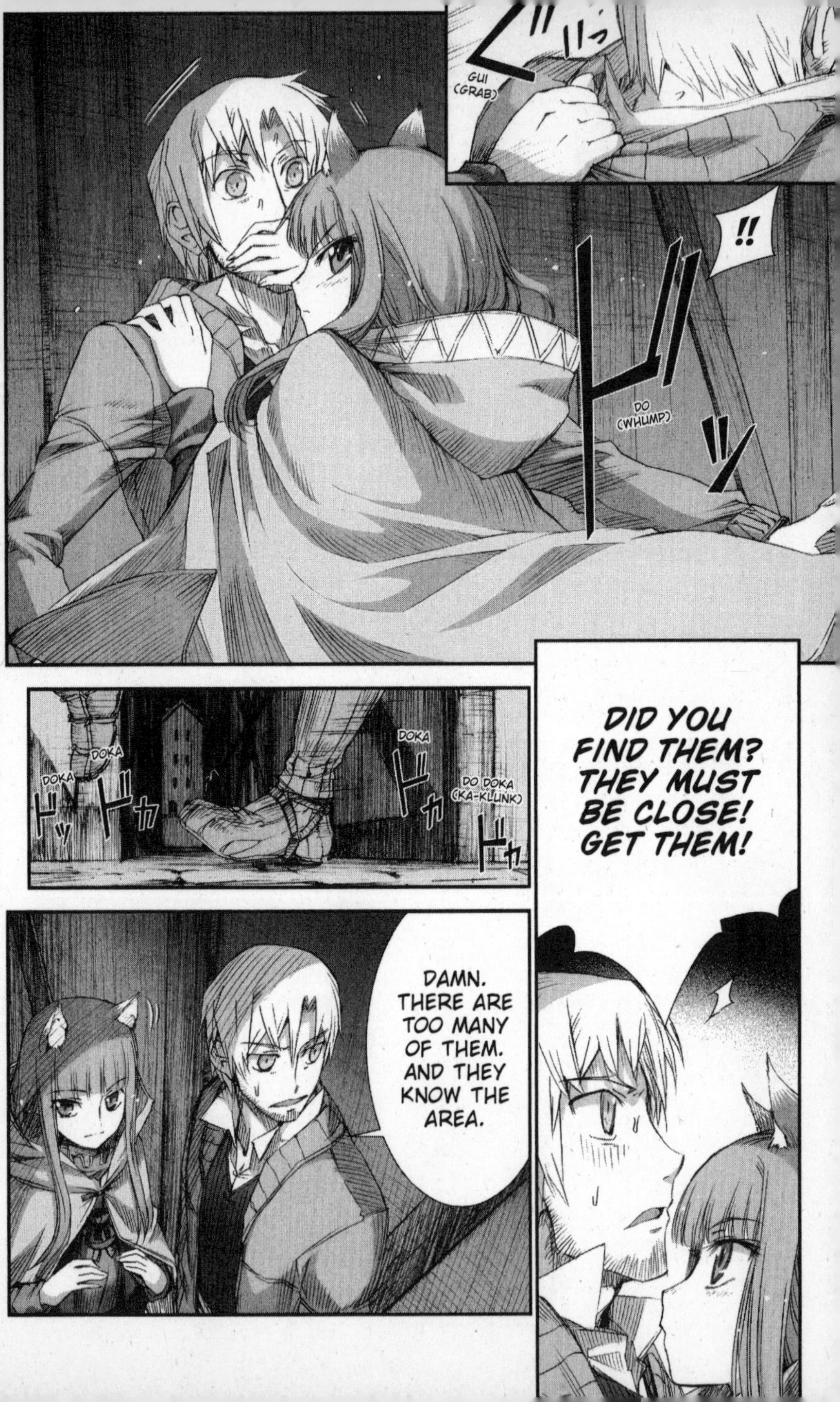
GUI (GRAB)
!!
DO (WHUMP)
DID YOU FIND THEM? THEY MUST BE CLOSE! GET THEM!
DO DOKA (KA-KLUNK)
DOKA
DOKA
DOKA
DAMN. THERE ARE TOO MANY OF THEM. AND THEY KNOW THE AREA.

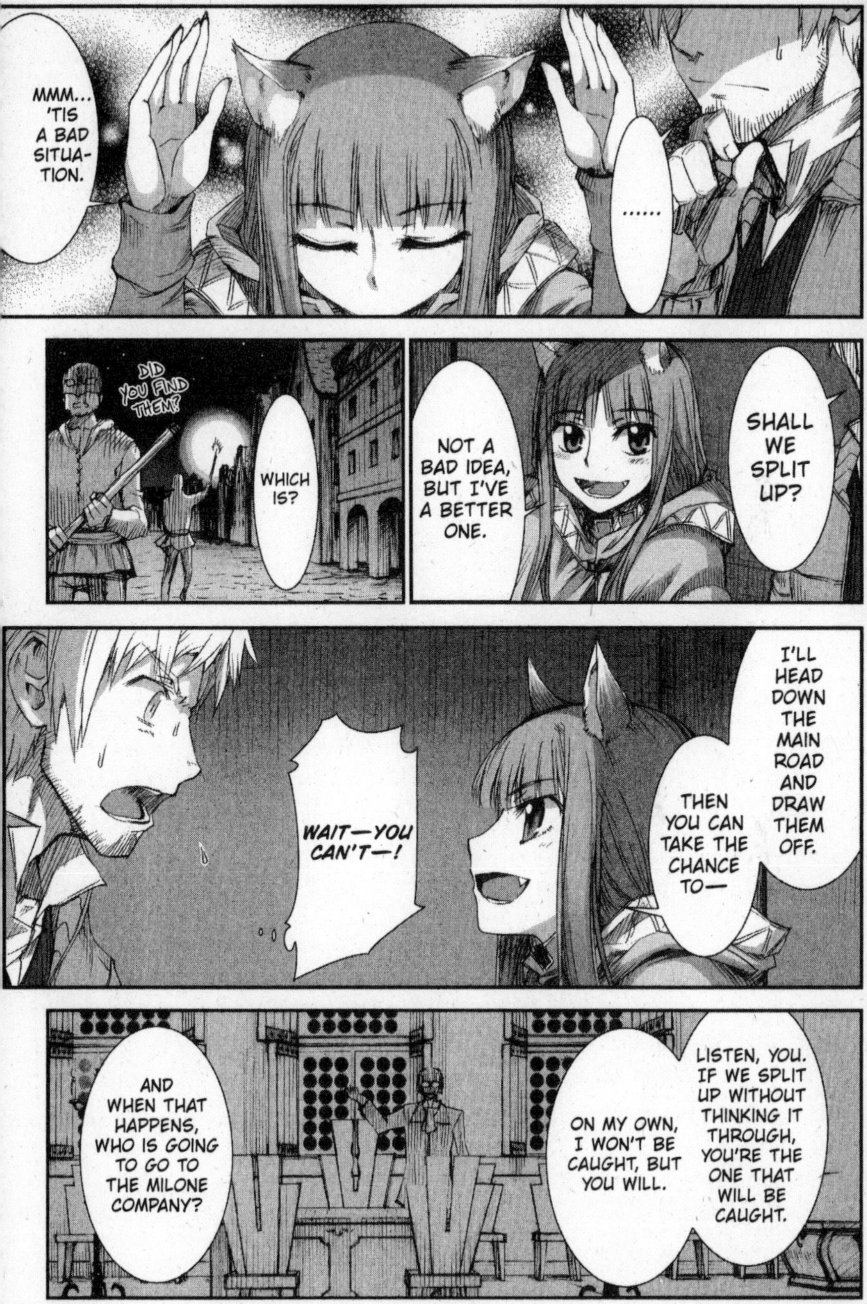
......
MMM... 'TIS A BAD SITUATION.
SHALL WE SPLIT UP?
NOT A BAD IDEA, BUT I'VE A BETTER ONE.
WHICH IS?
DID YOU FIND THEM?
I'LL HEAD DOWN THE MAIN ROAD AND DRAW THEM OFF.
THEN YOU CAN TAKE THE CHANCE TO—
WAIT—YOU CAN'T—!
LISTEN, YOU. IF WE SPLIT UP WITHOUT THINKING IT THROUGH, YOU'RE THE ONE THAT WILL BE CAUGHT.
ON MY OWN, I WON'T BE CAUGHT, BUT YOU WILL.
AND WHEN THAT HAPPENS, WHO IS GOING TO GO TO THE MILONE COMPANY?

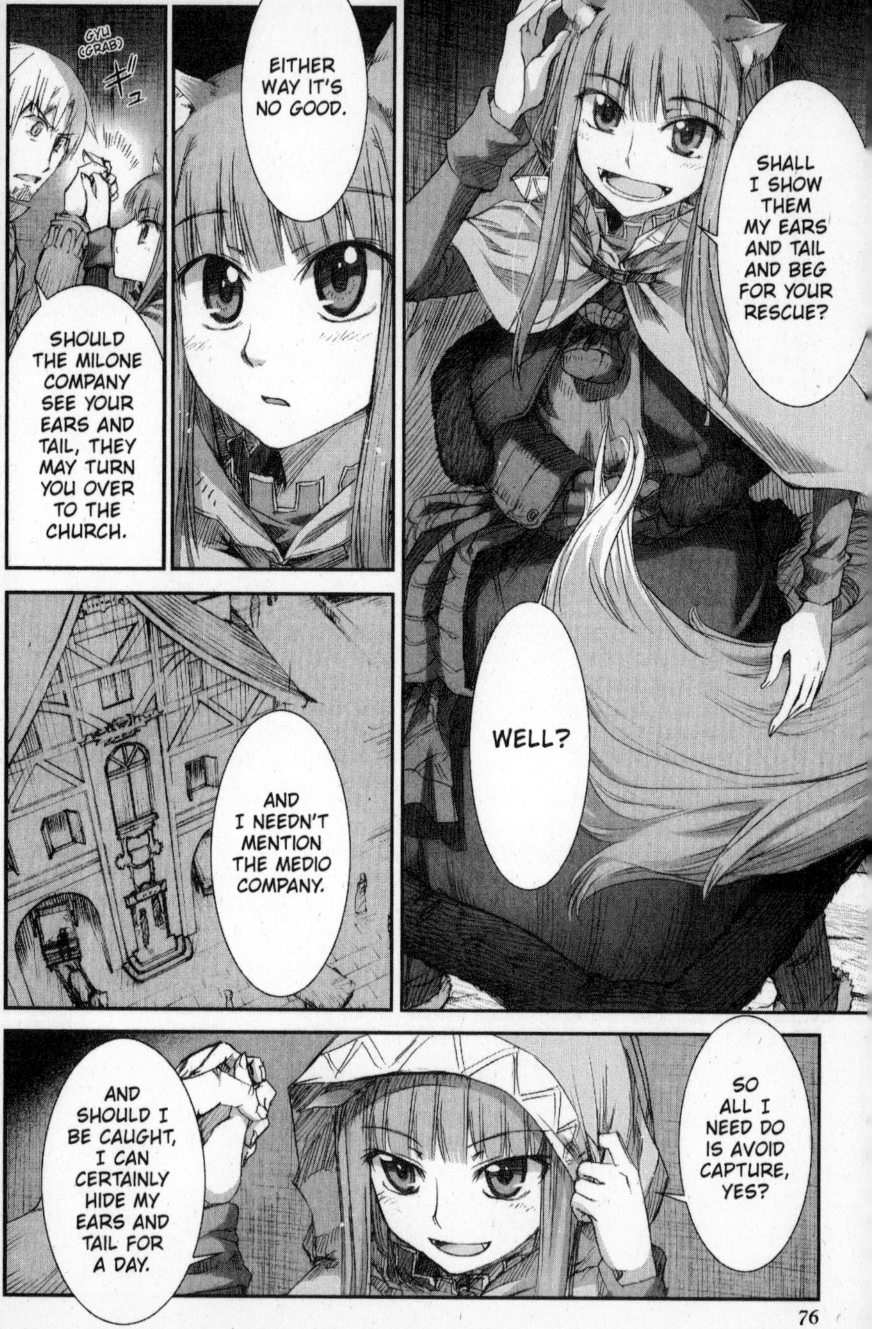
SHALL I SHOW THEM MY EARS AND TAIL AND BEG FOR YOUR RESCUE?
WELL?
EITHER WAY IT'S NO GOOD.
GYU (GRAB)
ギュ
SHOULD THE MILONE COMPANY SEE YOUR EARS AND TAIL, THEY MAY TURN YOU OVER TO THE CHURCH.
AND I NEEDN'T MENTION THE MEDIO COMPANY.
SO ALL I NEED DO IS AVOID CAPTURE, YES?
AND SHOULD I BE CAUGHT, I CAN CERTAINLY HIDE MY EARS AND TAIL FOR A DAY.

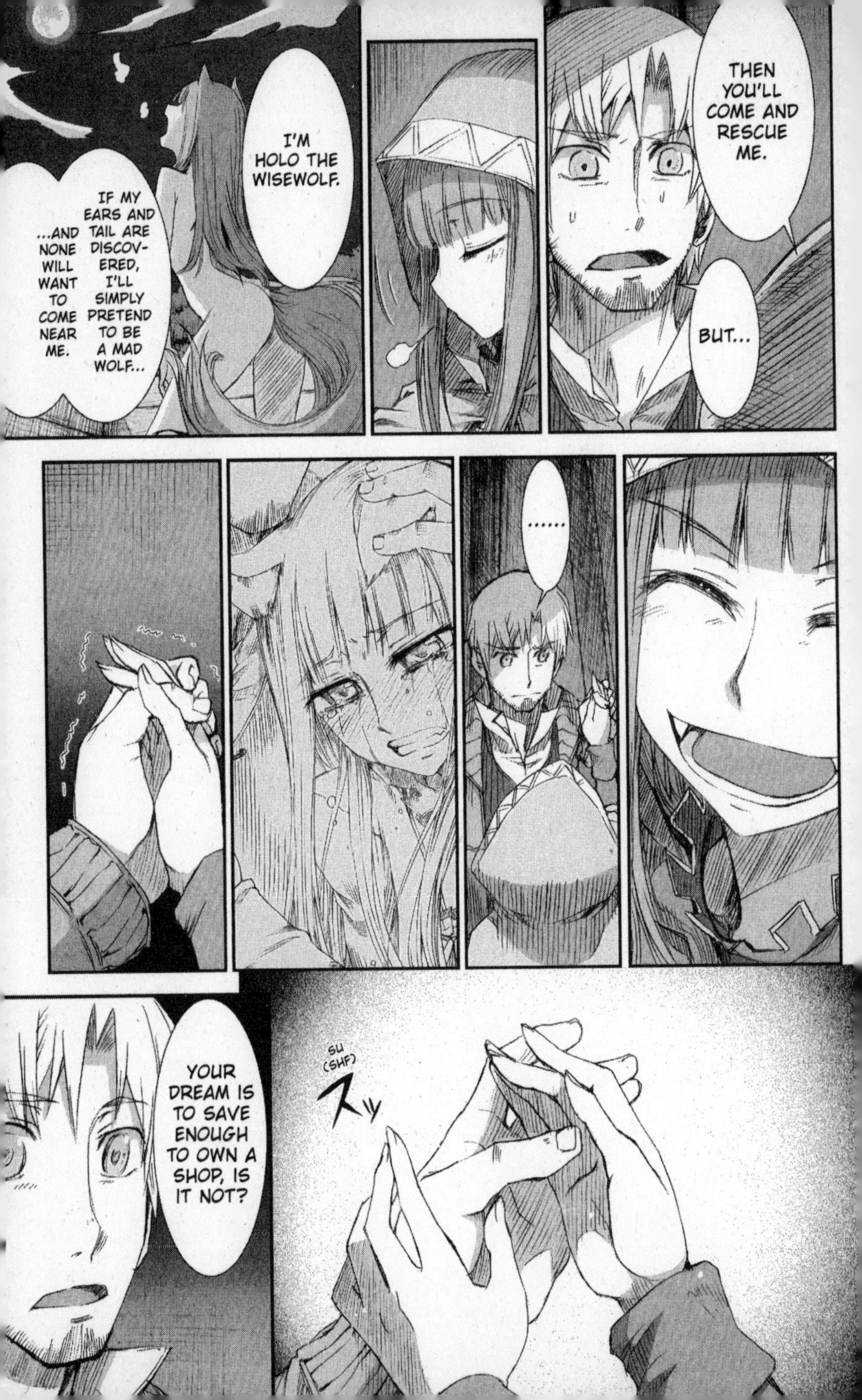
THEN YOU'LL COME AND RESCUE ME.
BUT...
I'M HOLO THE WISEWOLF.
IF MY EARS AND TAIL ARE DISCOVERED, I'LL SIMPLY PRETEND TO BE A MAD WOLF...
...AND NONE WILL WANT TO COME NEAR ME.
......
スッ
SU (SHF)
YOUR DREAM IS TO SAVE ENOUGH TO OWN A SHOP, IS IT NOT?

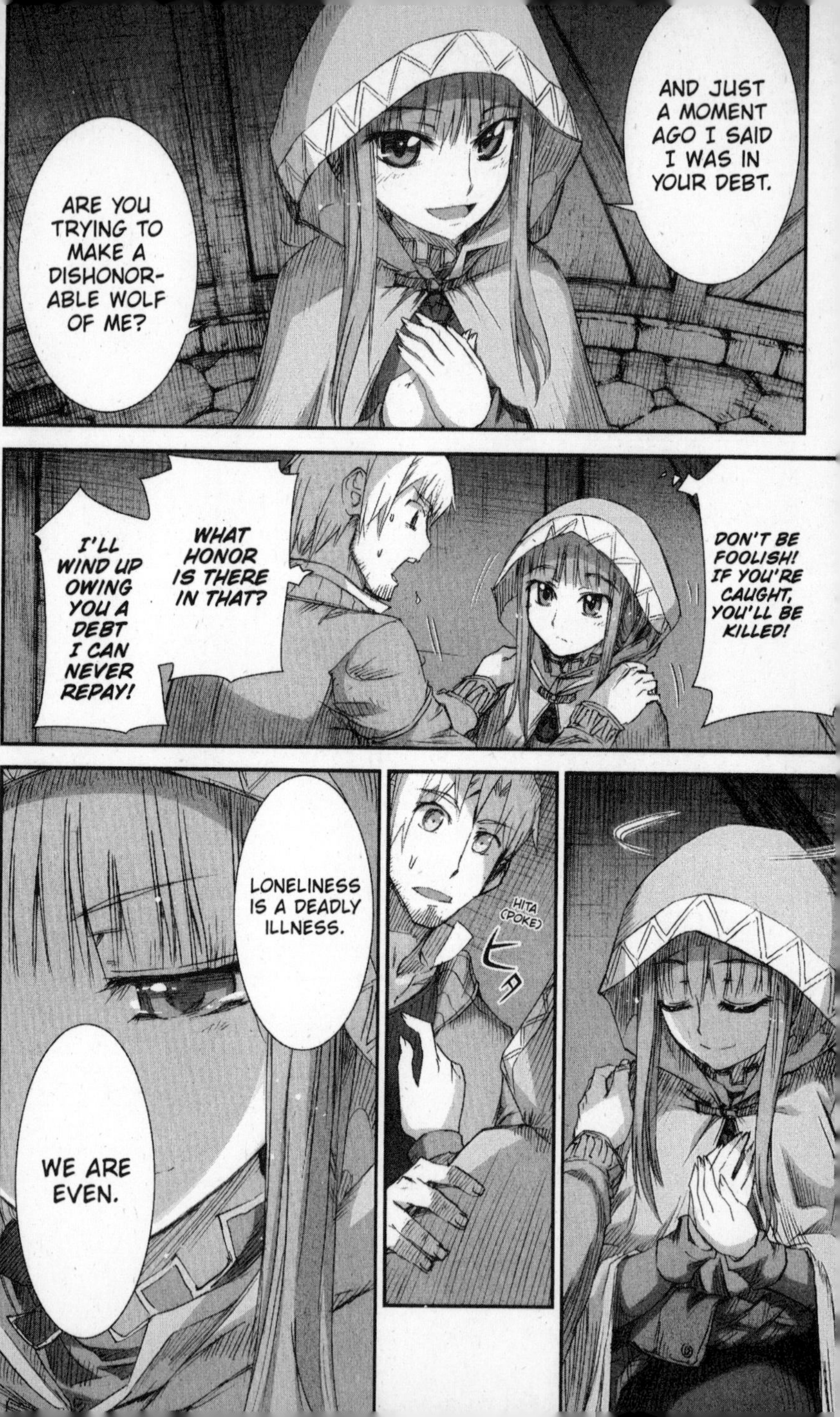
AND JUST A MOMENT AGO I SAID I WAS IN YOUR DEBT.
ARE YOU TRYING TO MAKE A DISHONOR-ABLE WOLF OF ME?
DON'T BE FOOLISH! IF YOU'RE CAUGHT, YOU'LL BE KILLED!
WHAT HONOR IS THERE IN THAT?
I'LL WIND UP OWING YOU A DEBT I CAN NEVER REPAY!
HITA (POKE)
LONELINESS IS A DEADLY ILLNESS.
WE ARE EVEN.

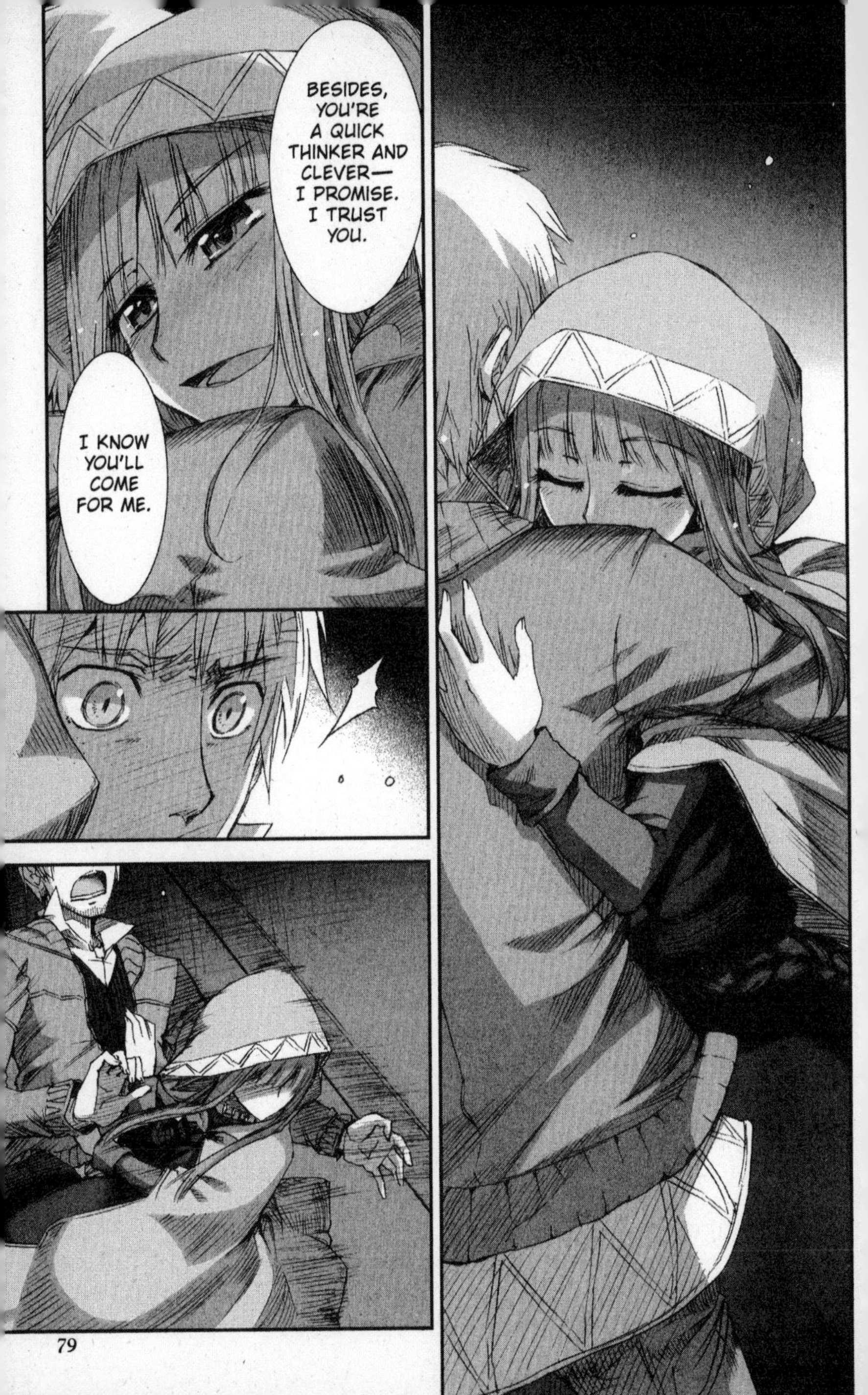
BESIDES, YOU'RE A QUICK THINKER AND CLEVER— I PROMISE. I TRUST YOU.
I KNOW YOU'LL COME FOR ME.
...

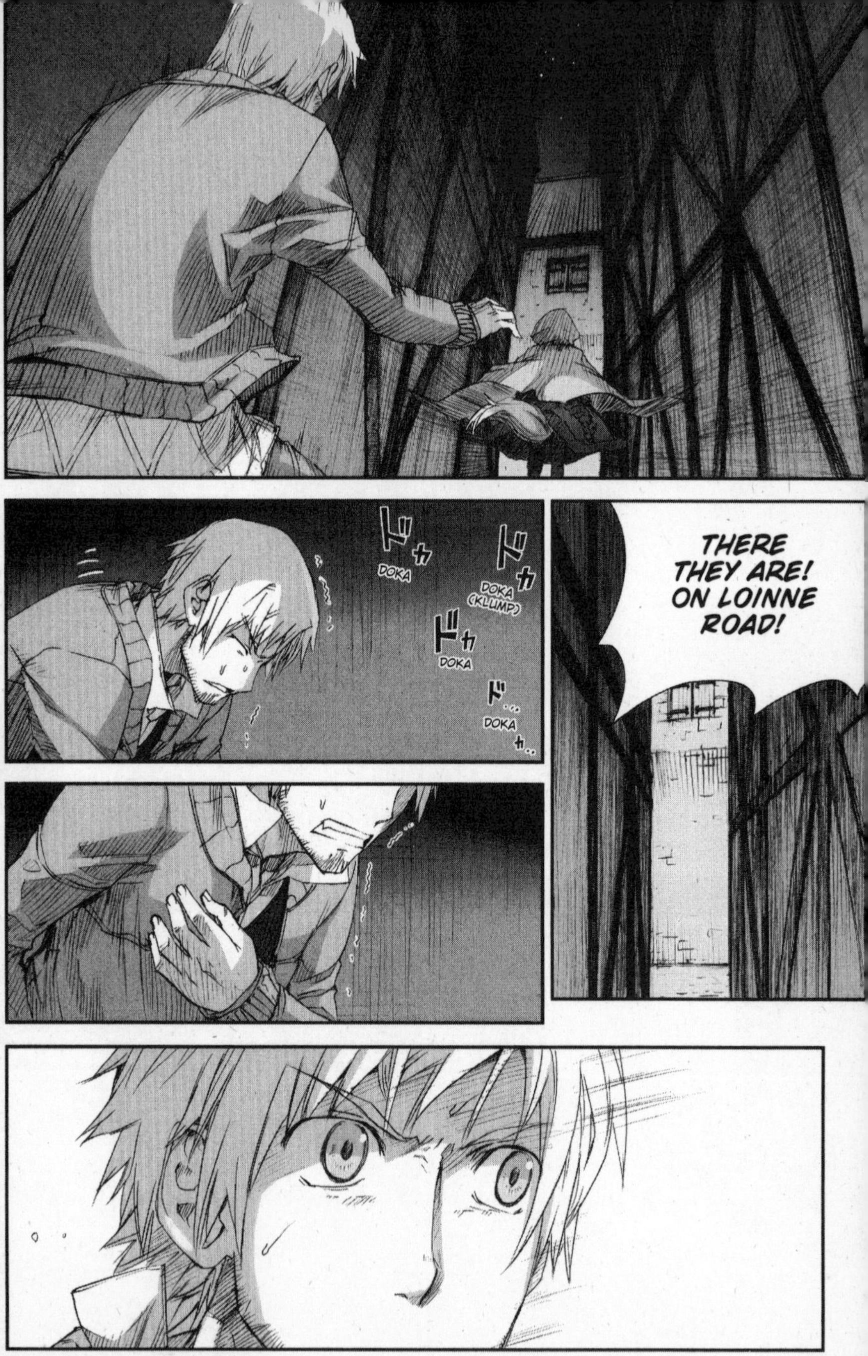
THERE THEY ARE! ON LOINNE ROAD!
DOKA (KLUMP)
DOKA
DOKA
DOKA

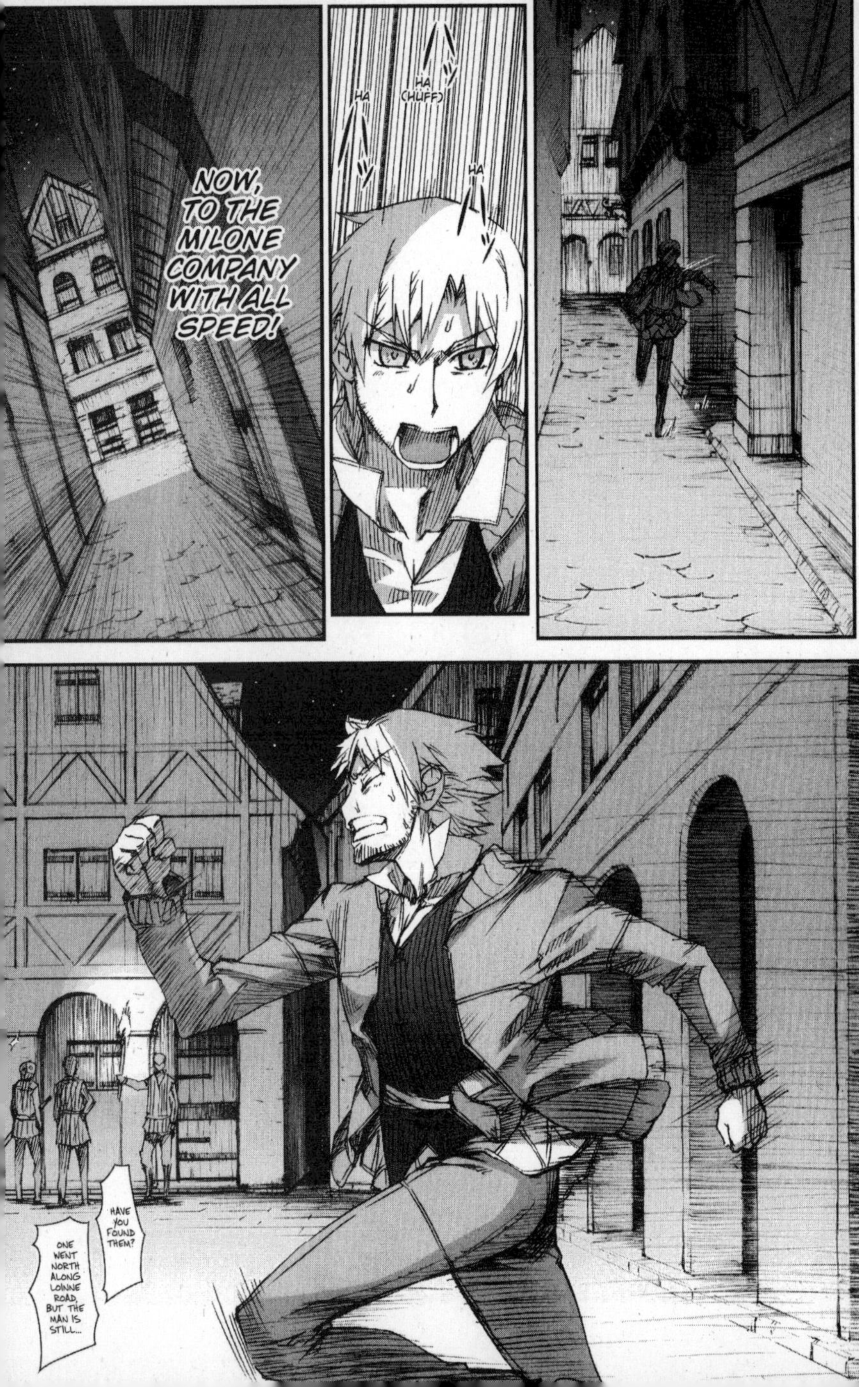
HA (HUFF)
HA
HA
NOW, TO THE MILONE COMPANY WITH ALL SPEED!
HAVE YOU FOUND THEM?
ONE WENT NORTH ALONG LOINNE ROAD, BUT THE MAN IS STILL...

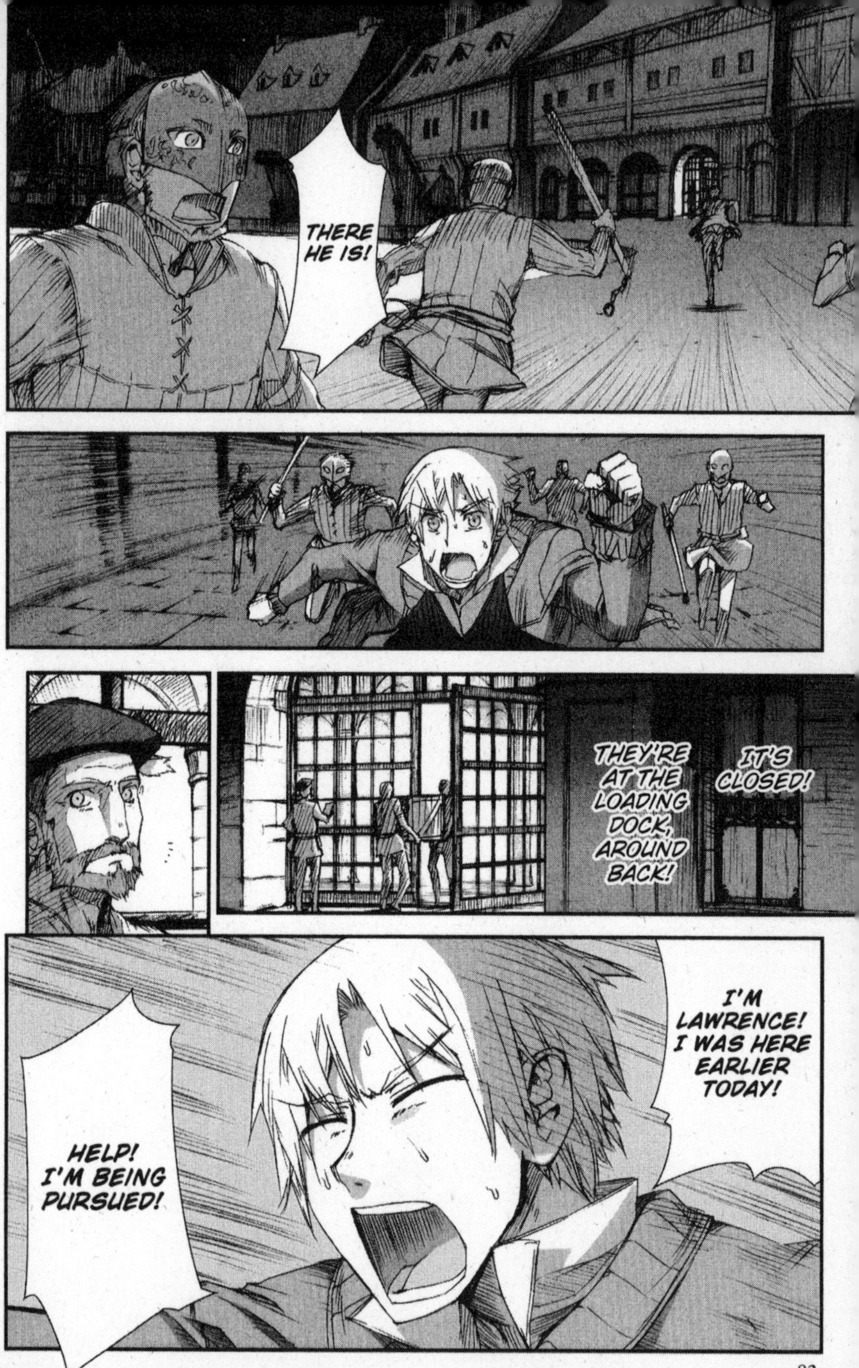
THERE HE IS!
IT'S CLOSED!
THEY'RE AT THE LOADING DOCK, AROUND BACK!
I'M LAWRENCE! I WAS HERE EARLIER TODAY!
HELP! I'M BEING PURSUED!

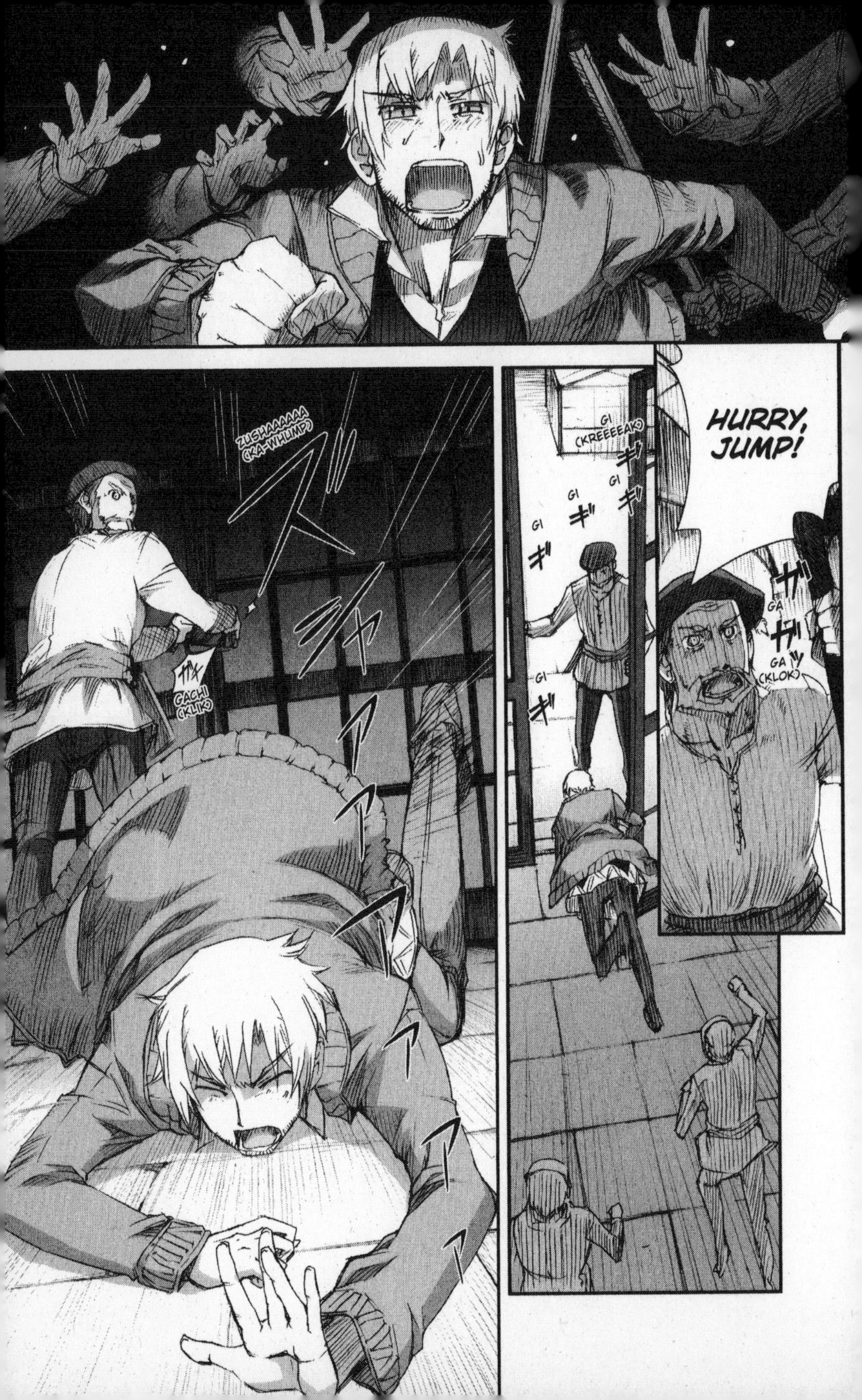
HURRY, JUMP!
GA
GA
(KLOK)
GI
(KREEEEAK)
GI
GI
GI
GI
ZUSHAAAAAA
(KA-WHUMP)
GACHI
(KLIK)

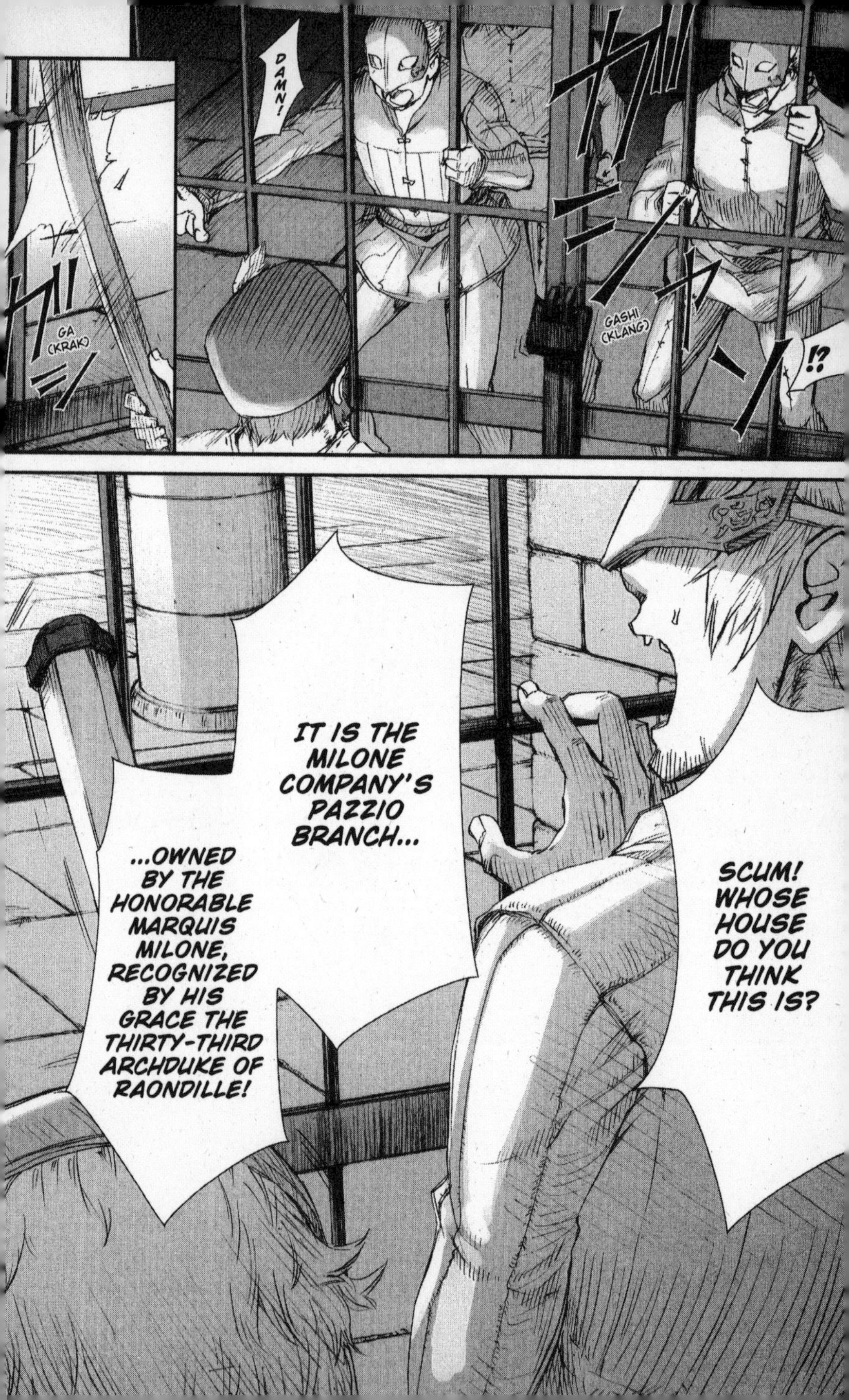
GASHI (KLANG)
!?
DAMN!
GA (KRAK)
SCUM! WHOSE HOUSE DO YOU THINK THIS IS?
IT IS THE MILONE COMPANY'S PAZZIO BRANCH...
...OWNED BY THE HONORABLE MARQUIS MILONE, RECOGNIZED BY HIS GRACE THE THIRTY-THIRD ARCHDUKE OF RAONDILLE!

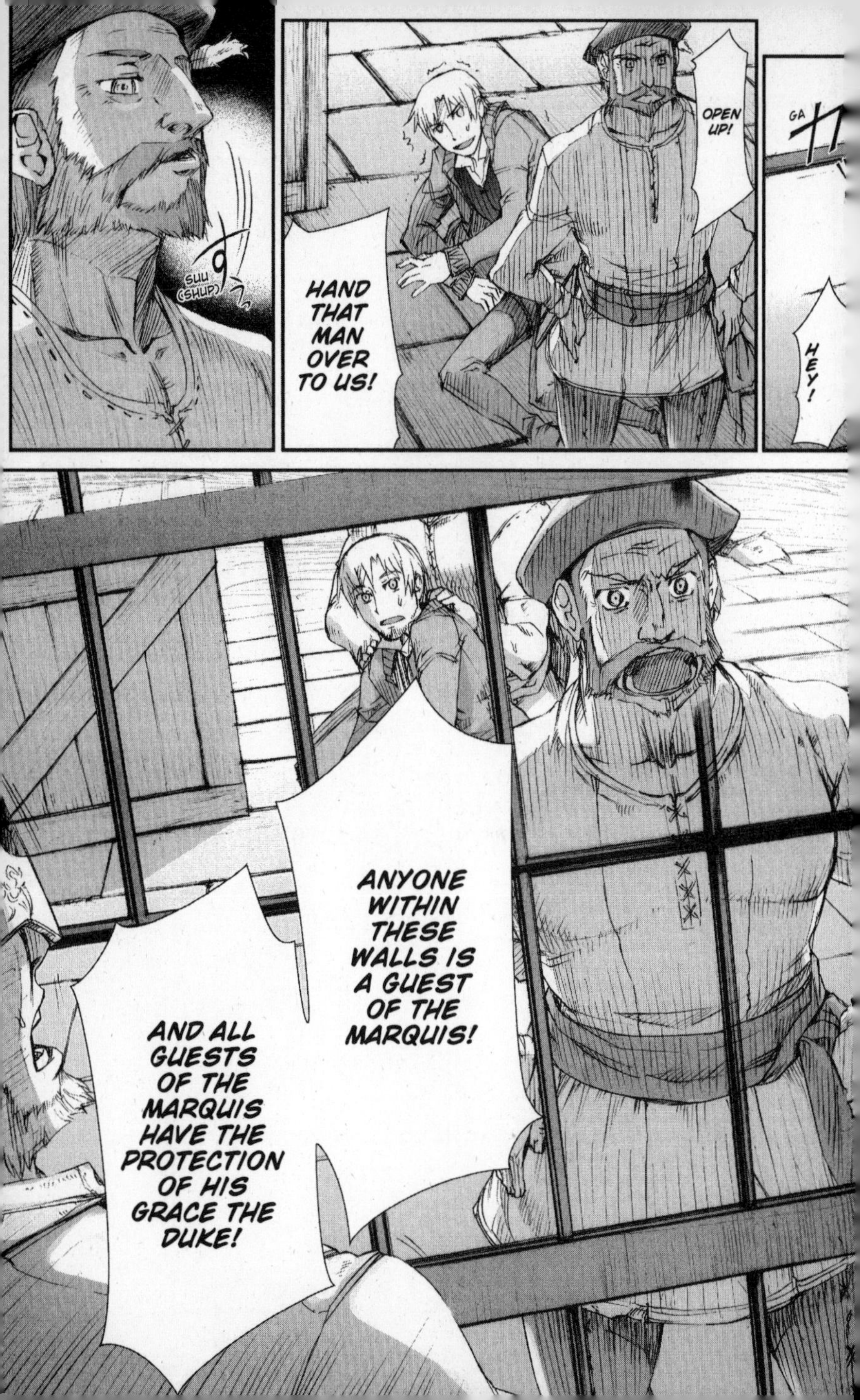
GA
HEY!
OPEN UP!
HAND THAT MAN OVER TO US!
SUU (SHUP)
ANYONE WITHIN THESE WALLS IS A GUEST OF THE MARQUIS!
AND ALL GUESTS OF THE MARQUIS HAVE THE PROTECTION OF HIS GRACE THE DUKE!

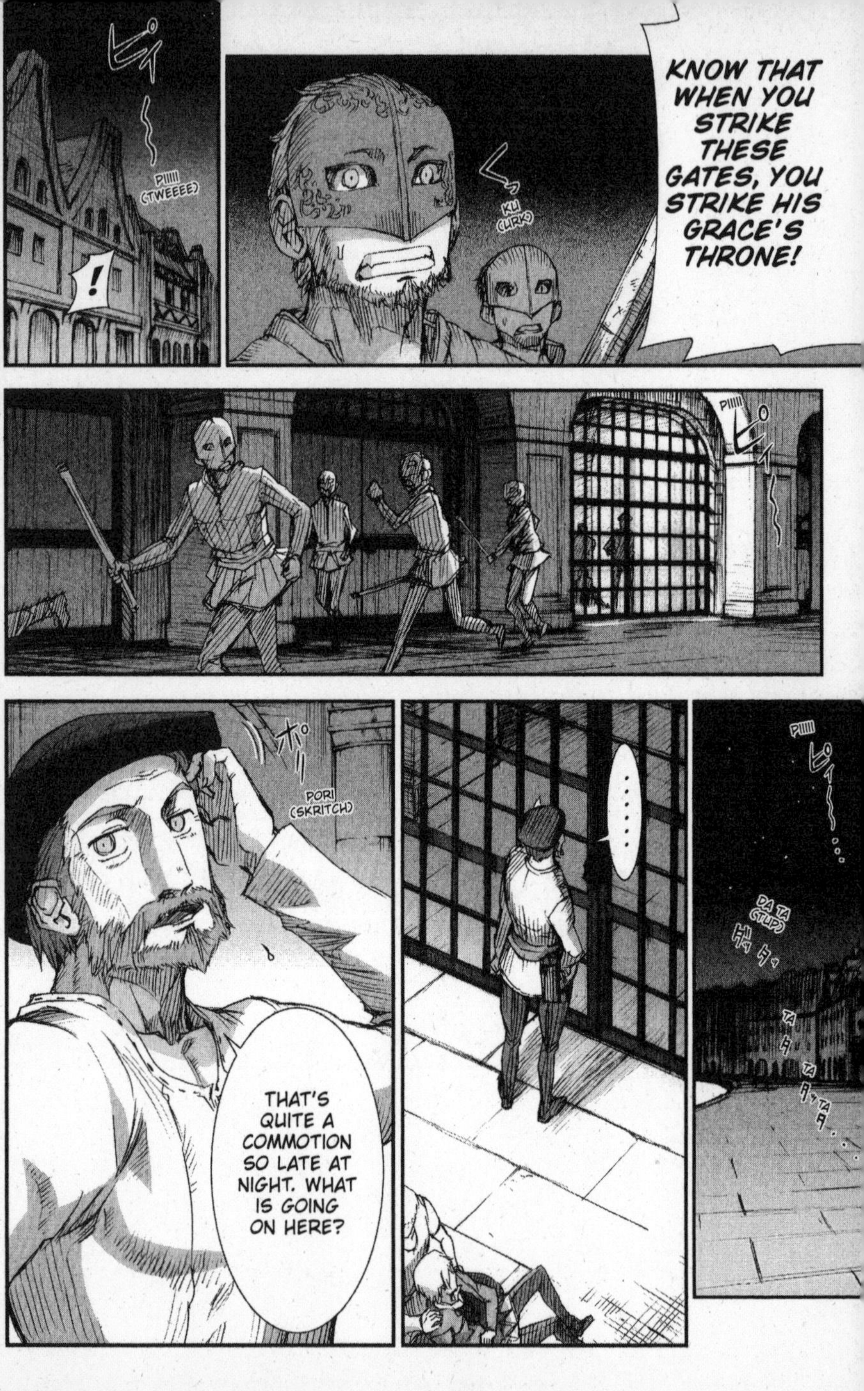
KNOW THAT WHEN YOU STRIKE THESE GATES, YOU STRIKE HIS GRACE'S THRONE!
KU (URK)
PIIII (TWEEEE)
!
PIIII
PIIII
DA TA (TUP)
TA TA TA
......
PORI (SKRITCH)
THAT'S QUITE A COMMOTION SO LATE AT NIGHT. WHAT IS GOING ON HERE?

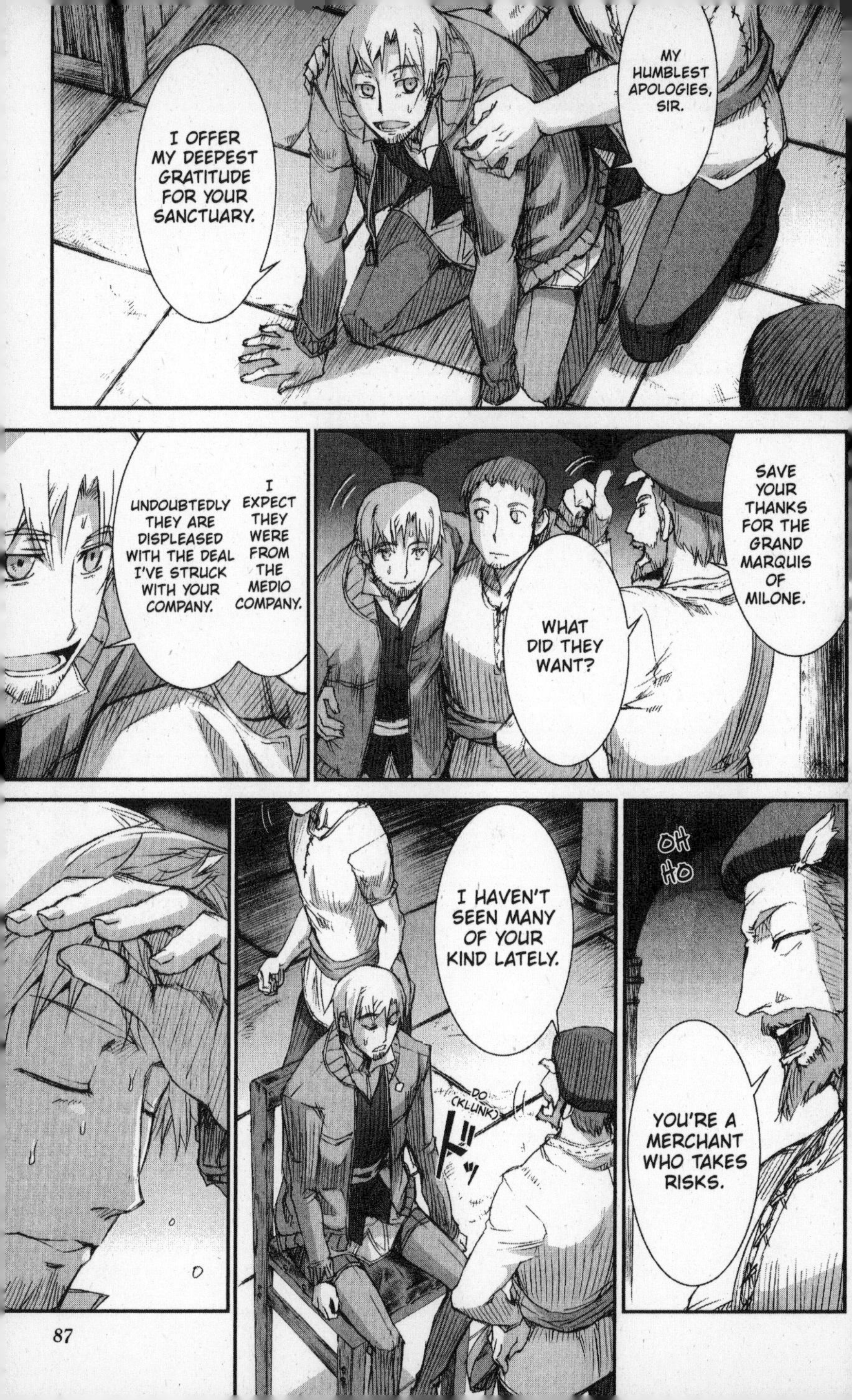
MY HUMBLEST APOLOGIES, SIR.
I OFFER MY DEEPEST GRATITUDE FOR YOUR SANCTUARY.
SAVE YOUR THANKS FOR THE GRAND MARQUIS OF MILONE.
WHAT DID THEY WANT?
I EXPECT THEY WERE FROM THE MEDIO COMPANY.
UNDOUBTEDLY THEY ARE DISPLEASED WITH THE DEAL I'VE STRUCK WITH YOUR COMPANY.
OH HO
YOU'RE A MERCHANT WHO TAKES RISKS.
I HAVEN'T SEEN MANY OF YOUR KIND LATELY.
DO (KLUNK)
ドッ

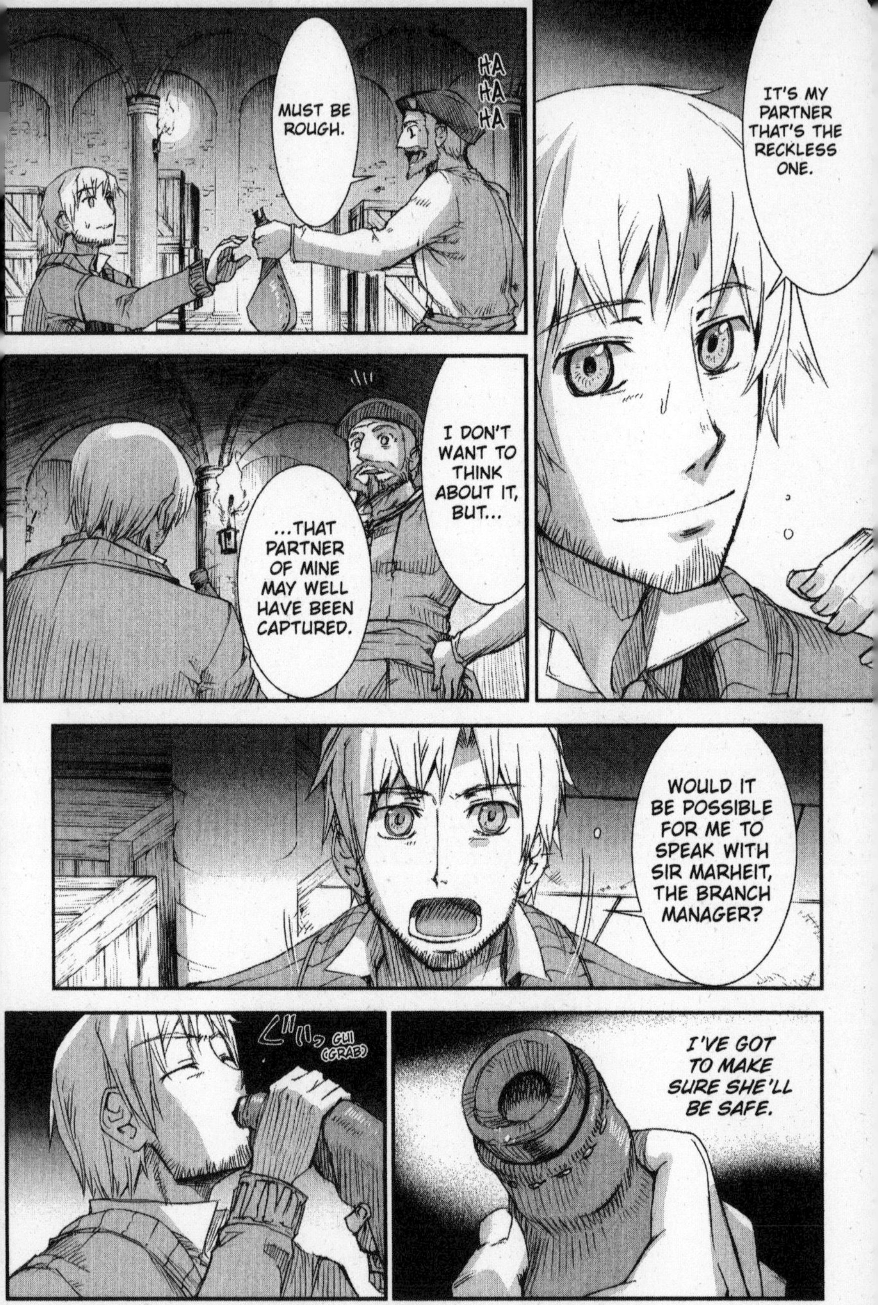
IT'S MY PARTNER THAT'S THE RECKLESS ONE.
MUST BE ROUGH.
HA HA HA
I DON'T WANT TO THINK ABOUT IT, BUT...
...THAT PARTNER OF MINE MAY WELL HAVE BEEN CAPTURED.
WOULD IT BE POSSIBLE FOR ME TO SPEAK WITH SIR MARHEIT, THE BRANCH MANAGER?
I'VE GOT TO MAKE SURE SHE'LL BE SAFE.
GUI (GRAB)

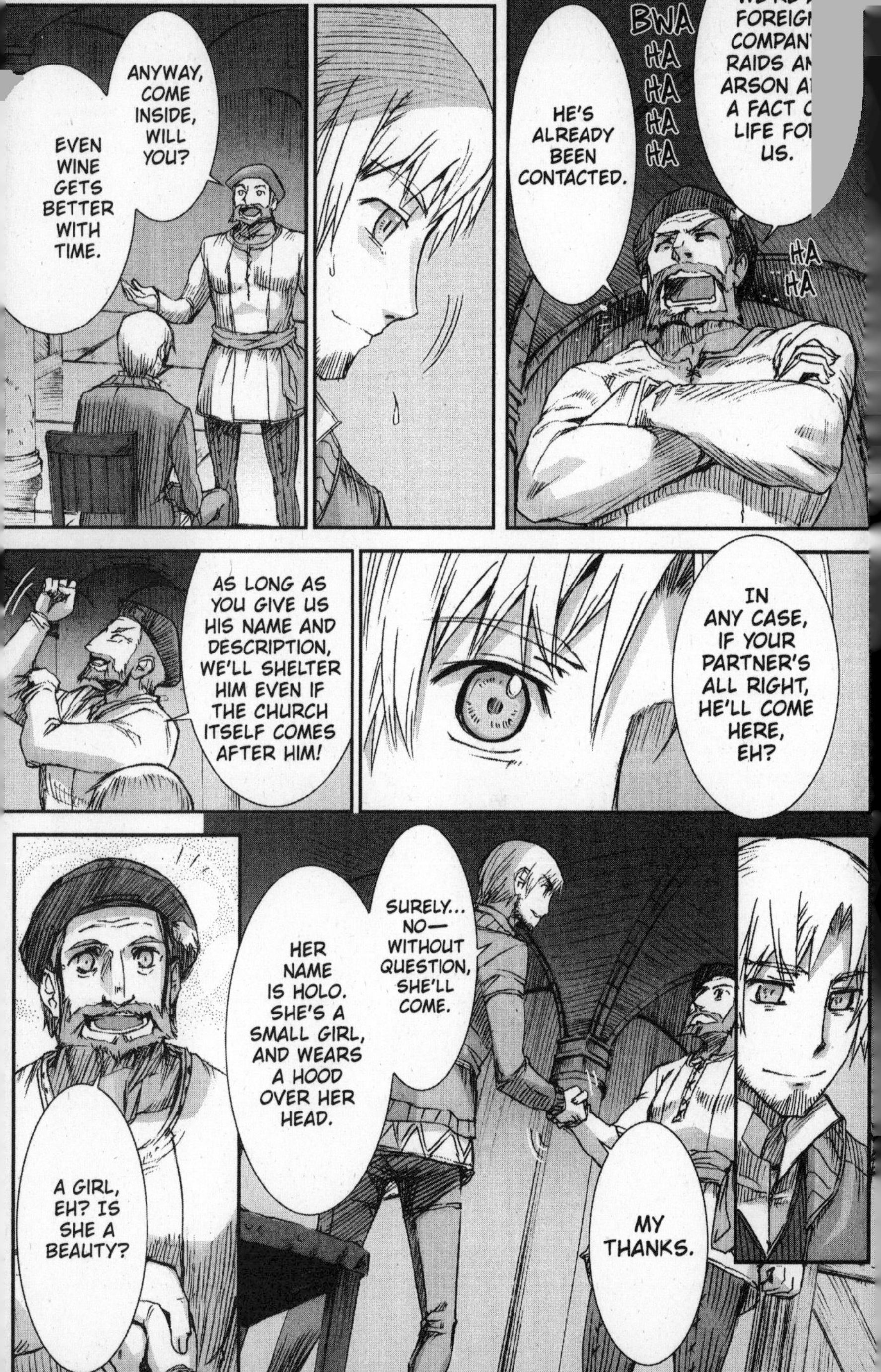
WE'RE A FOREIG COMPAN RAIDS AN ARSON A A FACT O LIFE FO US.
BWA HA HA HA HA HA
HE'S ALREADY BEEN CONTACTED.
HA HA
ANYWAY, COME INSIDE, WILL YOU?
EVEN WINE GETS BETTER WITH TIME.
IN ANY CASE, IF YOUR PARTNER'S ALL RIGHT, HE'LL COME HERE, EH?
AS LONG AS YOU GIVE US HIS NAME AND DESCRIPTION, WE'LL SHELTER HIM EVEN IF THE CHURCH ITSELF COMES AFTER HIM!
SURELY... NO— WITHOUT QUESTION, SHE'LL COME.
HER NAME IS HOLO. SHE'S A SMALL GIRL, AND WEARS A HOOD OVER HER HEAD.
MY THANKS.
A GIRL, EH? IS SHE A BEAUTY?

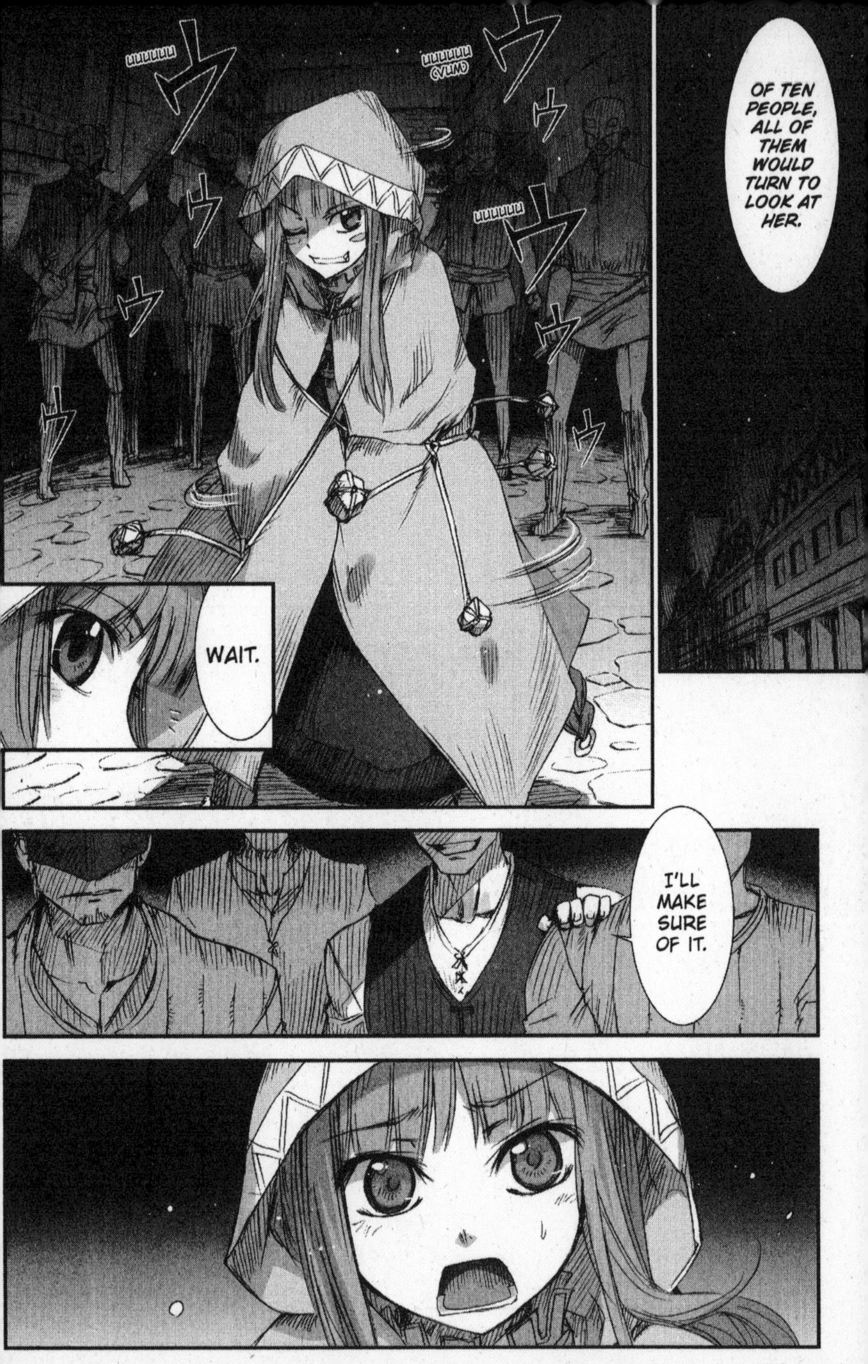
OF TEN PEOPLE, ALL OF THEM WOULD TURN TO LOOK AT HER.
WAIT.
I'LL MAKE SURE OF IT.

SPICE & WOLF

SPICE & WOLF

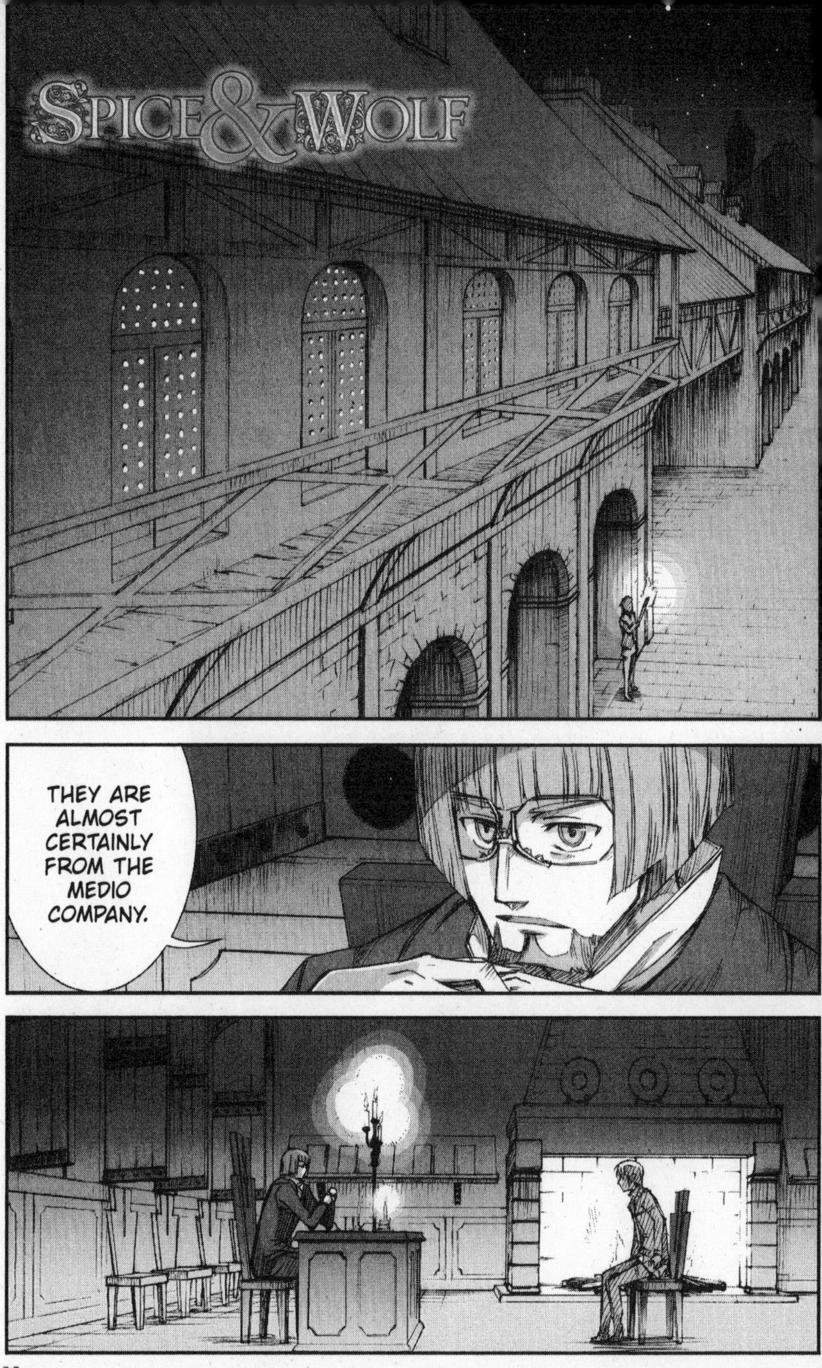
SPICE & WOLF
THEY ARE ALMOST CERTAINLY FROM THE MEDIO COMPANY.

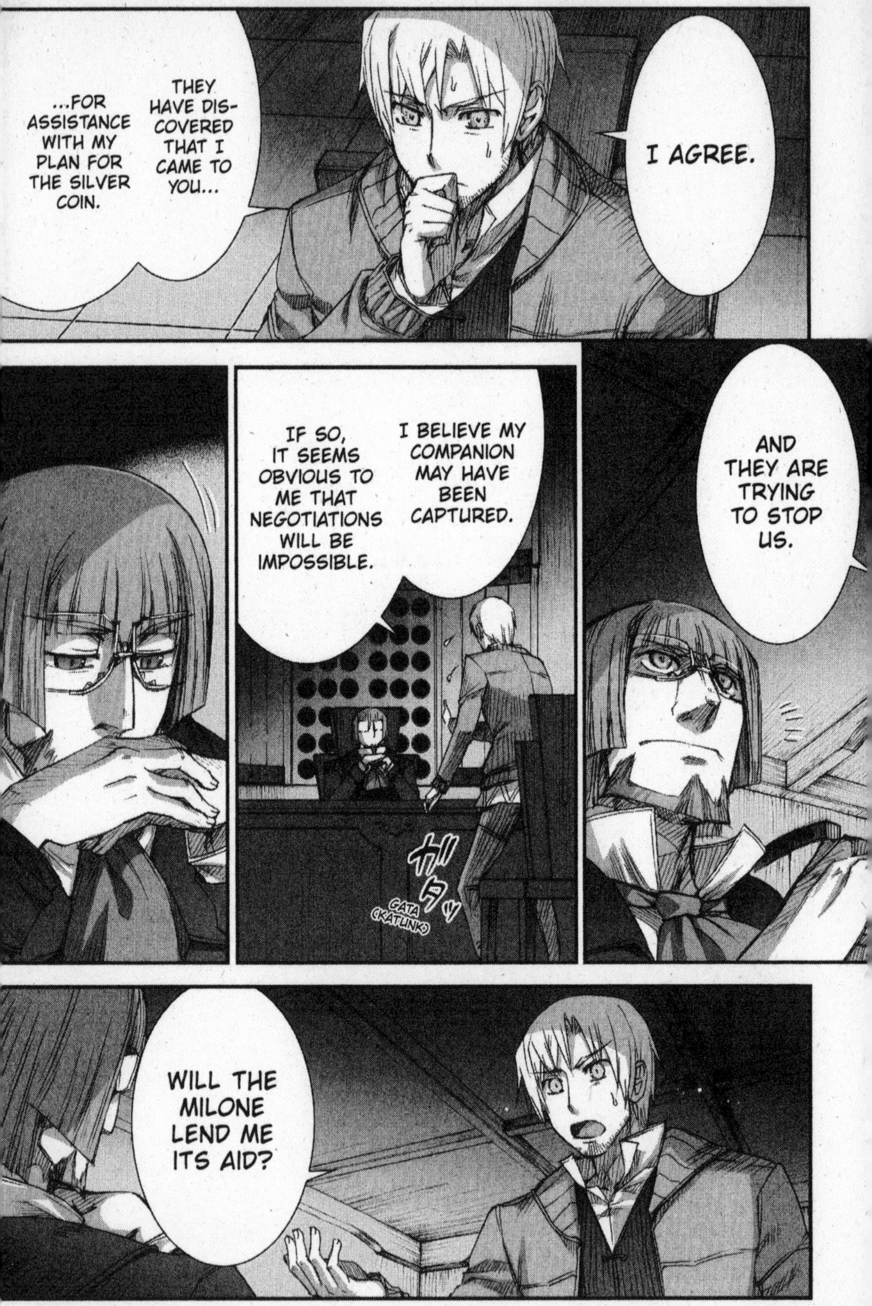
I AGREE.
THEY HAVE DIS-COVERED THAT I CAME TO YOU...
...FOR ASSISTANCE WITH MY PLAN FOR THE SILVER COIN.
AND THEY ARE TRYING TO STOP US.
I BELIEVE MY COMPANION MAY HAVE BEEN CAPTURED.
IF SO, IT SEEMS OBVIOUS TO ME THAT NEGOTIATIONS WILL BE IMPOSSIBLE.
ガタッ
GATA (KATUNK)
WILL THE MILONE LEND ME ITS AID?

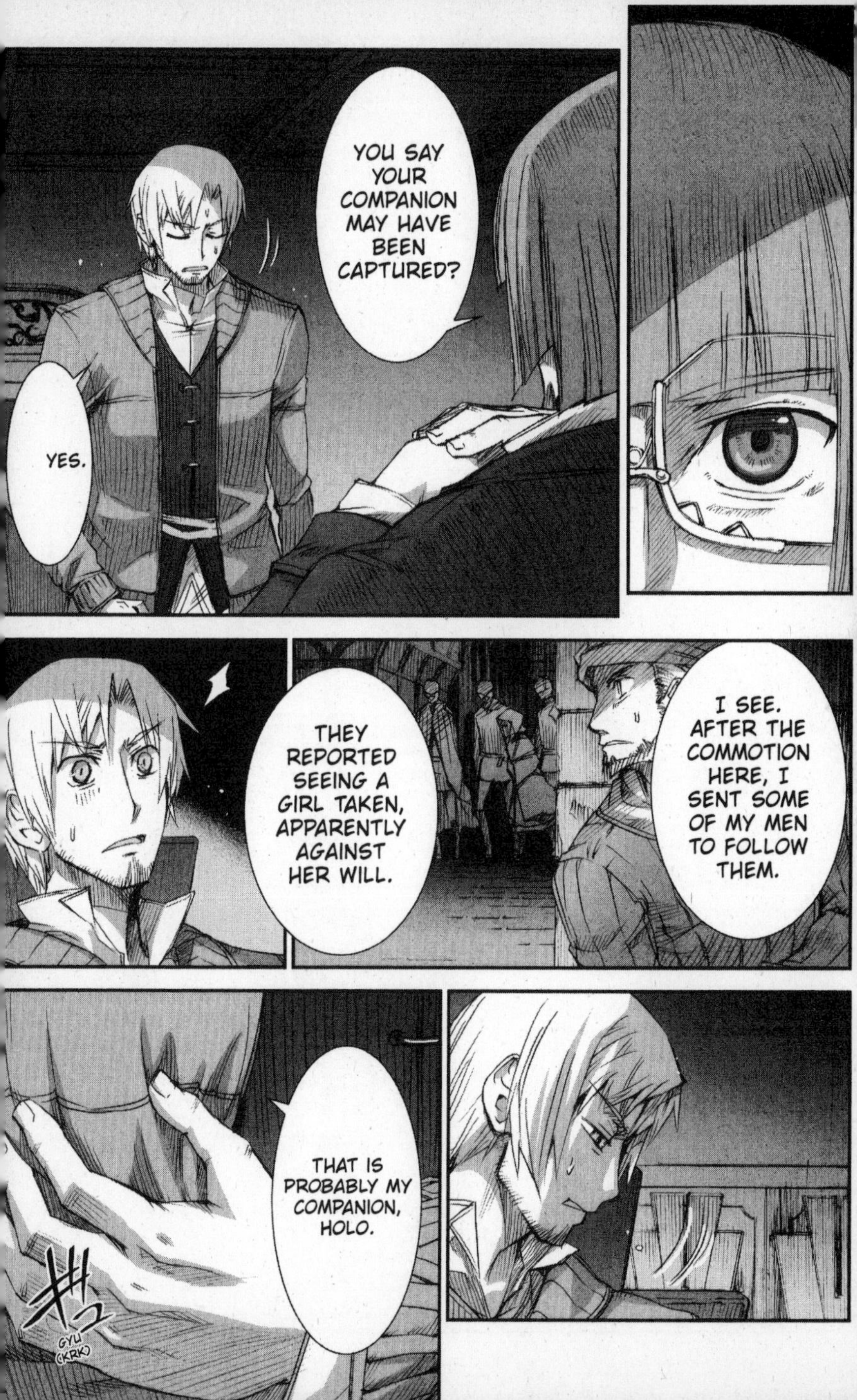
YOU SAY YOUR COMPANION MAY HAVE BEEN CAPTURED?
YES.
I SEE. AFTER THE COMMOTION HERE, I SENT SOME OF MY MEN TO FOLLOW THEM.
THEY REPORTED SEEING A GIRL TAKEN, APPARENTLY AGAINST HER WILL.
THAT IS PROBABLY MY COMPANION, HOLO.
GYU (KRK)

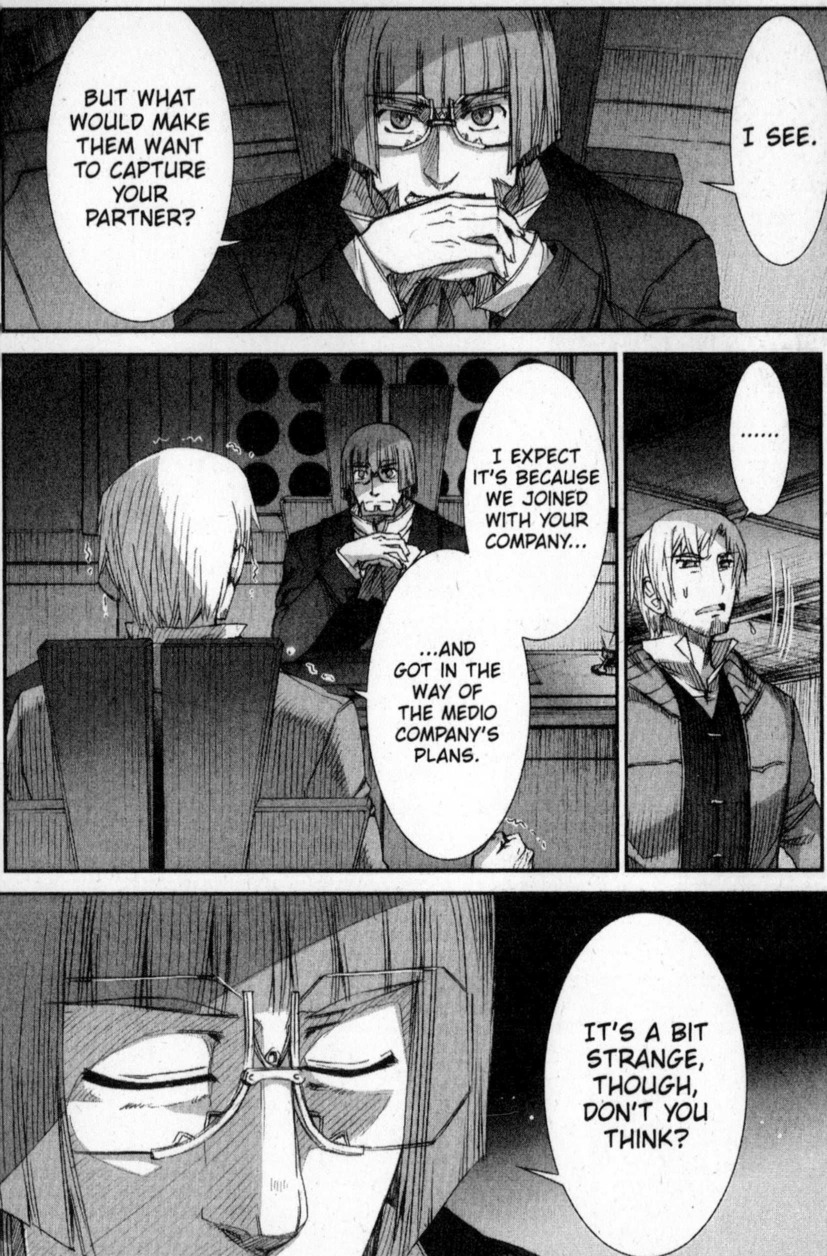
I SEE.
BUT WHAT WOULD MAKE THEM WANT TO CAPTURE YOUR PARTNER?
......
I EXPECT IT'S BECAUSE WE JOINED WITH YOUR COMPANY...
...AND GOT IN THE WAY OF THE MEDIO COMPANY'S PLANS.
IT'S A BIT STRANGE, THOUGH, DON'T YOU THINK?

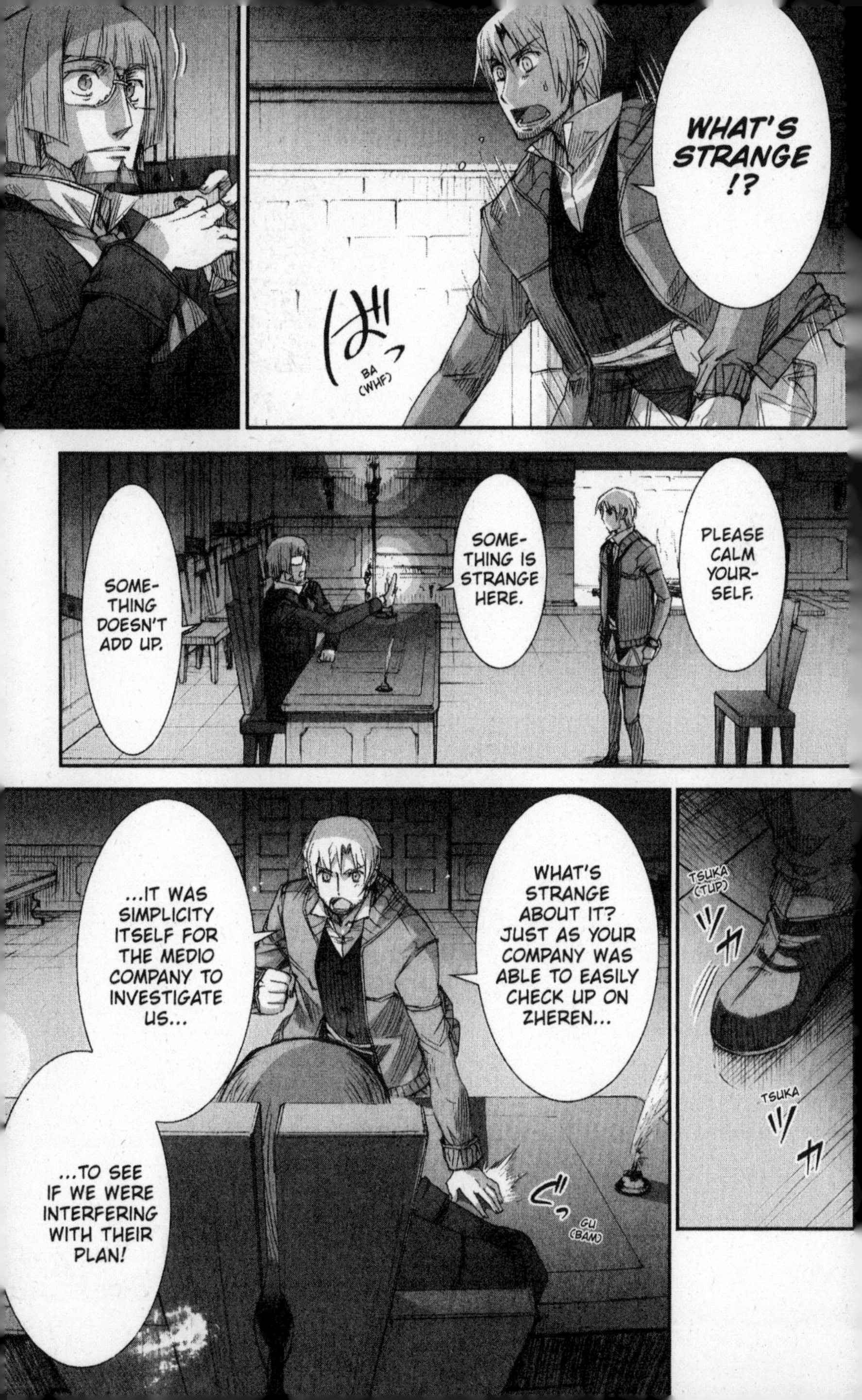
WHAT'S STRANGE !?
ばっ
BA (WHF)
PLEASE CALM YOUR-SELF.
SOME-THING IS STRANGE HERE.
SOME-THING DOESN'T ADD UP.
ツカ
TSUKA (TUP)
ツカ
TSUKA
WHAT'S STRANGE ABOUT IT? JUST AS YOUR COMPANY WAS ABLE TO EASILY CHECK UP ON ZHEREN...
...IT WAS SIMPLICITY ITSELF FOR THE MEDIO COMPANY TO INVESTIGATE US...
...TO SEE IF WE WERE INTERFERING WITH THEIR PLAN!
ぐっ
GU (BAM)

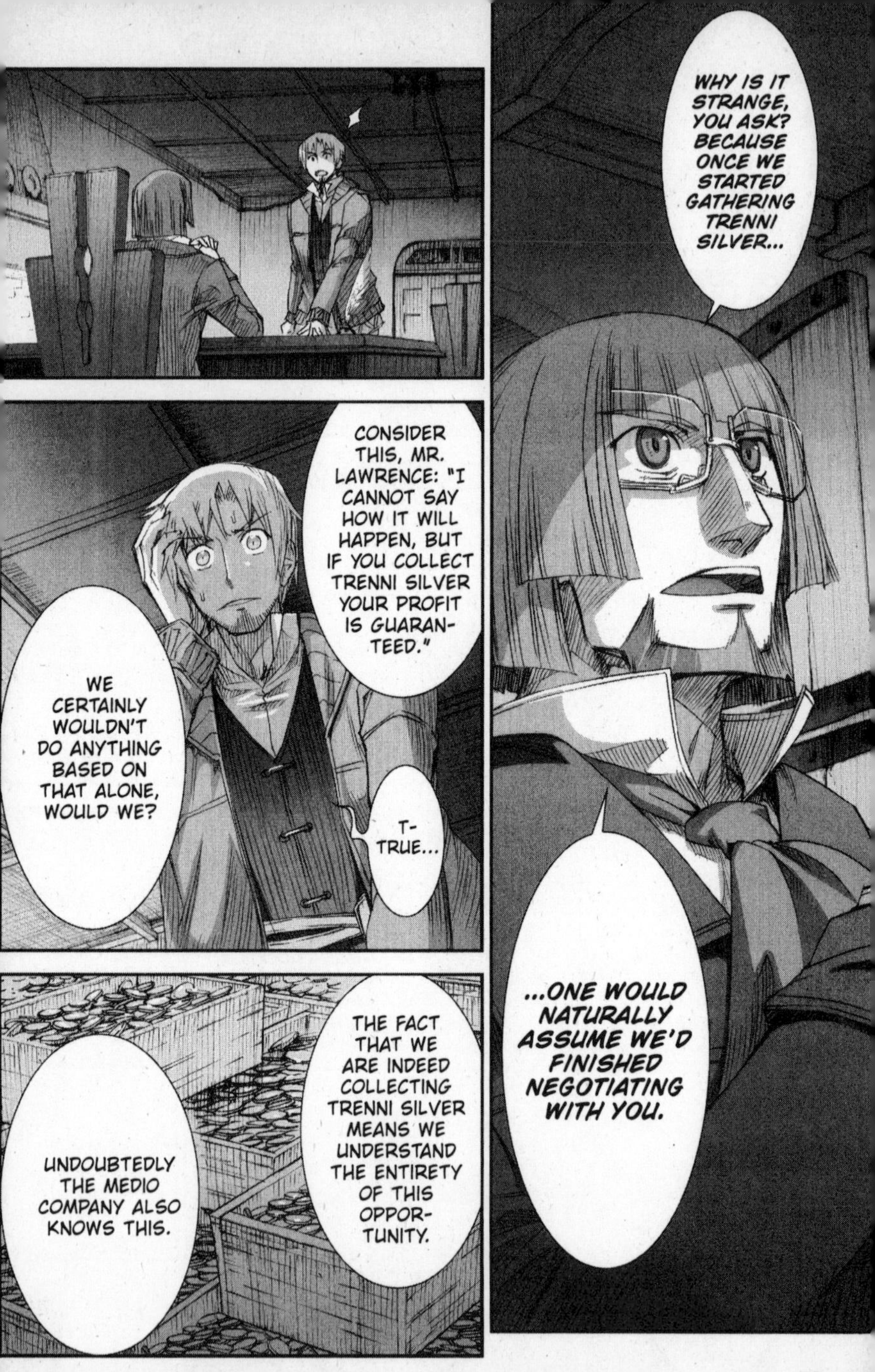
WHY IS IT STRANGE, YOU ASK? BECAUSE ONCE WE STARTED GATHERING TRENNI SILVER...
...ONE WOULD NATURALLY ASSUME WE'D FINISHED NEGOTIATING WITH YOU.
CONSIDER THIS, MR. LAWRENCE: "I CANNOT SAY HOW IT WILL HAPPEN, BUT IF YOU COLLECT TRENNI SILVER YOUR PROFIT IS GUARAN-TEED."
WE CERTAINLY WOULDN'T DO ANYTHING BASED ON THAT ALONE, WOULD WE?
T-TRUE...
THE FACT THAT WE ARE INDEED COLLECTING TRENNI SILVER MEANS WE UNDERSTAND THE ENTIRETY OF THIS OPPOR-TUNITY.
UNDOUBTEDLY THE MEDIO COMPANY ALSO KNOWS THIS.

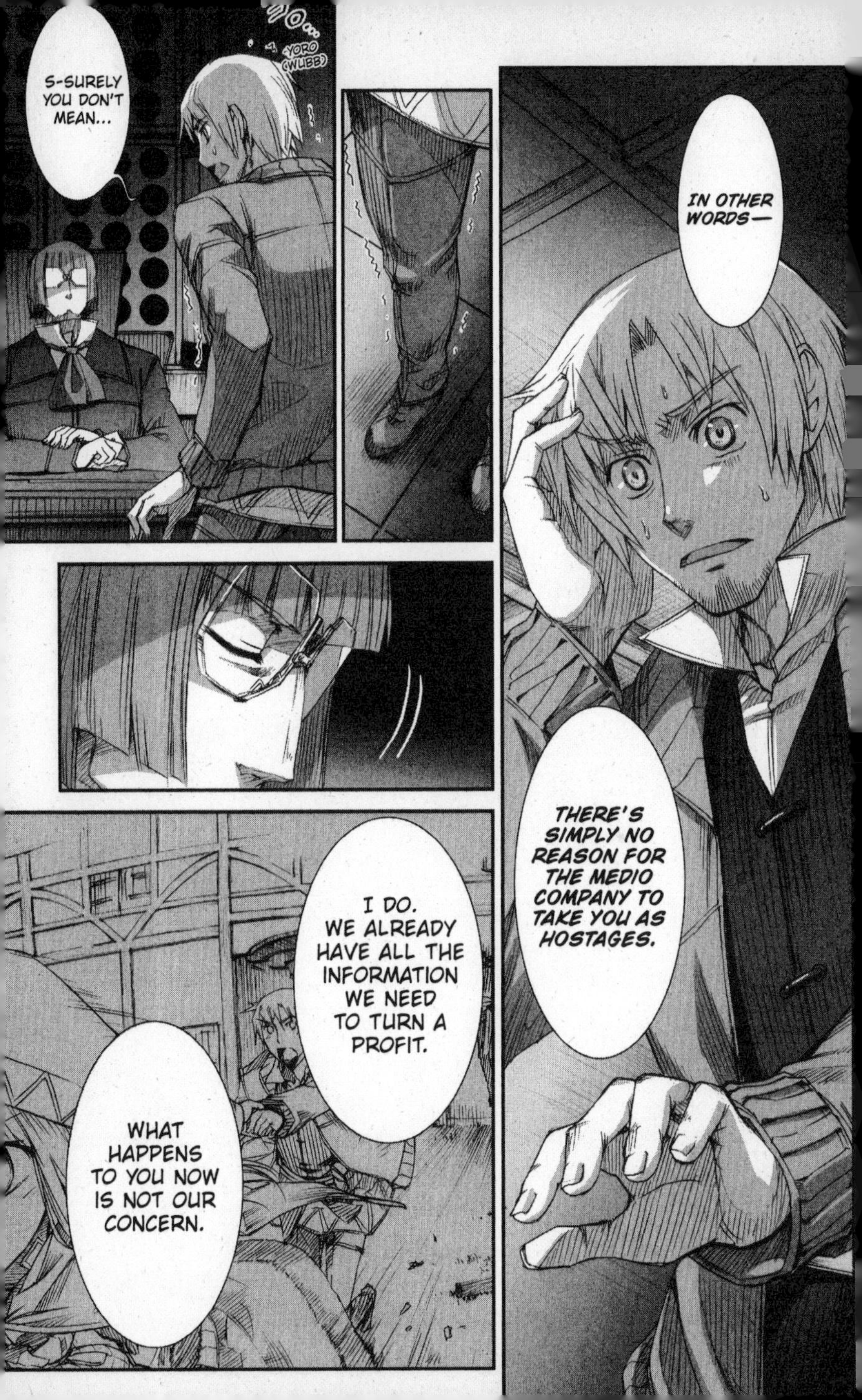
IN OTHER WORDS—
THERE'S SIMPLY NO REASON FOR THE MEDIO COMPANY TO TAKE YOU AS HOSTAGES.
YORO (WUBB)
S-SURELY YOU DON'T MEAN...
I DO. WE ALREADY HAVE ALL THE INFORMATION WE NEED TO TURN A PROFIT.
WHAT HAPPENS TO YOU NOW IS NOT OUR CONCERN.

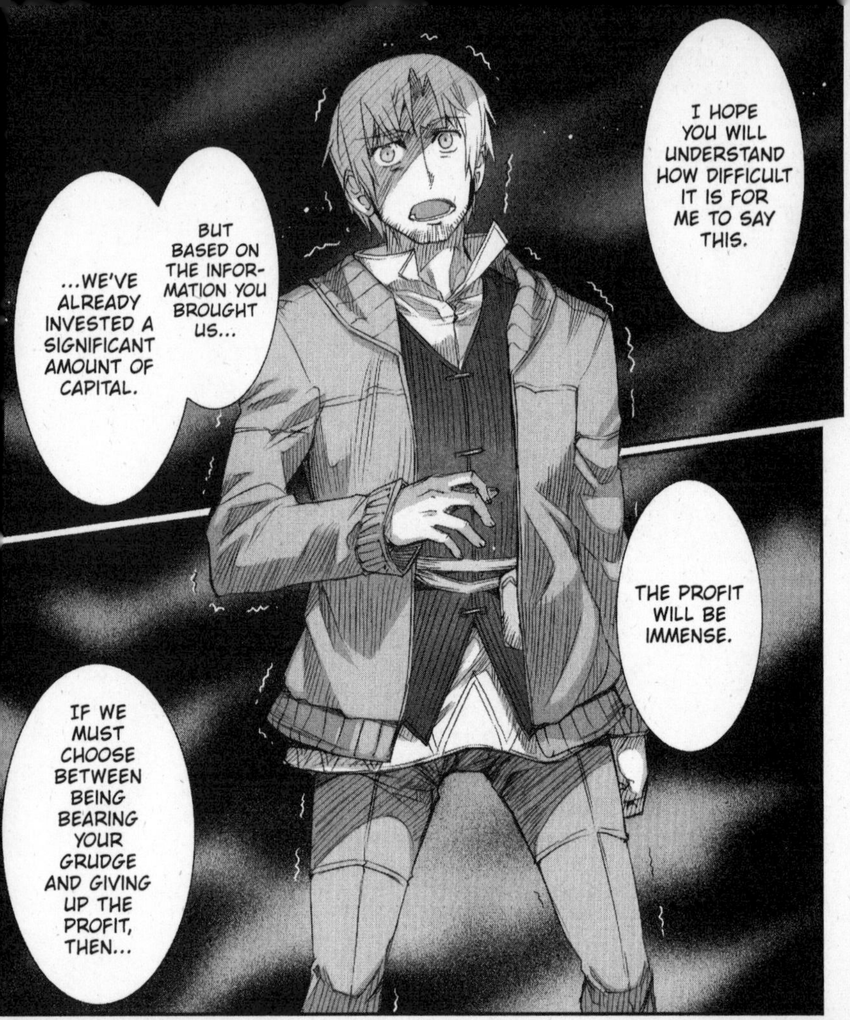
I HOPE YOU WILL UNDERSTAND HOW DIFFICULT IT IS FOR ME TO SAY THIS.
BUT BASED ON THE INFOR-MATION YOU BROUGHT US...
...WE'VE ALREADY INVESTED A SIGNIFICANT AMOUNT OF CAPITAL.
THE PROFIT WILL BE IMMENSE.
IF WE MUST CHOOSE BETWEEN BEING BEARING YOUR GRUDGE AND GIVING UP THE PROFIT, THEN...
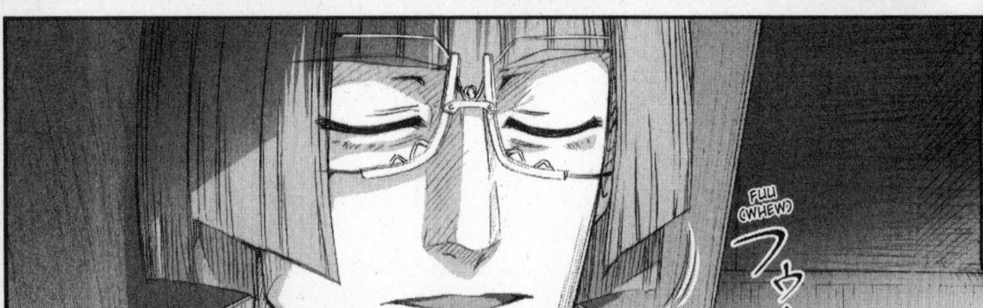
FUU (WHEW)

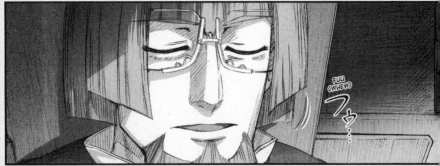

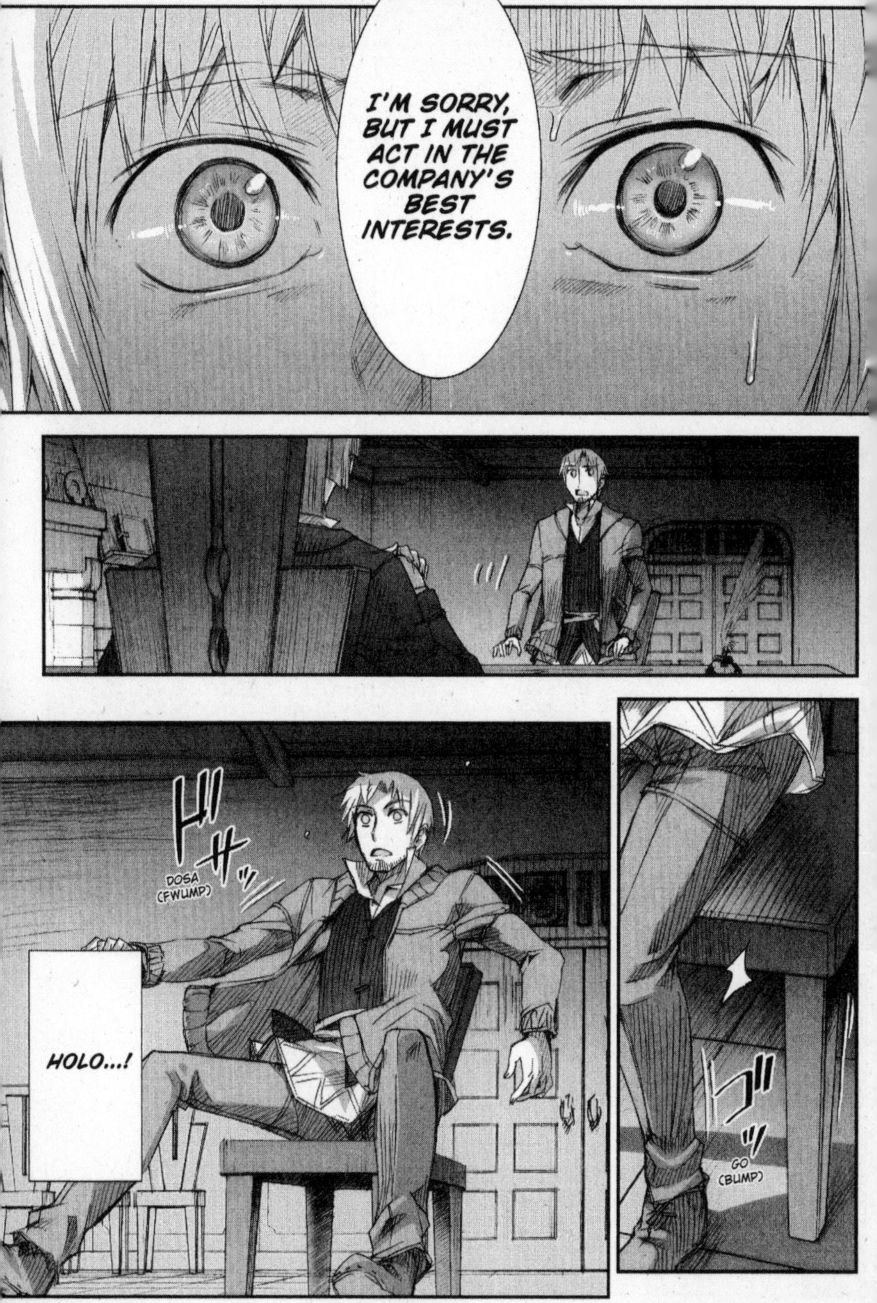
I'M SORRY, BUT I MUST ACT IN THE COMPANY'S BEST INTERESTS.
GO (BUMP)
DOSA (FWUMP)
HOLO...!

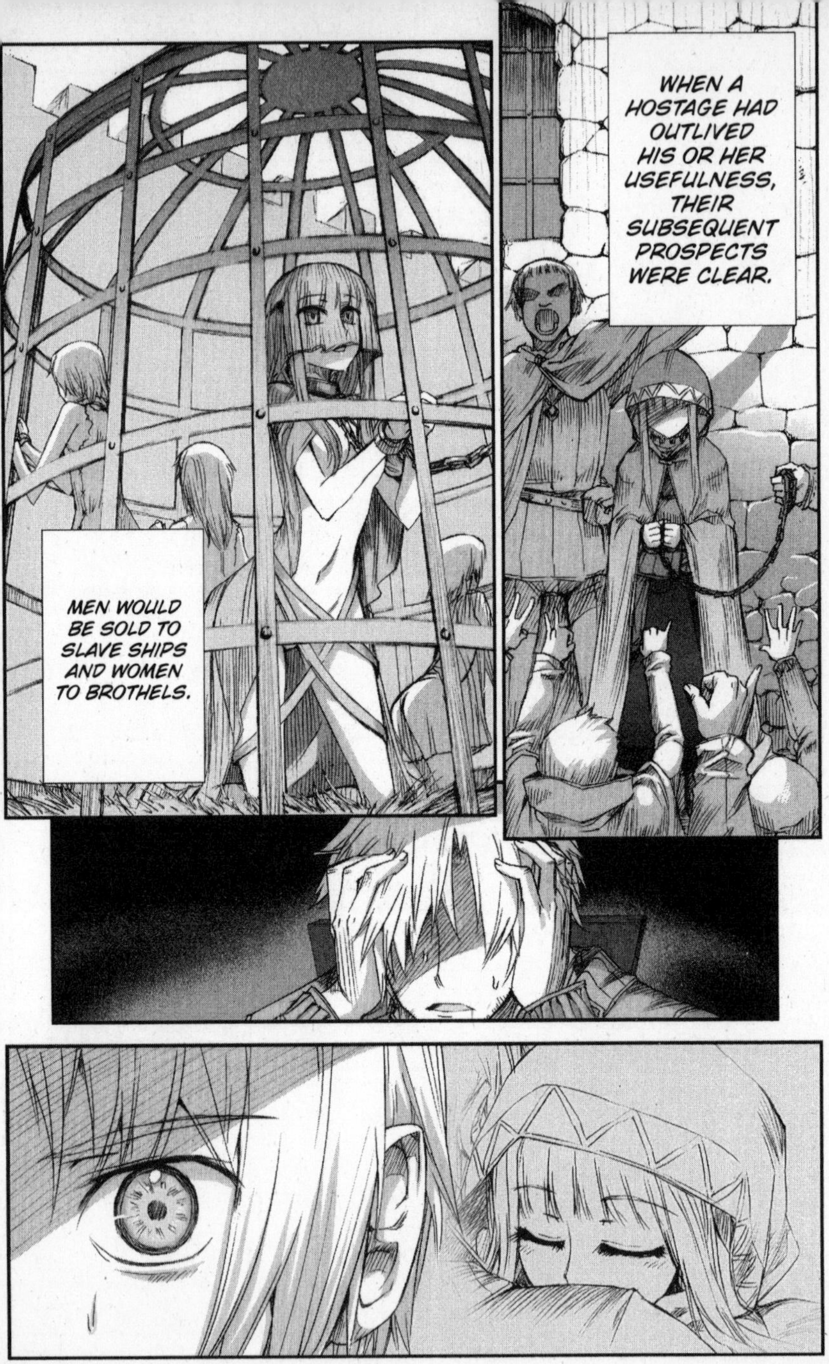
WHEN A HOSTAGE HAD OUTLIVED HIS OR HER USEFULNESS, THEIR SUBSEQUENT PROSPECTS WERE CLEAR.
MEN WOULD BE SOLD TO SLAVE SHIPS AND WOMEN TO BROTHELS.

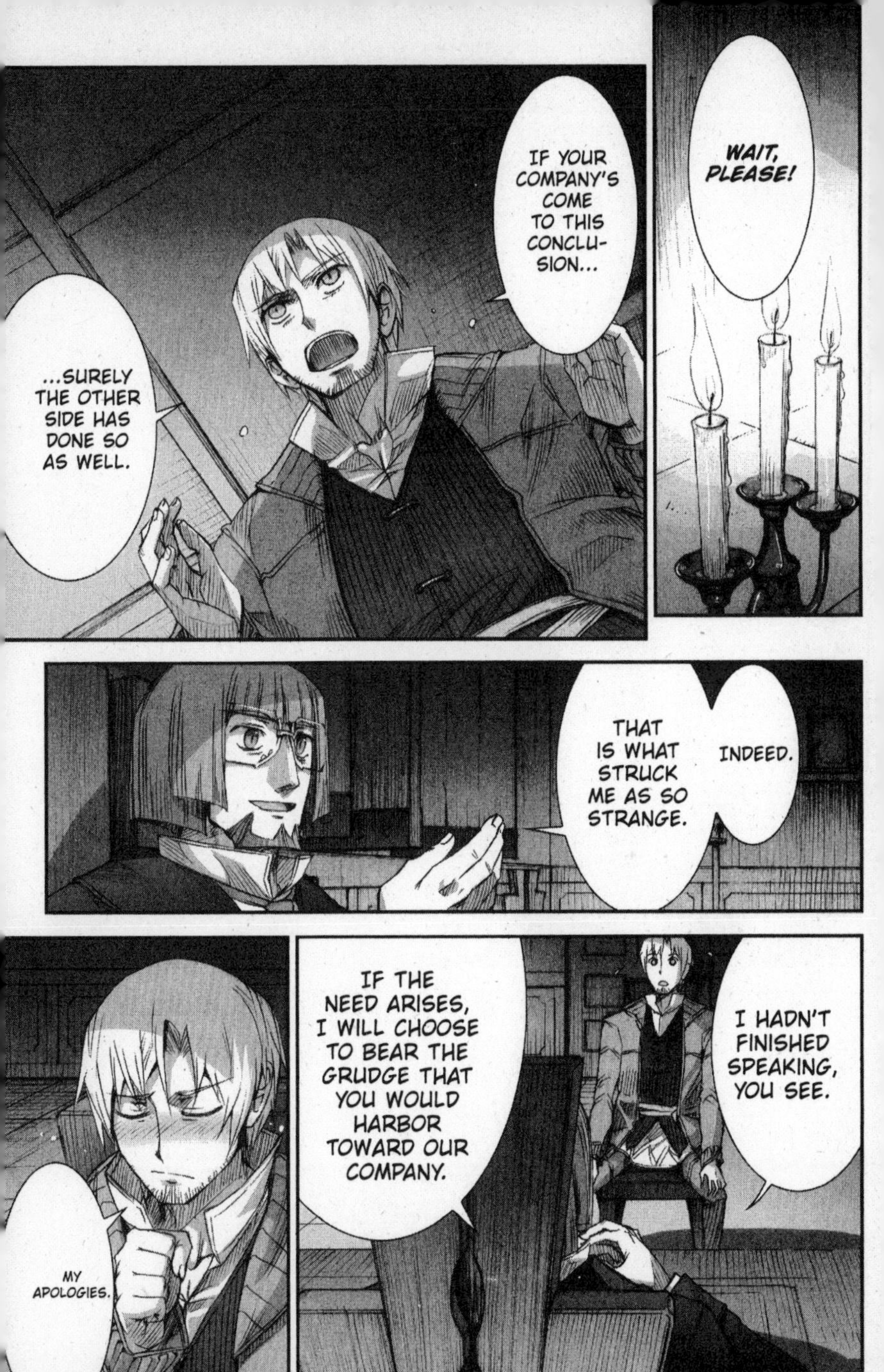
WAIT, PLEASE!
IF YOUR COMPANY'S COME TO THIS CONCLUSION...
...SURELY THE OTHER SIDE HAS DONE SO AS WELL.
INDEED.
THAT IS WHAT STRUCK ME AS SO STRANGE.
I HADN'T FINISHED SPEAKING, YOU SEE.
IF THE NEED ARISES, I WILL CHOOSE TO BEAR THE GRUDGE THAT YOU WOULD HARBOR TOWARD OUR COMPANY.
MY APOLOGIES.

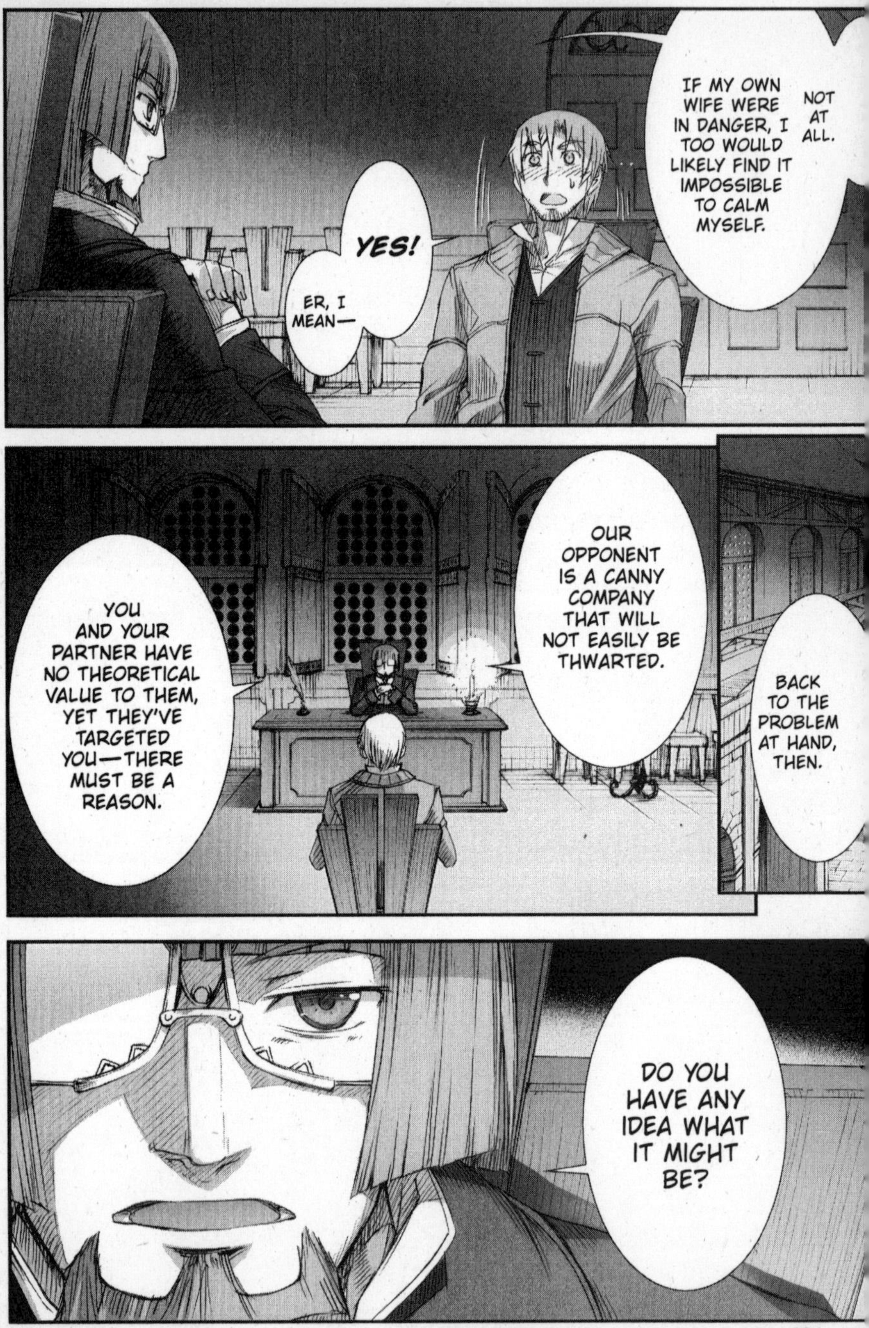
NOT AT ALL.
IF MY OWN WIFE WERE IN DANGER, I TOO WOULD LIKELY FIND IT IMPOSSIBLE TO CALM MYSELF.
YES!
ER, I MEAN—
BACK TO THE PROBLEM AT HAND, THEN.
OUR OPPONENT IS A CANNY COMPANY THAT WILL NOT EASILY BE THWARTED.
YOU AND YOUR PARTNER HAVE NO THEORETICAL VALUE TO THEM, YET THEY'VE TARGETED YOU—THERE MUST BE A REASON.
DO YOU HAVE ANY IDEA WHAT IT MIGHT BE?

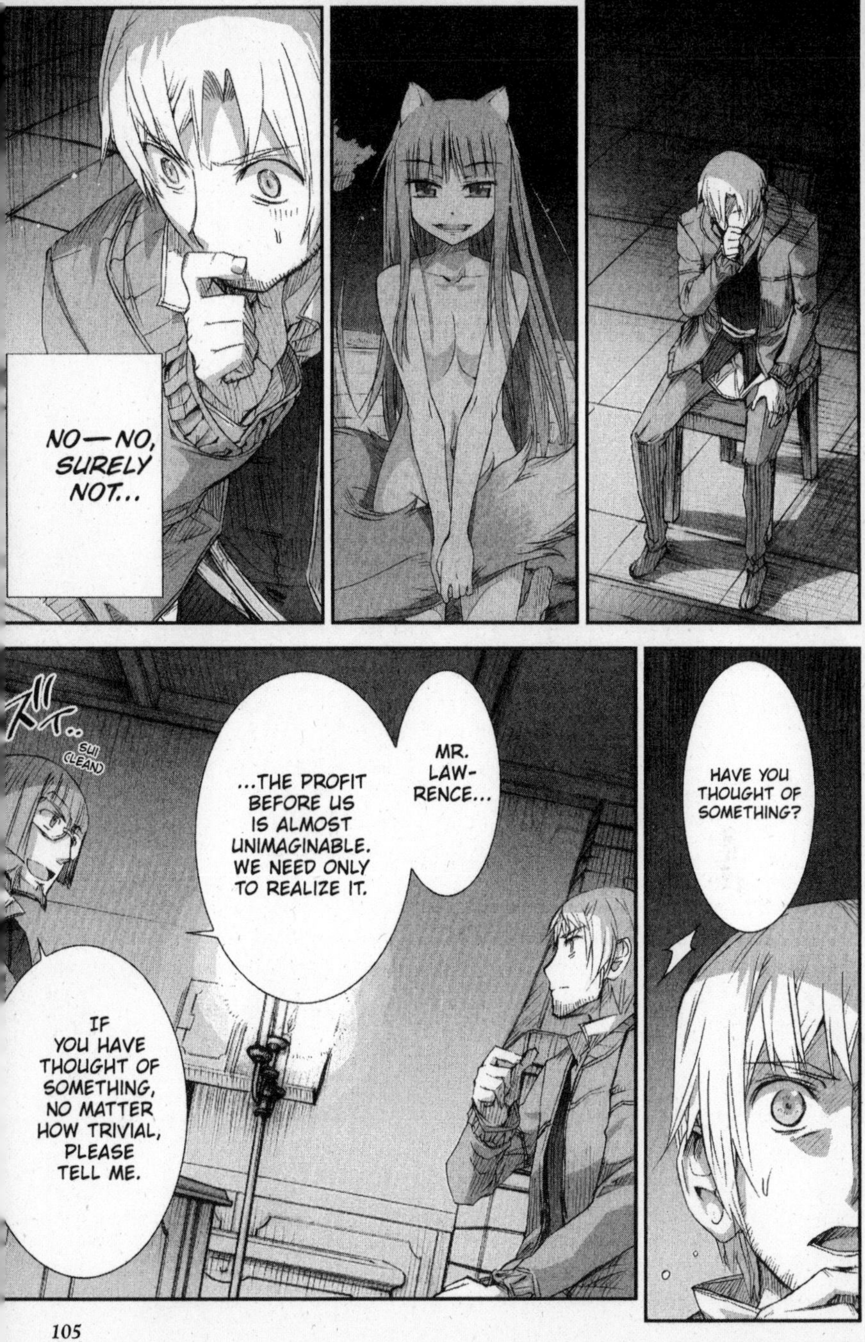
NO—NO, SURELY NOT...
HAVE YOU THOUGHT OF SOMETHING?
MR. LAWRENCE...
...THE PROFIT BEFORE US IS ALMOST UNIMAGINABLE. WE NEED ONLY TO REALIZE IT.
SUI (LEAN)
IF YOU HAVE THOUGHT OF SOMETHING, NO MATTER HOW TRIVIAL, PLEASE TELL ME.

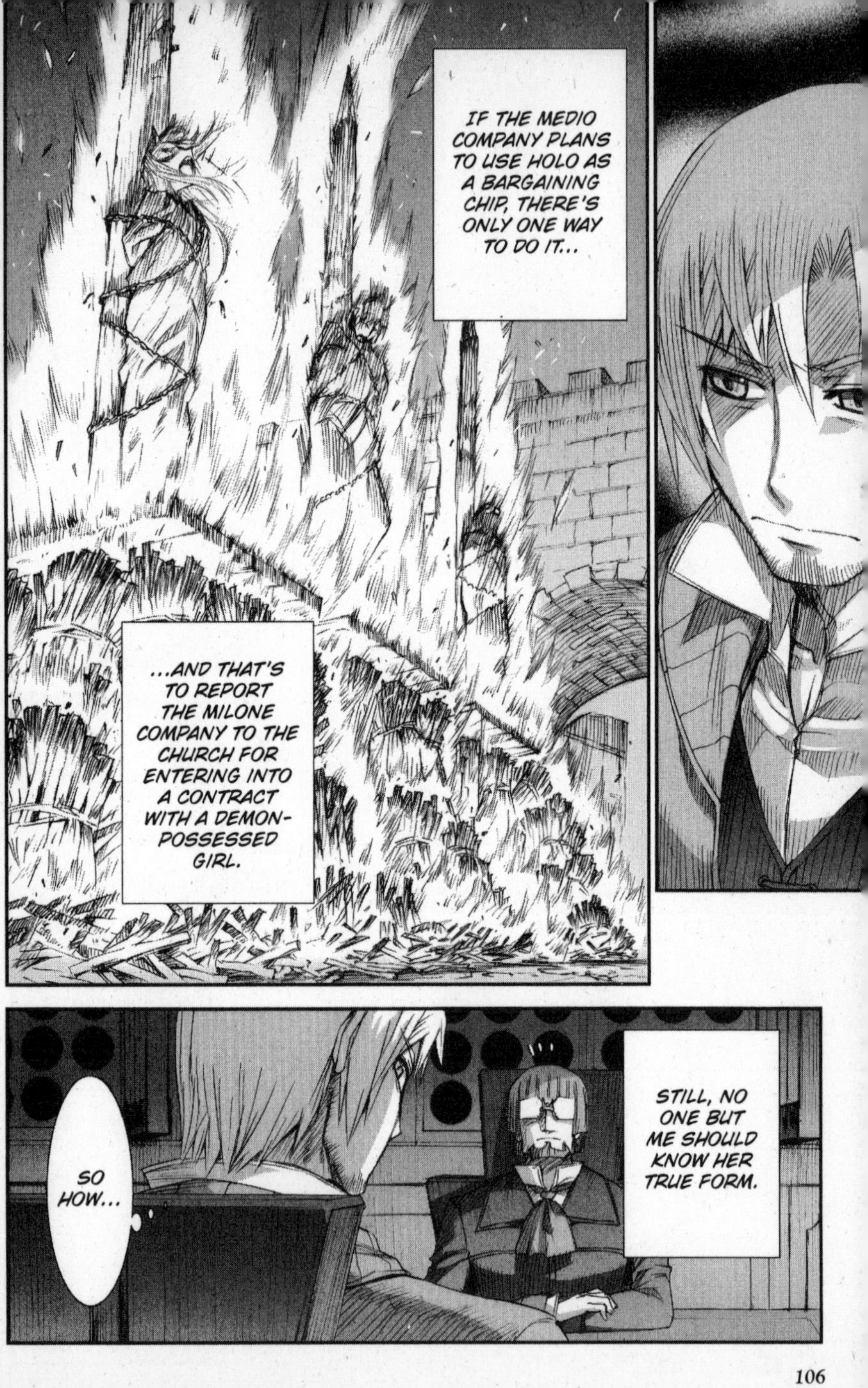
IF THE MEDIO COMPANY PLANS TO USE HOLO AS A BARGAINING CHIP, THERE'S ONLY ONE WAY TO DO IT...
...AND THAT'S TO REPORT THE MILONE COMPANY TO THE CHURCH FOR ENTERING INTO A CONTRACT WITH A DEMON-POSSESSED GIRL.
STILL, NO ONE BUT ME SHOULD KNOW HER TRUE FORM.
SO HOW...

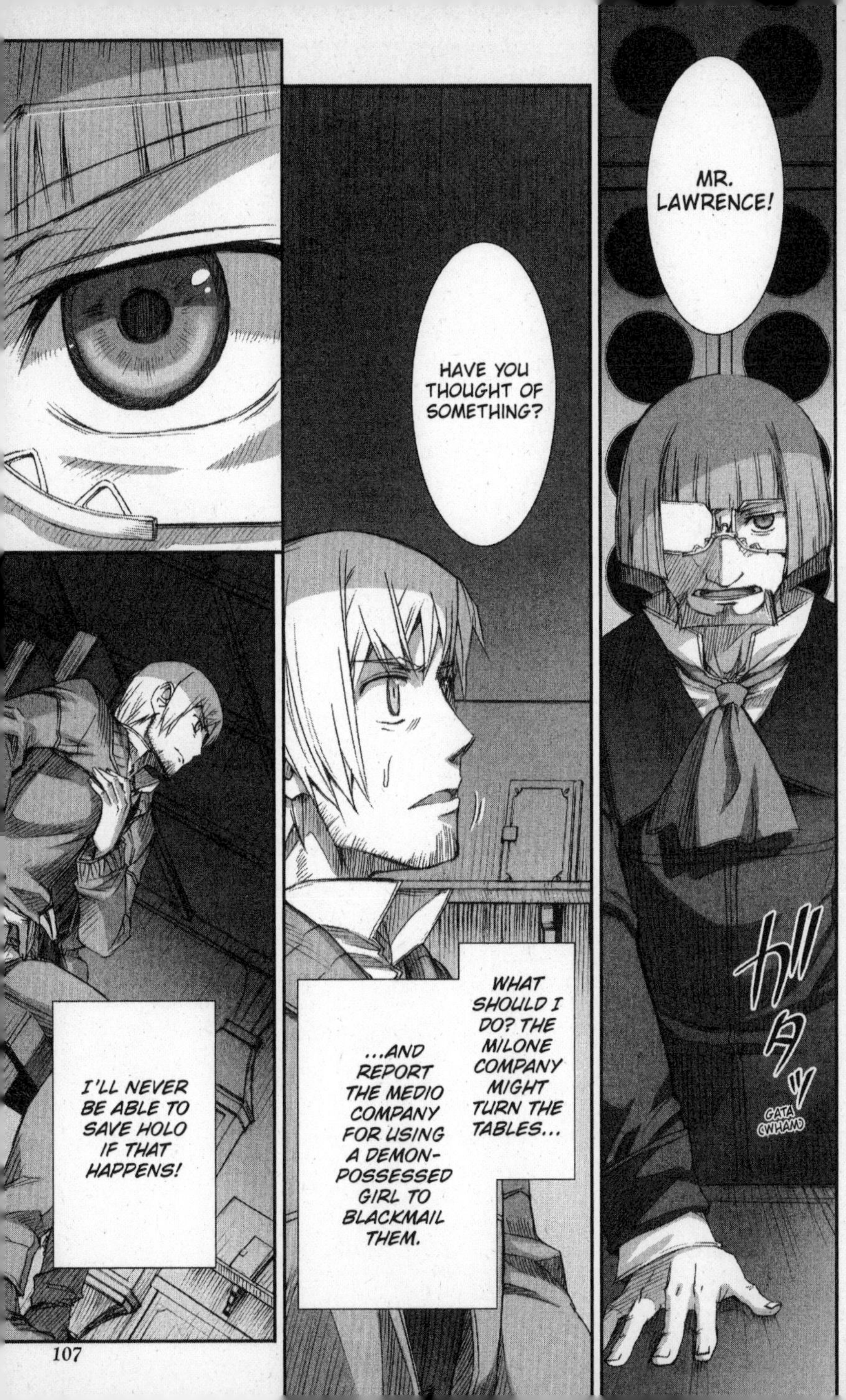
MR. LAWRENCE!
ガタッ
GATA (WHAM)
HAVE YOU THOUGHT OF SOMETHING?
WHAT SHOULD I DO? THE MILONE COMPANY MIGHT TURN THE TABLES...
...AND REPORT THE MEDIO COMPANY FOR USING A DEMON-POSSESSED GIRL TO BLACKMAIL THEM.
I'LL NEVER BE ABLE TO SAVE HOLO IF THAT HAPPENS!

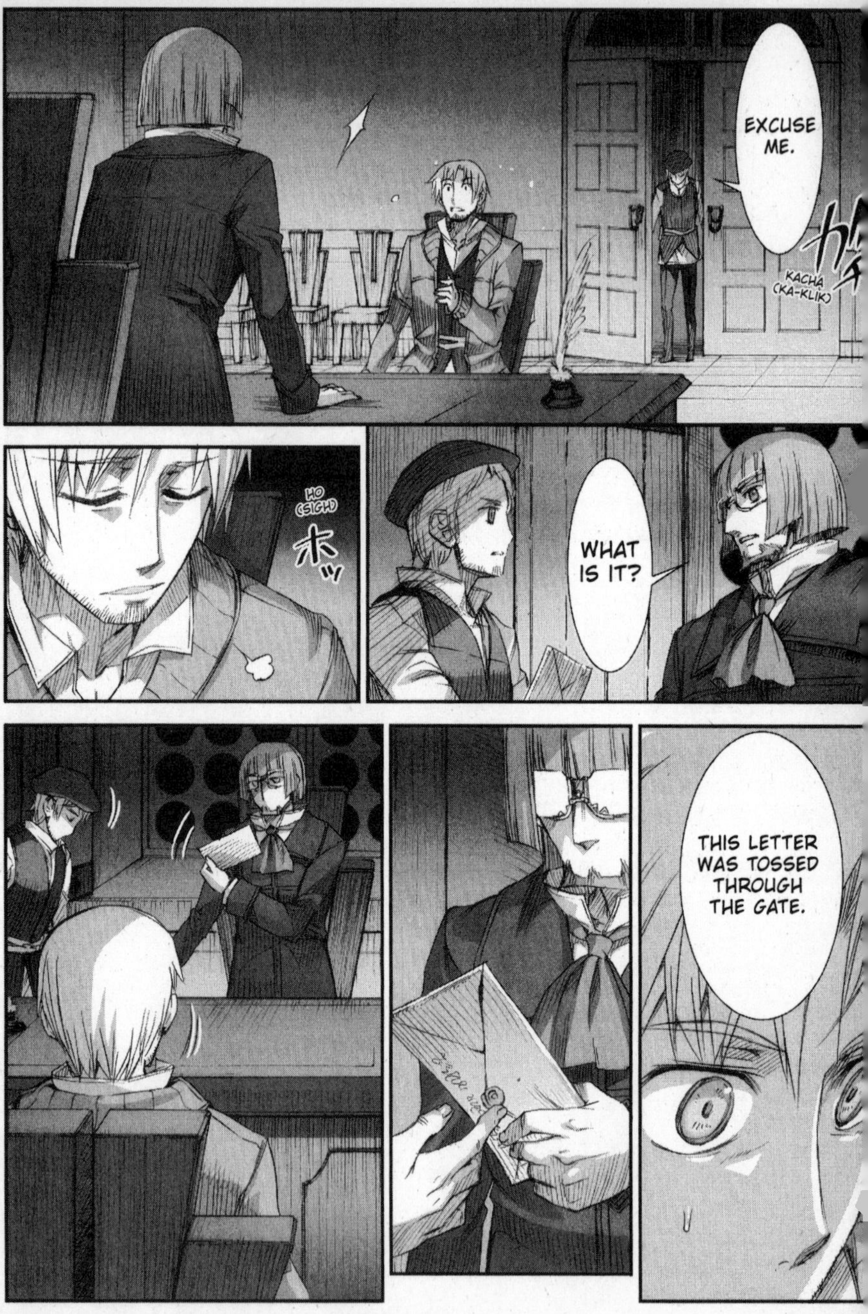
KACHA (KA-KLIK)
EXCUSE ME.
WHAT IS IT?
HO (SIGH)
THIS LETTER WAS TOSSED THROUGH THE GATE.

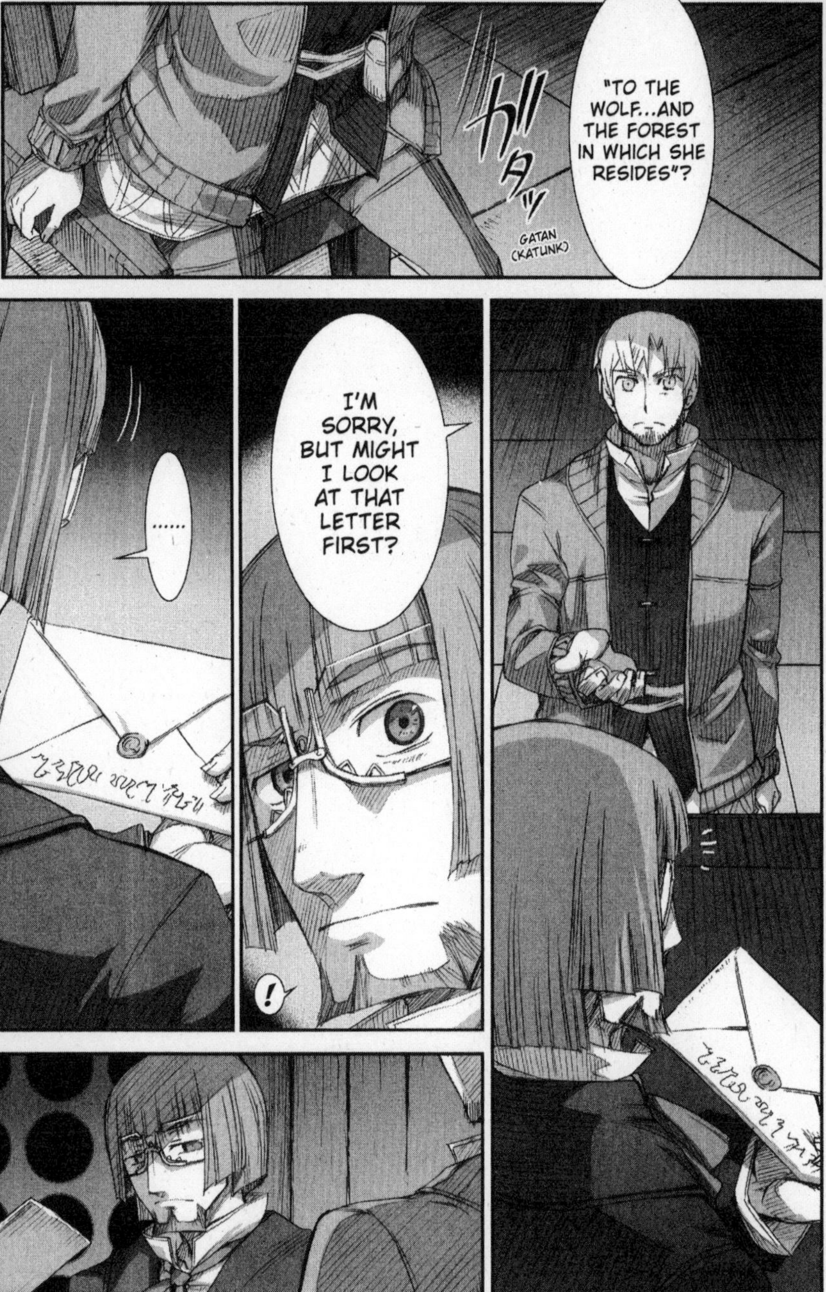
"TO THE WOLF...AND THE FOREST IN WHICH SHE RESIDES"?
ガタッ
GATAN (KATUNK)
I'M SORRY, BUT MIGHT I LOOK AT THAT LETTER FIRST?
!
......

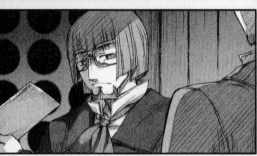

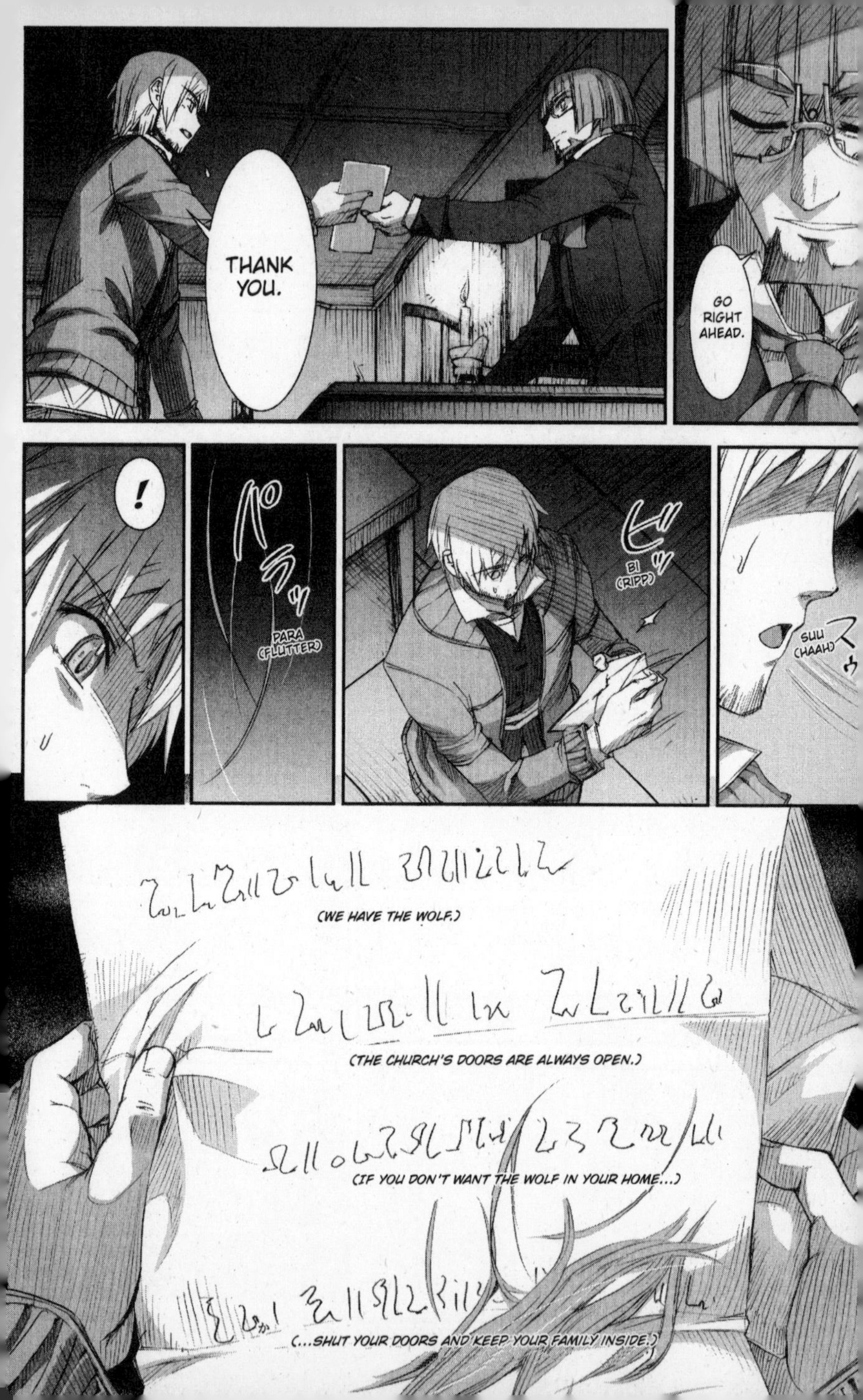
GO RIGHT AHEAD.
THANK YOU.
SUU (HAAH)
BI (RIPP)
PARA (FLUTTER)
!
(WE HAVE THE WOLF.)
(THE CHURCH'S DOORS ARE ALWAYS OPEN.)
(IF YOU DON'T WANT THE WOLF IN YOUR HOME...)
(...SHUT YOUR DOORS AND KEEP YOUR FAMILY INSIDE.)

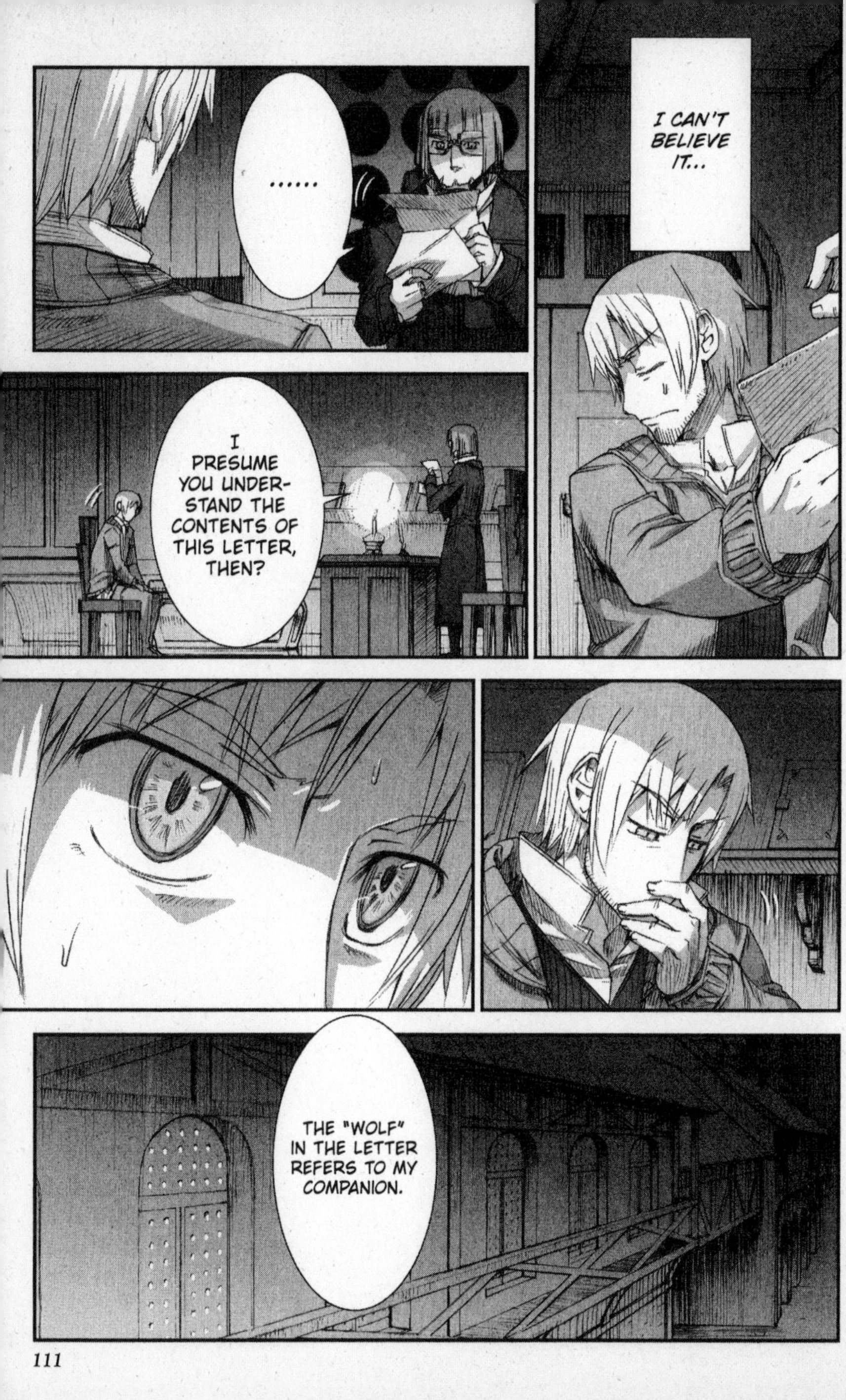
I CAN'T BELIEVE IT...
......
I PRESUME YOU UNDERSTAND THE CONTENTS OF THIS LETTER, THEN?
THE "WOLF" IN THE LETTER REFERS TO MY COMPANION.

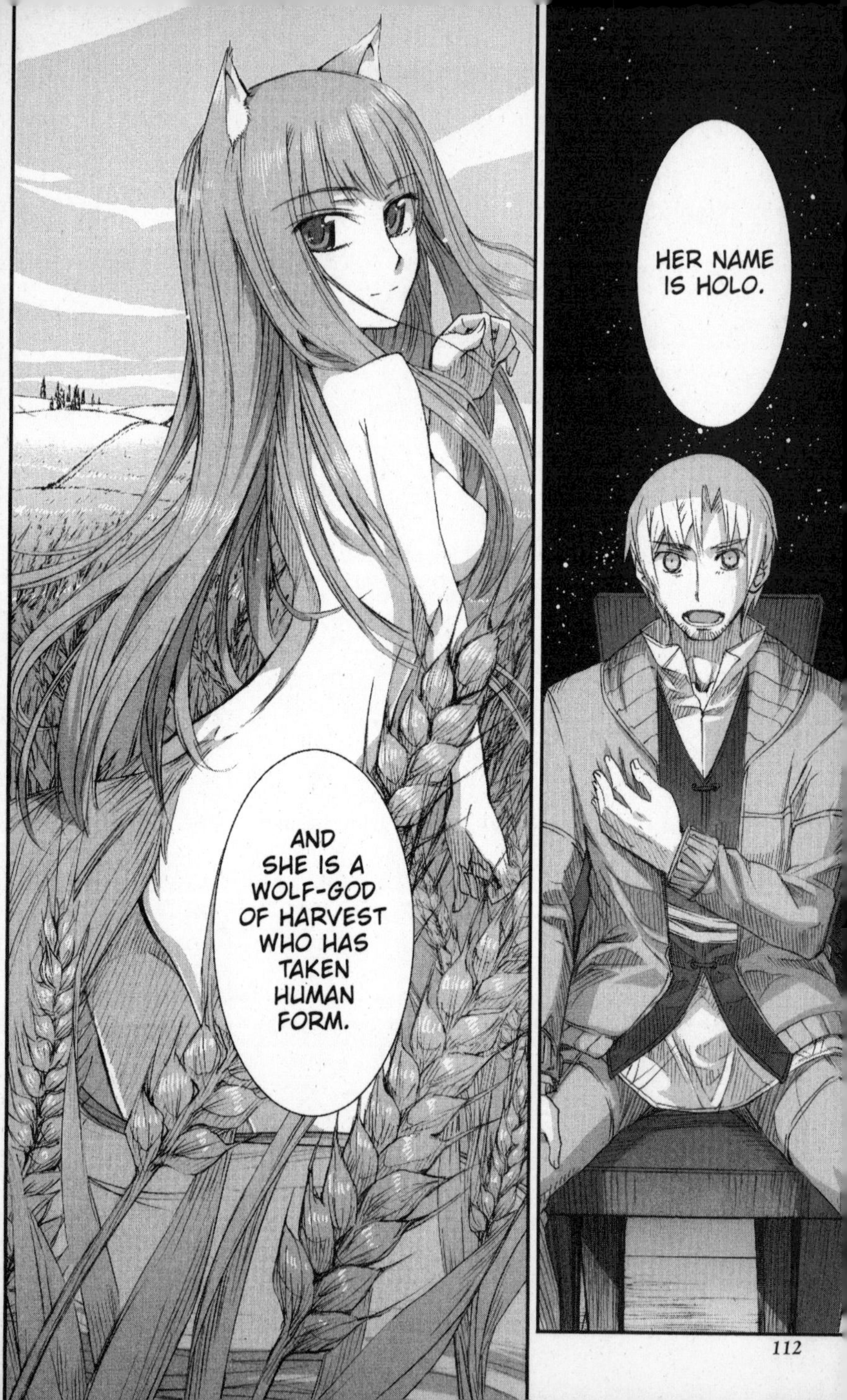
HER NAME IS HOLO.
AND SHE IS A WOLF-GOD OF HARVEST WHO HAS TAKEN HUMAN FORM.

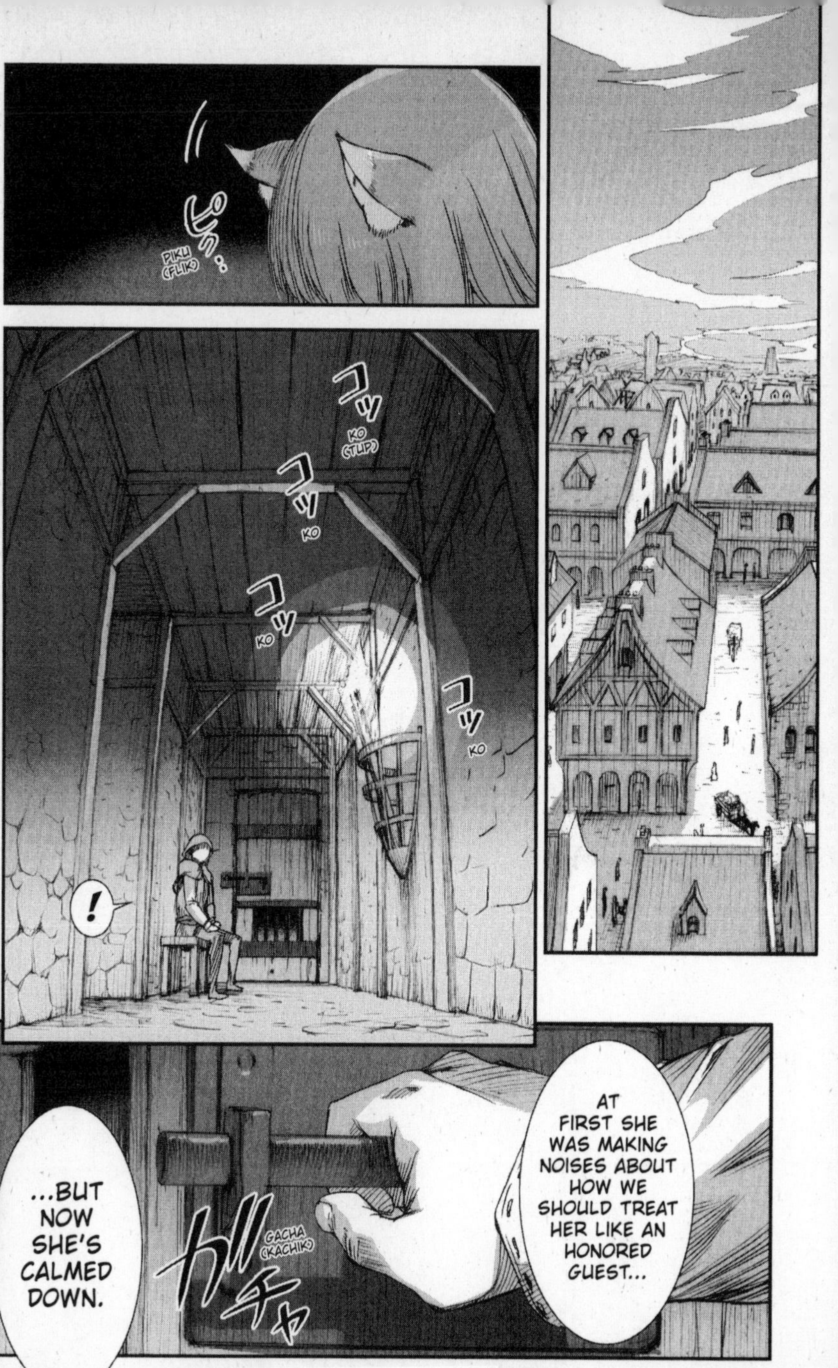

ピク..
PIKU (FLIK)
コッ
KO (TUP)
コッ
KO
コッ
KO
コッ
KO
!
AT FIRST SHE WAS MAKING NOISES ABOUT HOW WE SHOULD TREAT HER LIKE AN HONORED GUEST...
カチャ
GACHA (KACHIK)
...BUT NOW SHE'S CALMED DOWN.

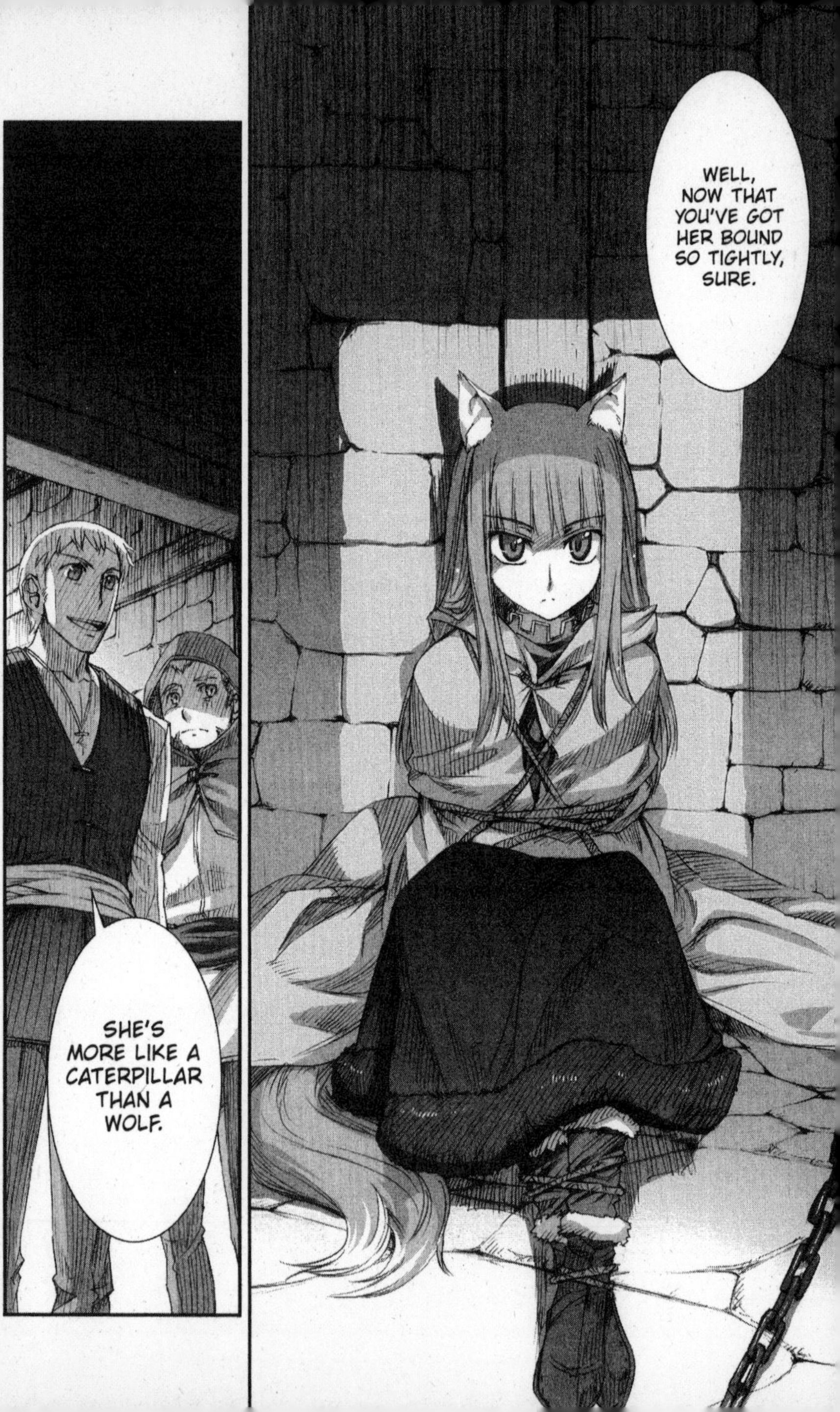
WELL, NOW THAT YOU'VE GOT HER BOUND SO TIGHTLY, SURE.
SHE'S MORE LIKE A CATERPILLAR THAN A WOLF.

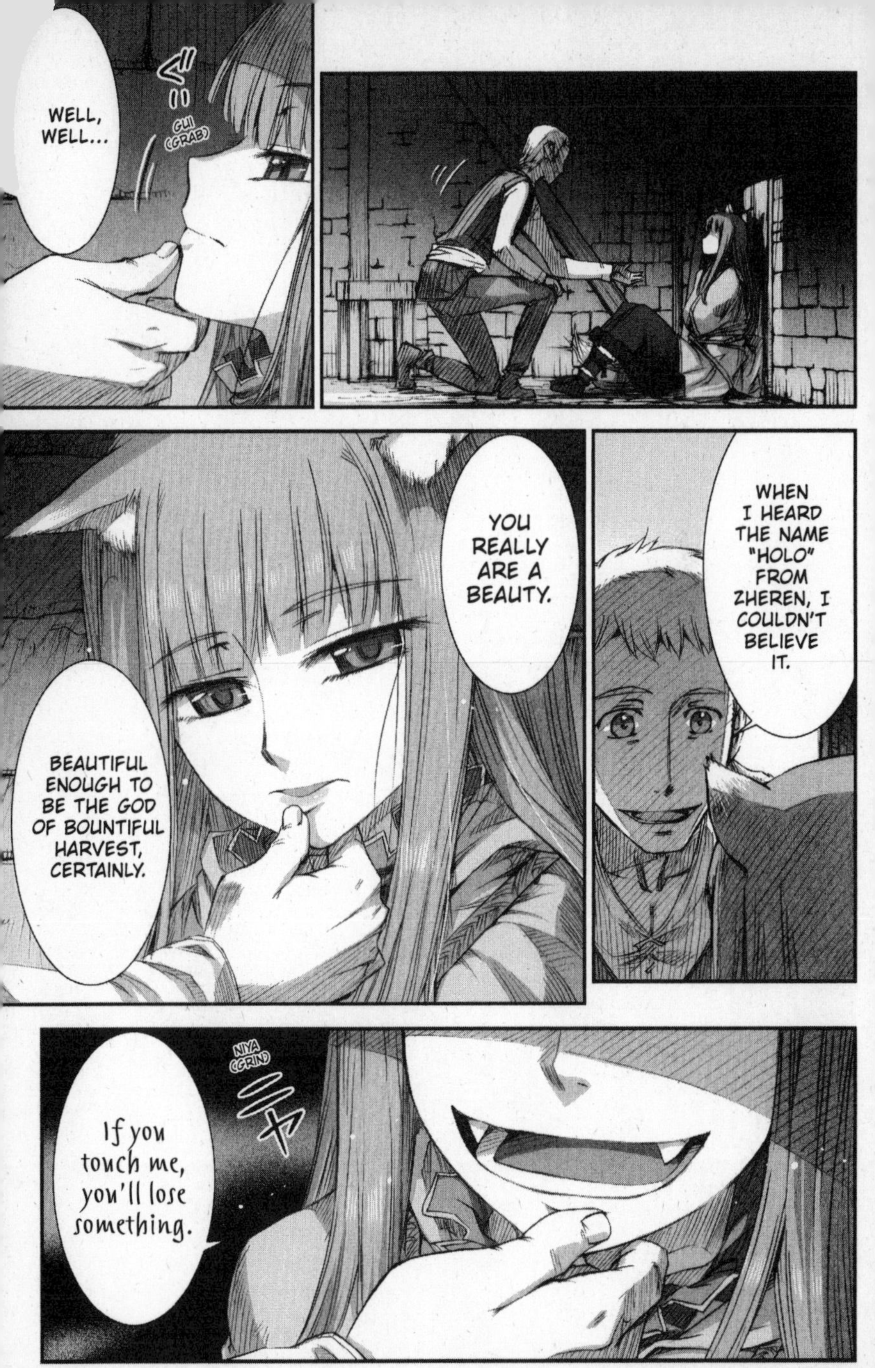
GUI (GRAB)
WELL, WELL...
WHEN I HEARD THE NAME "HOLO" FROM ZHEREN, I COULDN'T BELIEVE IT.
YOU REALLY ARE A BEAUTY.
BEAUTIFUL ENOUGH TO BE THE GOD OF BOUNTIFUL HARVEST, CERTAINLY.
NIYA (GRIN)
If you touch me, you'll lose something.

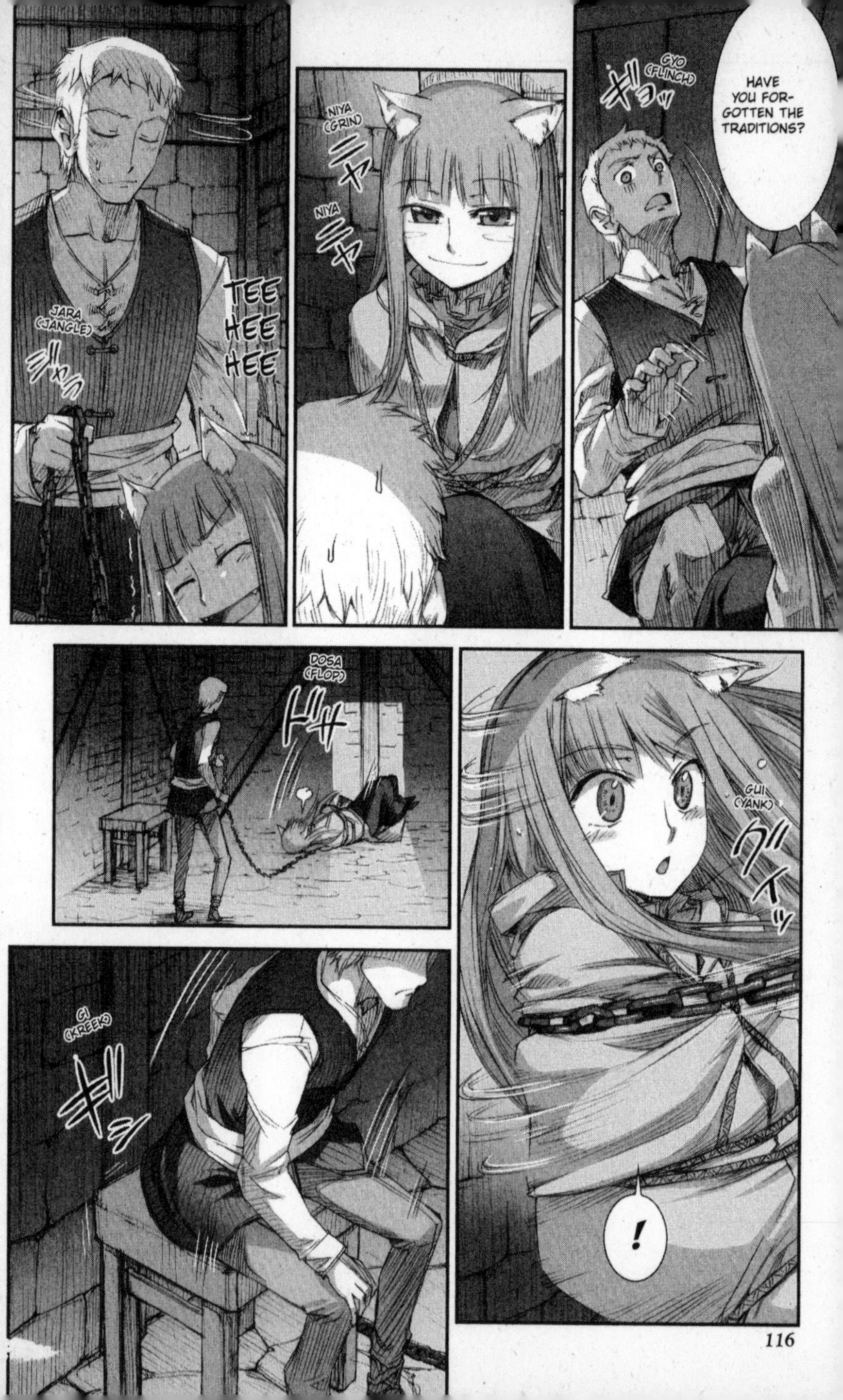
HAVE YOU FOR-GOTTEN THE TRADITIONS?
GYO (FLINCH)
NIYA (GRIN)
NIYA
JARA (JANGLE)
TEE HEE HEE
GUI (YANK)
!
DOSA (FLOP)
GI (KREEK)

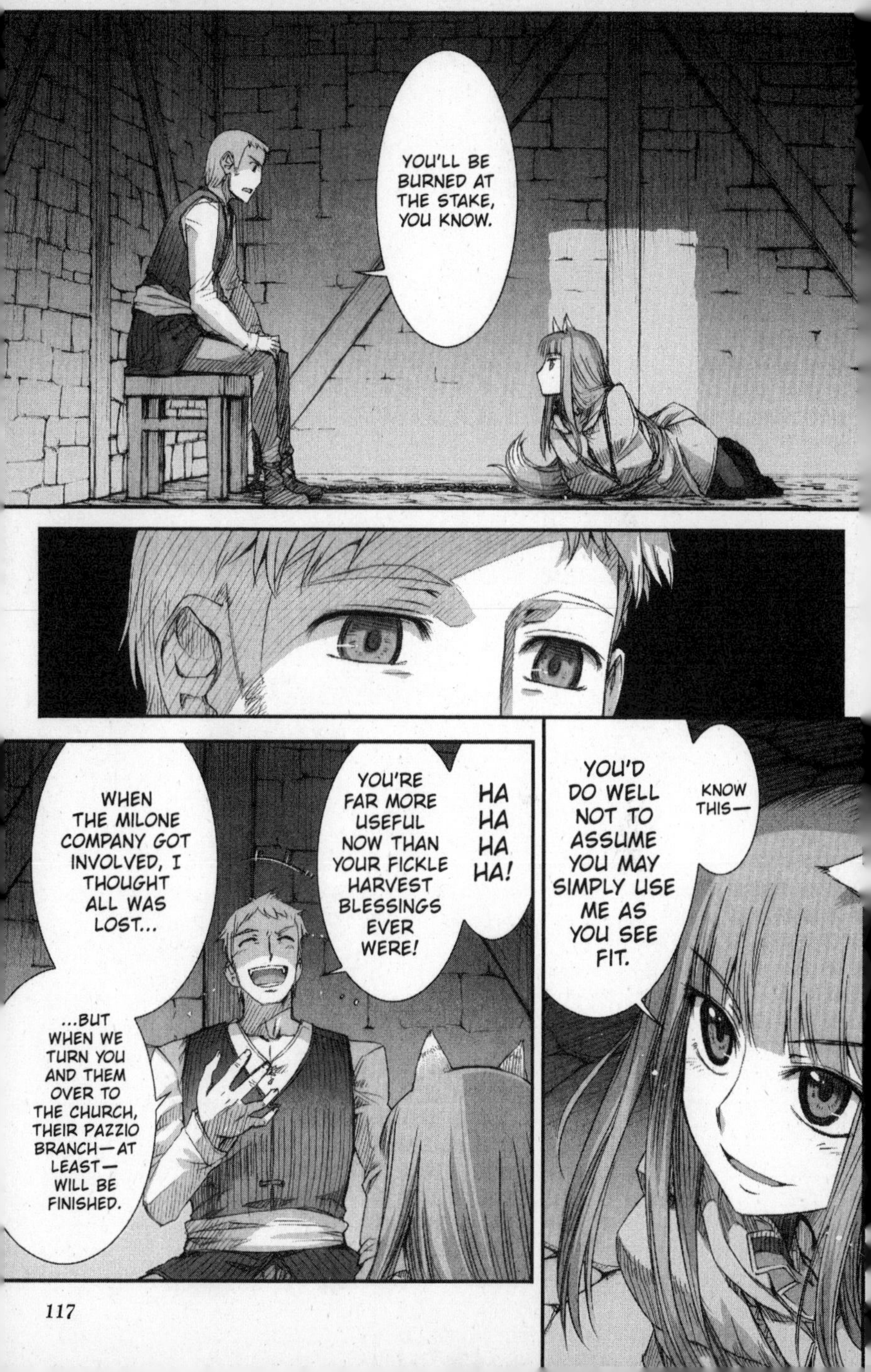
YOU'LL BE BURNED AT THE STAKE, YOU KNOW.
KNOW THIS—
YOU'D DO WELL NOT TO ASSUME YOU MAY SIMPLY USE ME AS YOU SEE FIT.
HA HA HA HA!
YOU'RE FAR MORE USEFUL NOW THAN YOUR FICKLE HARVEST BLESSINGS EVER WERE!
WHEN THE MILONE COMPANY GOT INVOLVED, I THOUGHT ALL WAS LOST...
...BUT WHEN WE TURN YOU AND THEM OVER TO THE CHURCH, THEIR PAZZIO BRANCH—AT LEAST—WILL BE FINISHED.

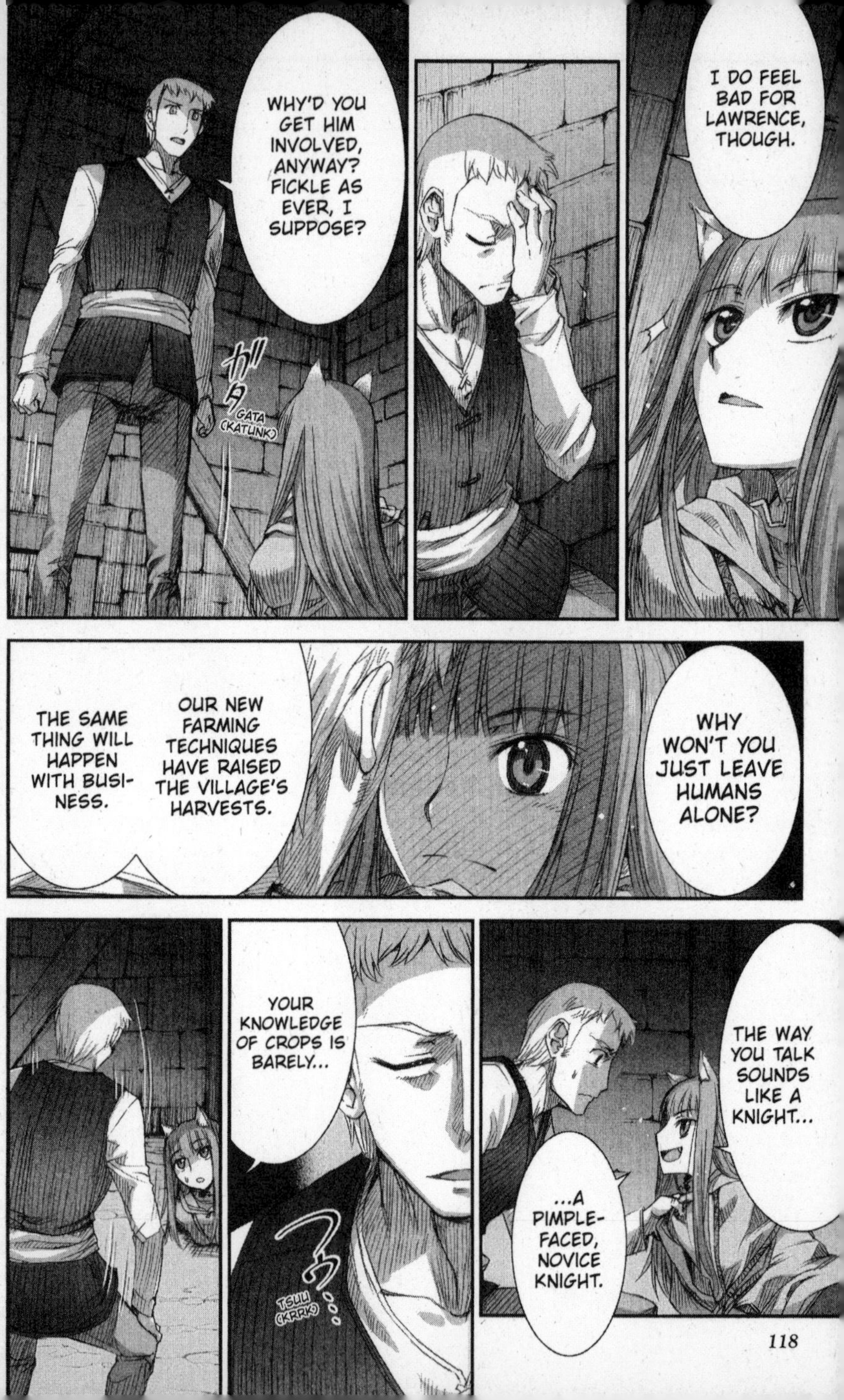
I DO FEEL BAD FOR LAWRENCE, THOUGH.
WHY'D YOU GET HIM INVOLVED, ANYWAY? FICKLE AS EVER, I SUPPOSE?
GATA (KATUNK)
WHY WON'T YOU JUST LEAVE HUMANS ALONE?
OUR NEW FARMING TECHNIQUES HAVE RAISED THE VILLAGE'S HARVESTS.
THE SAME THING WILL HAPPEN WITH BUSI-NESS.
THE WAY YOU TALK SOUNDS LIKE A KNIGHT...
...A PIMPLE-FACED, NOVICE KNIGHT.
YOUR KNOWLEDGE OF CROPS IS BARELY...
TSUU (KRRK)

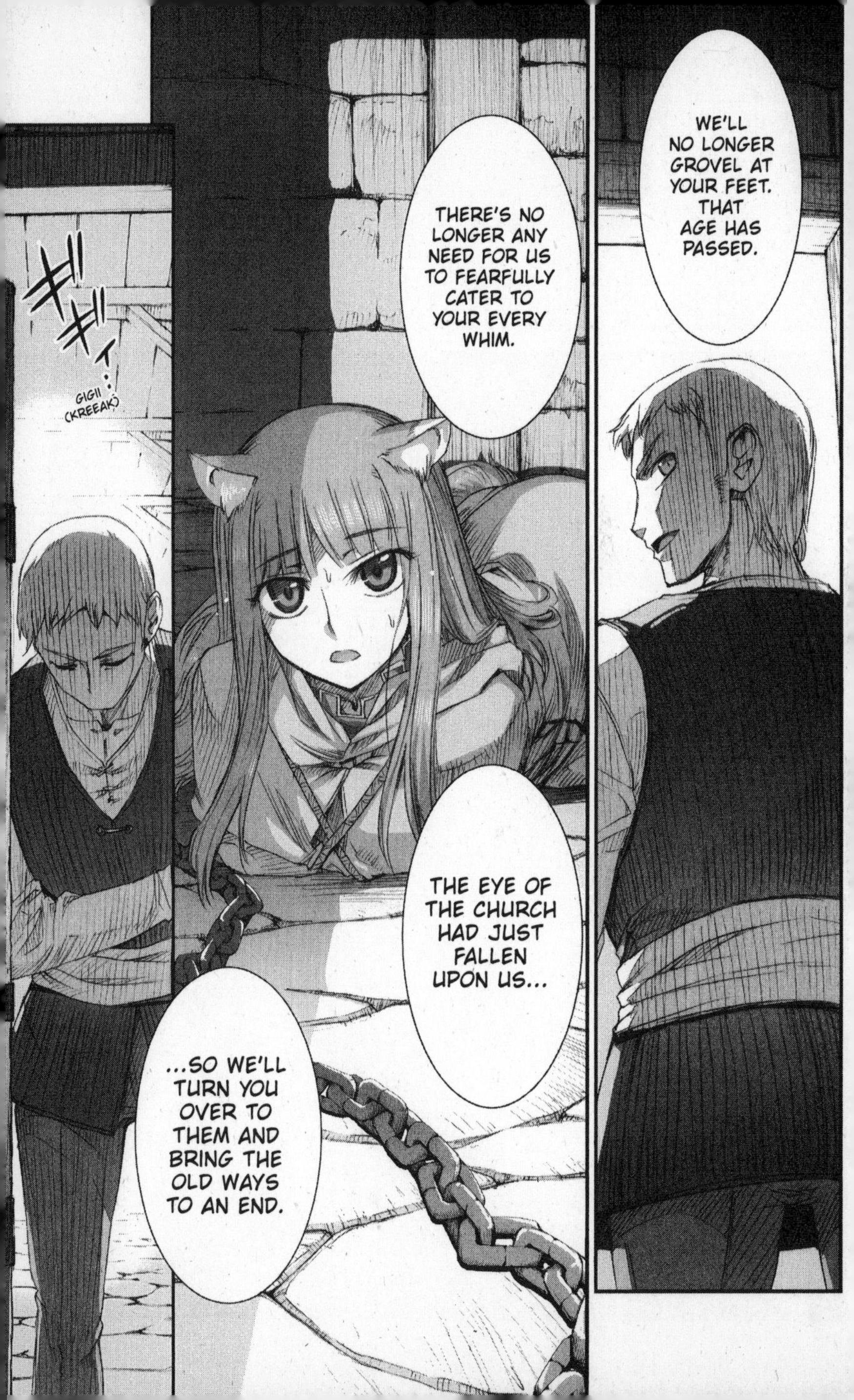
WE'LL NO LONGER GROVEL AT YOUR FEET. THAT AGE HAS PASSED.
THERE'S NO LONGER ANY NEED FOR US TO FEARFULLY CATER TO YOUR EVERY WHIM.
THE EYE OF THE CHURCH HAD JUST FALLEN UPON US...
...SO WE'LL TURN YOU OVER TO THEM AND BRING THE OLD WAYS TO AN END.
ギギィ…
GIGII (KREEAK)

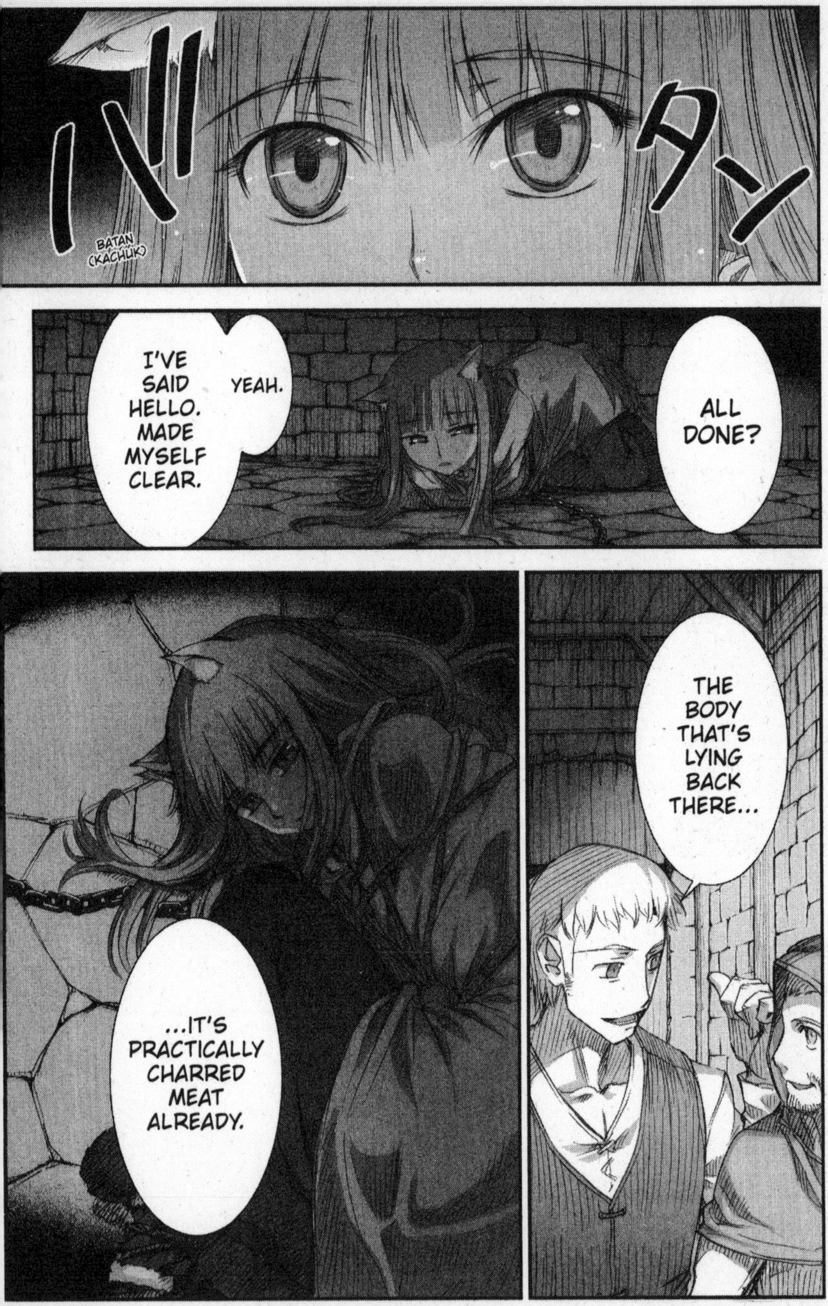
バタン
BATAN (KACHUK)
ALL DONE?
YEAH.
I'VE SAID HELLO. MADE MYSELF CLEAR.
THE BODY THAT'S LYING BACK THERE...
...IT'S PRACTICALLY CHARRED MEAT ALREADY.

SPICE & WOLF

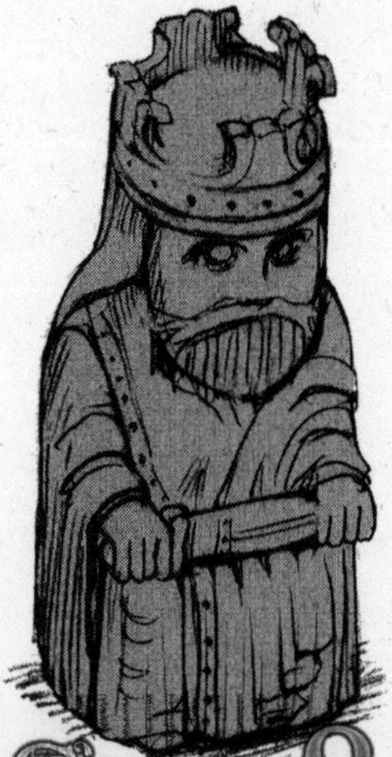

SPICE & WOLF

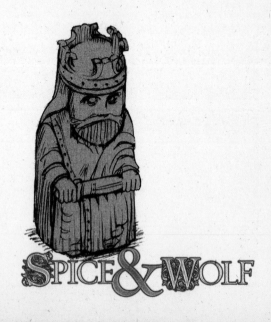

HOLO IS NOT HUMAN.

SHE IS A WOLF WHO HAS TAKEN HUMAN FORM.

GASA
(FLUTTER)

GASA

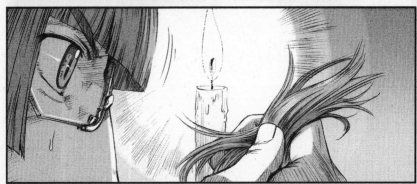

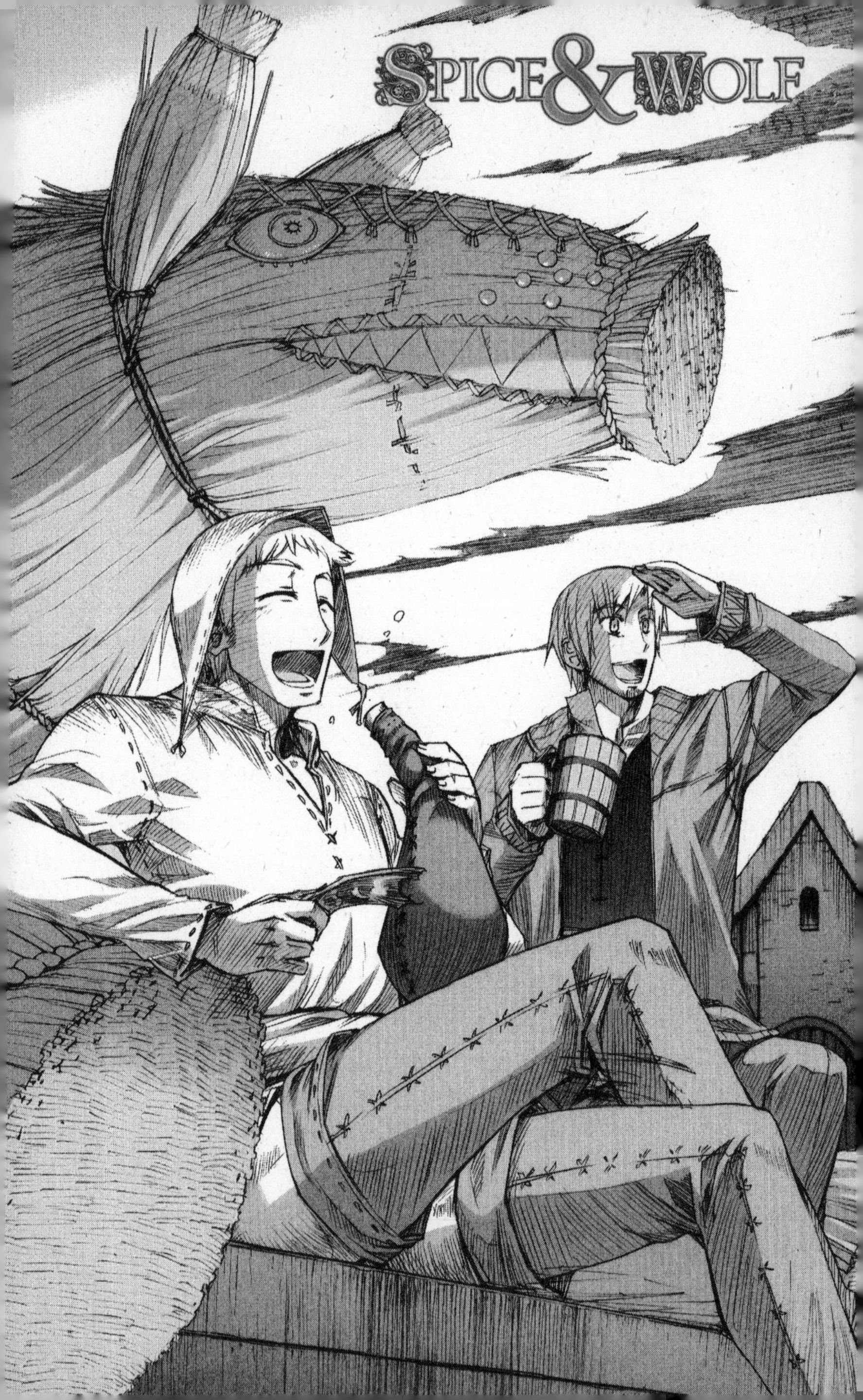
SPICE&WOLF

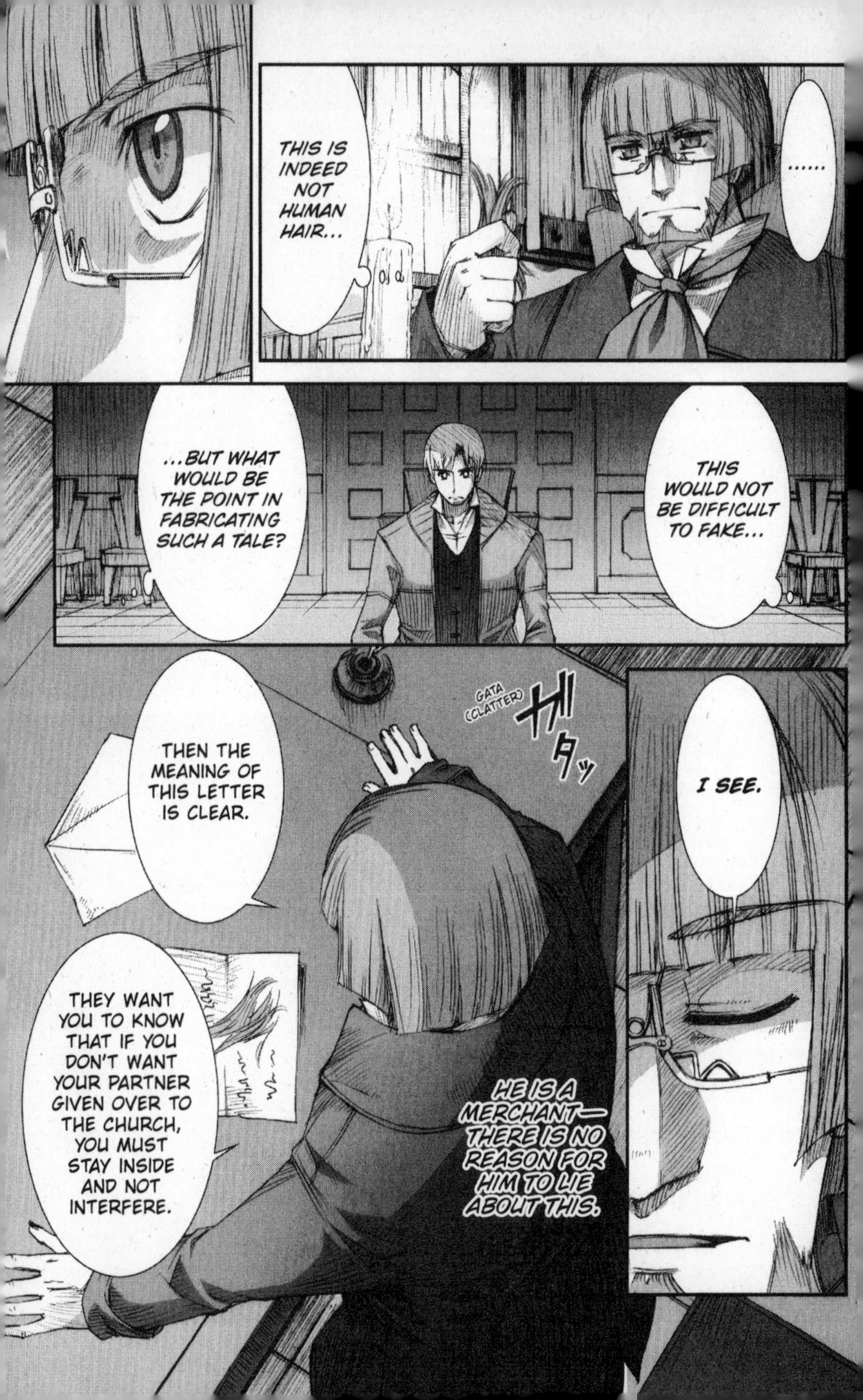
......
THIS IS INDEED NOT HUMAN HAIR...
THIS WOULD NOT BE DIFFICULT TO FAKE...
...BUT WHAT WOULD BE THE POINT IN FABRICATING SUCH A TALE?
I SEE.
HE IS A MERCHANT— THERE IS NO REASON FOR HIM TO LIE ABOUT THIS.
GATA (CLATTER)
THEN THE MEANING OF THIS LETTER IS CLEAR.
THEY WANT YOU TO KNOW THAT IF YOU DON'T WANT YOUR PARTNER GIVEN OVER TO THE CHURCH, YOU MUST STAY INSIDE AND NOT INTERFERE.

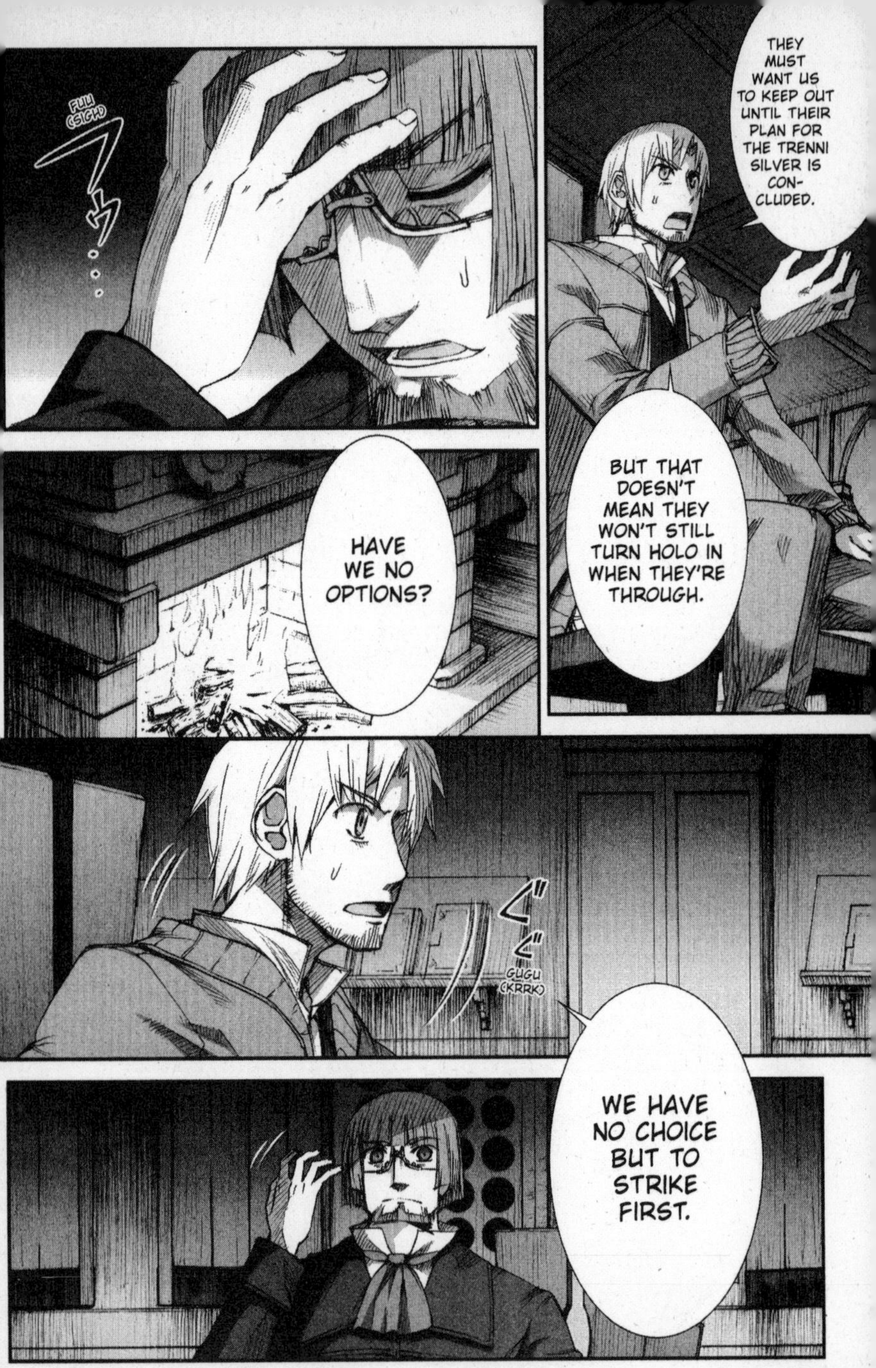
THEY MUST WANT US TO KEEP OUT UNTIL THEIR PLAN FOR THE TRENNI SILVER IS CON-CLUDED.
BUT THAT DOESN'T MEAN THEY WON'T STILL TURN HOLO IN WHEN THEY'RE THROUGH.
FUU (SIGH)
HAVE WE NO OPTIONS?
GUGU (KRRK)
WE HAVE NO CHOICE BUT TO STRIKE FIRST.

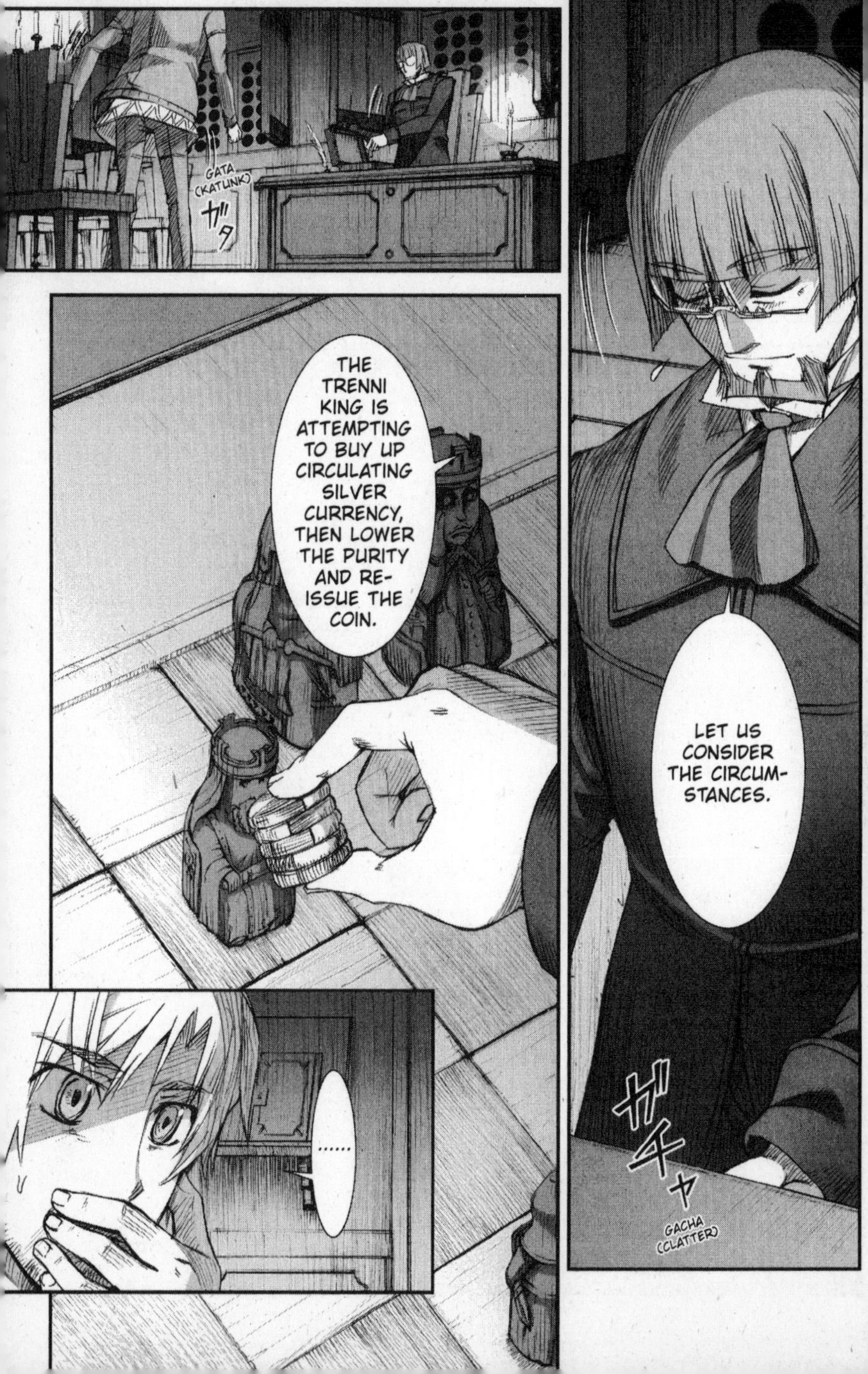
LET US CONSIDER THE CIRCUM-STANCES.
ガチャ
GACHA (CLATTER)
GATA (KATUNK)
ガタ
THE TRENNI KING IS ATTEMPTING TO BUY UP CIRCULATING SILVER CURRENCY, THEN LOWER THE PURITY AND RE-ISSUE THE COIN.
......

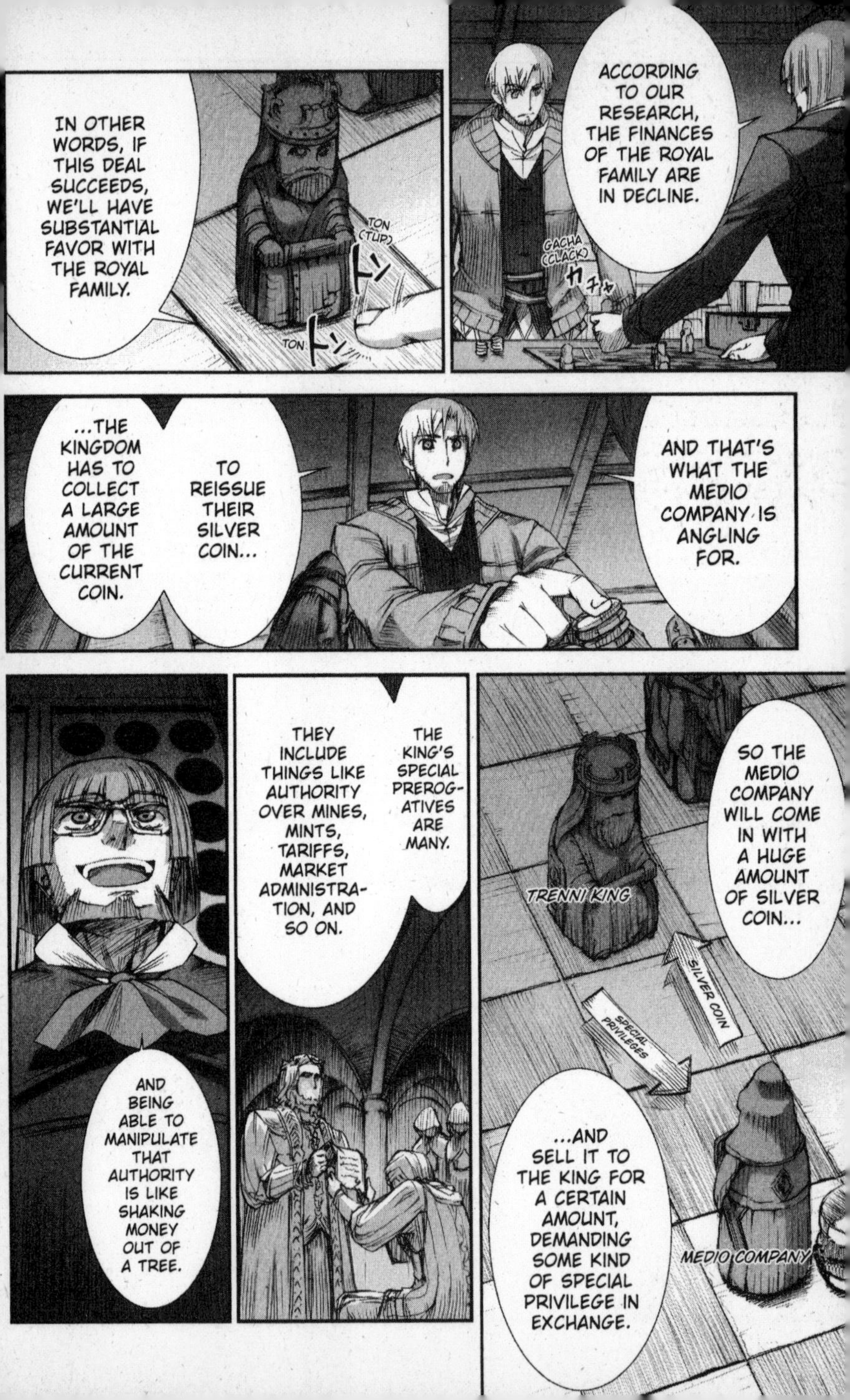
ACCORDING TO OUR RESEARCH, THE FINANCES OF THE ROYAL FAMILY ARE IN DECLINE.
GACHA (CLACK) カチャ
IN OTHER WORDS, IF THIS DEAL SUCCEEDS, WE'LL HAVE SUBSTANTIAL FAVOR WITH THE ROYAL FAMILY.
TON (TUP) トン
TON トン
AND THAT'S WHAT THE MEDIO COMPANY IS ANGLING FOR.
TO REISSUE THEIR SILVER COIN...
...THE KINGDOM HAS TO COLLECT A LARGE AMOUNT OF THE CURRENT COIN.
SO THE MEDIO COMPANY WILL COME IN WITH A HUGE AMOUNT OF SILVER COIN...
TRENNI KING
SILVER COIN
SPECIAL PRIVILEGES
...AND SELL IT TO THE KING FOR A CERTAIN AMOUNT, DEMANDING SOME KIND OF SPECIAL PRIVILEGE IN EXCHANGE.
MEDIO COMPANY
THE KING'S SPECIAL PREROGATIVES ARE MANY.
THEY INCLUDE THINGS LIKE AUTHORITY OVER MINES, MINTS, TARIFFS, MARKET ADMINISTRATION, AND SO ON.
AND BEING ABLE TO MANIPULATE THAT AUTHORITY IS LIKE SHAKING MONEY OUT OF A TREE.

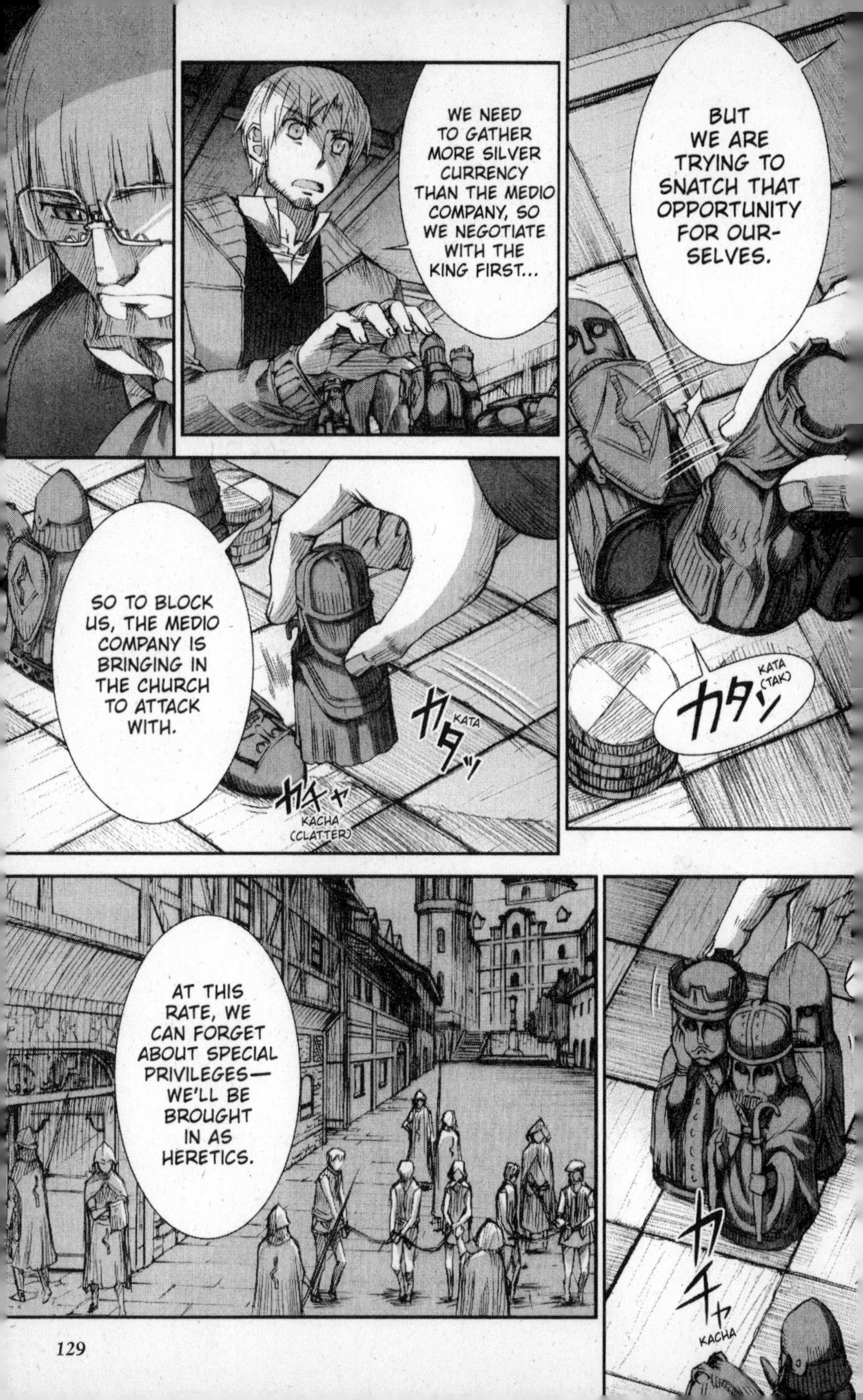
WE NEED TO GATHER MORE SILVER CURRENCY THAN THE MEDIO COMPANY, SO WE NEGOTIATE WITH THE KING FIRST...
BUT WE ARE TRYING TO SNATCH THAT OPPORTUNITY FOR OUR-SELVES.
カタン KATA (TAK)
SO TO BLOCK US, THE MEDIO COMPANY IS BRINGING IN THE CHURCH TO ATTACK WITH.
カタッ KATA
カチャ KACHA (CLATTER)
カチャ KACHA
AT THIS RATE, WE CAN FORGET ABOUT SPECIAL PRIVILEGES— WE'LL BE BROUGHT IN AS HERETICS.

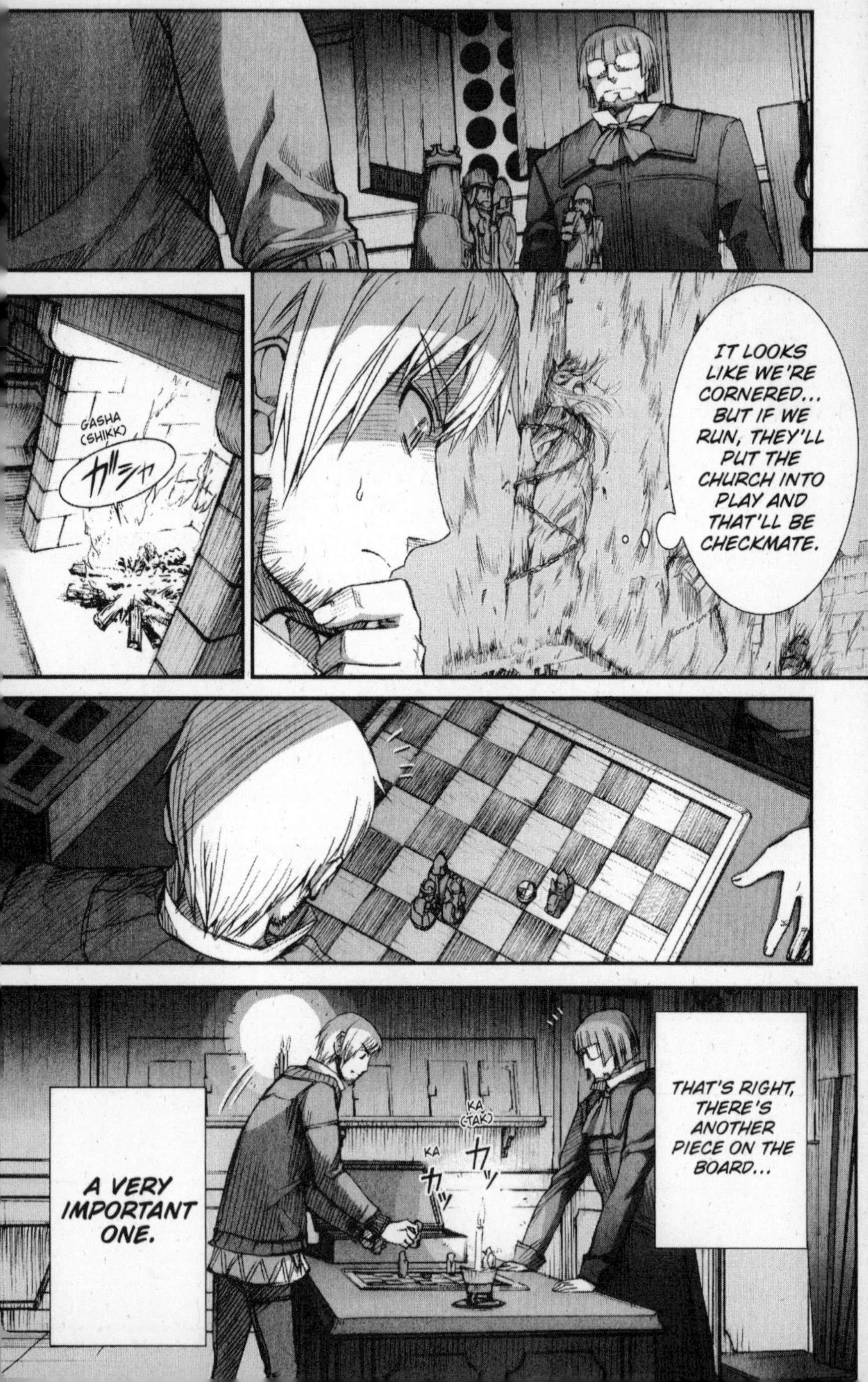
IT LOOKS LIKE WE'RE CORNERED... BUT IF WE RUN, THEY'LL PUT THE CHURCH INTO PLAY AND THAT'LL BE CHECKMATE.
GASHA (SHIKK)
ガシャ
THAT'S RIGHT, THERE'S ANOTHER PIECE ON THE BOARD...
KA (TAK)
カッ
KA
カッ
A VERY IMPORTANT ONE.

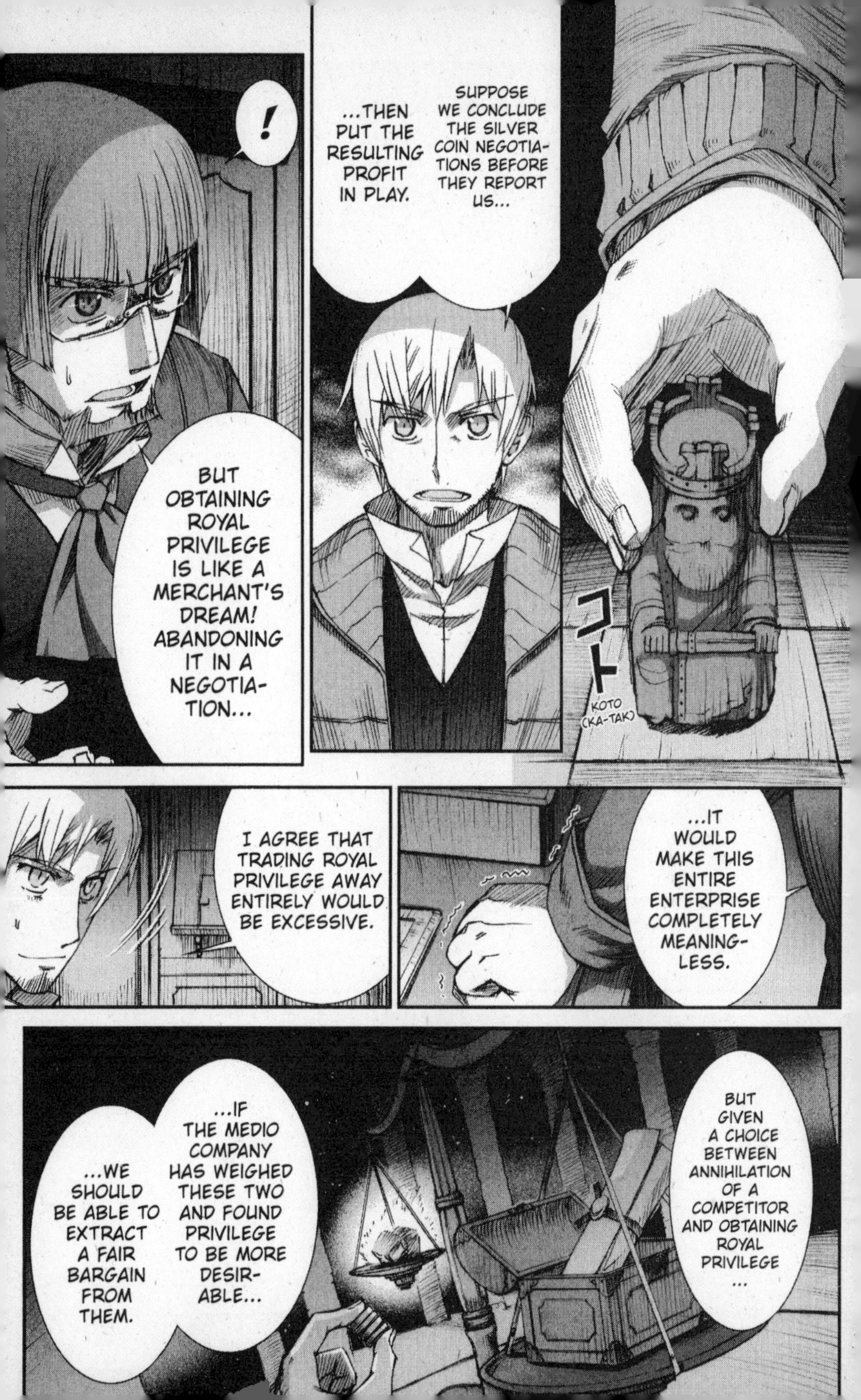
コト
KOTO (KA-TAK)
SUPPOSE WE CONCLUDE THE SILVER COIN NEGOTIATIONS BEFORE THEY REPORT US...
...THEN PUT THE RESULTING PROFIT IN PLAY.
!
BUT OBTAINING ROYAL PRIVILEGE IS LIKE A MERCHANT'S DREAM! ABANDONING IT IN A NEGOTIATION...
...IT WOULD MAKE THIS ENTIRE ENTERPRISE COMPLETELY MEANINGLESS.
I AGREE THAT TRADING ROYAL PRIVILEGE AWAY ENTIRELY WOULD BE EXCESSIVE.
BUT GIVEN A CHOICE BETWEEN ANNIHILATION OF A COMPETITOR AND OBTAINING ROYAL PRIVILEGE...
...IF THE MEDIO COMPANY HAS WEIGHED THESE TWO AND FOUND PRIVILEGE TO BE MORE DESIRABLE...
...WE SHOULD BE ABLE TO EXTRACT A FAIR BARGAIN FROM THEM.

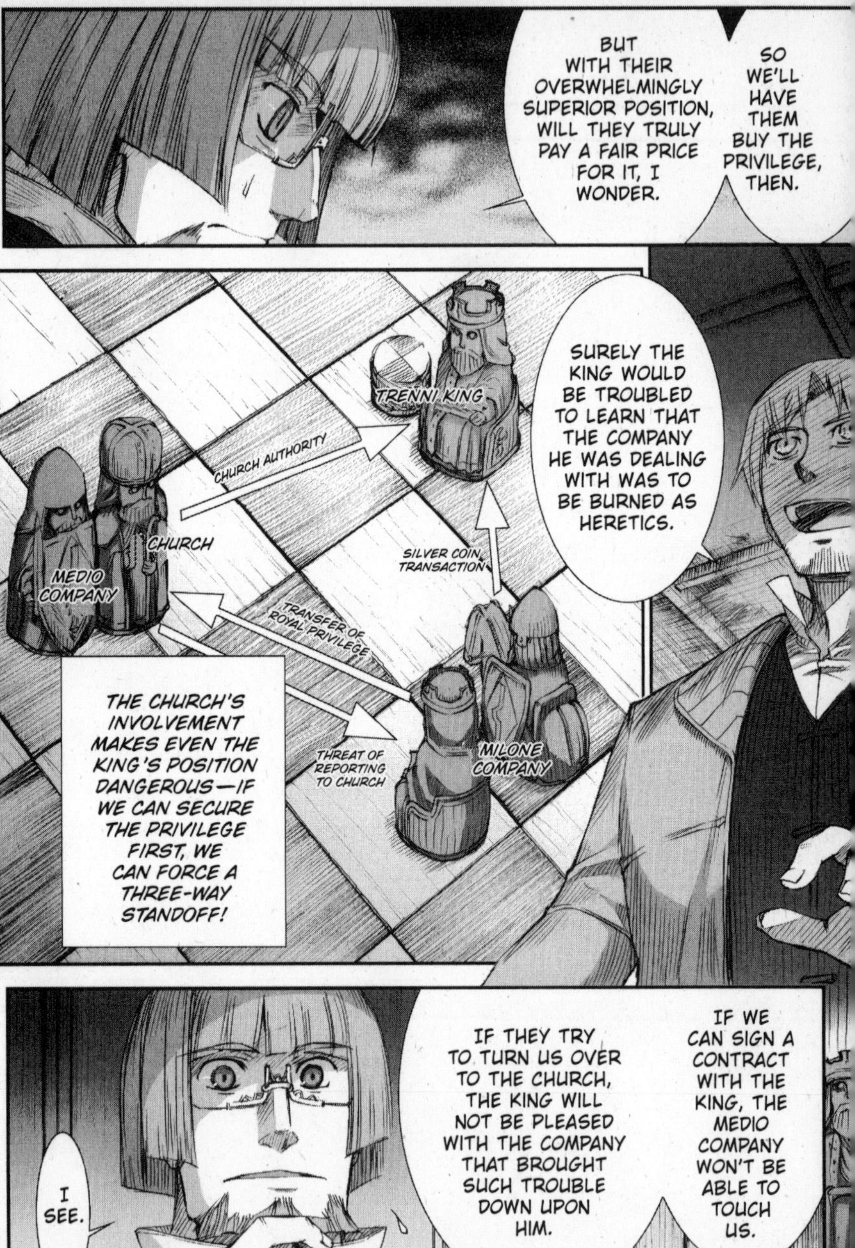
SO WE'LL HAVE THEM BUY THE PRIVILEGE, THEN.
BUT WITH THEIR OVERWHELMINGLY SUPERIOR POSITION, WILL THEY TRULY PAY A FAIR PRICE FOR IT, I WONDER.
SURELY THE KING WOULD BE TROUBLED TO LEARN THAT THE COMPANY HE WAS DEALING WITH WAS TO BE BURNED AS HERETICS.
TRENNI KING
CHURCH AUTHORITY
CHURCH
MEDIO COMPANY
SILVER COIN TRANSACTION
TRANSFER OF ROYAL PRIVILEGE
THREAT OF REPORTING TO CHURCH
MILONE COMPANY
THE CHURCH'S INVOLVEMENT MAKES EVEN THE KING'S POSITION DANGEROUS—IF WE CAN SECURE THE PRIVILEGE FIRST, WE CAN FORCE A THREE-WAY STANDOFF!
IF WE CAN SIGN A CONTRACT WITH THE KING, THE MEDIO COMPANY WON'T BE ABLE TO TOUCH US.
IF THEY TRY TO TURN US OVER TO THE CHURCH, THE KING WILL NOT BE PLEASED WITH THE COMPANY THAT BROUGHT SUCH TROUBLE DOWN UPON HIM.
I SEE.

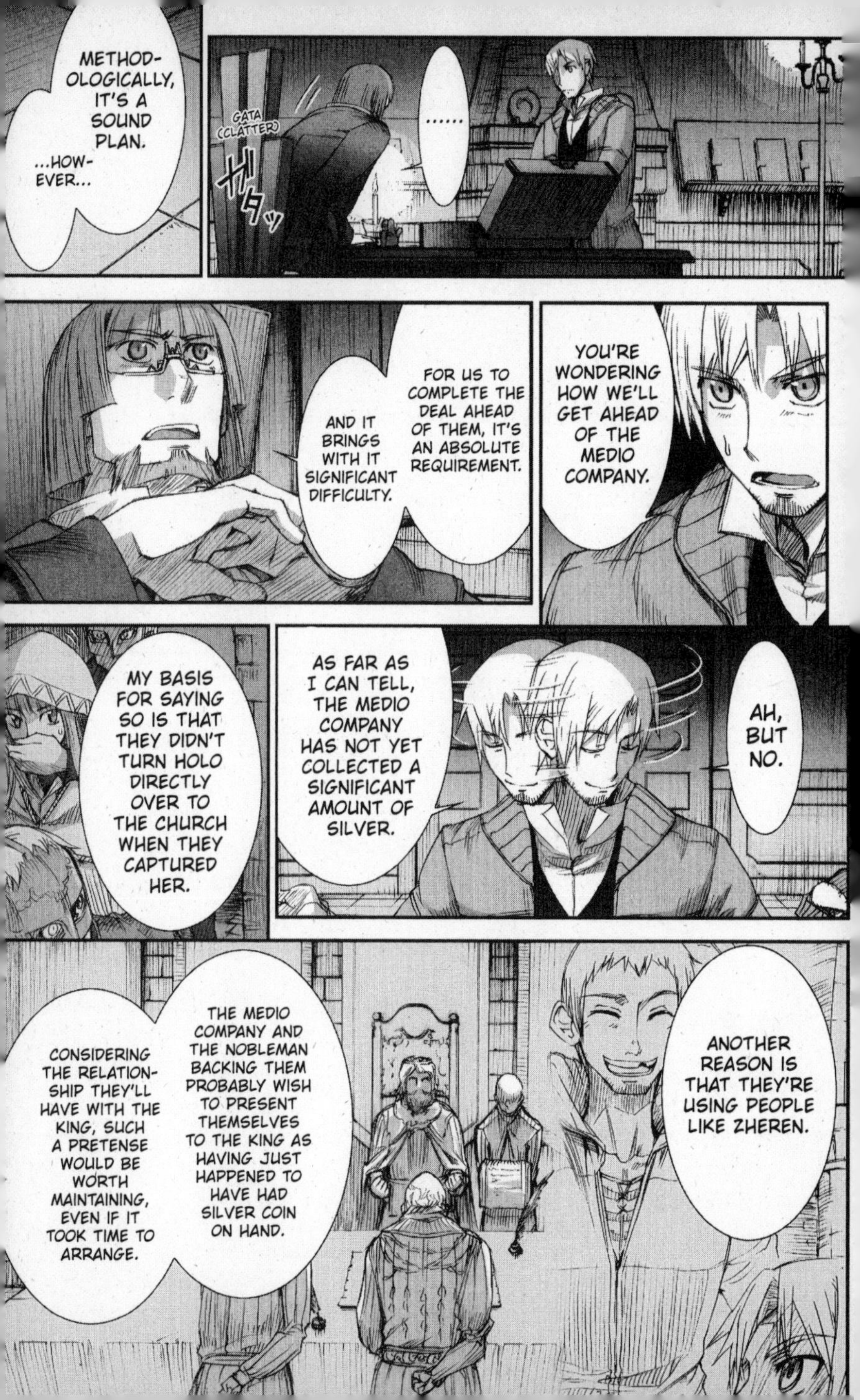
......
GATA (CLATTER)
METHODOLOGICALLY, IT'S A SOUND PLAN. ...HOWEVER...
YOU'RE WONDERING HOW WE'LL GET AHEAD OF THE MEDIO COMPANY.
FOR US TO COMPLETE THE DEAL AHEAD OF THEM, IT'S AN ABSOLUTE REQUIREMENT.
AND IT BRINGS WITH IT SIGNIFICANT DIFFICULTY.
AH, BUT NO.
AS FAR AS I CAN TELL, THE MEDIO COMPANY HAS NOT YET COLLECTED A SIGNIFICANT AMOUNT OF SILVER.
MY BASIS FOR SAYING SO IS THAT THEY DIDN'T TURN HOLO DIRECTLY OVER TO THE CHURCH WHEN THEY CAPTURED HER.
ANOTHER REASON IS THAT THEY'RE USING PEOPLE LIKE ZHEREN.
THE MEDIO COMPANY AND THE NOBLEMAN BACKING THEM PROBABLY WISH TO PRESENT THEMSELVES TO THE KING AS HAVING JUST HAPPENED TO HAVE HAD SILVER COIN ON HAND.
CONSIDERING THE RELATIONSHIP THEY'LL HAVE WITH THE KING, SUCH A PRETENSE WOULD BE WORTH MAINTAINING, EVEN IF IT TOOK TIME TO ARRANGE.

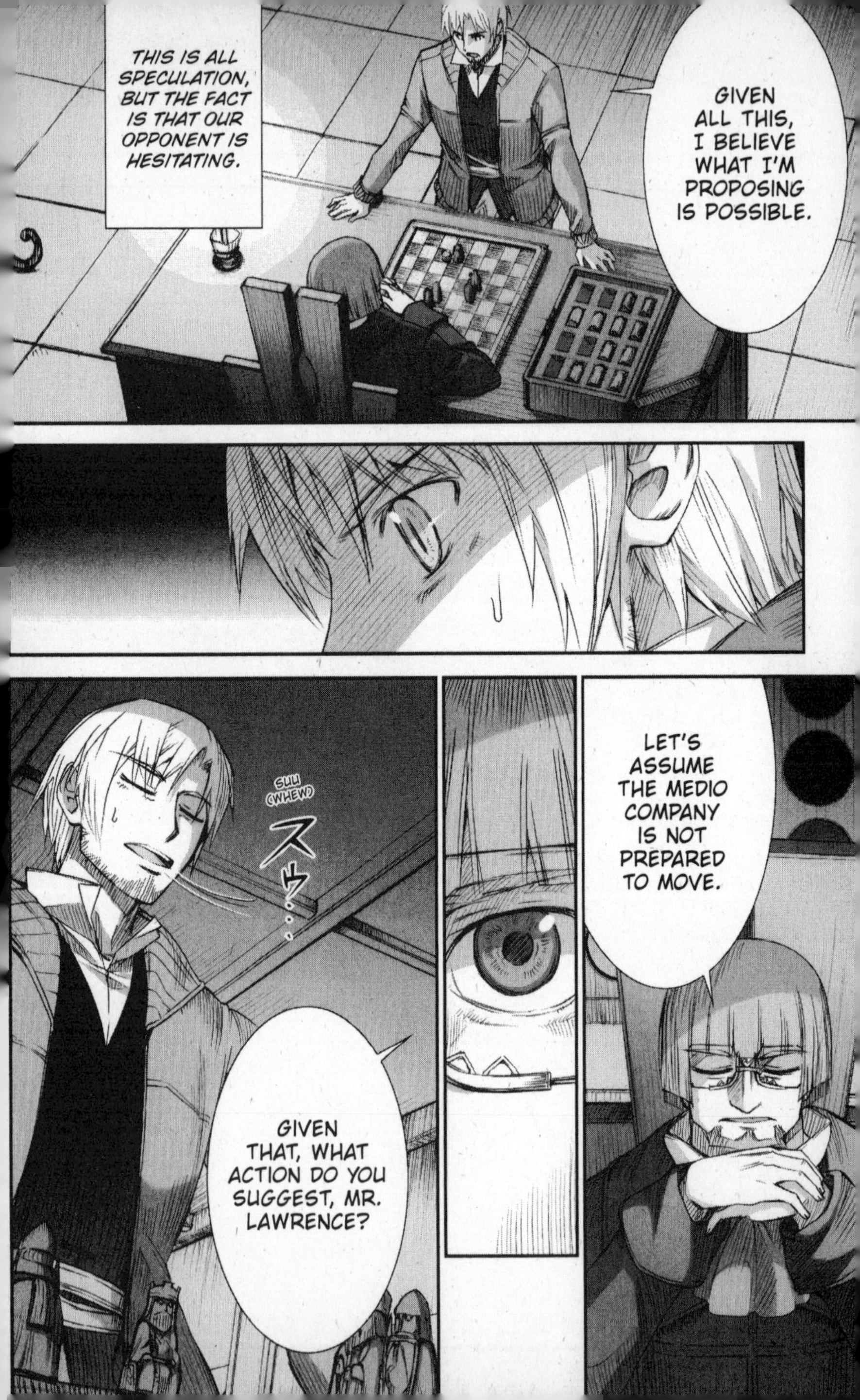
GIVEN ALL THIS, I BELIEVE WHAT I'M PROPOSING IS POSSIBLE.
THIS IS ALL SPECULATION, BUT THE FACT IS THAT OUR OPPONENT IS HESITATING.
LET'S ASSUME THE MEDIO COMPANY IS NOT PREPARED TO MOVE.
SUU (WHEW)
スゥ…
GIVEN THAT, WHAT ACTION DO YOU SUGGEST, MR. LAWRENCE?

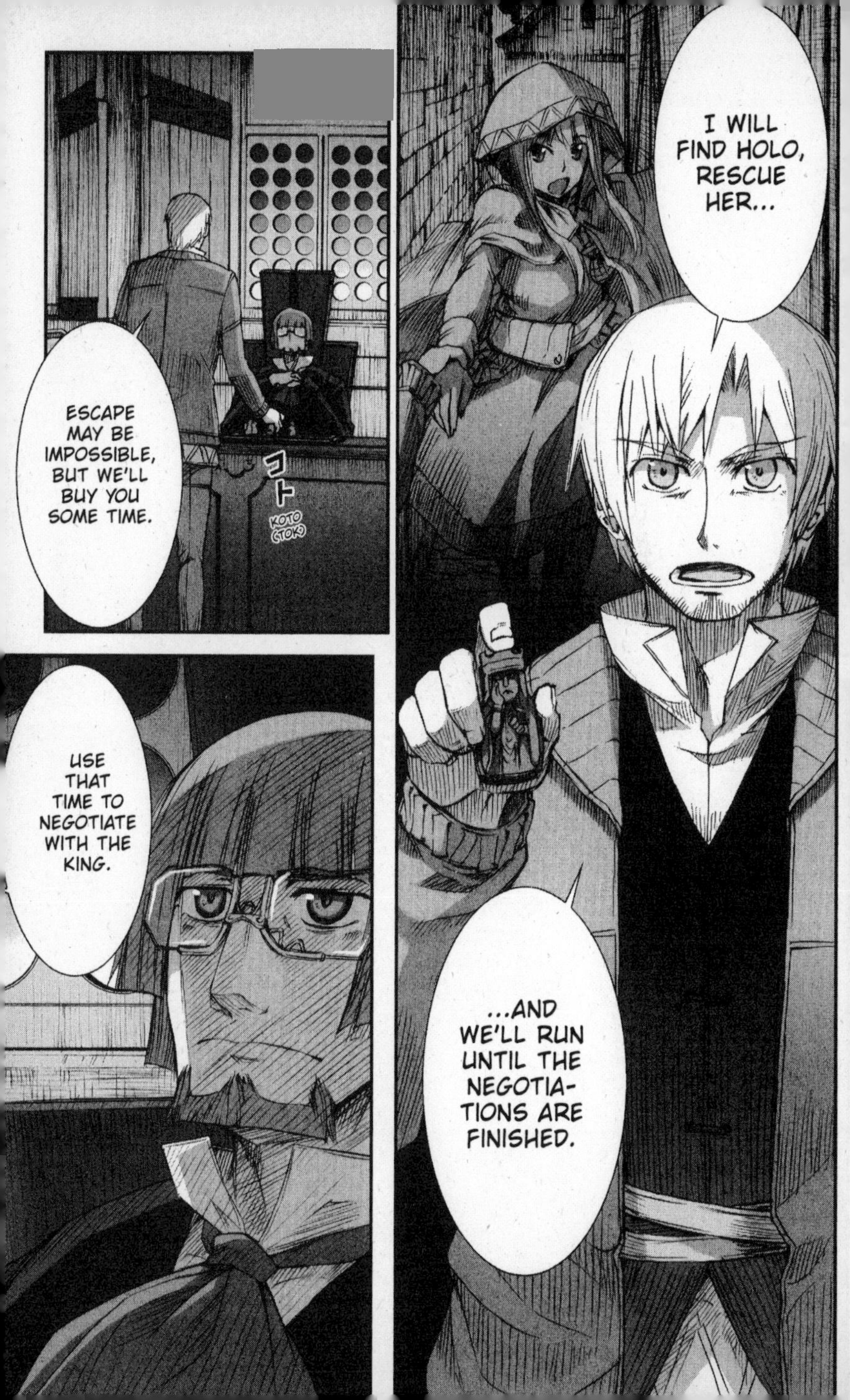
I WILL FIND HOLO, RESCUE HER...
...AND WE'LL RUN UNTIL THE NEGOTIATIONS ARE FINISHED.
ESCAPE MAY BE IMPOSSIBLE, BUT WE'LL BUY YOU SOME TIME.
コト
KOTO (TOK)
USE THAT TIME TO NEGOTIATE WITH THE KING.

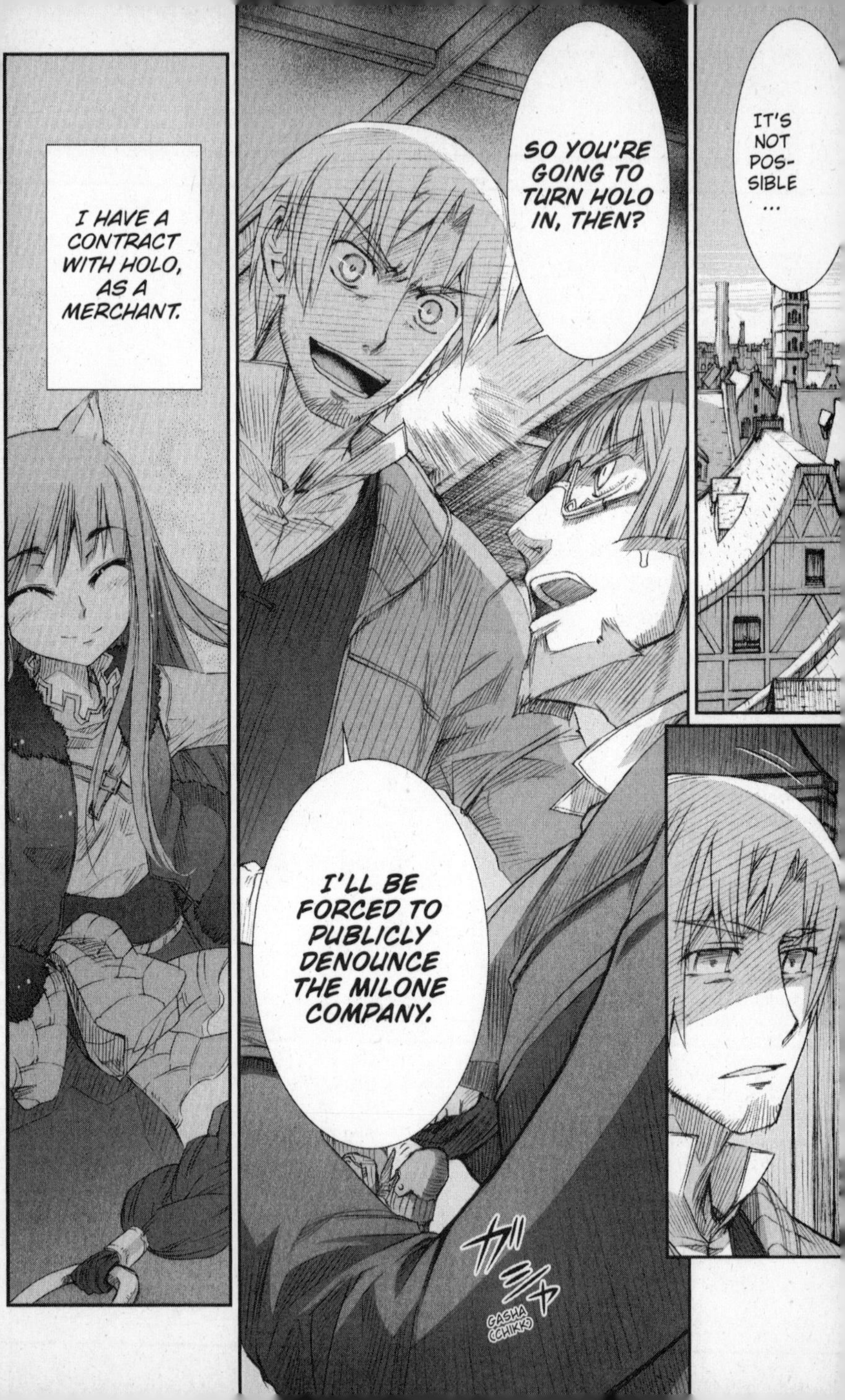
IT'S NOT POS-SIBLE ...
SO YOU'RE GOING TO TURN HOLO IN, THEN?
I'LL BE FORCED TO PUBLICLY DENOUNCE THE MILONE COMPANY.
GASHA (CHIKK)
I HAVE A CONTRACT WITH HOLO, AS A MERCHANT.

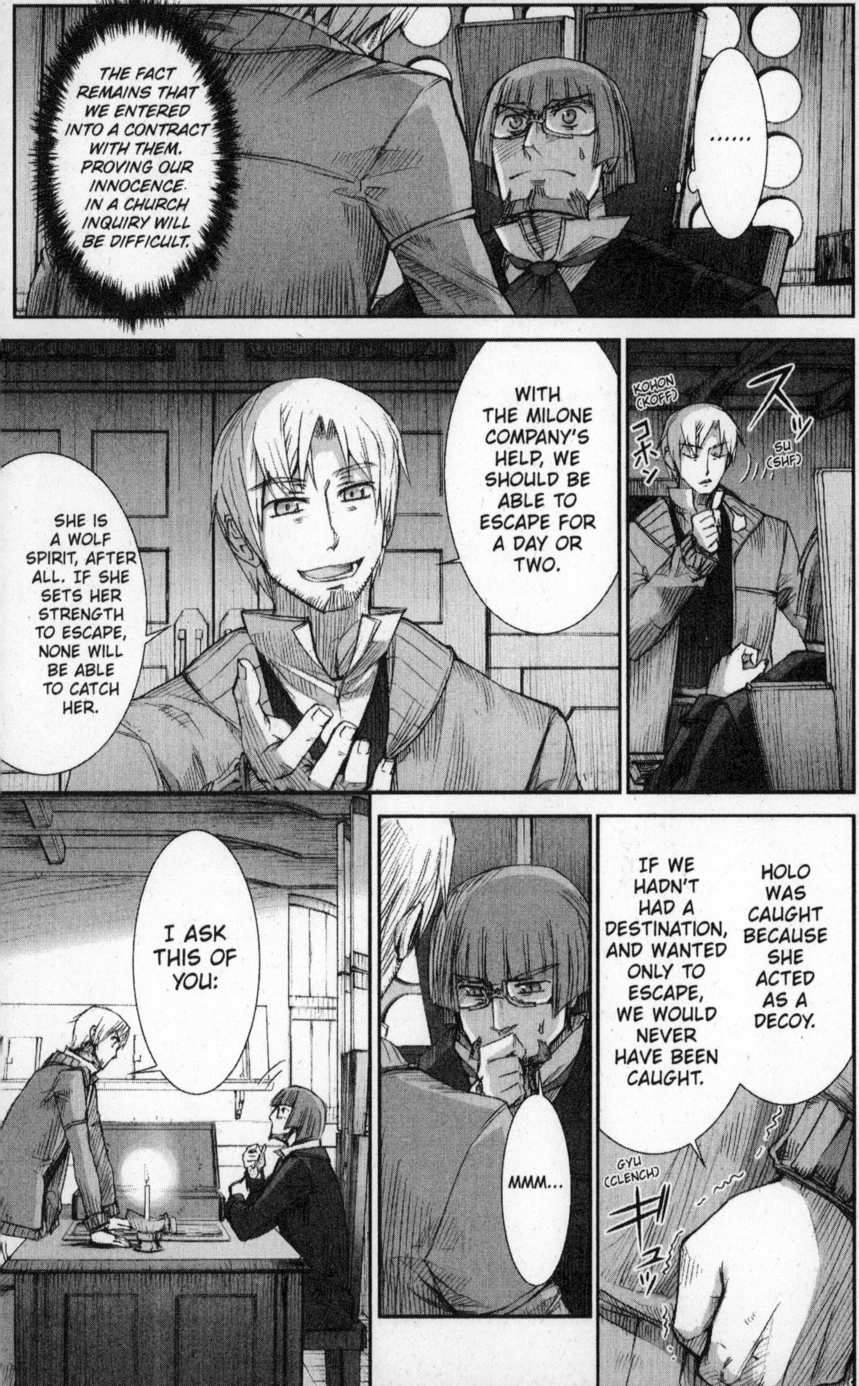
......
THE FACT REMAINS THAT WE ENTERED INTO A CONTRACT WITH THEM. PROVING OUR INNOCENCE IN A CHURCH INQUIRY WILL BE DIFFICULT.
スッ
SU (SHF)
コホン
KOHON (KOFF)
WITH THE MILONE COMPANY'S HELP, WE SHOULD BE ABLE TO ESCAPE FOR A DAY OR TWO.
SHE IS A WOLF SPIRIT, AFTER ALL. IF SHE SETS HER STRENGTH TO ESCAPE, NONE WILL BE ABLE TO CATCH HER.
HOLO WAS CAUGHT BECAUSE SHE ACTED AS A DECOY.
IF WE HADN'T HAD A DESTINATION, AND WANTED ONLY TO ESCAPE, WE WOULD NEVER HAVE BEEN CAUGHT.
GYU (CLENCH)
ギュッ
MMM...
I ASK THIS OF YOU:

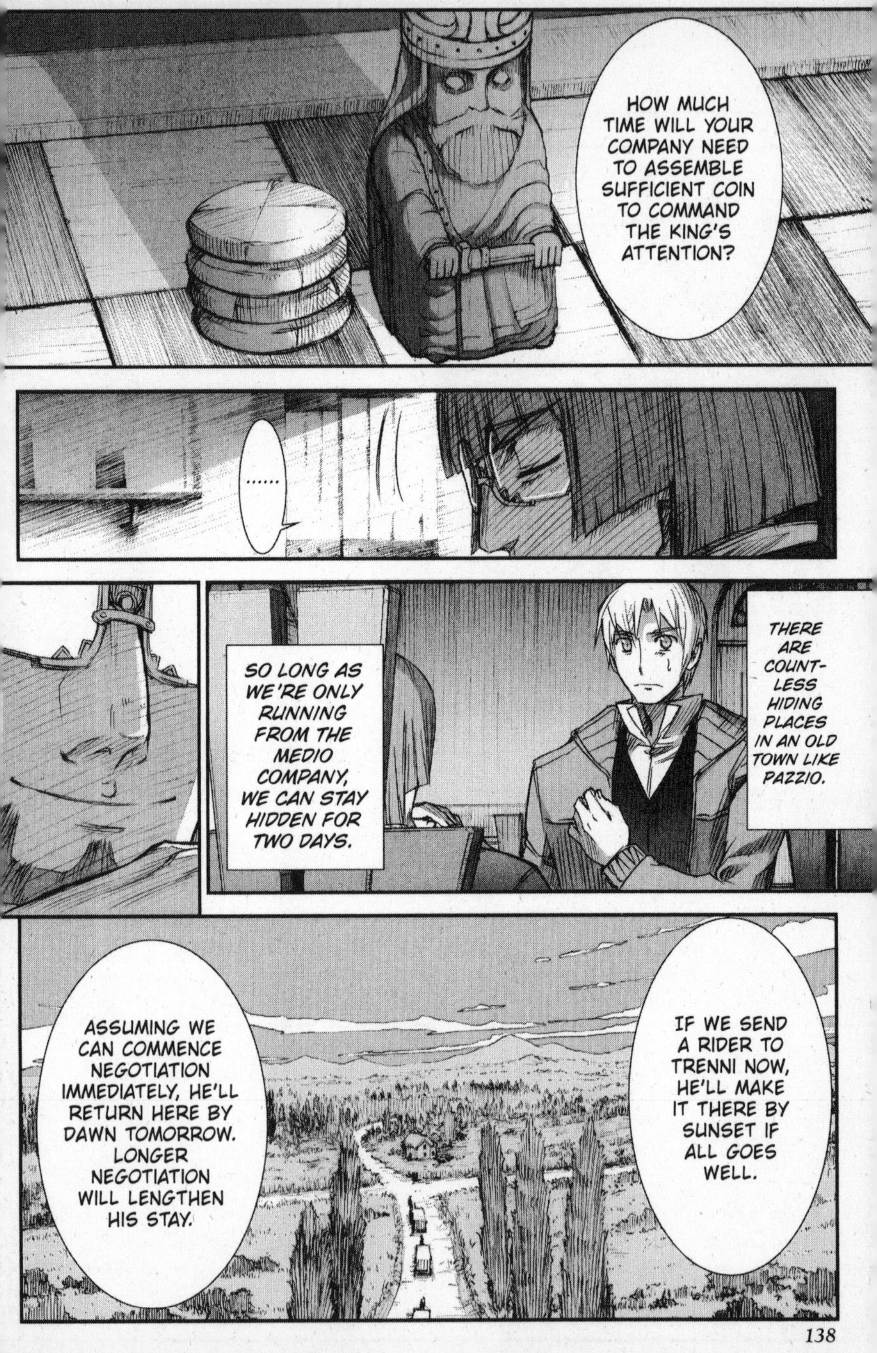
HOW MUCH TIME WILL YOUR COMPANY NEED TO ASSEMBLE SUFFICIENT COIN TO COMMAND THE KING'S ATTENTION?
......
THERE ARE COUNT-LESS HIDING PLACES IN AN OLD TOWN LIKE PAZZIO.
SO LONG AS WE'RE ONLY RUNNING FROM THE MEDIO COMPANY, WE CAN STAY HIDDEN FOR TWO DAYS.
IF WE SEND A RIDER TO TRENNI NOW, HE'LL MAKE IT THERE BY SUNSET IF ALL GOES WELL.
ASSUMING WE CAN COMMENCE NEGOTIATION IMMEDIATELY, HE'LL RETURN HERE BY DAWN TOMORROW. LONGER NEGOTIATION WILL LENGTHEN HIS STAY.

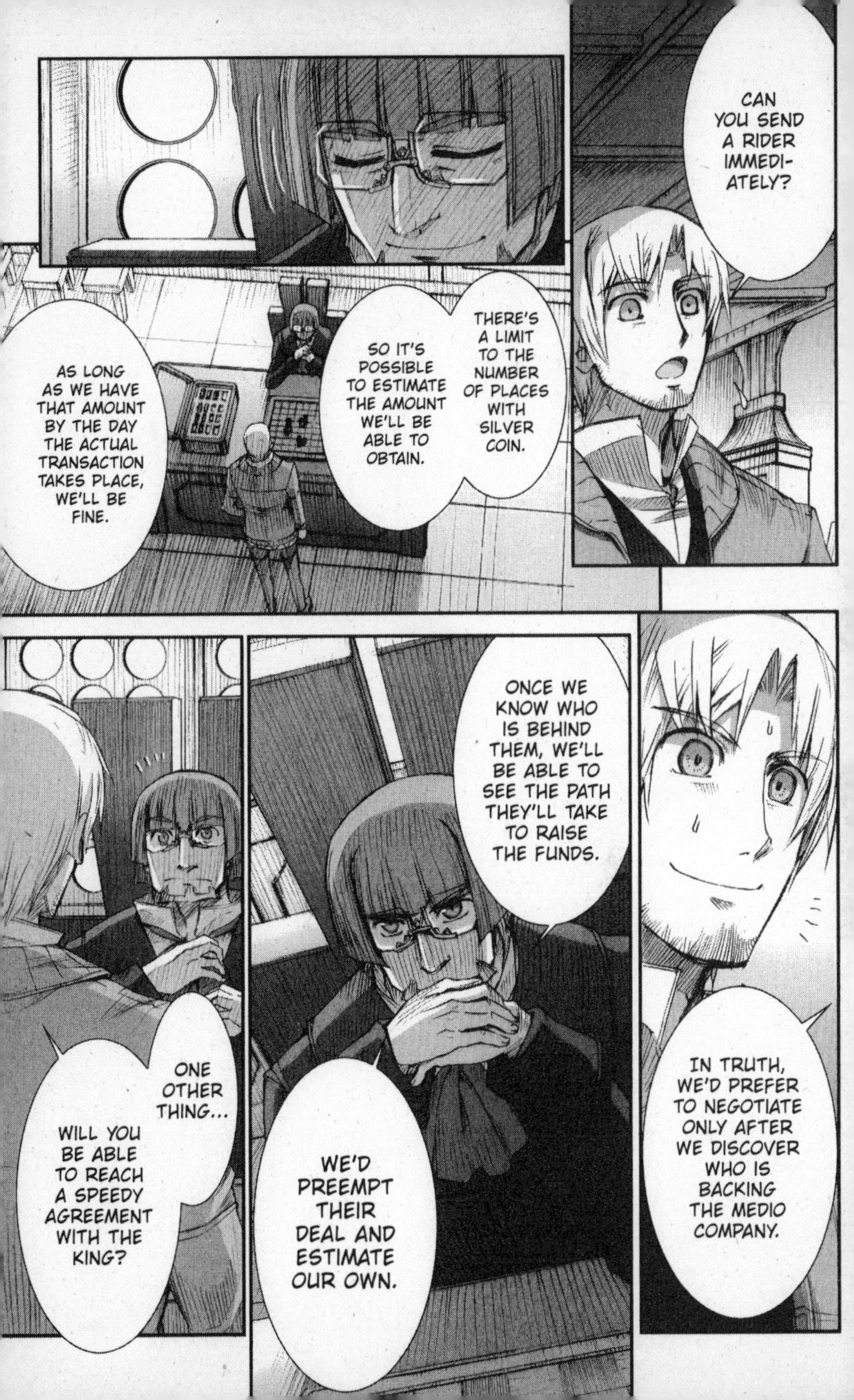
CAN YOU SEND A RIDER IMMEDI-ATELY?
THERE'S A LIMIT TO THE NUMBER OF PLACES WITH SILVER COIN.
SO IT'S POSSIBLE TO ESTIMATE THE AMOUNT WE'LL BE ABLE TO OBTAIN.
AS LONG AS WE HAVE THAT AMOUNT BY THE DAY THE ACTUAL TRANSACTION TAKES PLACE, WE'LL BE FINE.
IN TRUTH, WE'D PREFER TO NEGOTIATE ONLY AFTER WE DISCOVER WHO IS BACKING THE MEDIO COMPANY.
ONCE WE KNOW WHO IS BEHIND THEM, WE'LL BE ABLE TO SEE THE PATH THEY'LL TAKE TO RAISE THE FUNDS.
WE'D PREEMPT THEIR DEAL AND ESTIMATE OUR OWN.
ONE OTHER THING...
WILL YOU BE ABLE TO REACH A SPEEDY AGREEMENT WITH THE KING?

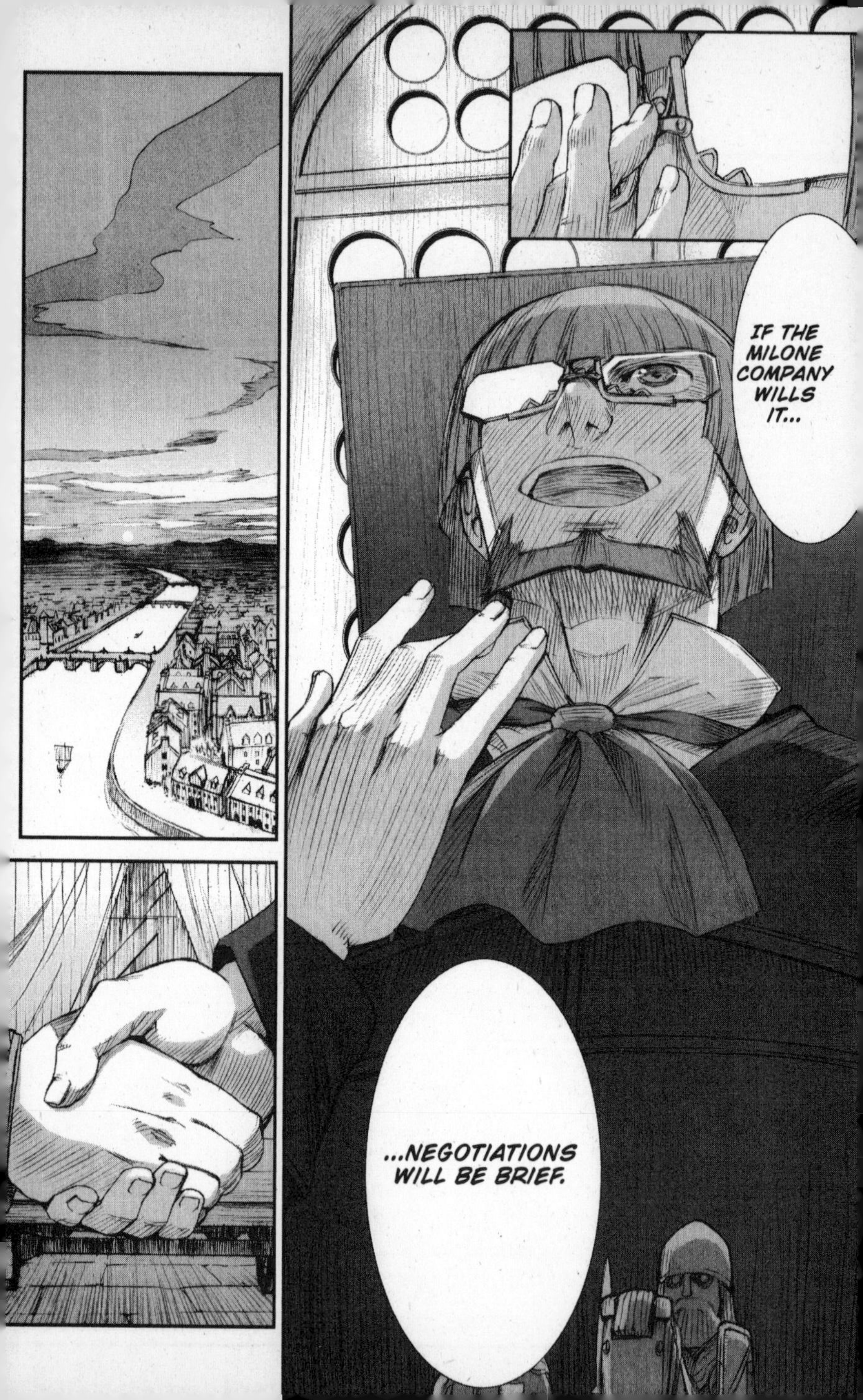
IF THE MILONE COMPANY WILLS IT...
...NEGOTIATIONS WILL BE BRIEF.

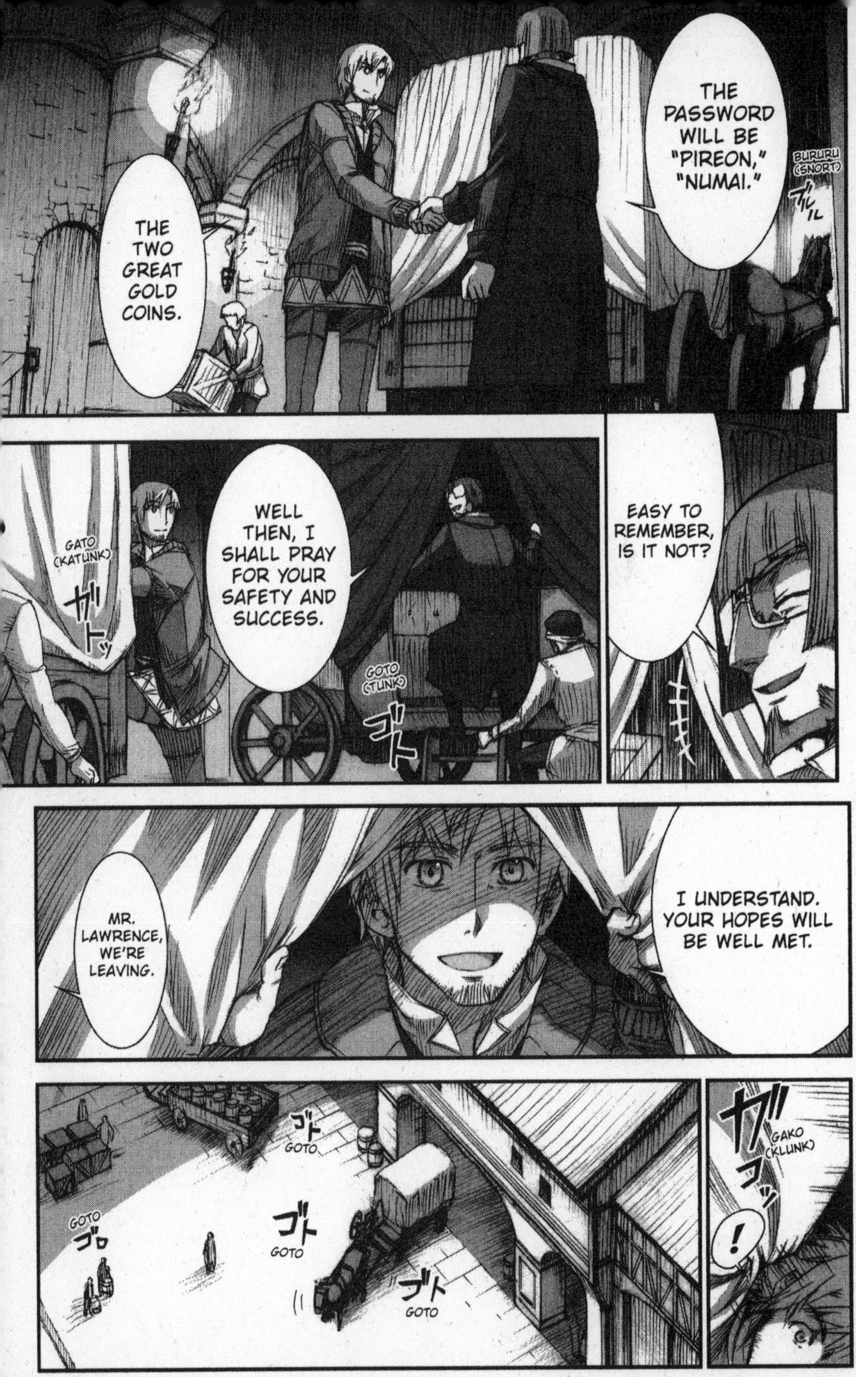
THE PASSWORD WILL BE "PIREON," "NUMAI."
BURURU (SNORT)
THE TWO GREAT GOLD COINS.
EASY TO REMEMBER, IS IT NOT?
WELL THEN, I SHALL PRAY FOR YOUR SAFETY AND SUCCESS.
GOTO (TUNK)
GATO (KATUNK)
I UNDERSTAND. YOUR HOPES WILL BE WELL MET.
MR. LAWRENCE, WE'RE LEAVING.
GAKO (KLUNK)
!
GOTO
GOTO
GOTO
GOTO

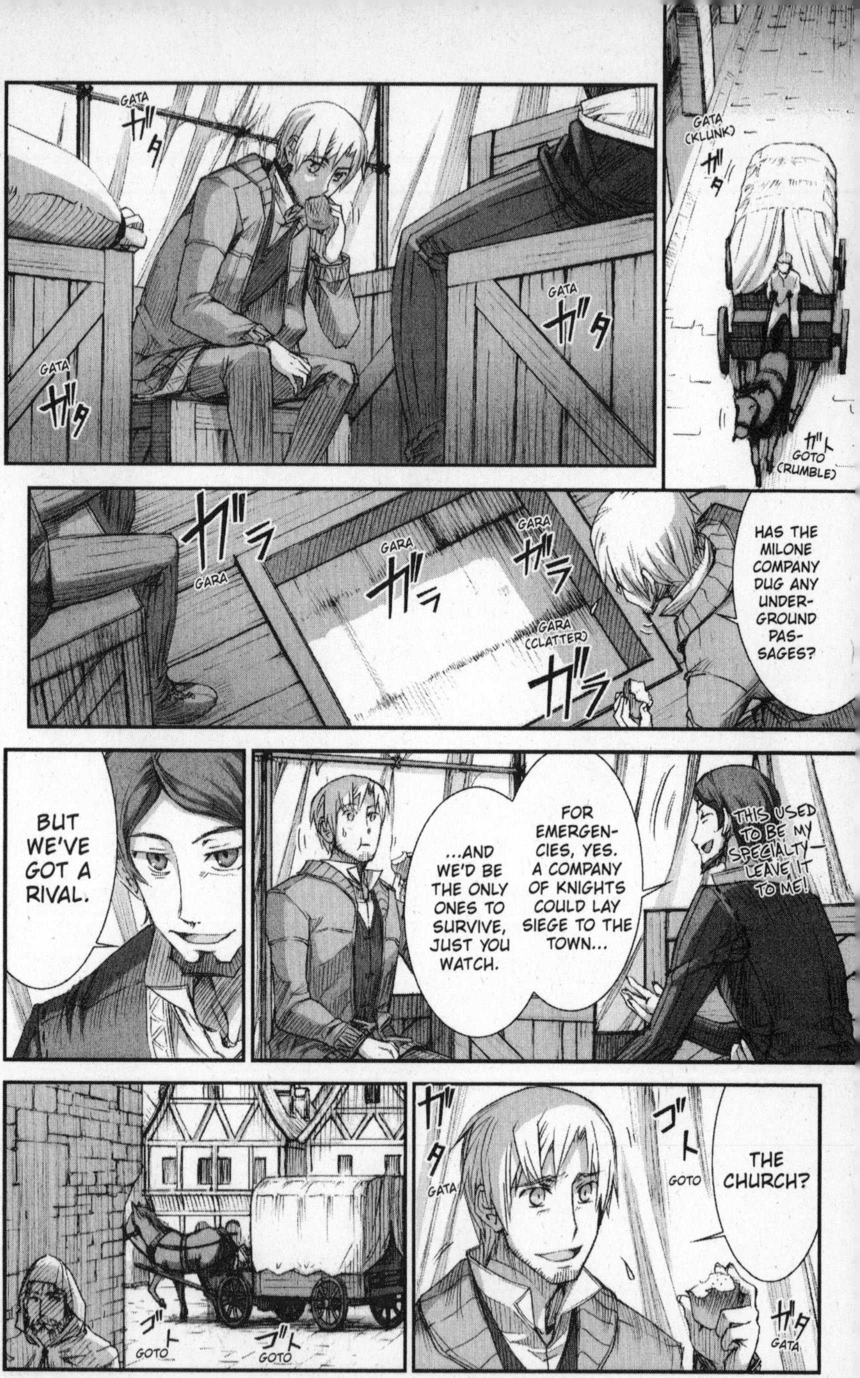
GATA (KLUNK)
GOTO (RUMBLE)
GATA
GATA
GATA
GARA
GARA
GARA
GARA (CLATTER)
HAS THE MILONE COMPANY DUG ANY UNDER-GROUND PAS-SAGES?
THIS USED TO BE MY SPECIALTY—LEAVE IT TO ME!
FOR EMERGEN-CIES, YES. A COMPANY OF KNIGHTS COULD LAY SIEGE TO THE TOWN...
...AND WE'D BE THE ONLY ONES TO SURVIVE, JUST YOU WATCH.
BUT WE'VE GOT A RIVAL.
GATA
GOTO
THE CHURCH?
GATA
GOTO
GOTO

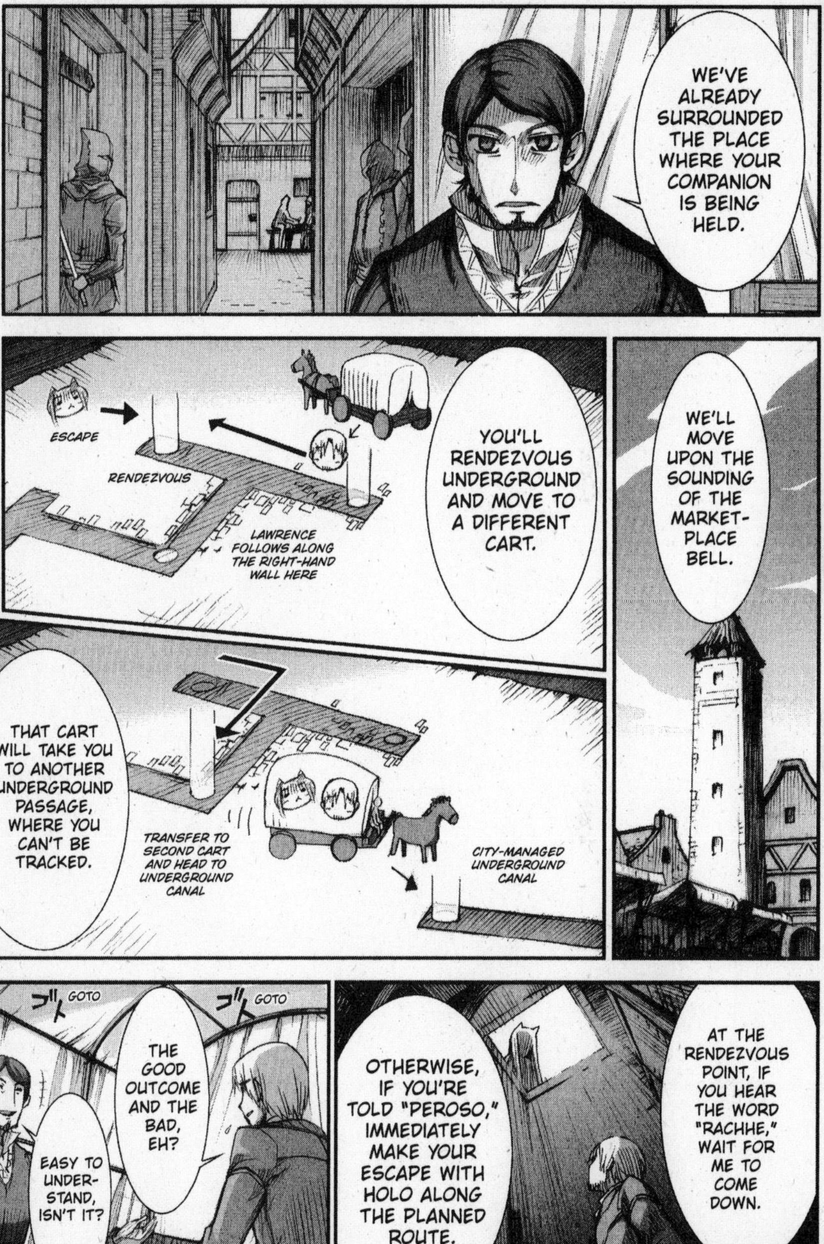
WE'VE ALREADY SURROUNDED THE PLACE WHERE YOUR COMPANION IS BEING HELD.
WE'LL MOVE UPON THE SOUNDING OF THE MARKET-PLACE BELL.
YOU'LL RENDEZVOUS UNDERGROUND AND MOVE TO A DIFFERENT CART.
ESCAPE
RENDEZVOUS
LAWRENCE FOLLOWS ALONG THE RIGHT-HAND WALL HERE
CITY-MANAGED UNDERGROUND CANAL
TRANSFER TO SECOND CART AND HEAD TO UNDERGROUND CANAL
THAT CART WILL TAKE YOU TO ANOTHER UNDERGROUND PASSAGE, WHERE YOU CAN'T BE TRACKED.
AT THE RENDEZVOUS POINT, IF YOU HEAR THE WORD "RACHHE," WAIT FOR ME TO COME DOWN.
OTHERWISE, IF YOU'RE TOLD "PEROSO," IMMEDIATELY MAKE YOUR ESCAPE WITH HOLO ALONG THE PLANNED ROUTE.
ゴト GOTO
ゴト GOTO
THE GOOD OUTCOME AND THE BAD, EH?
EASY TO UNDER-STAND, ISN'T IT?

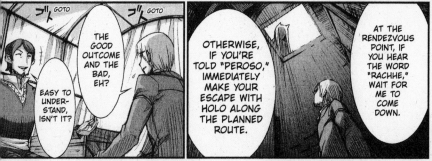

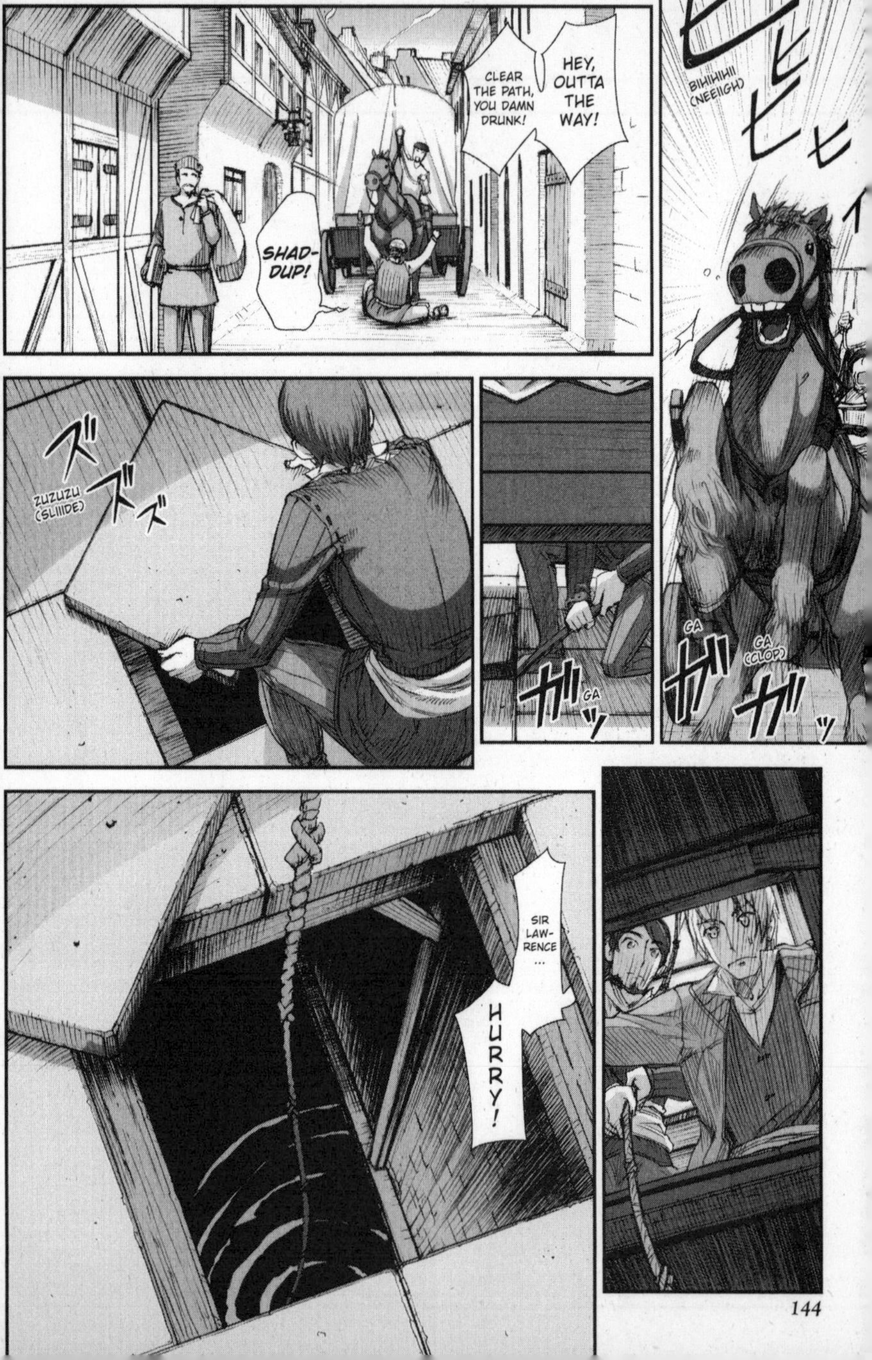
BIHIHIHII (NEEIIGH)
GA
GA (CLOP)
HEY, OUTTA THE WAY!
CLEAR THE PATH, YOU DAMN DRUNK!
SHAD-DUP!
GA
ZUZUZU (SLIIIDE)
SIR LAW-RENCE ...
HURRY!

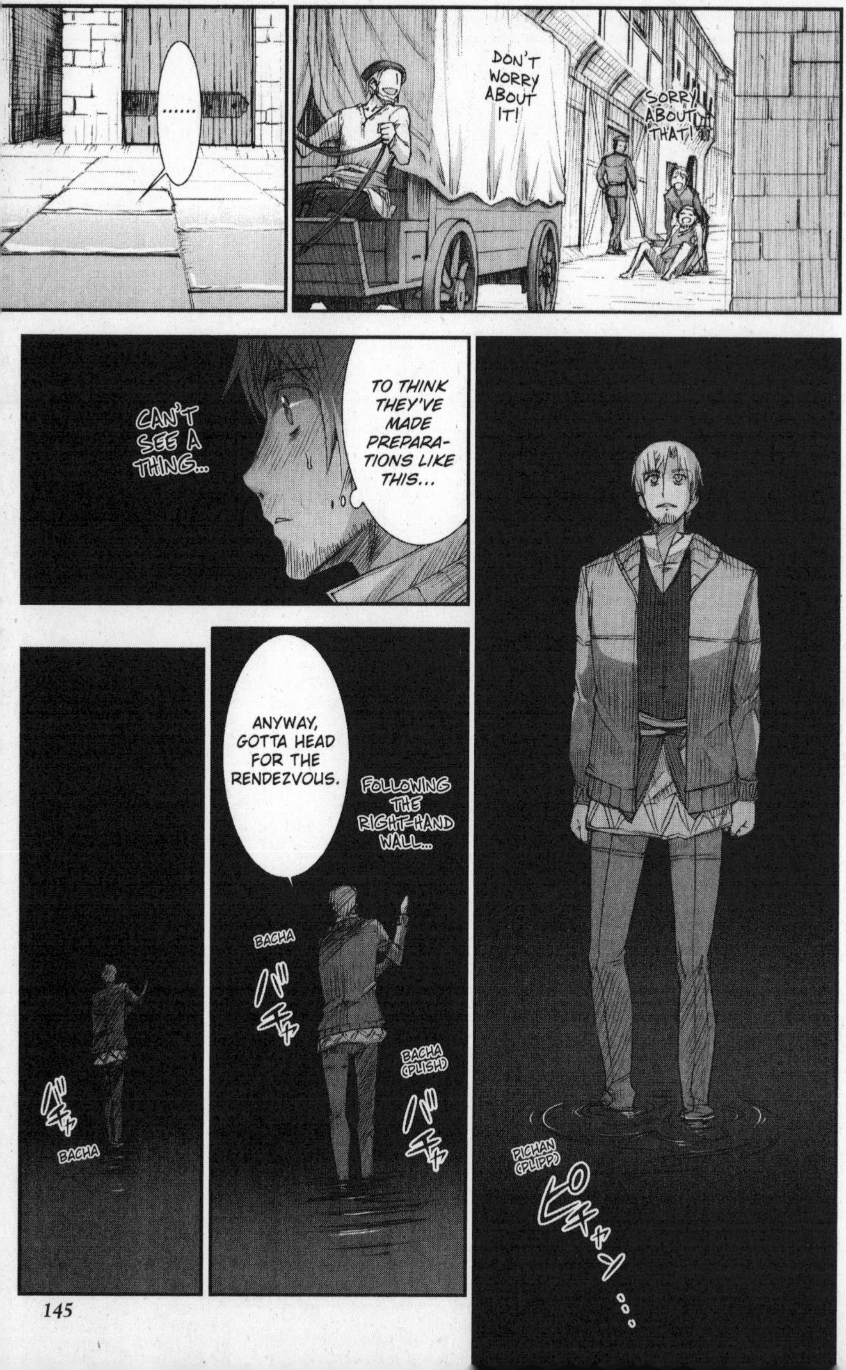
SORRY ABOUT THAT!
DON'T WORRY ABOUT IT!
......
PICHAN (PLIPP)
TO THINK THEY'VE MADE PREPARATIONS LIKE THIS...
CAN'T SEE A THING...
ANYWAY, GOTTA HEAD FOR THE RENDEZVOUS.
FOLLOWING THE RIGHT-HAND WALL...
BACHA
BACHA (PLISH)
BACHA

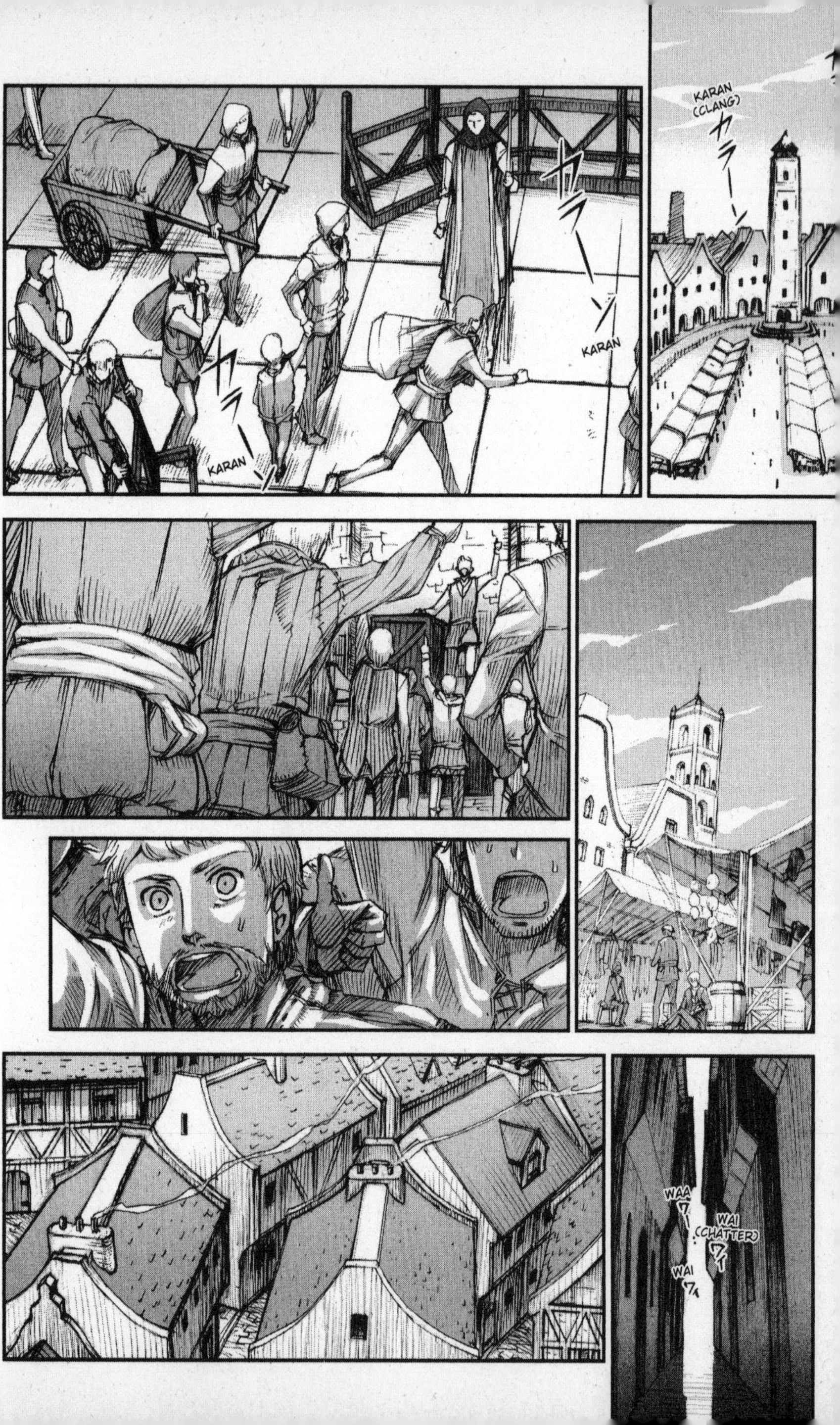
KARAN (CLANG)
カラーン
KARAN
カラーン
KARAN
カラーン
WAA
ワ
WAI (CHATTER)
ワイ
WAI
ワイ

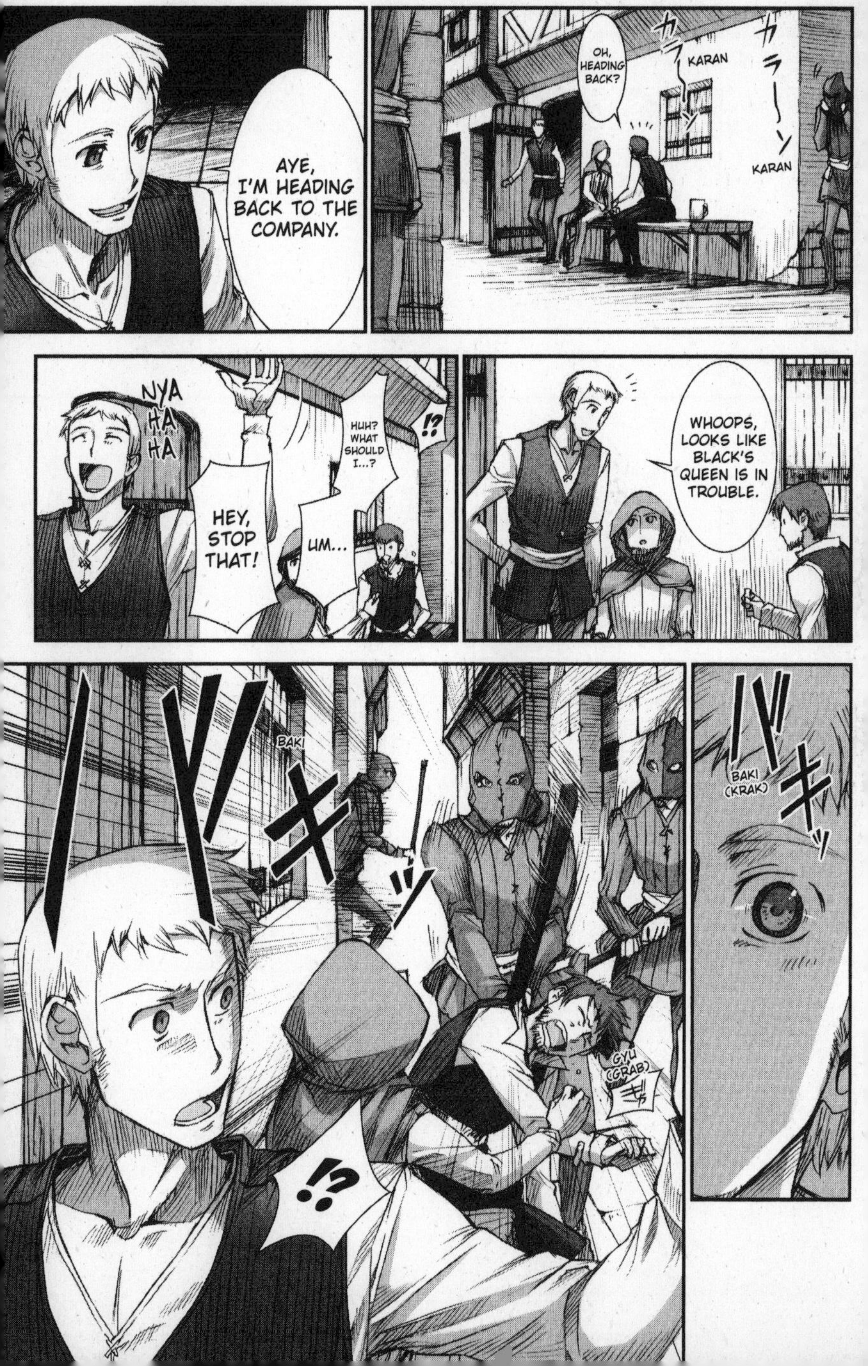
OH, HEADING BACK?
KARAN
KARAN
AYE, I'M HEADING BACK TO THE COMPANY.
WHOOPS, LOOKS LIKE BLACK'S QUEEN IS IN TROUBLE.
!?
HUH? WHAT SHOULD I...?
NYA HA HA HA
HEY, STOP THAT!
UM...
BAKI (KRAK)
BAKI
GYU (GRAB)
!?

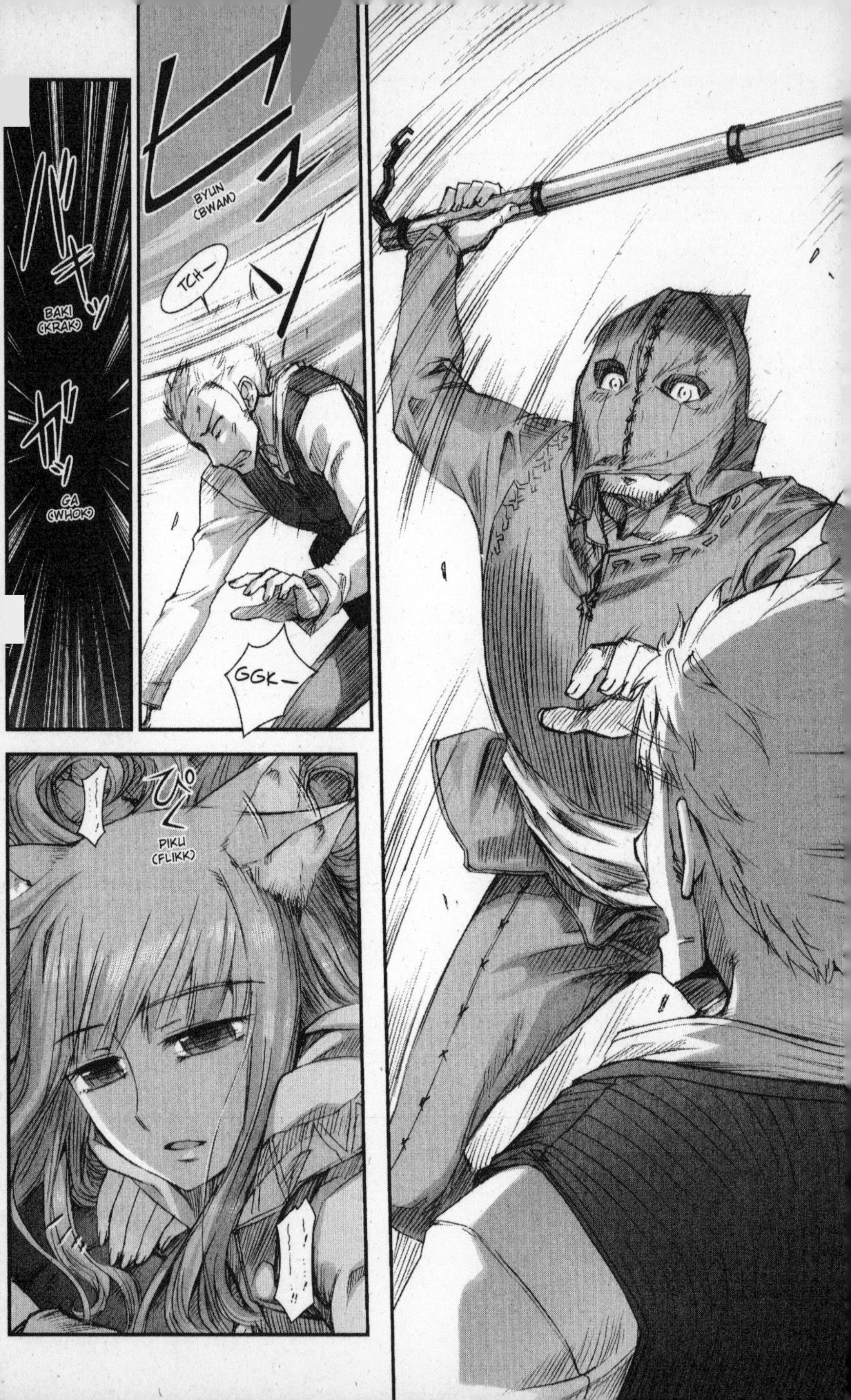
BYUN (BWAM)
TCH—
GGK—
BAKI (KRAK)
GA (WHOK)
PIKU (FLIKK)

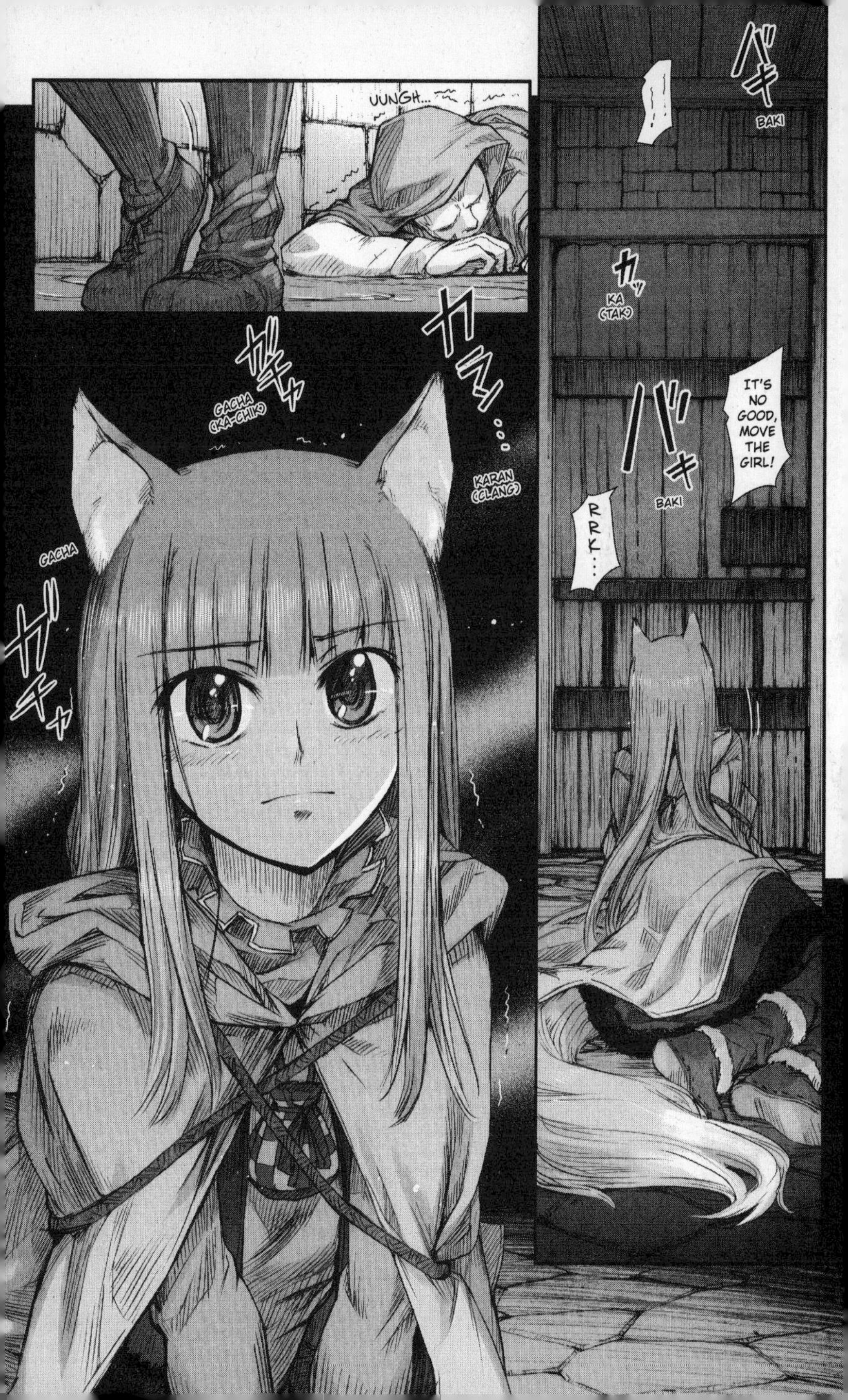
バキ
BAKI
カッ
KA (TAK)
IT'S NO GOOD, MOVE THE GIRL!
バキ
BAKI
RRK...
UUNGH...
カラン...
KARAN (CLANG)
ガチャ
GACHA (KA-CHIK)
GACHA
ガチャ

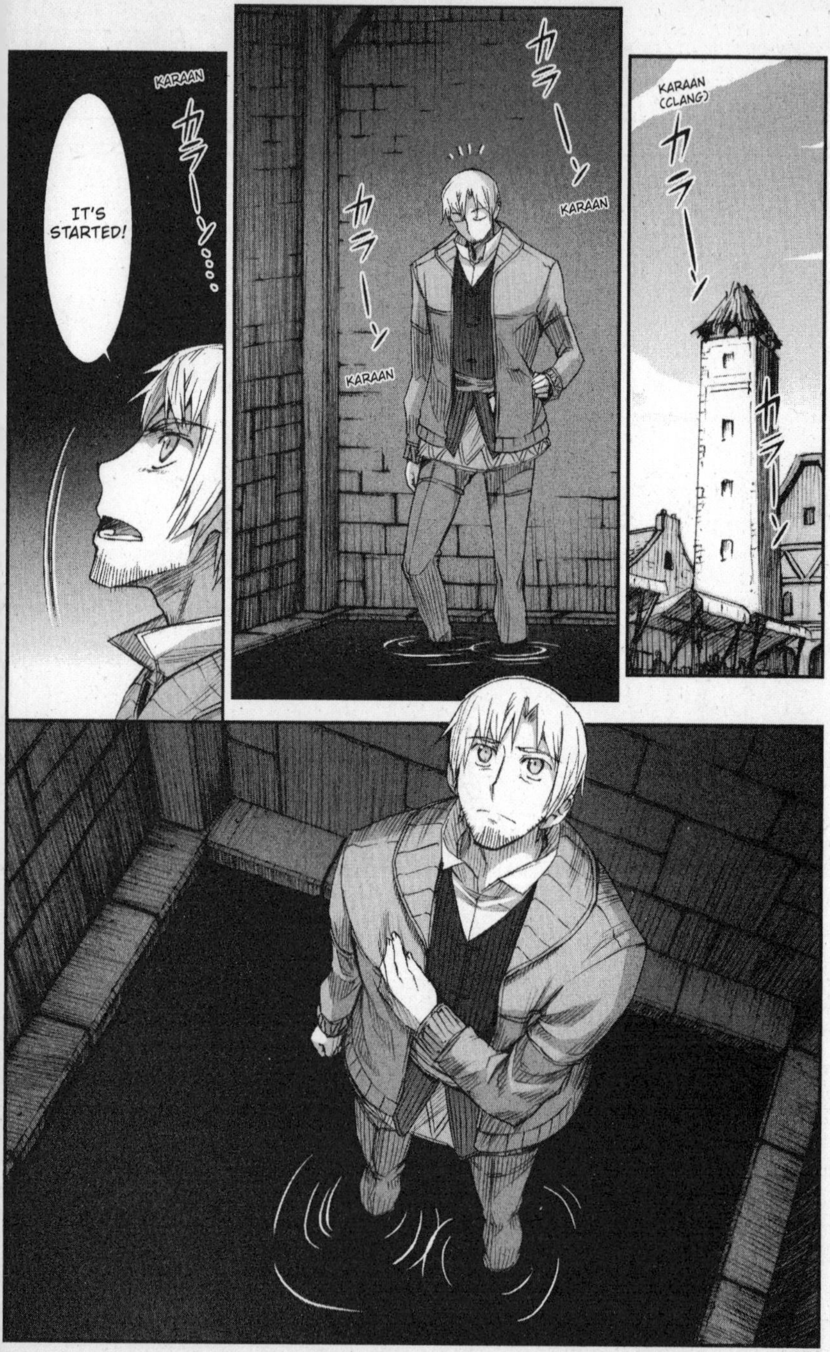
KARAAN (CLANG)
KARAAN
KARAAN
KARAAN
IT'S STARTED!

SPICE & WOLF

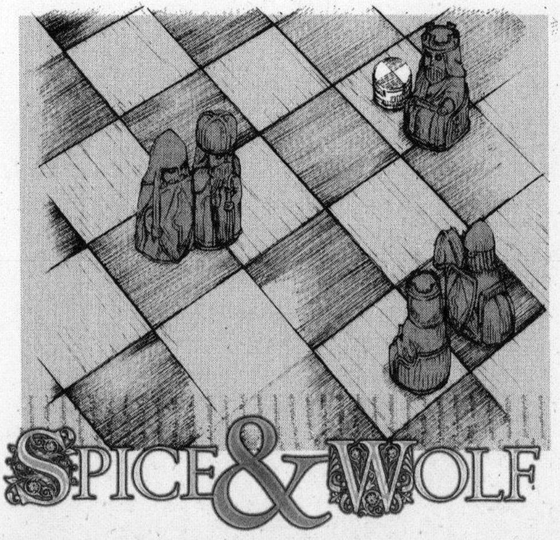
SPICE & WOLF

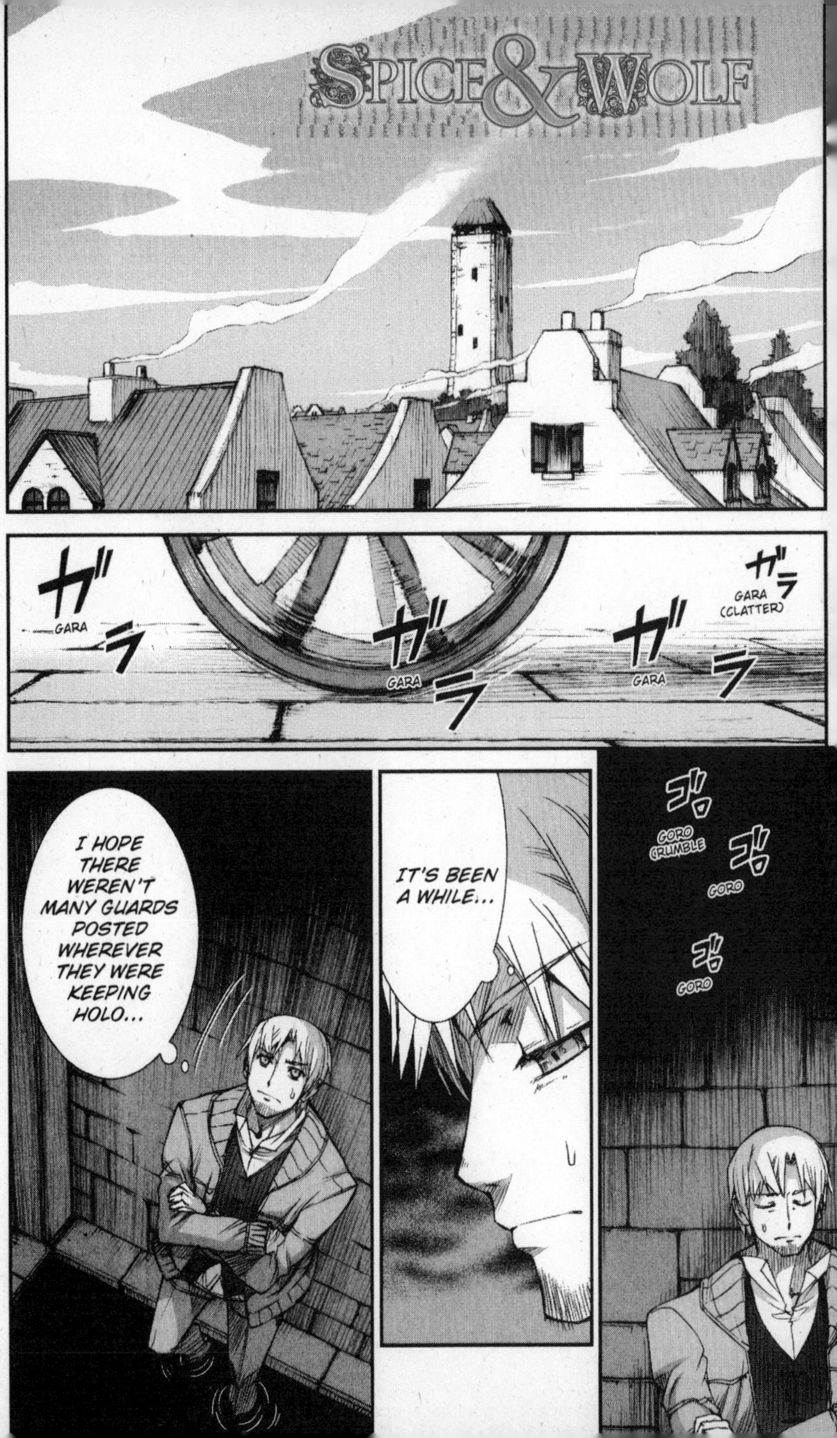

SPICE & WOLF
ガラ
GARA (CLATTER)
ガラ
GARA
ガラ
GARA
ガラ
GARA
ゴロ
GORO CRUMBLE
ゴロ
GORO
ゴロ
GORO
IT'S BEEN A WHILE...
I HOPE THERE WEREN'T MANY GUARDS POSTED WHEREVER THEY WERE KEEPING HOLO...

BUN
BUN
(FWIP)

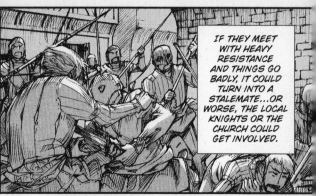

IF THEY MEET WITH HEAVY RESISTANCE AND THINGS GO BADLY, IT COULD TURN INTO A STALEMATE...OR WORSE, THE LOCAL KNIGHTS OR THE CHURCH COULD GET INVOLVED.

....

NUMAI!

...PIREON!

RACHHE!

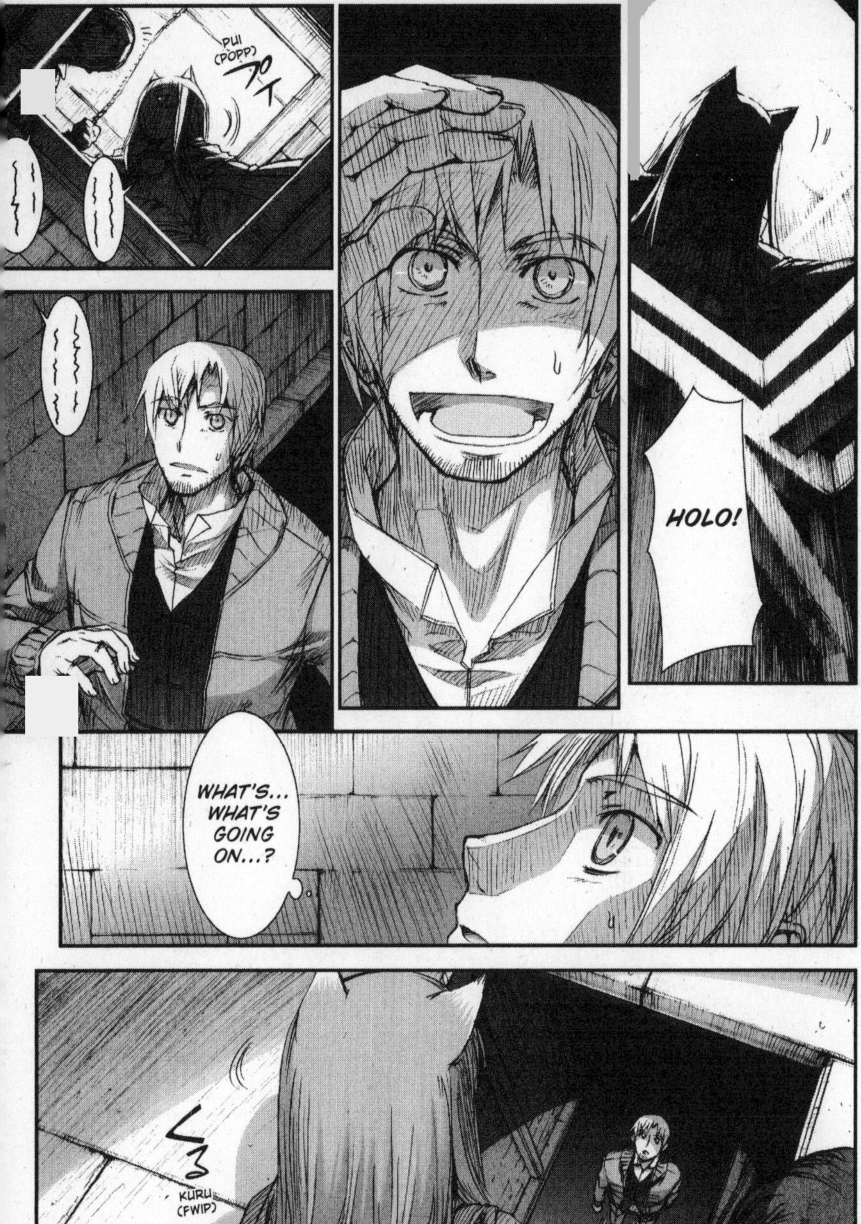
PUI (POPP)
HOLO!
WHAT'S... WHAT'S GOING ON...?
KURU (FWIP)

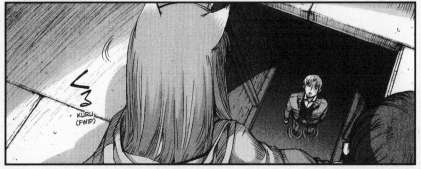

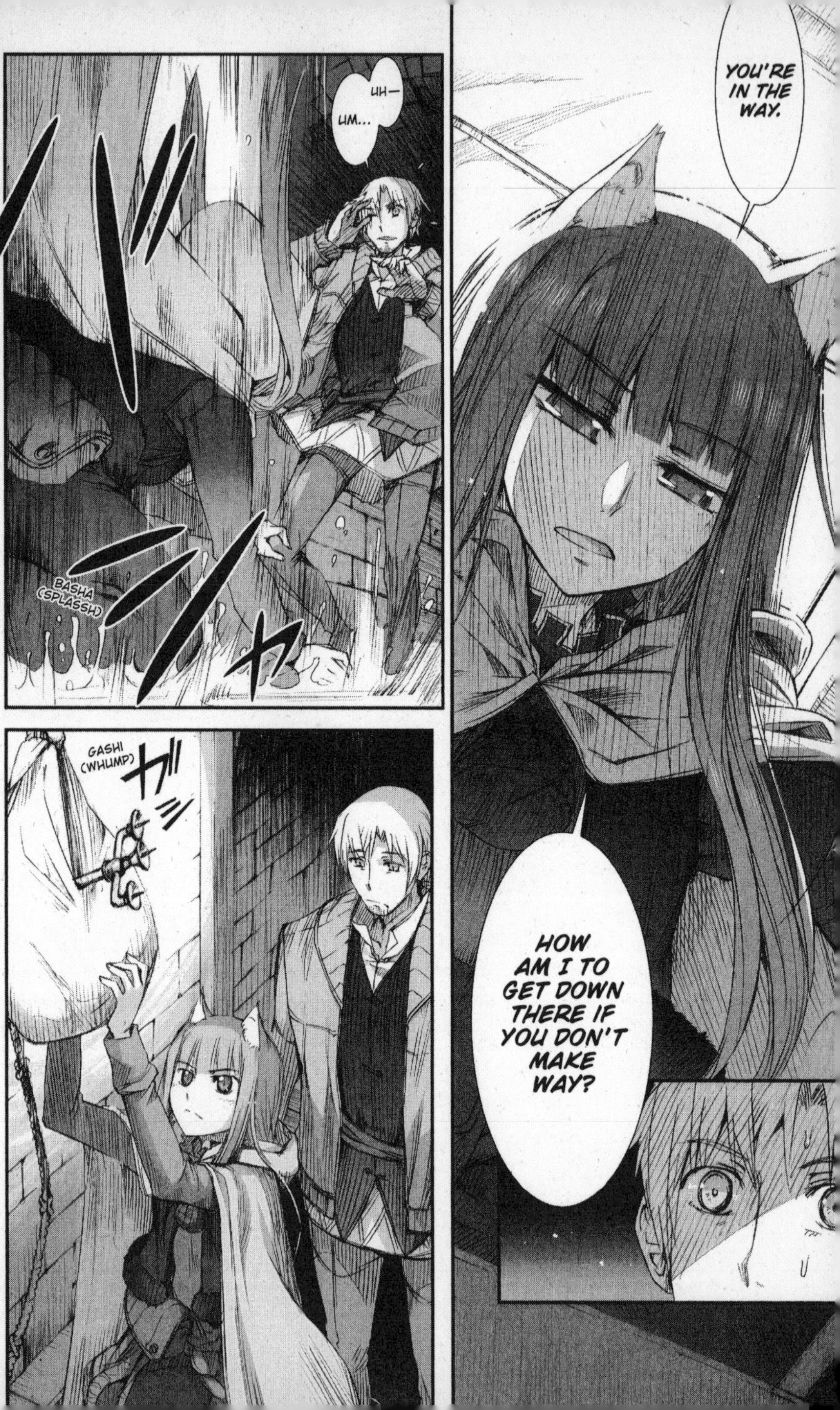
YOU'RE IN THE WAY.
HOW AM I TO GET DOWN THERE IF YOU DON'T MAKE WAY?
UH— UM...
BASHA (SPLASSH)
GASHI (WHUMP)

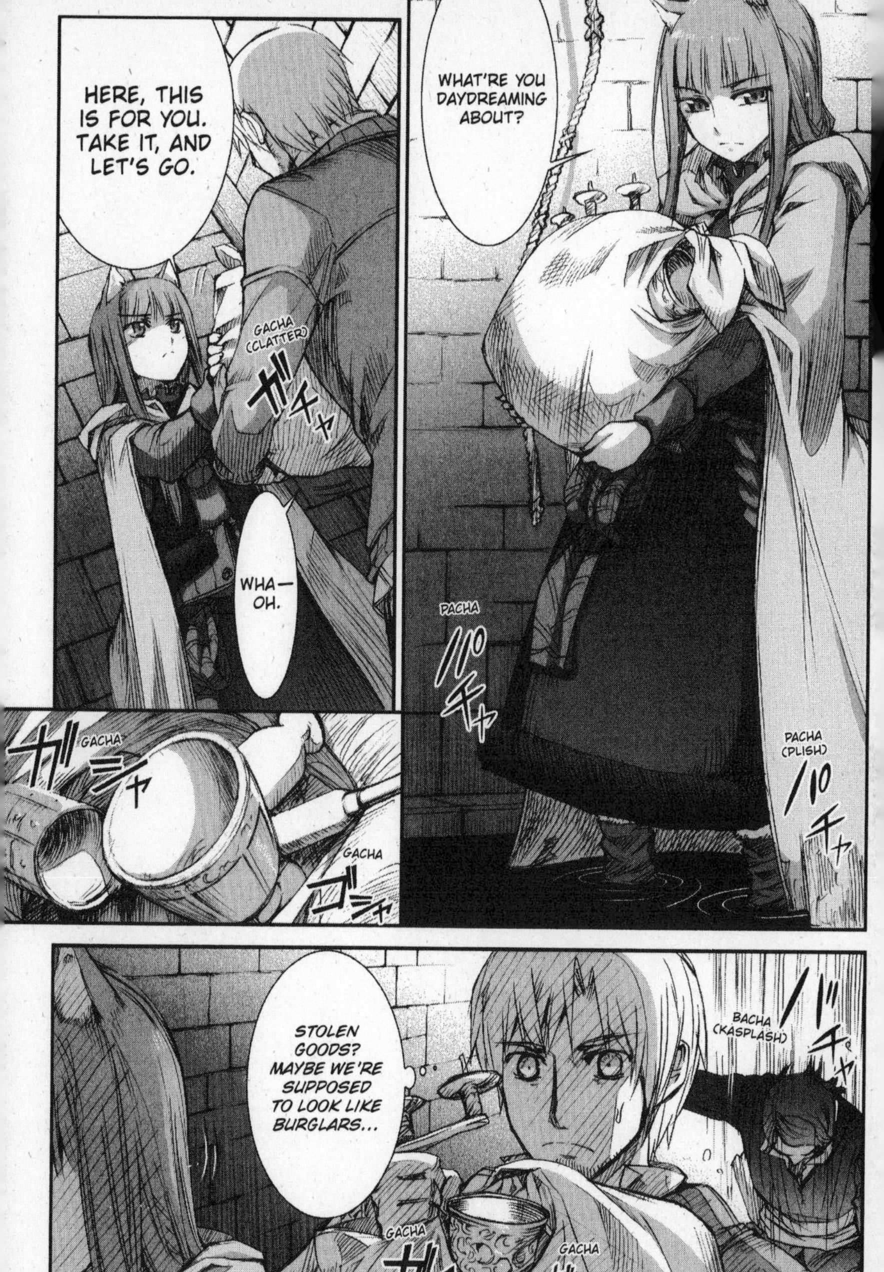
WHAT'RE YOU DAYDREAMING ABOUT?
PACHA
PACHA (PLISH)
HERE, THIS IS FOR YOU. TAKE IT, AND LET'S GO.
GACHA (CLATTER)
WHA— OH.
GACHA
GACHA
BACHA (KASPLASH)
STOLEN GOODS? MAYBE WE'RE SUPPOSED TO LOOK LIKE BURGLARS...
GACHA
GACHA

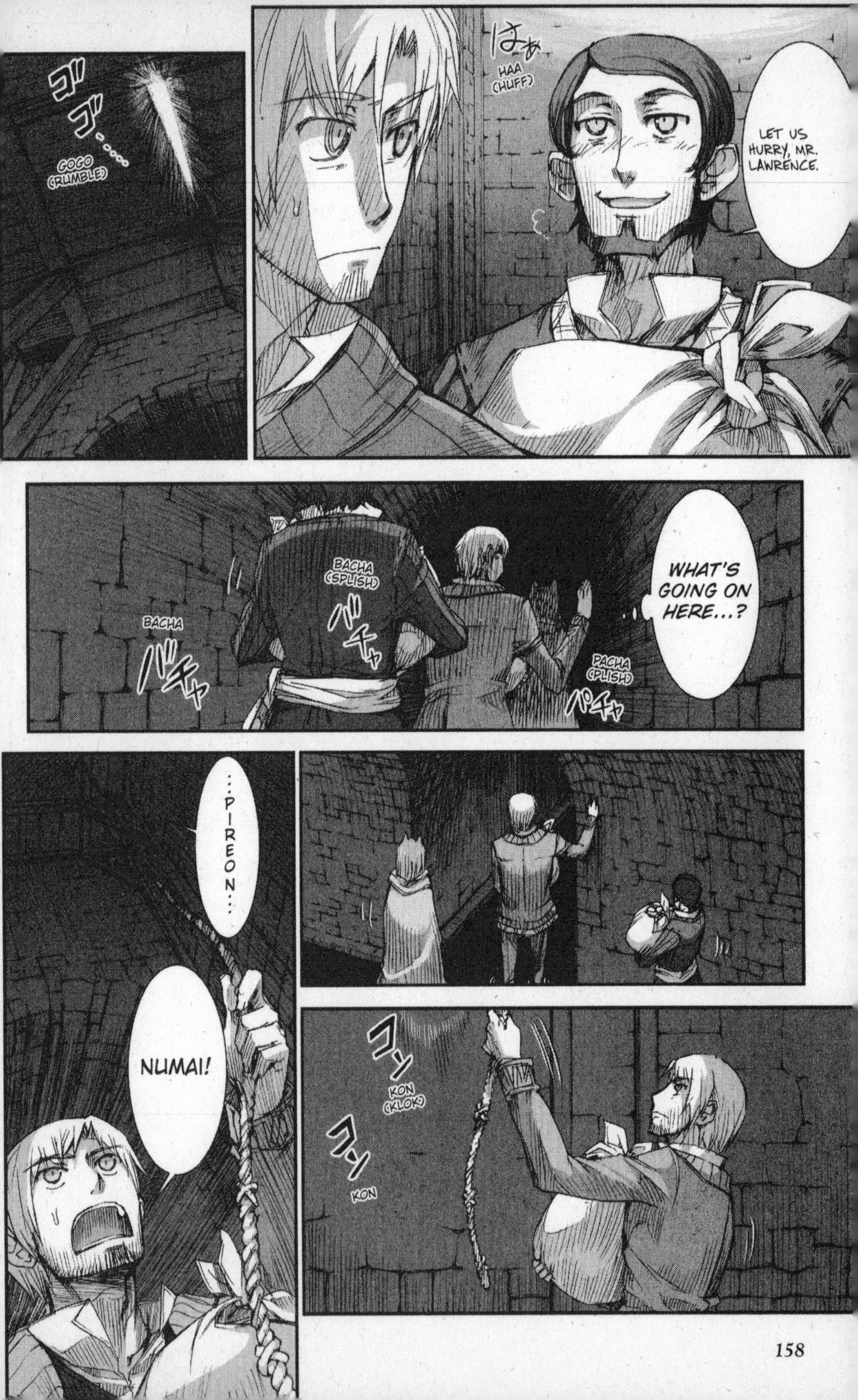
LET US HURRY, MR. LAWRENCE.
HAA (HUFF)
GOGO (RUMBLE)
WHAT'S GOING ON HERE...?
PACHA (PLISH)
BACHA (SPLISH)
BACHA
KON (KLOK)
KON
...PIREON...
NUMAI!

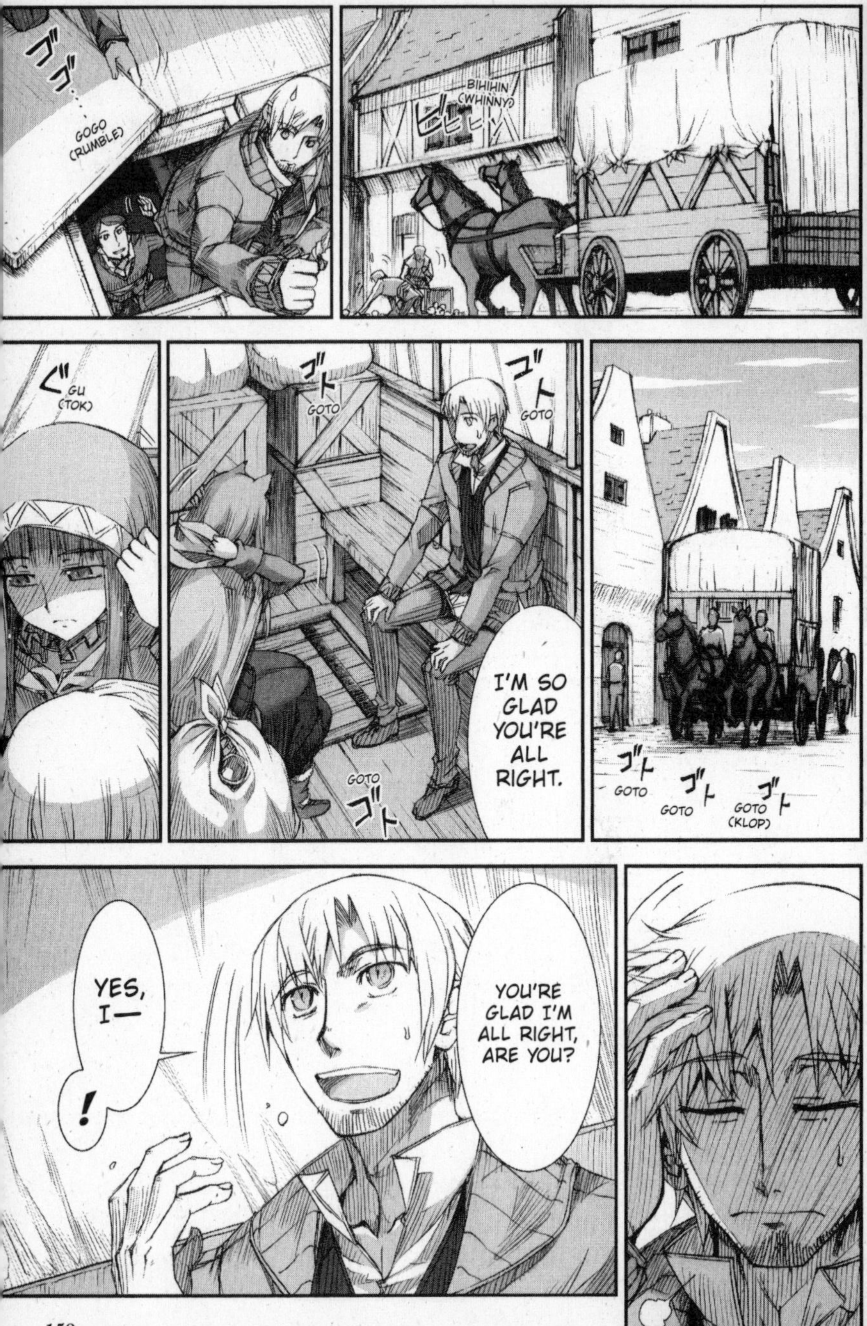
BIHIHIN (WHINNY)
GOGO (RUMBLE)
GOTO
GOTO
GOTO (KLOP)
GOTO
GOTO
I'M SO GLAD YOU'RE ALL RIGHT.
GOTO
GU (TOK)
YOU'RE GLAD I'M ALL RIGHT, ARE YOU?
YES, I—
!

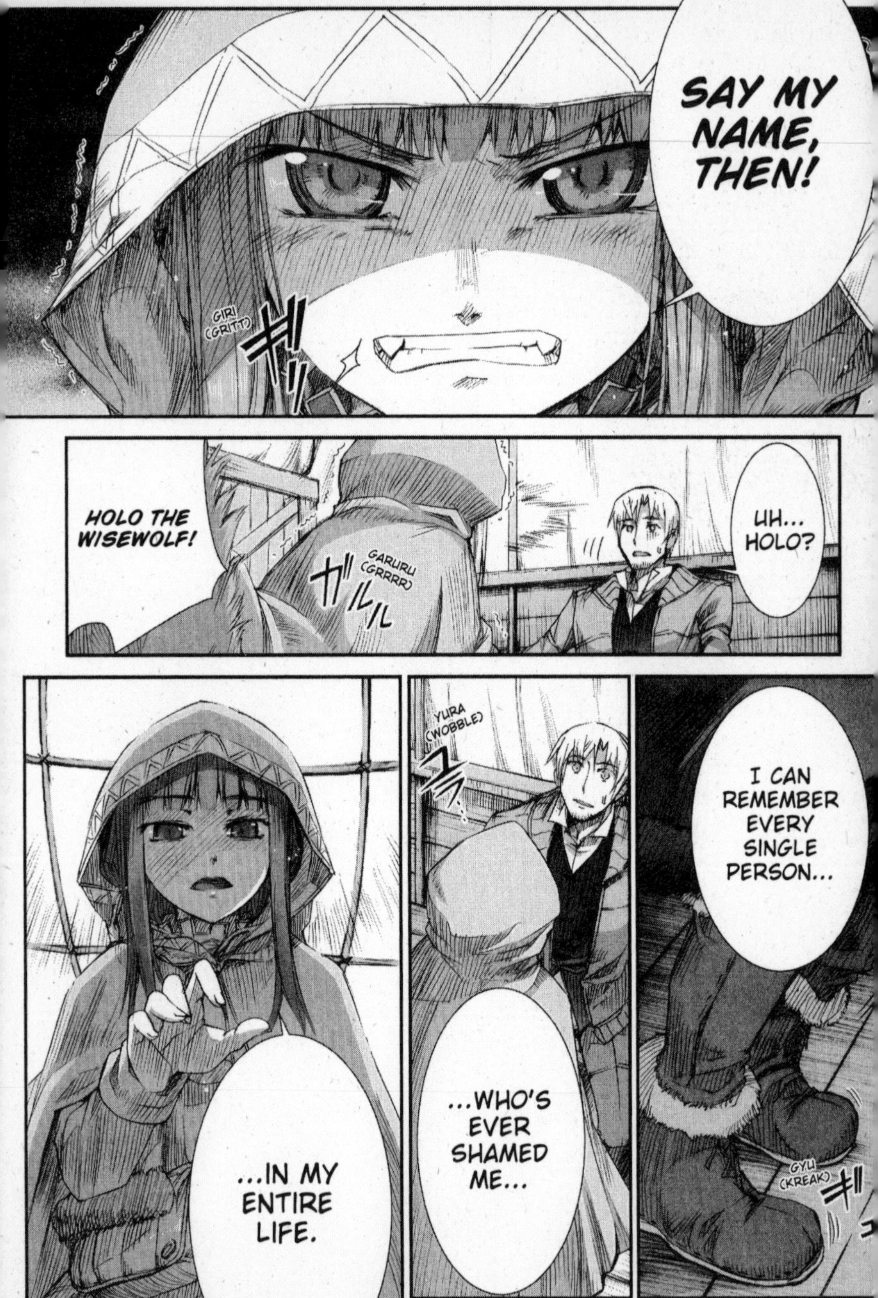
SAY MY NAME, THEN!
GIRI (GRITT)
UH... HOLO?
GARURU (GRRRR)
HOLO THE WISEWOLF!
I CAN REMEMBER EVERY SINGLE PERSON...
GYU (KREAK)
YURA (WOBBLE)
...WHO'S EVER SHAMED ME...
...IN MY ENTIRE LIFE.

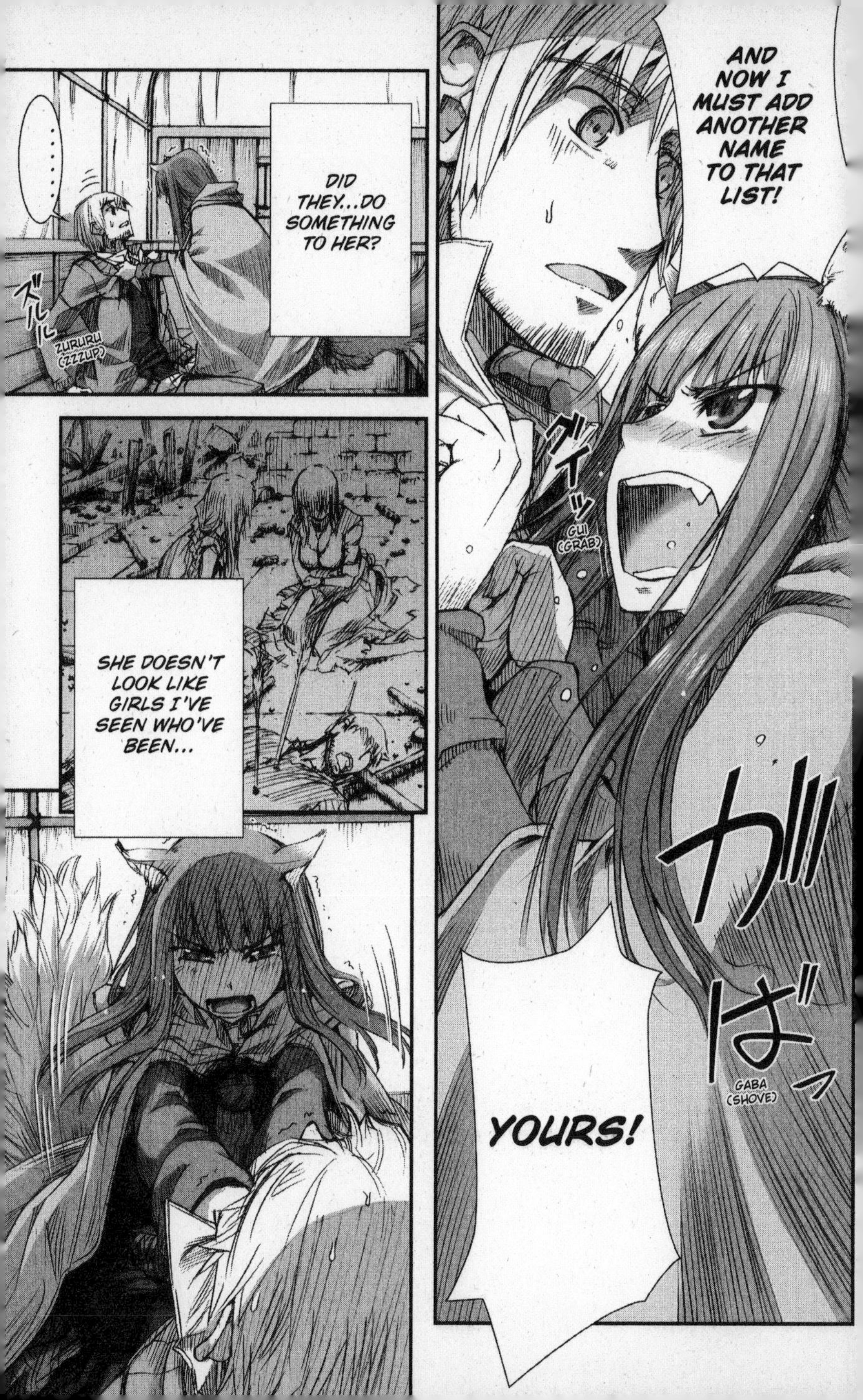
AND NOW I MUST ADD ANOTHER NAME TO THAT LIST!
グイッ
GUI (GRAB)
がばっ
GABA (SHOVE)
YOURS!
DID THEY...DO SOMETHING TO HER?
……
ズルル
ZURURU (ZZZZUP)
SHE DOESN'T LOOK LIKE GIRLS I'VE SEEN WHO'VE BEEN...

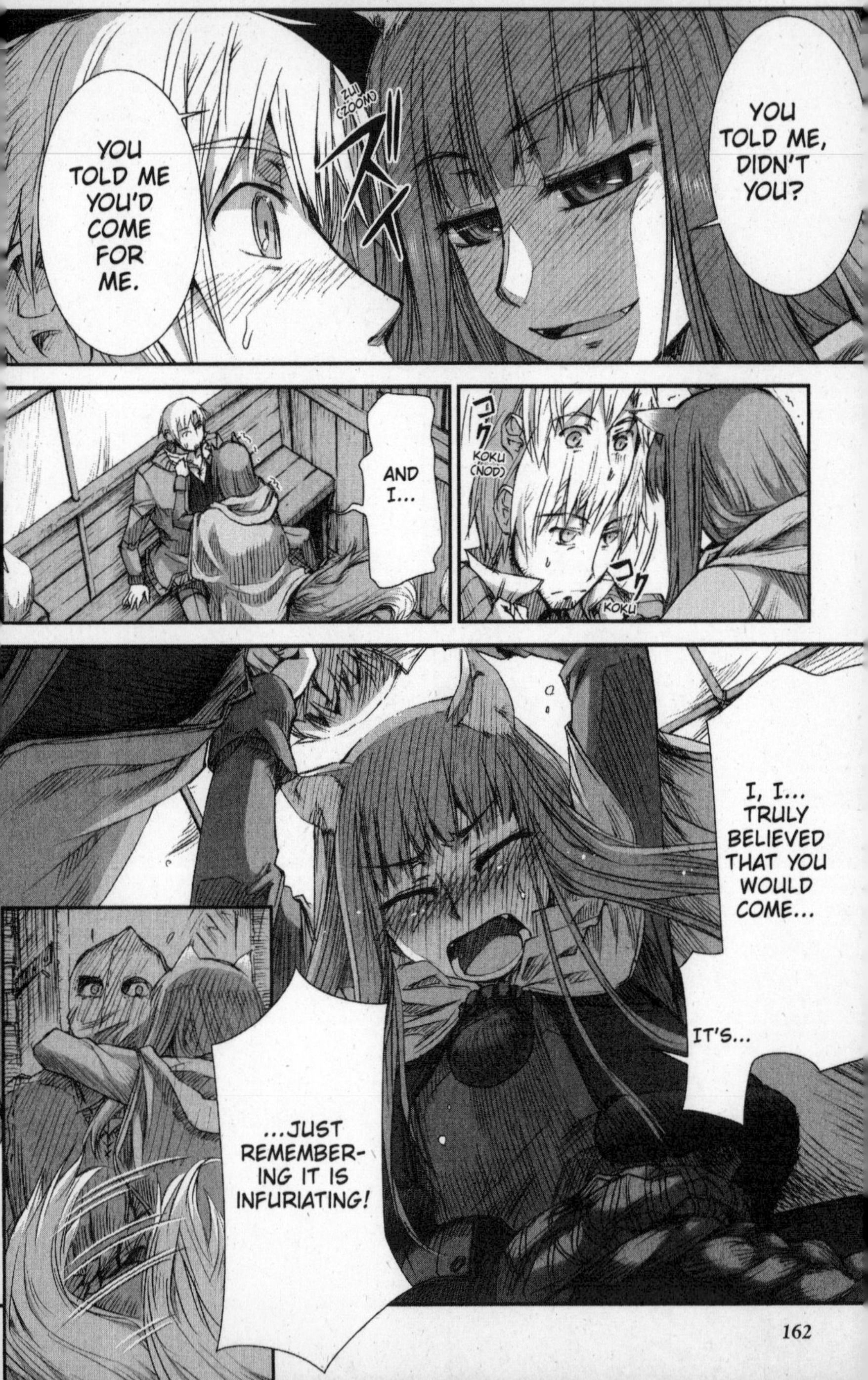
YOU TOLD ME, DIDN'T YOU?
ZUI (ZOOM)
YOU TOLD ME YOU'D COME FOR ME.
KOKU (NOD)
KOKU
AND I...
I, I... TRULY BELIEVED THAT YOU WOULD COME...
IT'S...
...JUST REMEMBER-ING IT IS INFURIATING!

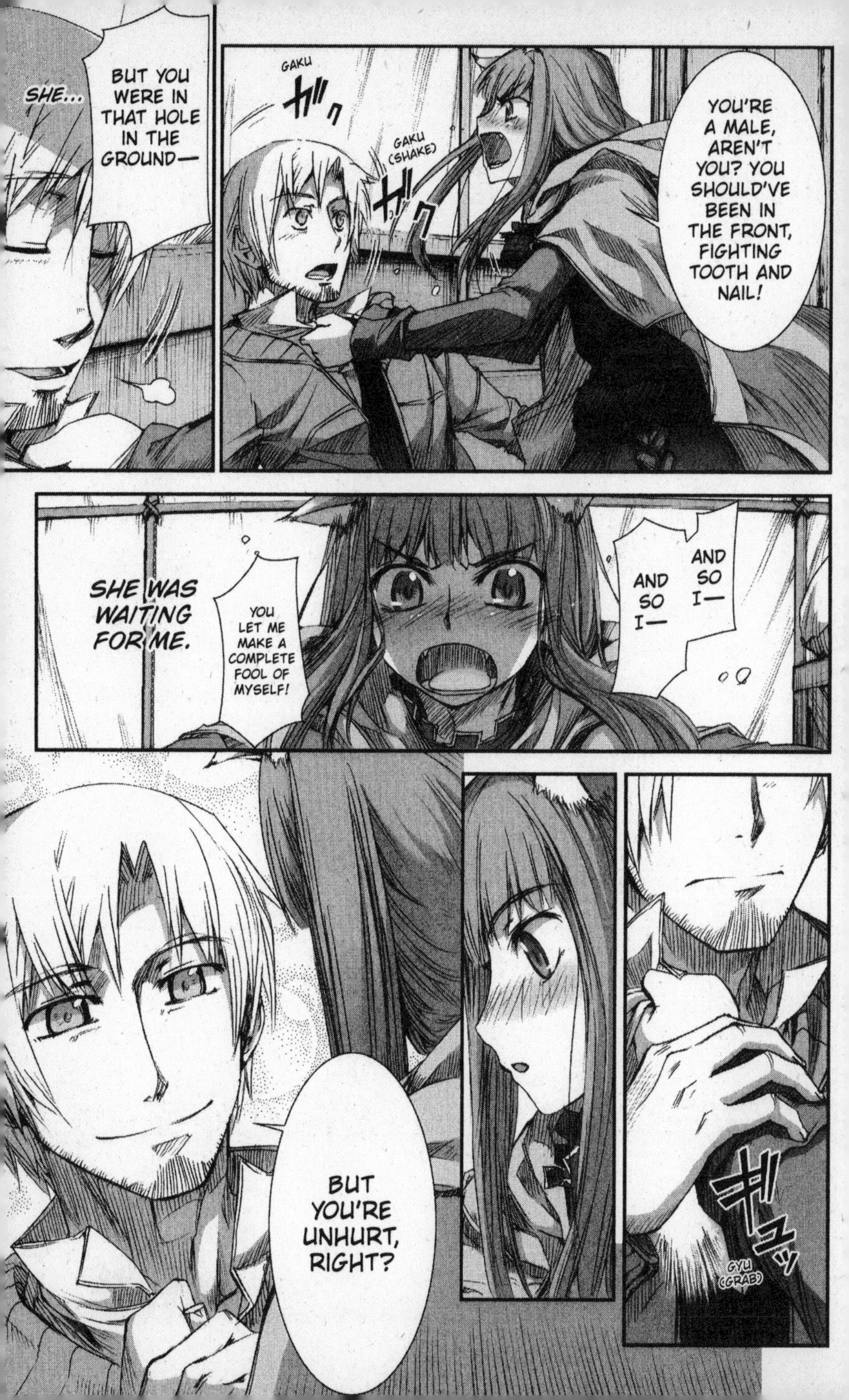
YOU'RE A MALE, AREN'T YOU? YOU SHOULD'VE BEEN IN THE FRONT, FIGHTING TOOTH AND NAIL!
GAKU
GAKU (SHAKE)
BUT YOU WERE IN THAT HOLE IN THE GROUND—
SHE...
AND SO I—
AND SO I—
YOU LET ME MAKE A COMPLETE FOOL OF MYSELF!
SHE WAS WAITING FOR ME.
GYU (GRAB)
BUT YOU'RE UNHURT, RIGHT?

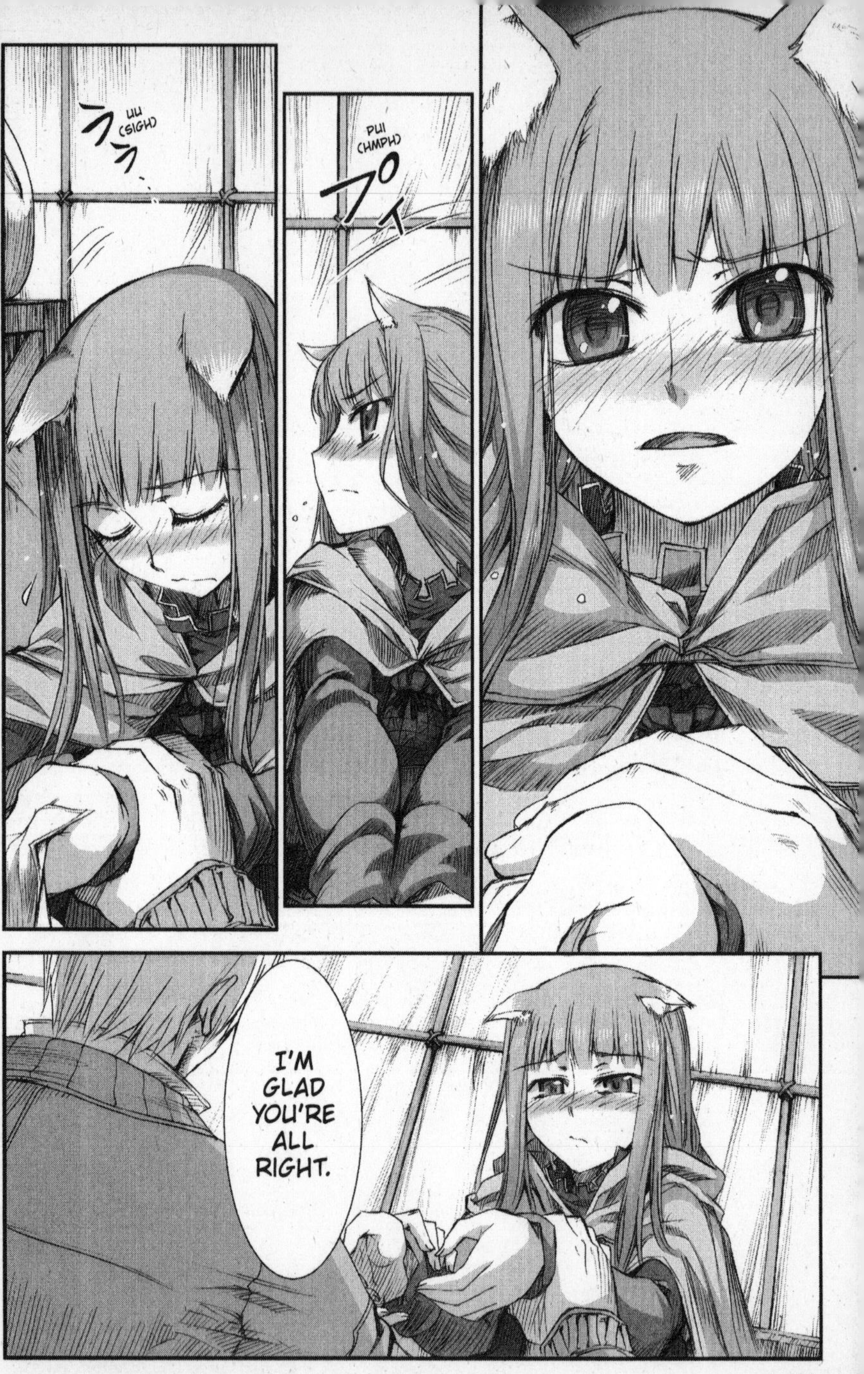
PUI (HMPH)
UU (SIGH)
I'M GLAD YOU'RE ALL RIGHT.

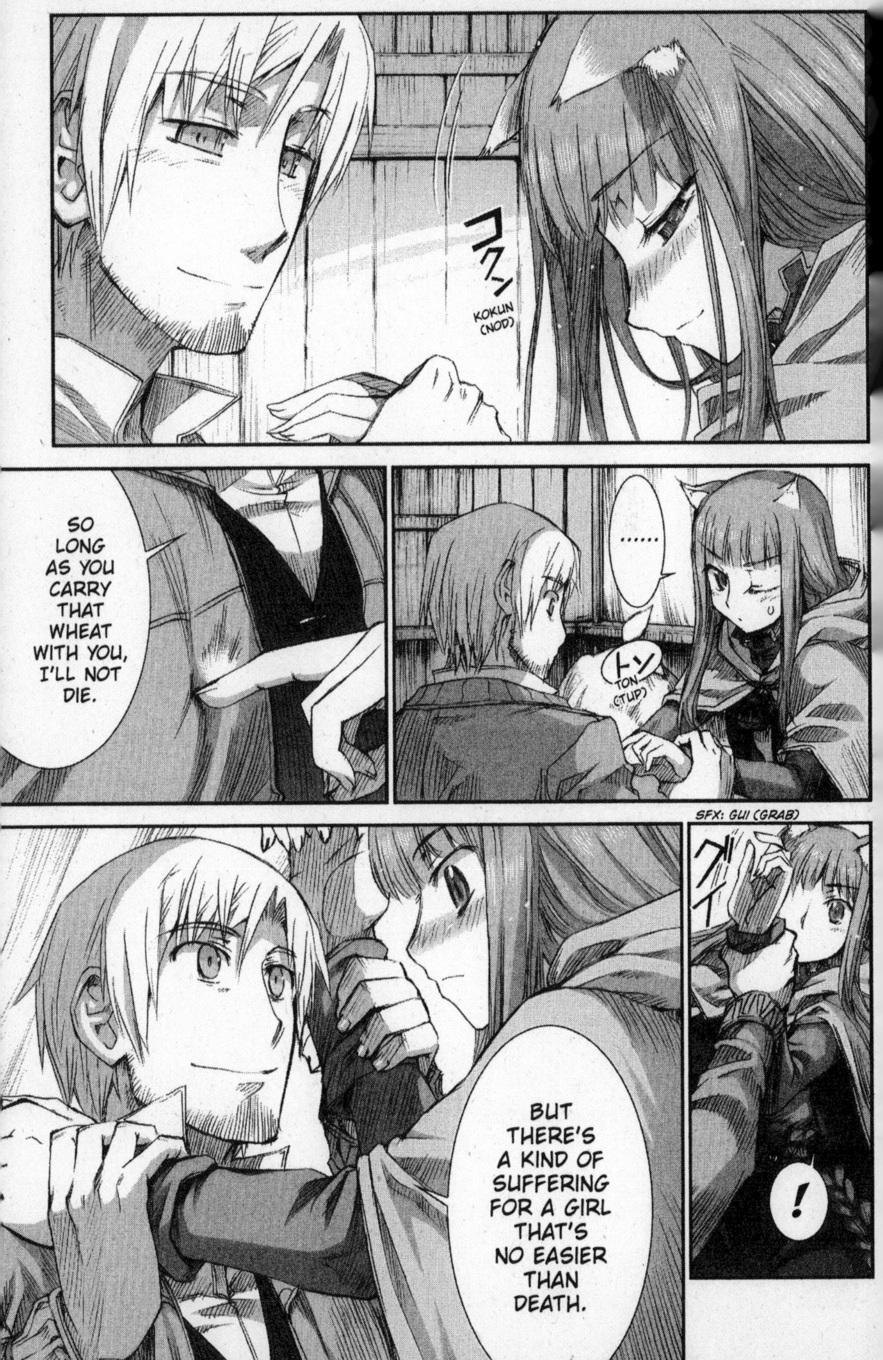

コクン
KOKUN
(NOD)
......
トン
TON
(TUP)
SO LONG AS YOU CARRY THAT WHEAT WITH YOU, I'LL NOT DIE.
SFX: GUI (GRAB)
グイ
!
BUT THERE'S A KIND OF SUFFERING FOR A GIRL THAT'S NO EASIER THAN DEATH.

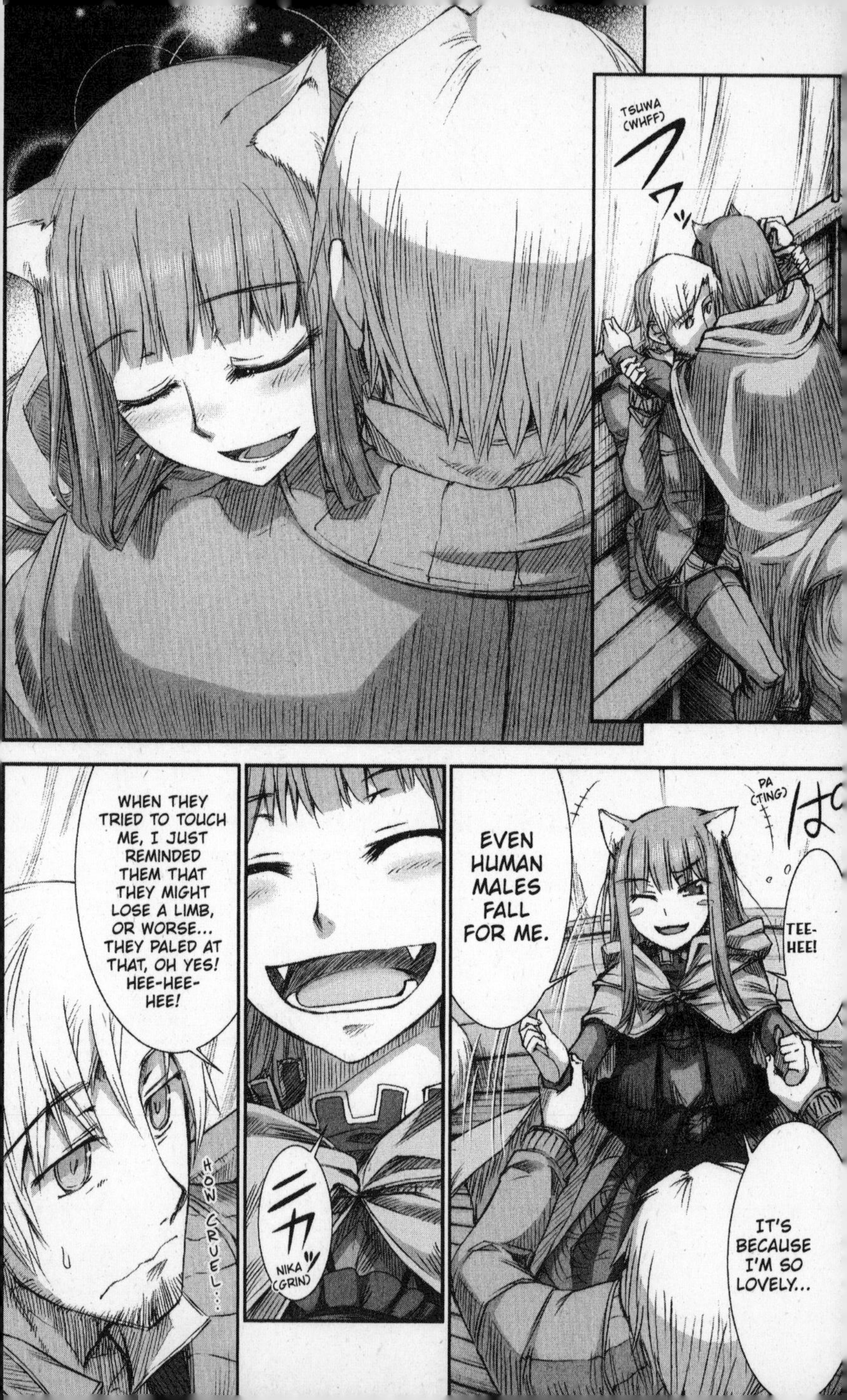
TSUWA (WHFF)
PA (TING)
TEE-HEE!
IT'S BECAUSE I'M SO LOVELY...
EVEN HUMAN MALES FALL FOR ME.
NIKA (GRIN)
WHEN THEY TRIED TO TOUCH ME, I JUST REMINDED THEM THAT THEY MIGHT LOSE A LIMB, OR WORSE... THEY PALED AT THAT, OH YES! HEE-HEE-HEE!
HOW CRUEL...

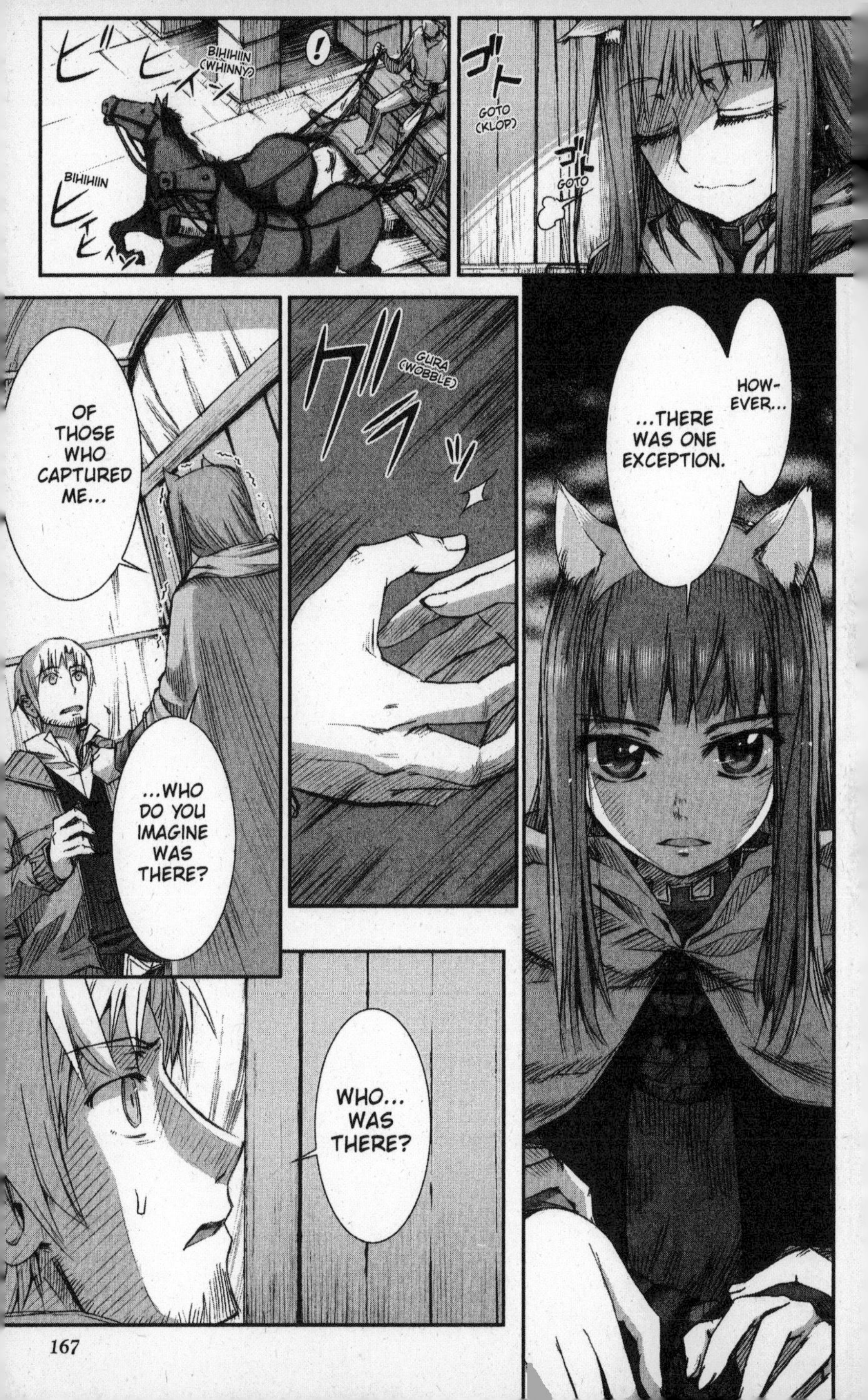
ゴト
GOTO (KLOP)
ゴト
GOTO
!
BIHIHIIN (WHINNY)
BIHIHIIN
HOW-EVER...
...THERE WAS ONE EXCEPTION.
GURA (WOBBLE)
OF THOSE WHO CAPTURED ME...
...WHO DO YOU IMAGINE WAS THERE?
WHO... WAS THERE?

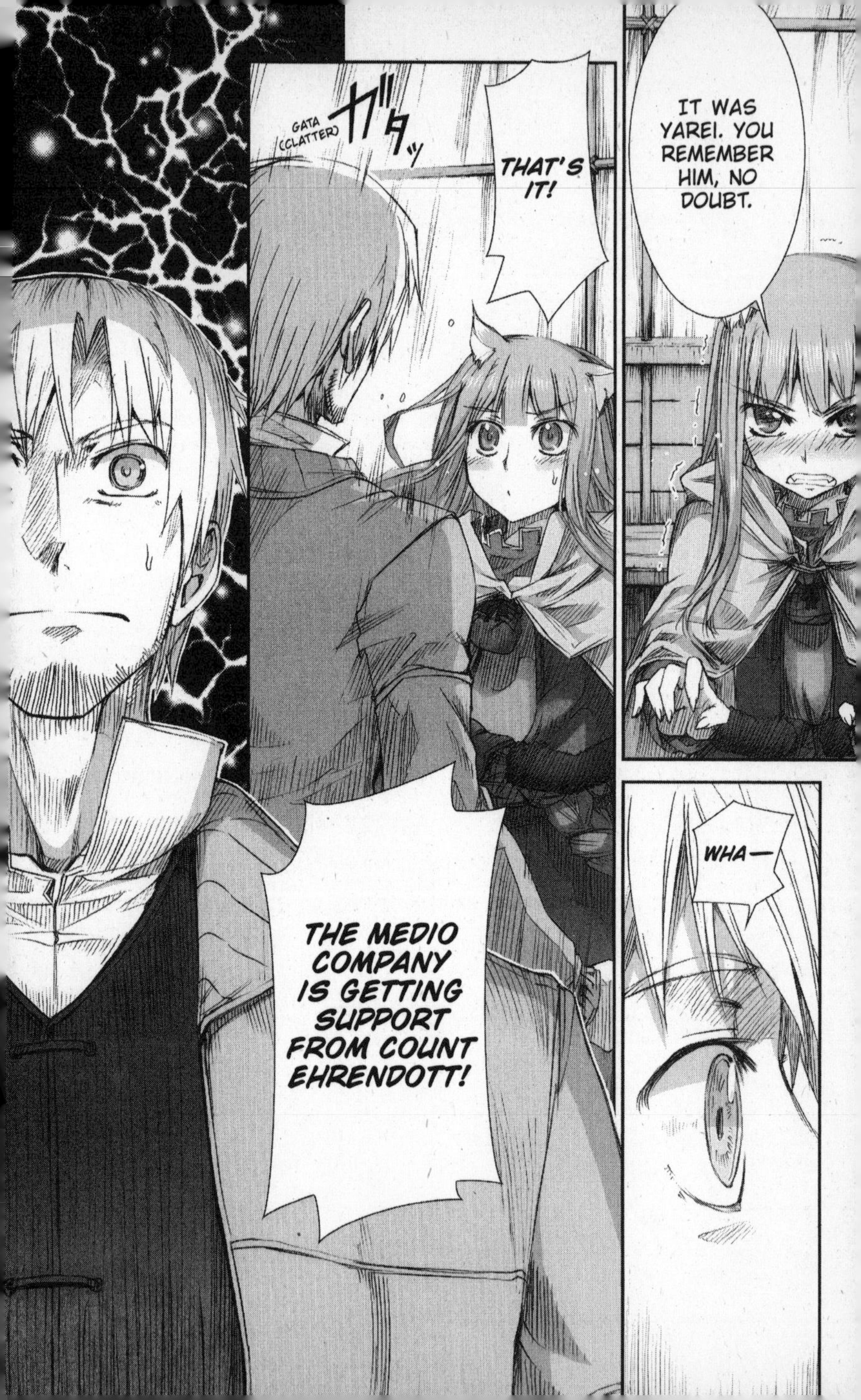
IT WAS YAREI. YOU REMEMBER HIM, NO DOUBT.
WHA—
GATA (CLATTER)
ガタッ
THAT'S IT!
THE MEDIO COMPANY IS GETTING SUPPORT FROM COUNT EHRENDOTT!

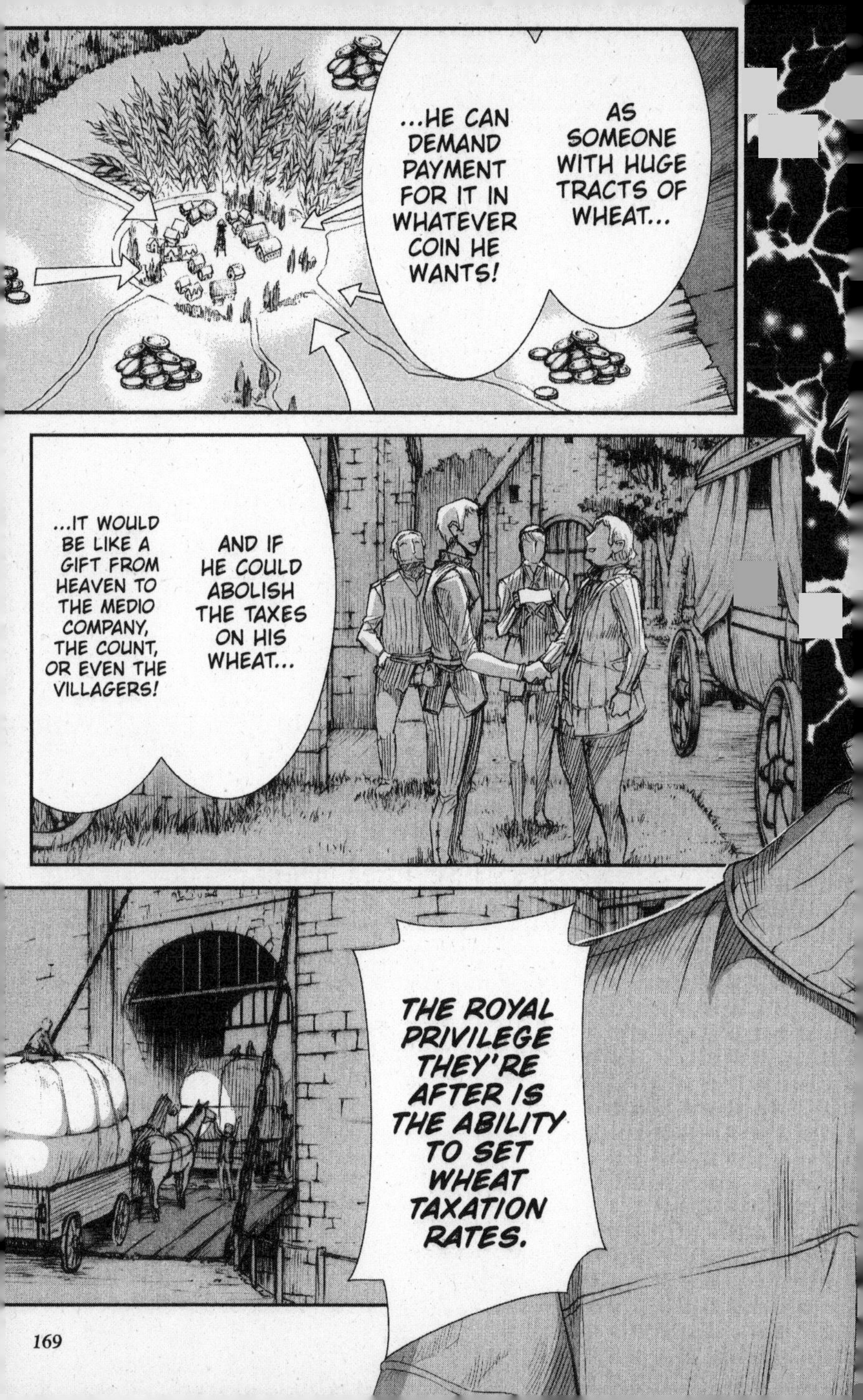
AS SOMEONE WITH HUGE TRACTS OF WHEAT...
...HE CAN DEMAND PAYMENT FOR IT IN WHATEVER COIN HE WANTS!
AND IF HE COULD ABOLISH THE TAXES ON HIS WHEAT...
...IT WOULD BE LIKE A GIFT FROM HEAVEN TO THE MEDIO COMPANY, THE COUNT, OR EVEN THE VILLAGERS!
THE ROYAL PRIVILEGE THEY'RE AFTER IS THE ABILITY TO SET WHEAT TAXATION RATES.

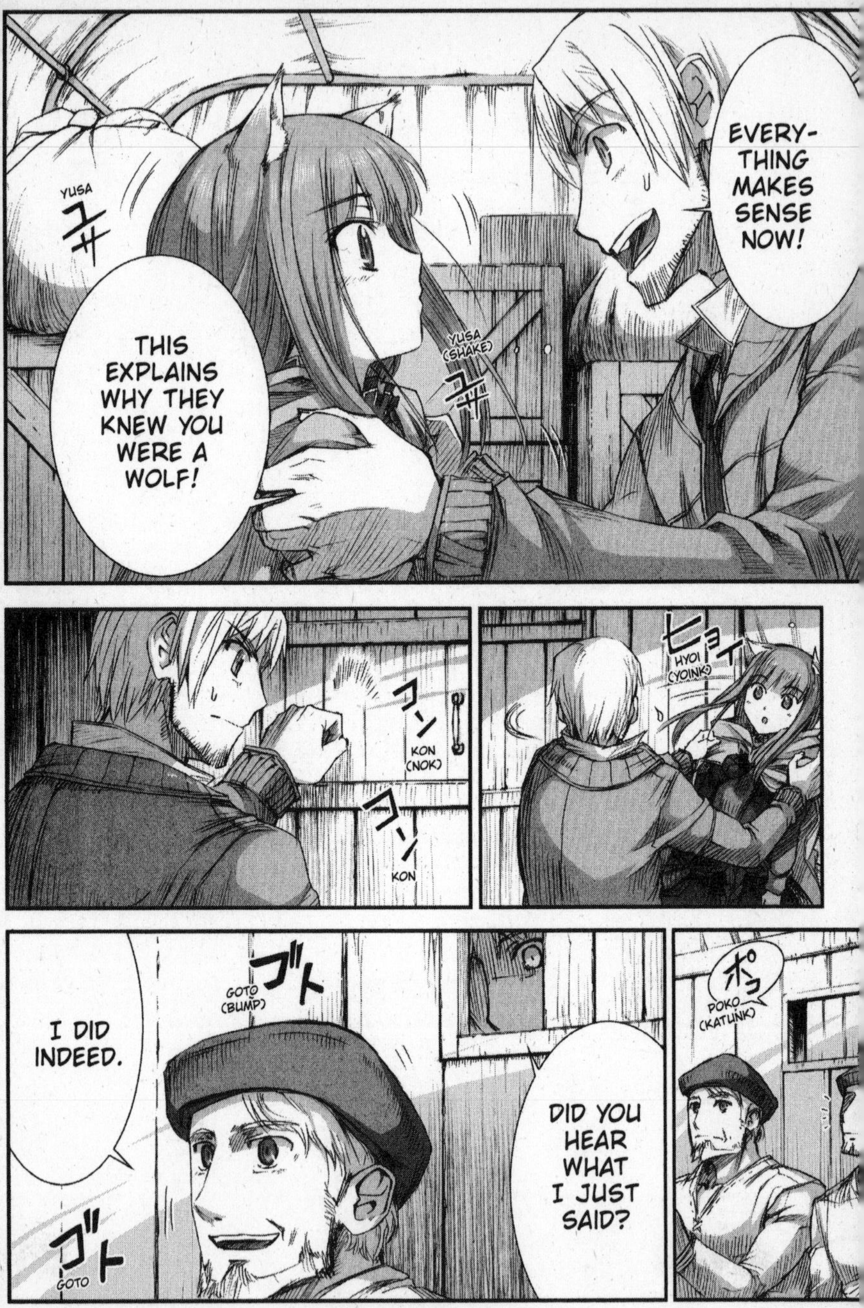
EVERY-THING MAKES SENSE NOW!
YUSA (SHAKE)
YUSA
THIS EXPLAINS WHY THEY KNEW YOU WERE A WOLF!
HYOI (YOINK)
KON (NOK)
KON
POKO (KATUNK)
DID YOU HEAR WHAT I JUST SAID?
GOTO (BUMP)
I DID INDEED.
GOTO

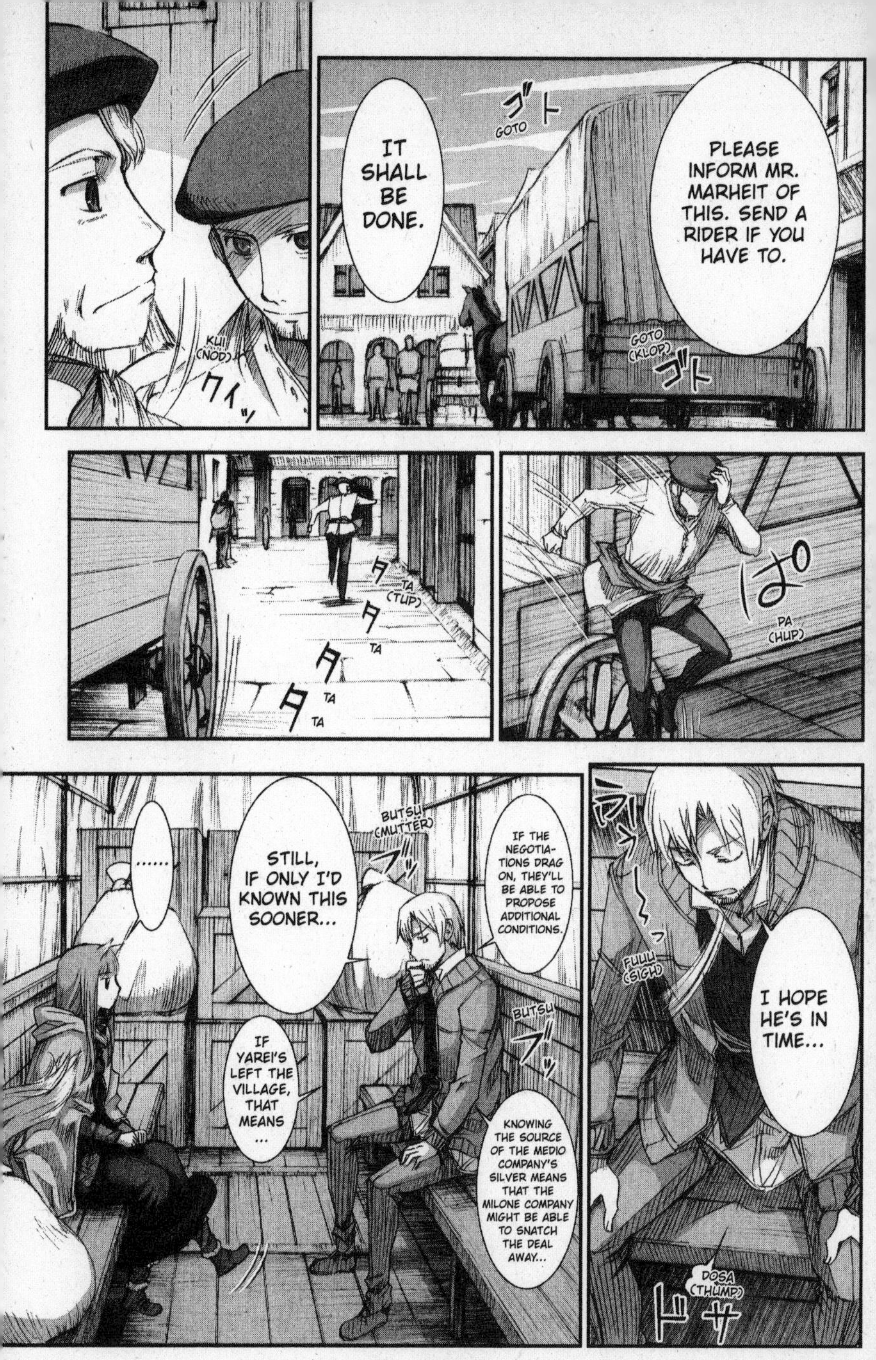
PLEASE INFORM MR. MARHEIT OF THIS. SEND A RIDER IF YOU HAVE TO.
GOTO
IT SHALL BE DONE.
GOTO (KLOP)
KUI (NOD)
PA (HUP)
TA (TUP)
TA
TA
TA
FUUU (SIGH)
I HOPE HE'S IN TIME...
DOSA (THUMP)
IF THE NEGOTIATIONS DRAG ON, THEY'LL BE ABLE TO PROPOSE ADDITIONAL CONDITIONS.
BUTSU (MUTTER)
STILL, IF ONLY I'D KNOWN THIS SOONER...
......
BUTSU
KNOWING THE SOURCE OF THE MEDIO COMPANY'S SILVER MEANS THAT THE MILONE COMPANY MIGHT BE ABLE TO SNATCH THE DEAL AWAY...
IF YAREI'S LEFT THE VILLAGE, THAT MEANS ...

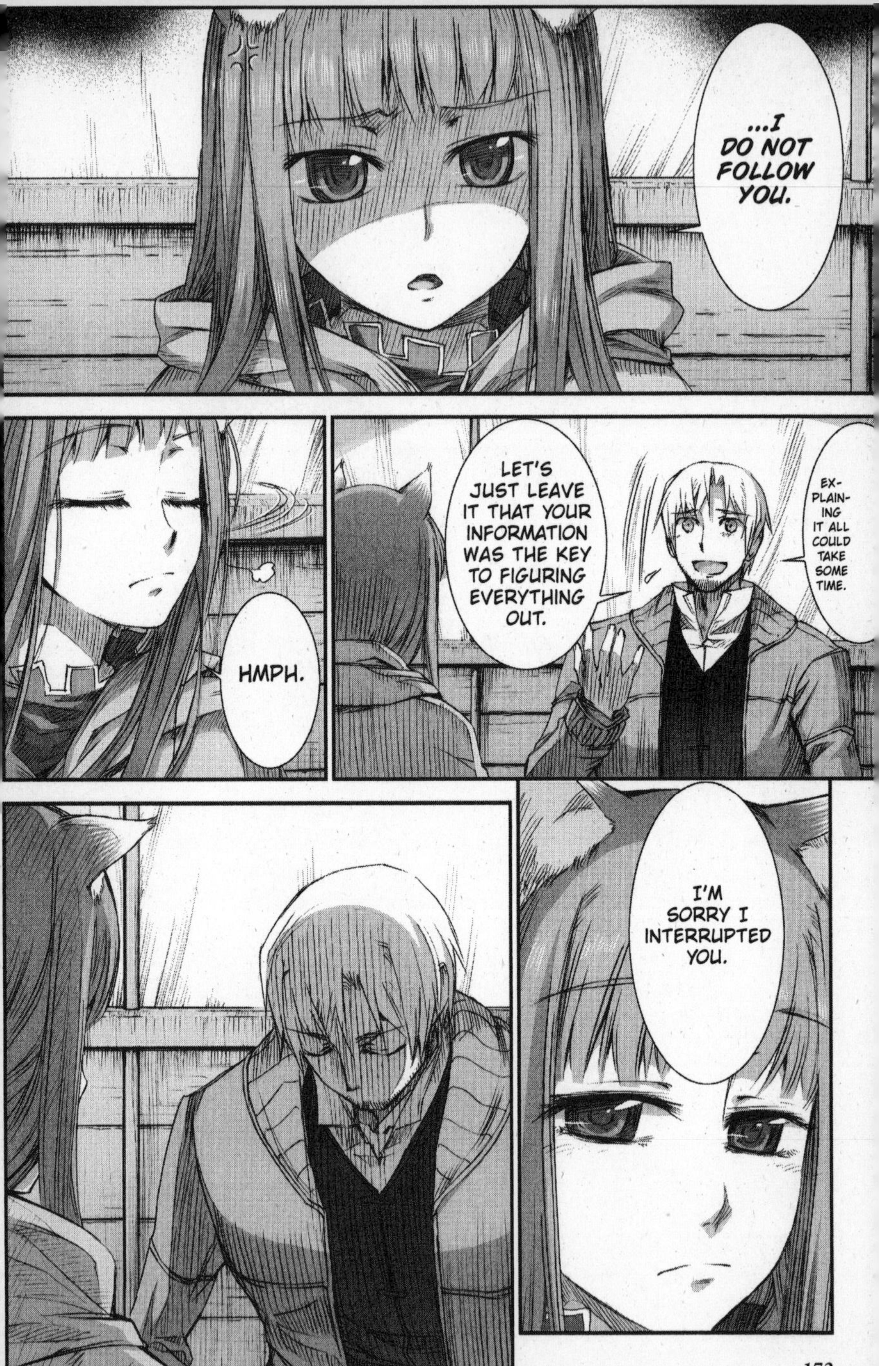
...I DO NOT FOLLOW YOU.
EX-PLAIN-ING IT ALL COULD TAKE SOME TIME.
LET'S JUST LEAVE IT THAT YOUR INFORMATION WAS THE KEY TO FIGURING EVERYTHING OUT.
HMPH.
I'M SORRY I INTERRUPTED YOU.

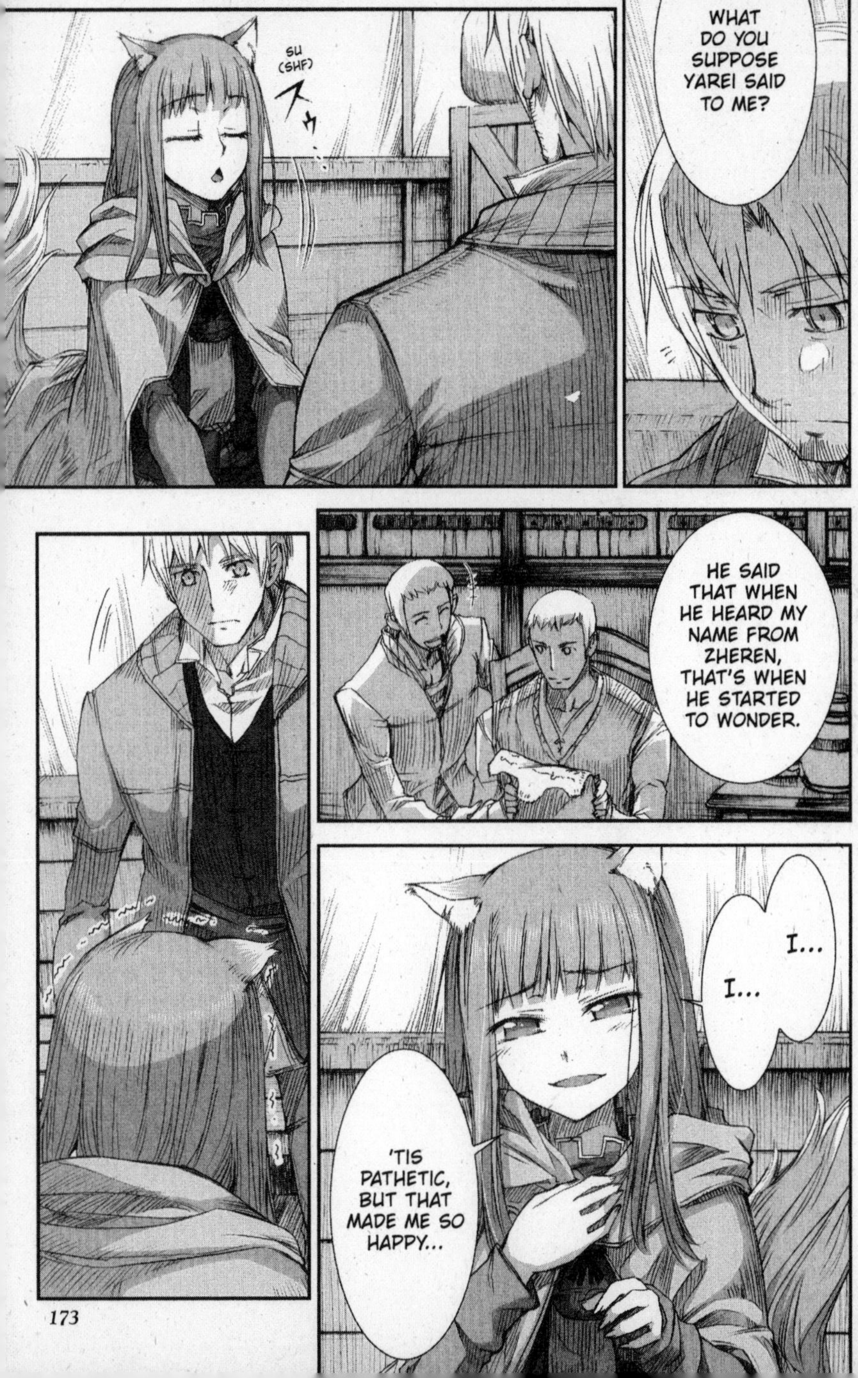
WHAT DO YOU SUPPOSE YAREI SAID TO ME?
SU (SHF)
スゥ…
HE SAID THAT WHEN HE HEARD MY NAME FROM ZHEREN, THAT'S WHEN HE STARTED TO WONDER.
I... I...
'TIS PATHETIC, BUT THAT MADE ME SO HAPPY...

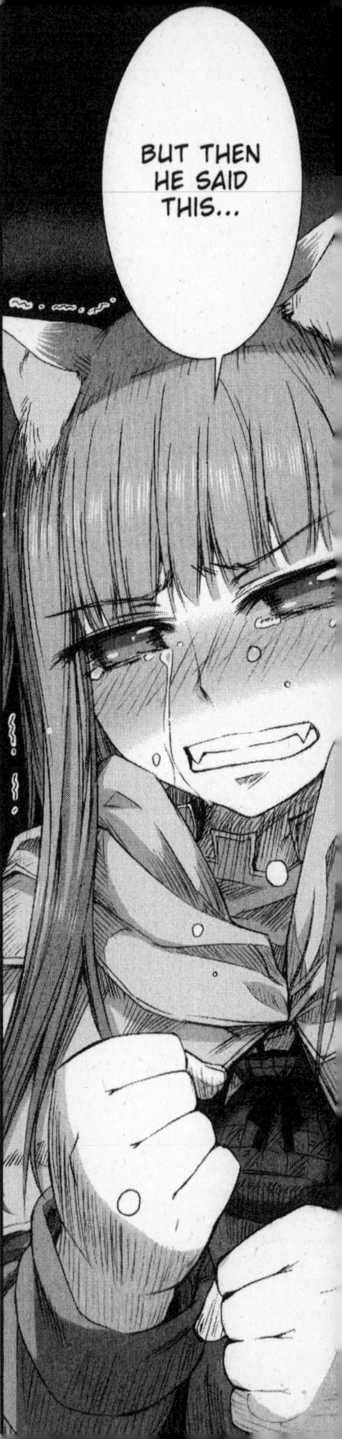
BUT THEN HE SAID THIS...
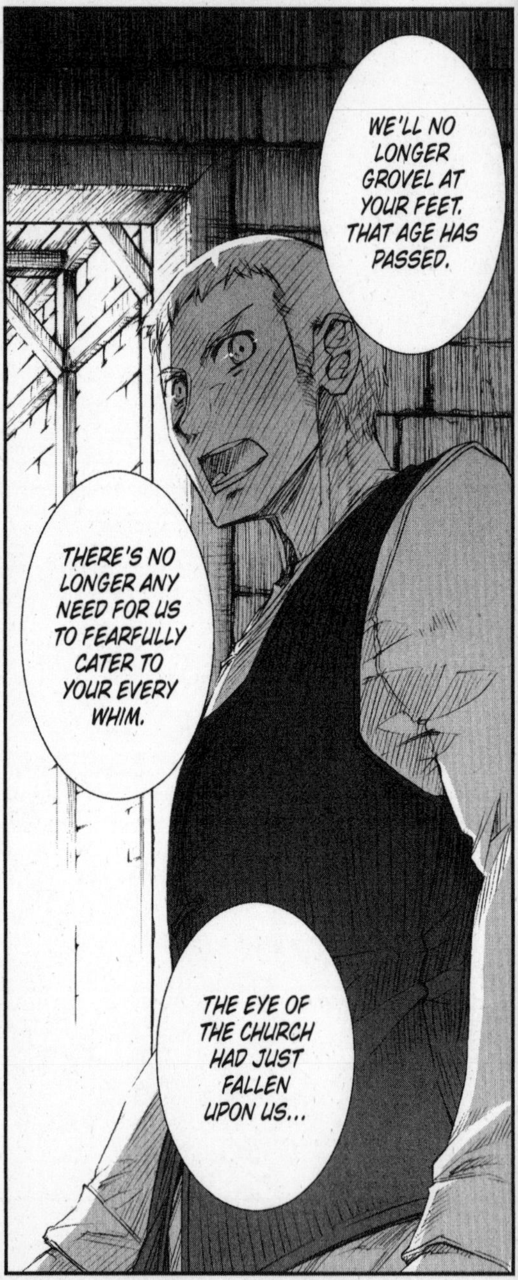
WE'LL NO LONGER GROVEL AT YOUR FEET. THAT AGE HAS PASSED.
THERE'S NO LONGER ANY NEED FOR US TO FEARFULLY CATER TO YOUR EVERY WHIM.
THE EYE OF THE CHURCH HAD JUST FALLEN UPON US...

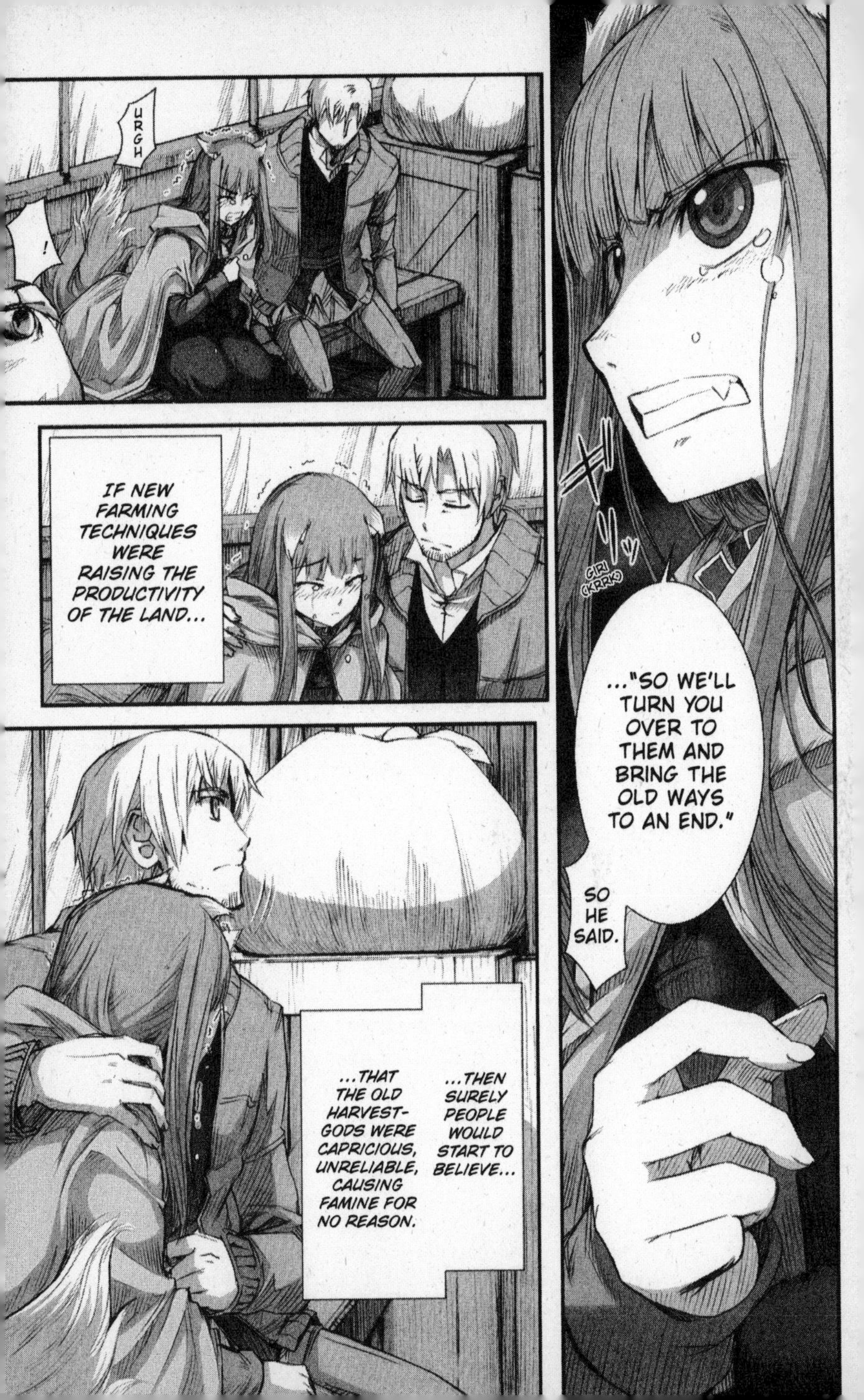
GIRI (KRRK)
..."SO WE'LL TURN YOU OVER TO THEM AND BRING THE OLD WAYS TO AN END."
SO HE SAID.
URGH
!
IF NEW FARMING TECHNIQUES WERE RAISING THE PRODUCTIVITY OF THE LAND...
...THEN SURELY PEOPLE WOULD START TO BELIEVE...
...THAT THE OLD HARVEST-GODS WERE CAPRICIOUS, UNRELIABLE, CAUSING FAMINE FOR NO REASON.

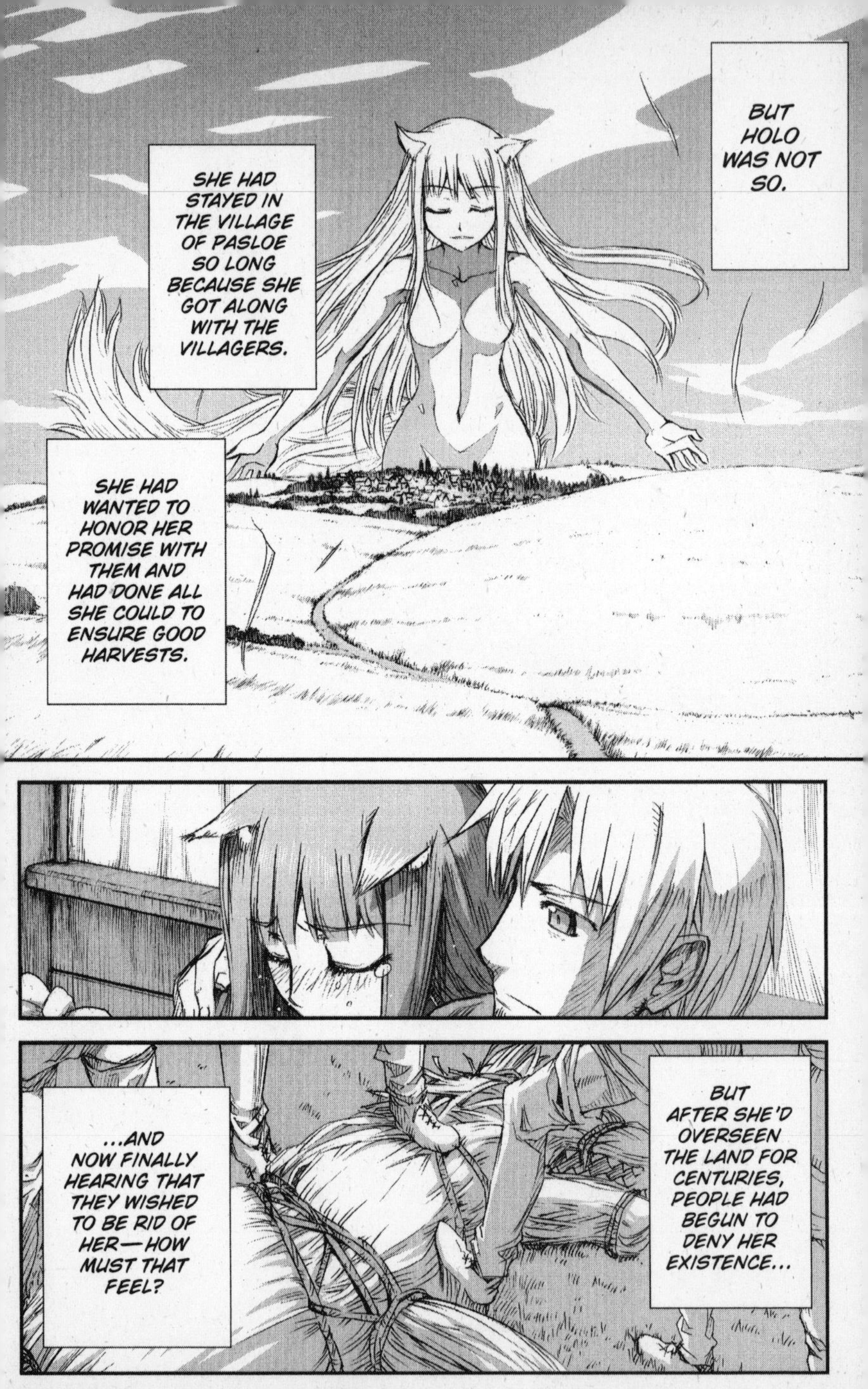
BUT HOLO WAS NOT SO.
SHE HAD STAYED IN THE VILLAGE OF PASLOE SO LONG BECAUSE SHE GOT ALONG WITH THE VILLAGERS.
SHE HAD WANTED TO HONOR HER PROMISE WITH THEM AND HAD DONE ALL SHE COULD TO ENSURE GOOD HARVESTS.
BUT AFTER SHE'D OVERSEEN THE LAND FOR CENTURIES, PEOPLE HAD BEGUN TO DENY HER EXISTENCE...
...AND NOW FINALLY HEARING THAT THEY WISHED TO BE RID OF HER—HOW MUST THAT FEEL?

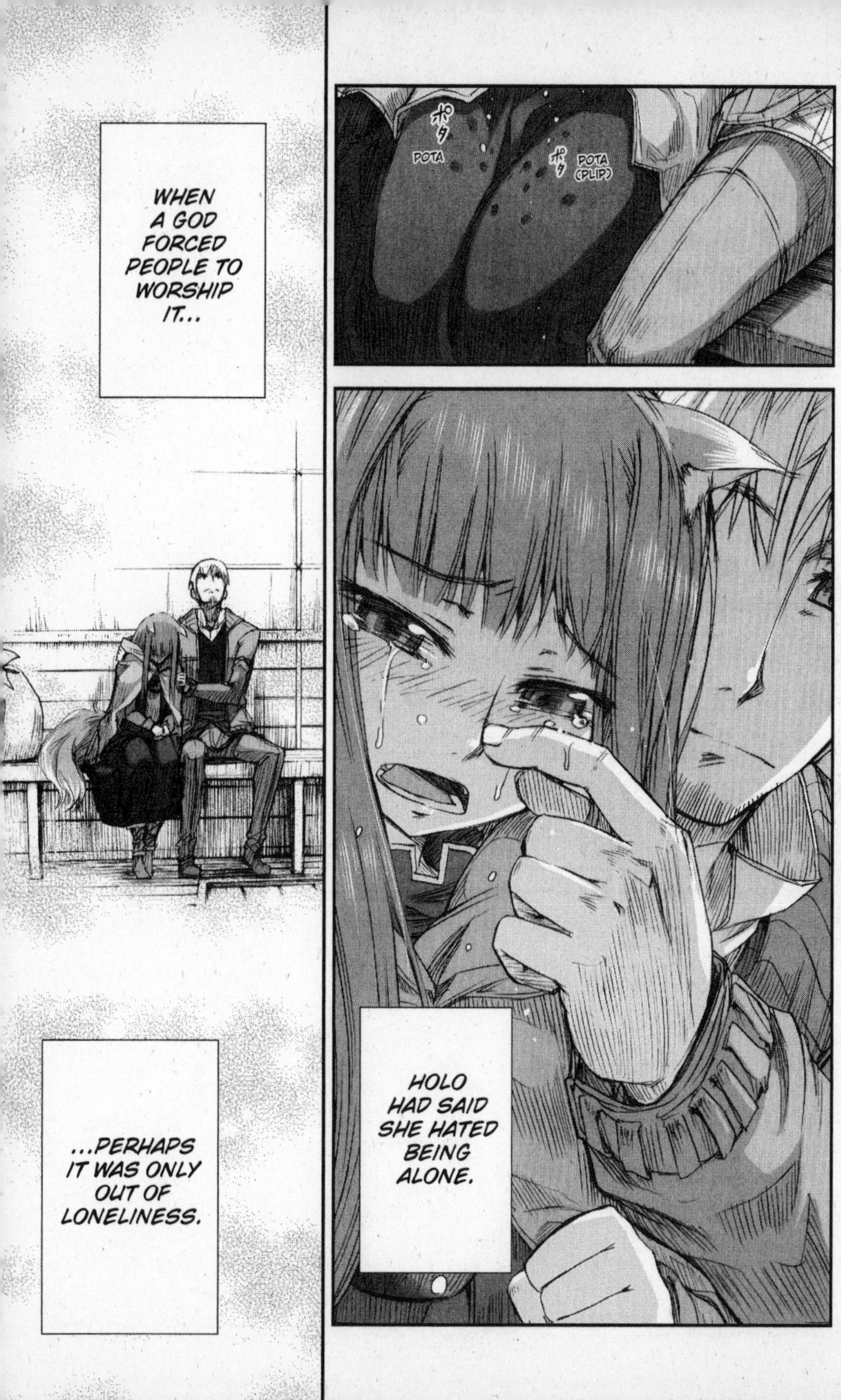
ポタ
POTA (PLIP)
ポタ
POTA
HOLO HAD SAID SHE HATED BEING ALONE.
WHEN A GOD FORCED PEOPLE TO WORSHIP IT...
...PERHAPS IT WAS ONLY OUT OF LONELINESS.

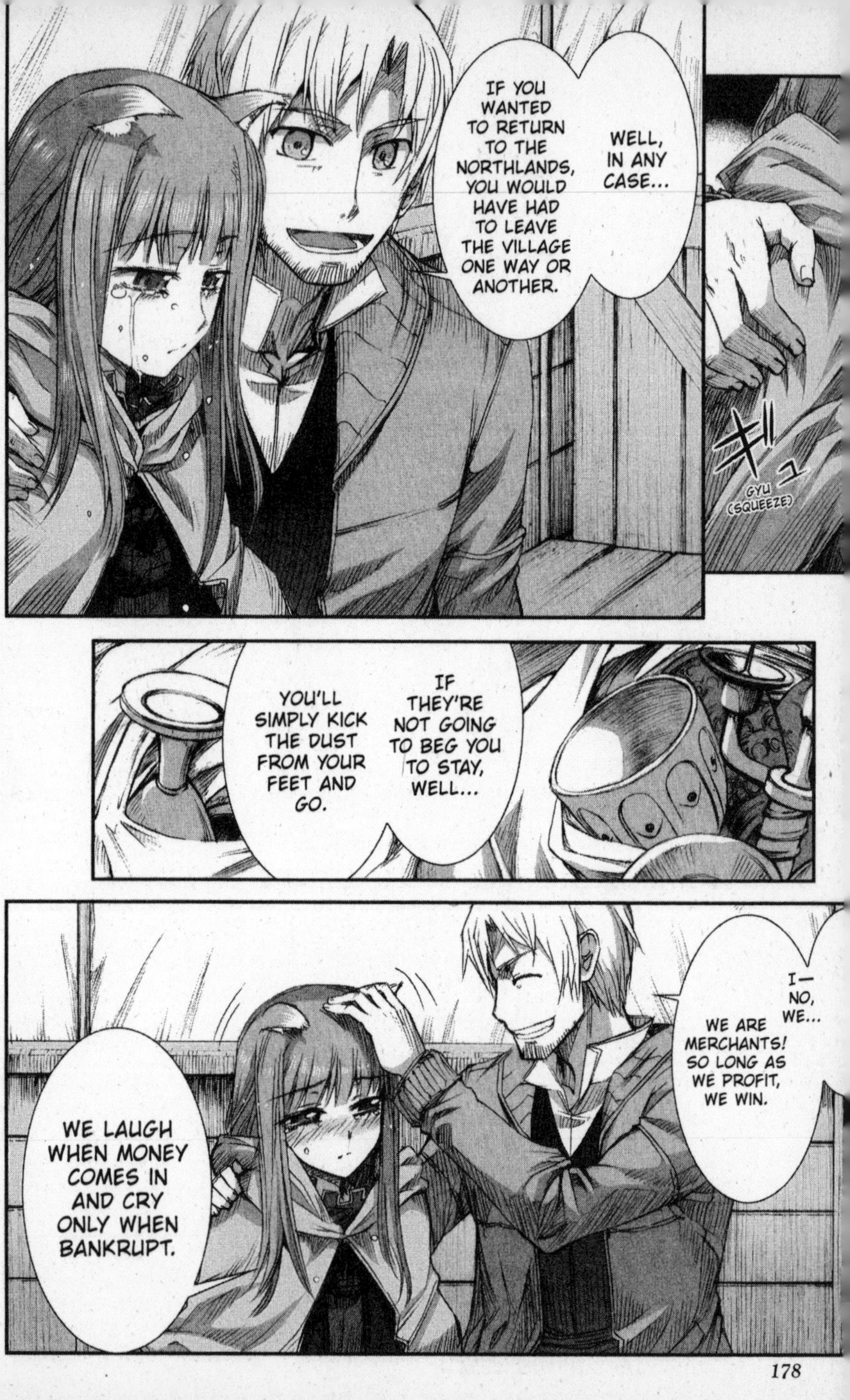
ギュ
GYU (SQUEEZE)
WELL, IN ANY CASE...
IF YOU WANTED TO RETURN TO THE NORTHLANDS, YOU WOULD HAVE HAD TO LEAVE THE VILLAGE ONE WAY OR ANOTHER.
IF THEY'RE NOT GOING TO BEG YOU TO STAY, WELL...
YOU'LL SIMPLY KICK THE DUST FROM YOUR FEET AND GO.
I— NO, WE...
WE ARE MERCHANTS! SO LONG AS WE PROFIT, WE WIN.
WE LAUGH WHEN MONEY COMES IN AND CRY ONLY WHEN BANKRUPT.

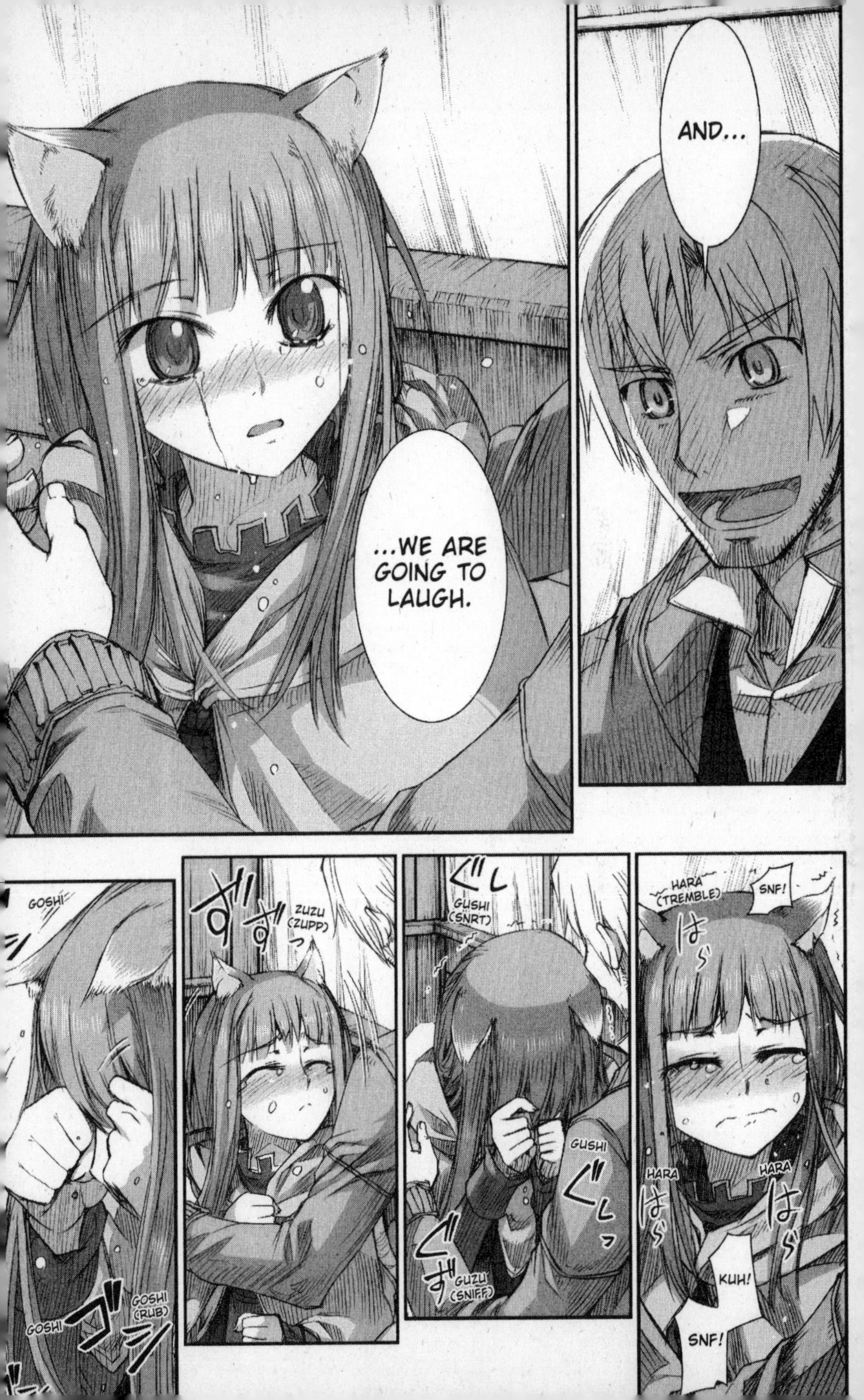
AND...
...WE ARE GOING TO LAUGH.
HARA (TREMBLE)
SNF!
HARA
HARA
KUH!
SNF!
GUSHI (SNRT)
GUSHI
GUZU (SNIFF)
ZUZU (ZUPP)
GOSHI
GOSHI (RUB)
GOSHI

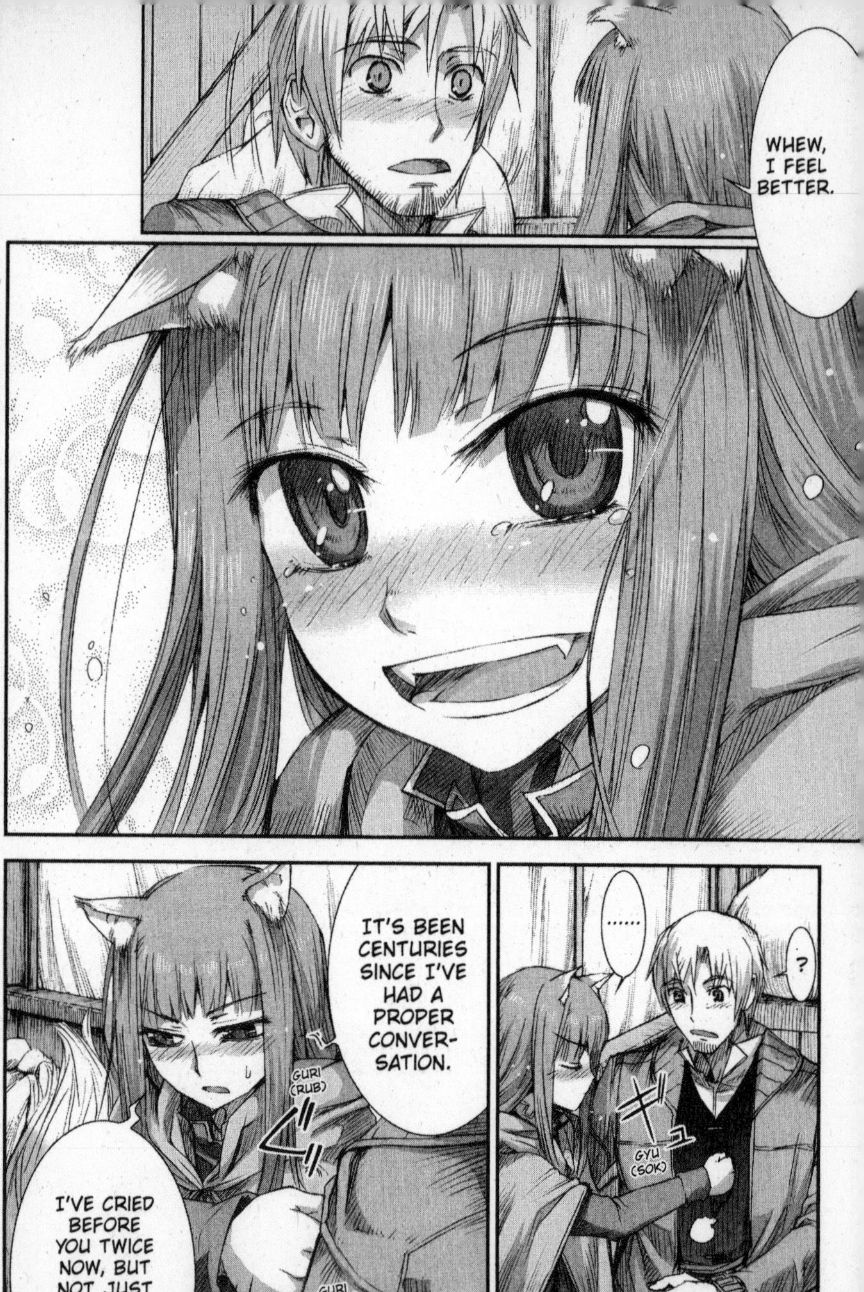
WHEW, I FEEL BETTER.
......
?
GYU (SOK)
IT'S BEEN CENTURIES SINCE I'VE HAD A PROPER CONVER-SATION.
GURI (RUB)
I'VE CRIED BEFORE YOU TWICE NOW, BUT NOT JUST BECAUSE YOU WERE THERE.
GURI

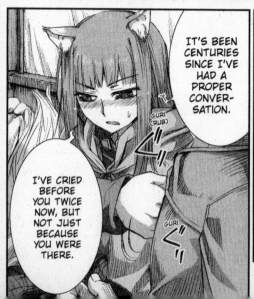

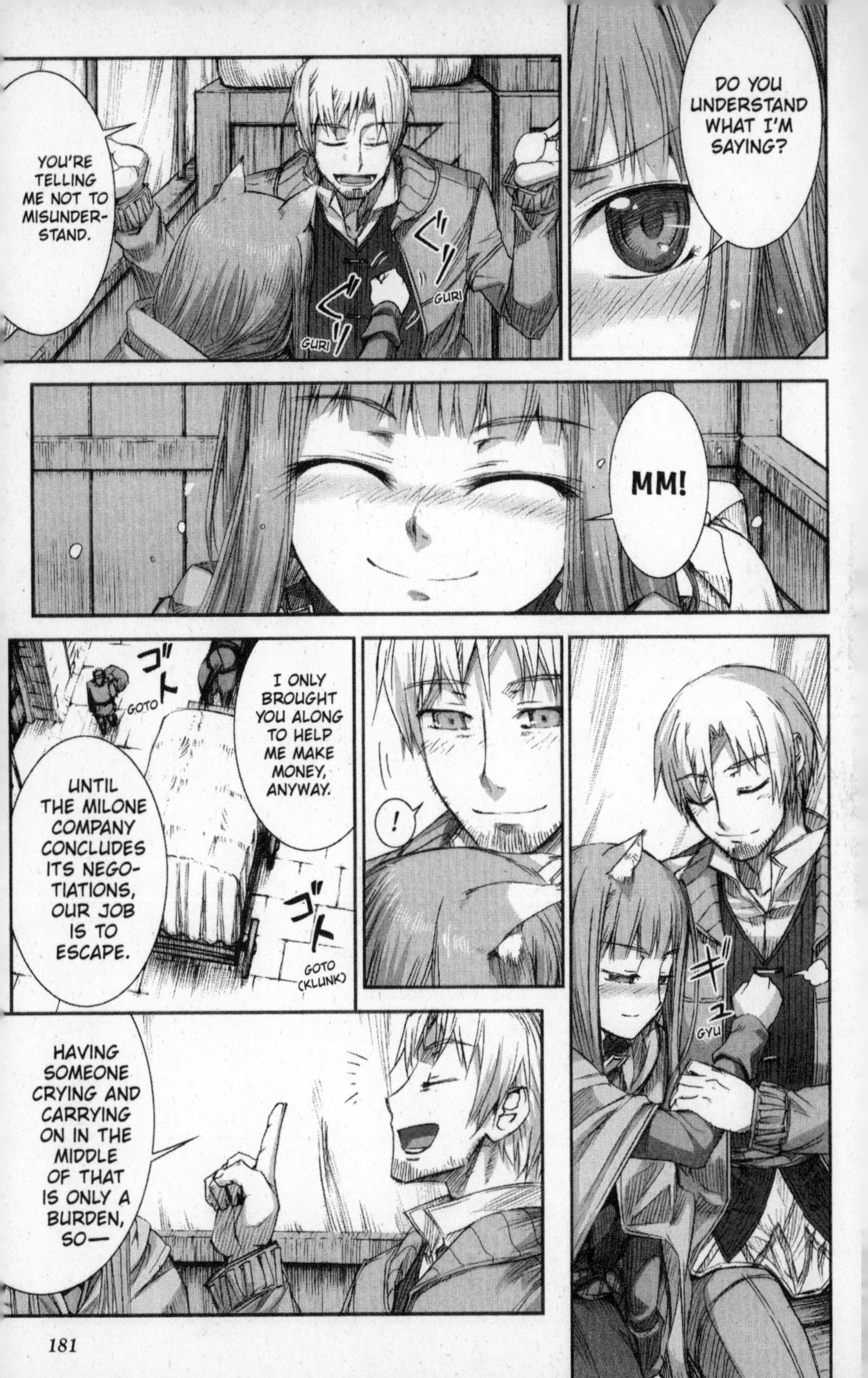
DO YOU UNDERSTAND WHAT I'M SAYING?
YOU'RE TELLING ME NOT TO MISUNDERSTAND.
ぐり GURI
ぐり GURI
MM!
ギュ GYU
!
ゴト GOTO (KLUNK)
ゴト GOTO
I ONLY BROUGHT YOU ALONG TO HELP ME MAKE MONEY, ANYWAY.
UNTIL THE MILONE COMPANY CONCLUDES ITS NEGOTIATIONS, OUR JOB IS TO ESCAPE.
HAVING SOMEONE CRYING AND CARRYING ON IN THE MIDDLE OF THAT IS ONLY A BURDEN, SO—

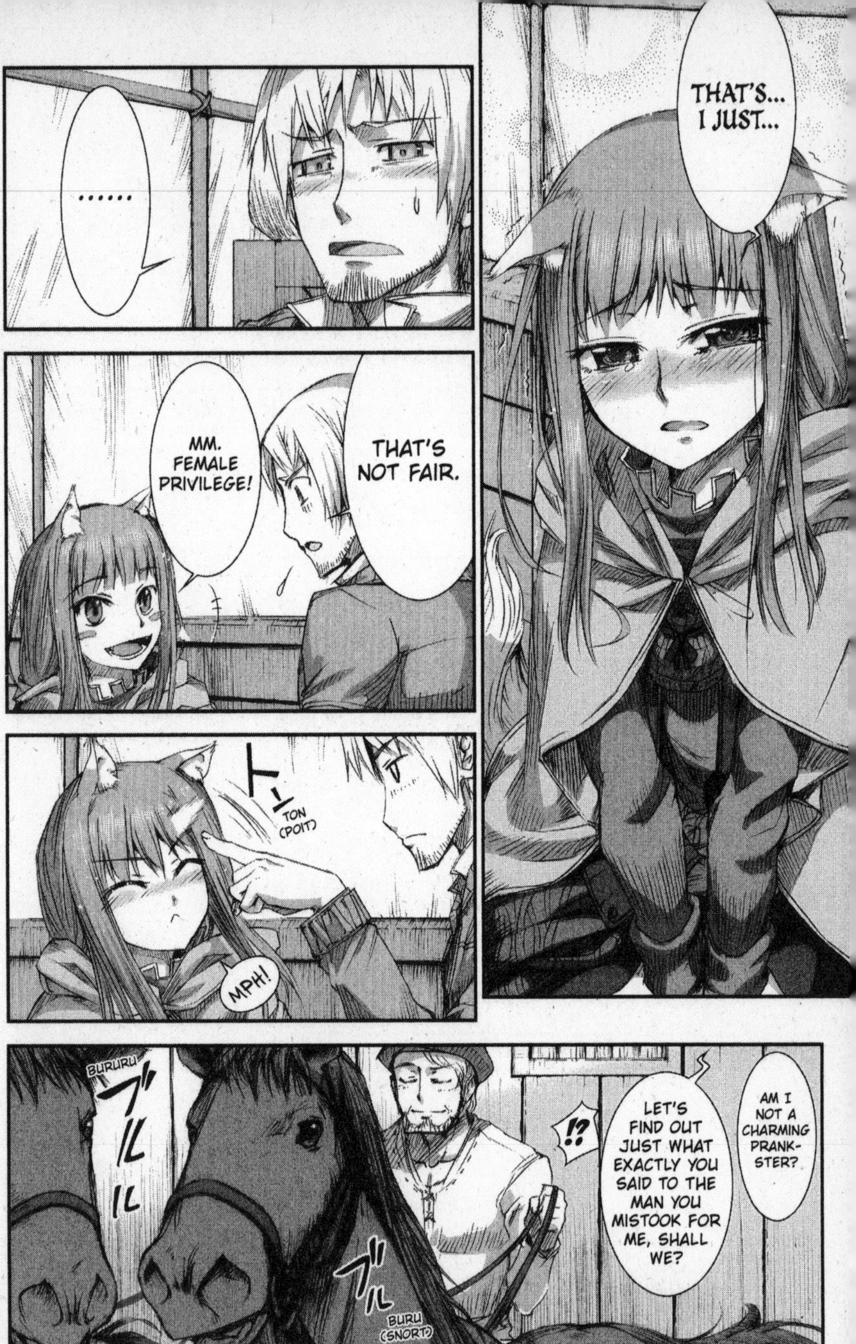
THAT'S... I JUST...
......
THAT'S NOT FAIR.
MM. FEMALE PRIVILEGE!
TON (POIT)
MPH!
AM I NOT A CHARMING PRANK-STER?
LET'S FIND OUT JUST WHAT EXACTLY YOU SAID TO THE MAN YOU MISTOOK FOR ME, SHALL WE?
!?
BURURU
BURU (SNORT)

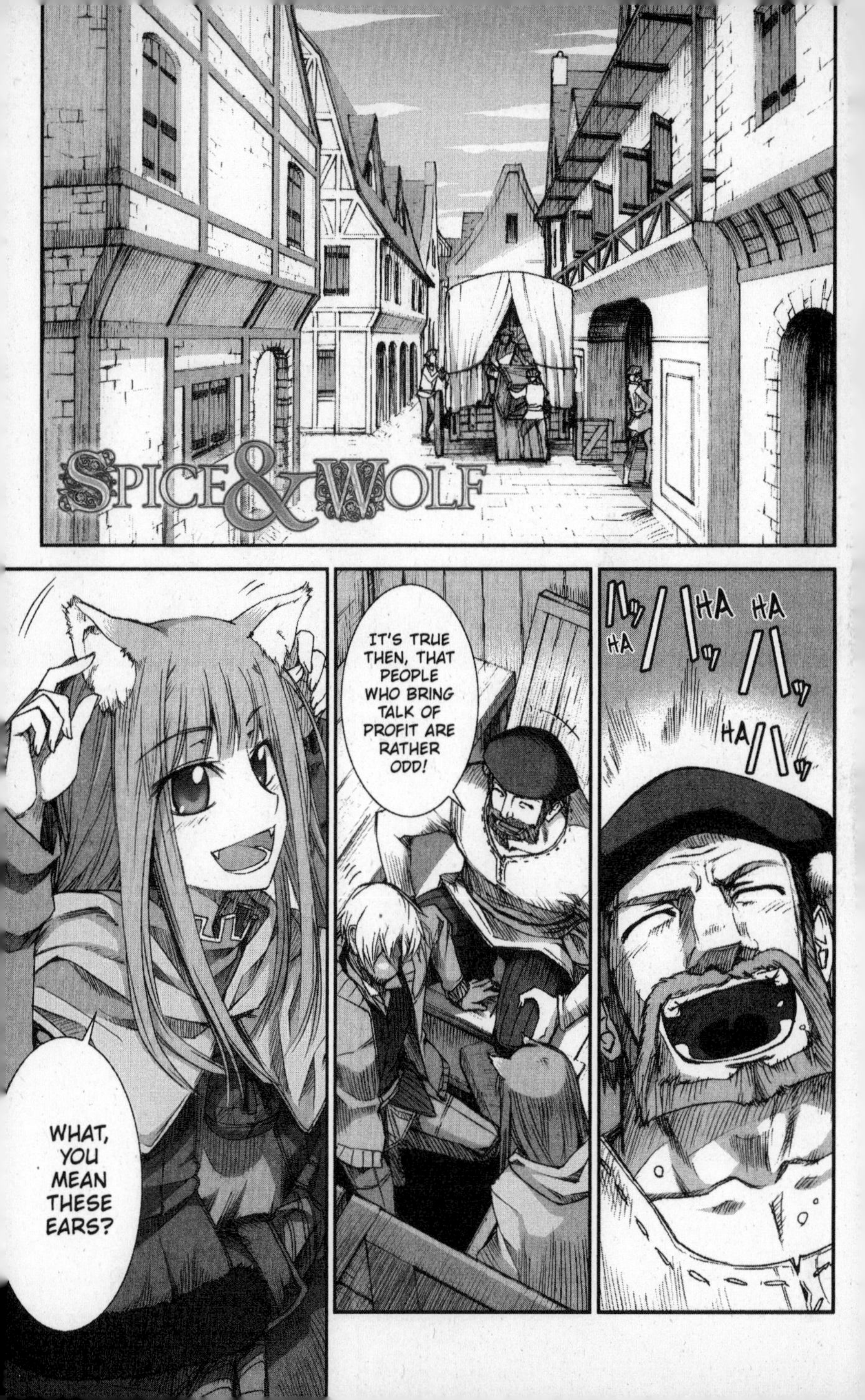
SPICE & WOLF
HA
HA
HA
HA
IT'S TRUE THEN, THAT PEOPLE WHO BRING TALK OF PROFIT ARE RATHER ODD!
WHAT, YOU MEAN THESE EARS?

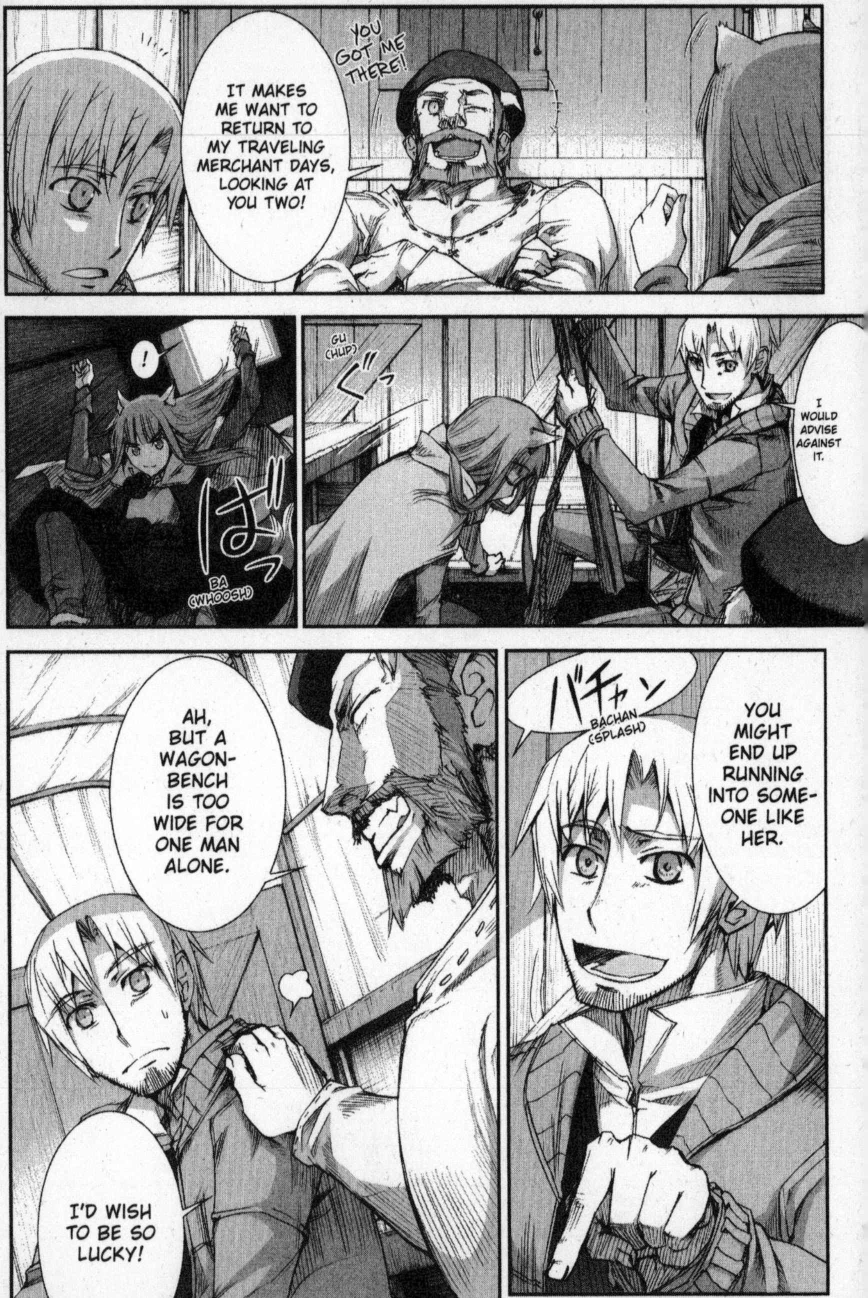
YOU GOT ME THERE!
IT MAKES ME WANT TO RETURN TO MY TRAVELING MERCHANT DAYS, LOOKING AT YOU TWO!
I WOULD ADVISE AGAINST IT.
ぐっ
GU (HUP)
!
ばっ
BA (WHOOSH)
バチャン
BACHAN (SPLASH)
YOU MIGHT END UP RUNNING INTO SOME-ONE LIKE HER.
AH, BUT A WAGON-BENCH IS TOO WIDE FOR ONE MAN ALONE.
I'D WISH TO BE SO LUCKY!

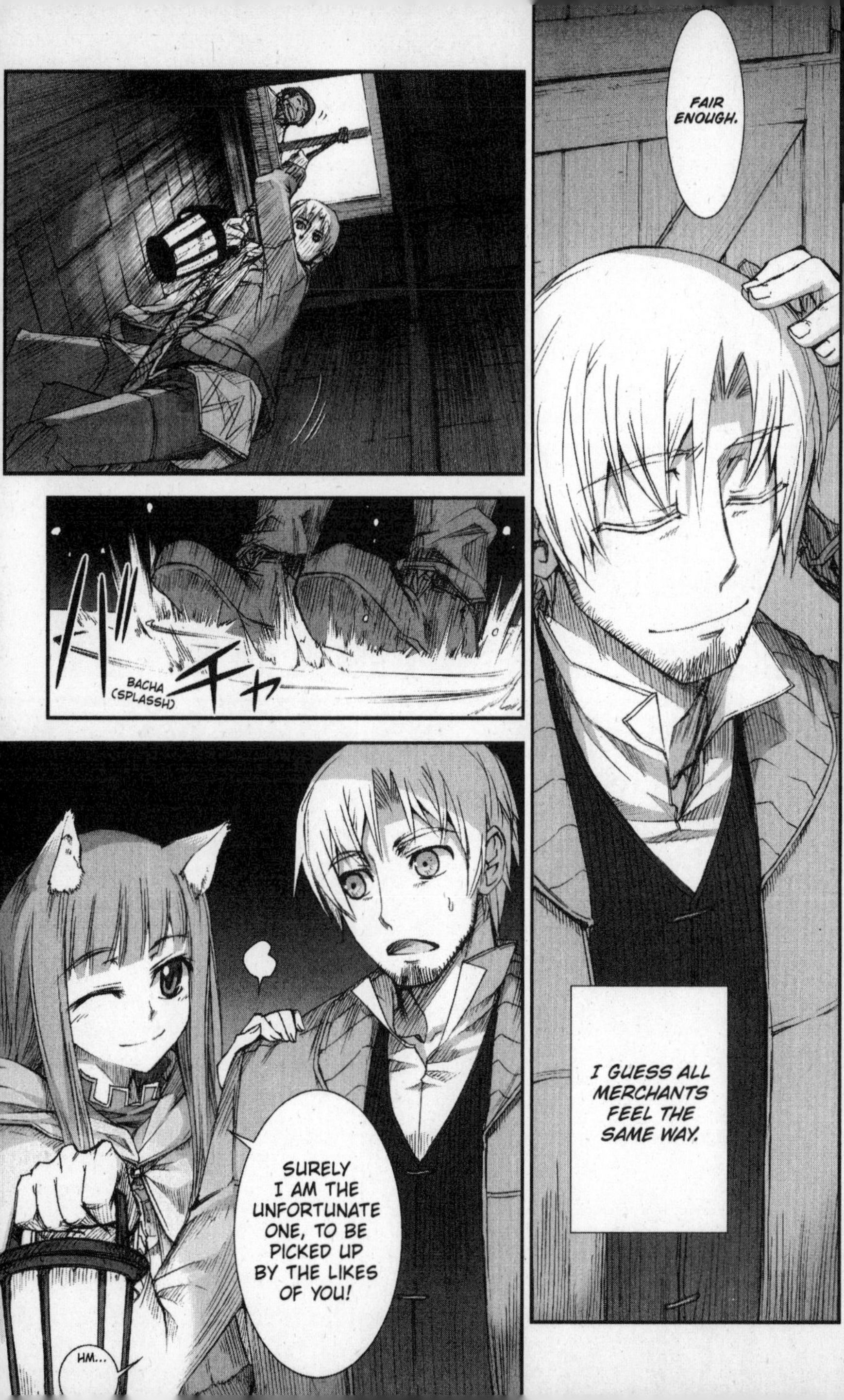
FAIR ENOUGH.
I GUESS ALL MERCHANTS FEEL THE SAME WAY.
BACHA (SPLASSH)
SURELY I AM THE UNFORTUNATE ONE, TO BE PICKED UP BY THE LIKES OF YOU!
HM...

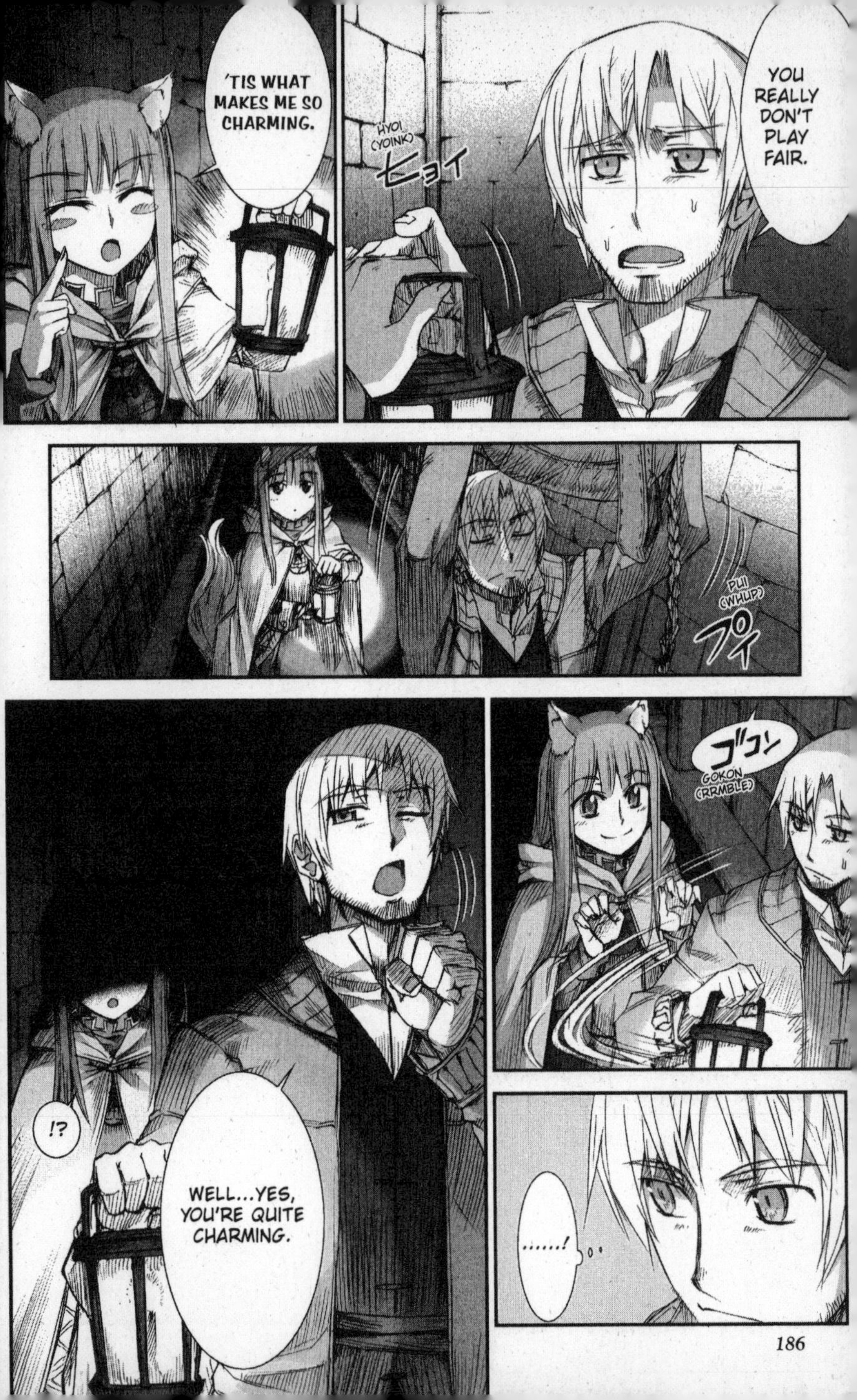
YOU REALLY DON'T PLAY FAIR.
HYOI (YOINK) ヒョイ
'TIS WHAT MAKES ME SO CHARMING.
PUI (WHUP) プイ
ゴコン GOKON (RRMBLE)
......!
WELL...YES, YOU'RE QUITE CHARMING.
!?

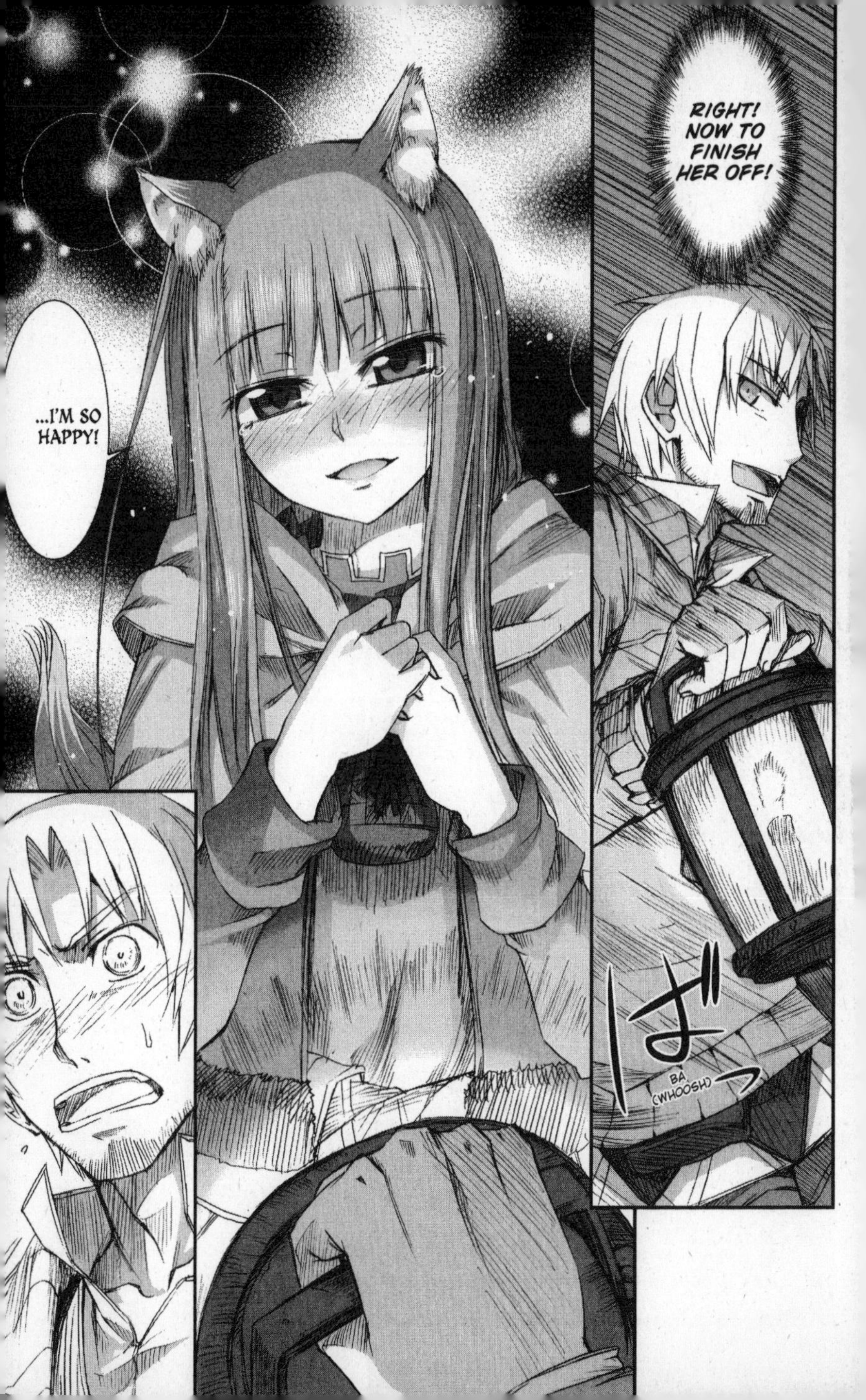
RIGHT! NOW TO FINISH HER OFF!
ばっ
BA (WHOOSH)
...I'M SO HAPPY!

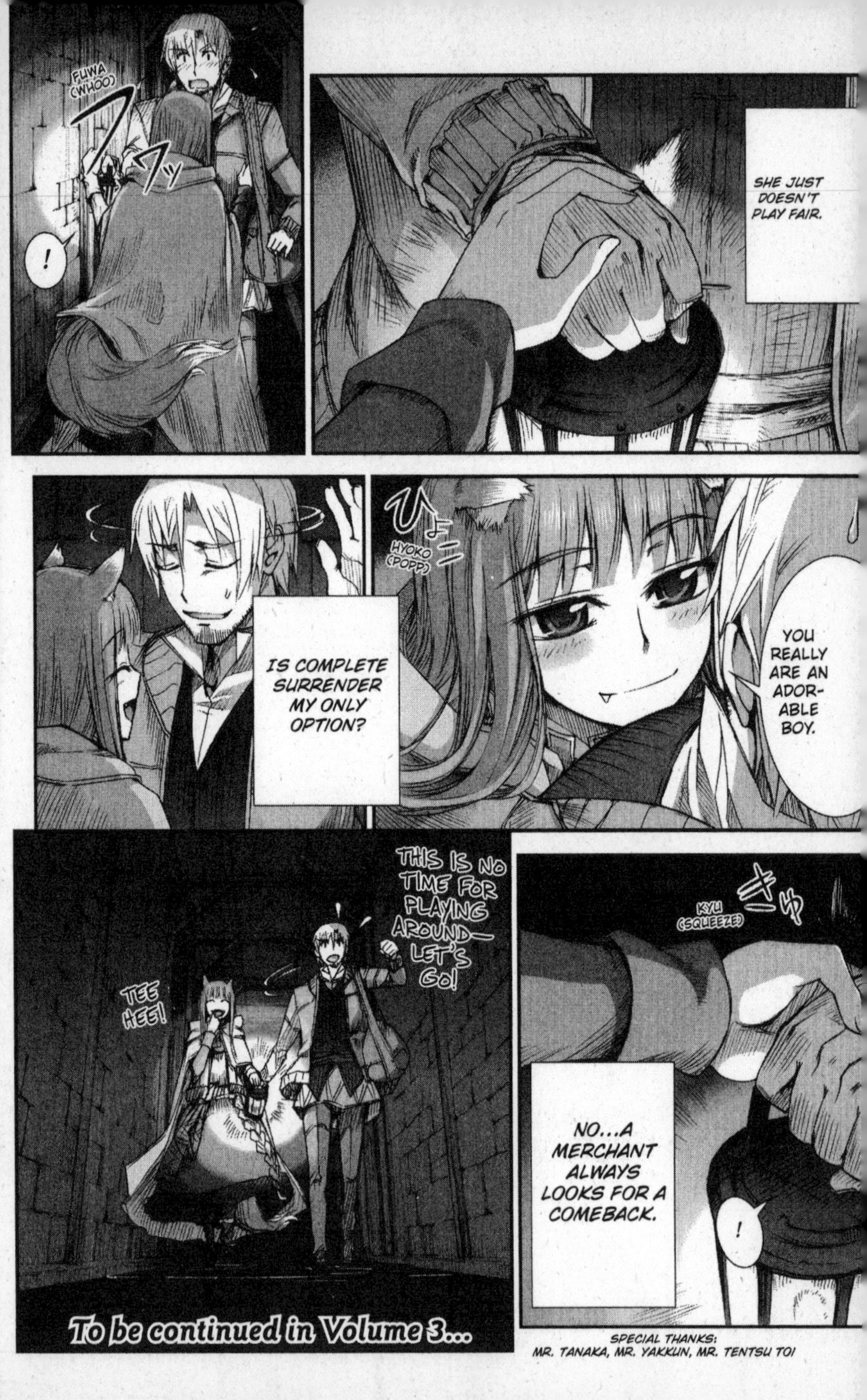
SHE JUST DOESN'T PLAY FAIR.
FUWA (WHOO)
!
HYOKO (POPP)
YOU REALLY ARE AN ADOR-ABLE BOY.
IS COMPLETE SURRENDER MY ONLY OPTION?
KYU (SQUEEZE)
NO...A MERCHANT ALWAYS LOOKS FOR A COMEBACK.
!
THIS IS NO TIME FOR PLAYING AROUND—LET'S GO!
TEE HEE!
To be continued in Volume 3...

SPECIAL THANKS:
MR. TANAKA, MR. YAKKUN, MR. TENTSU TOI

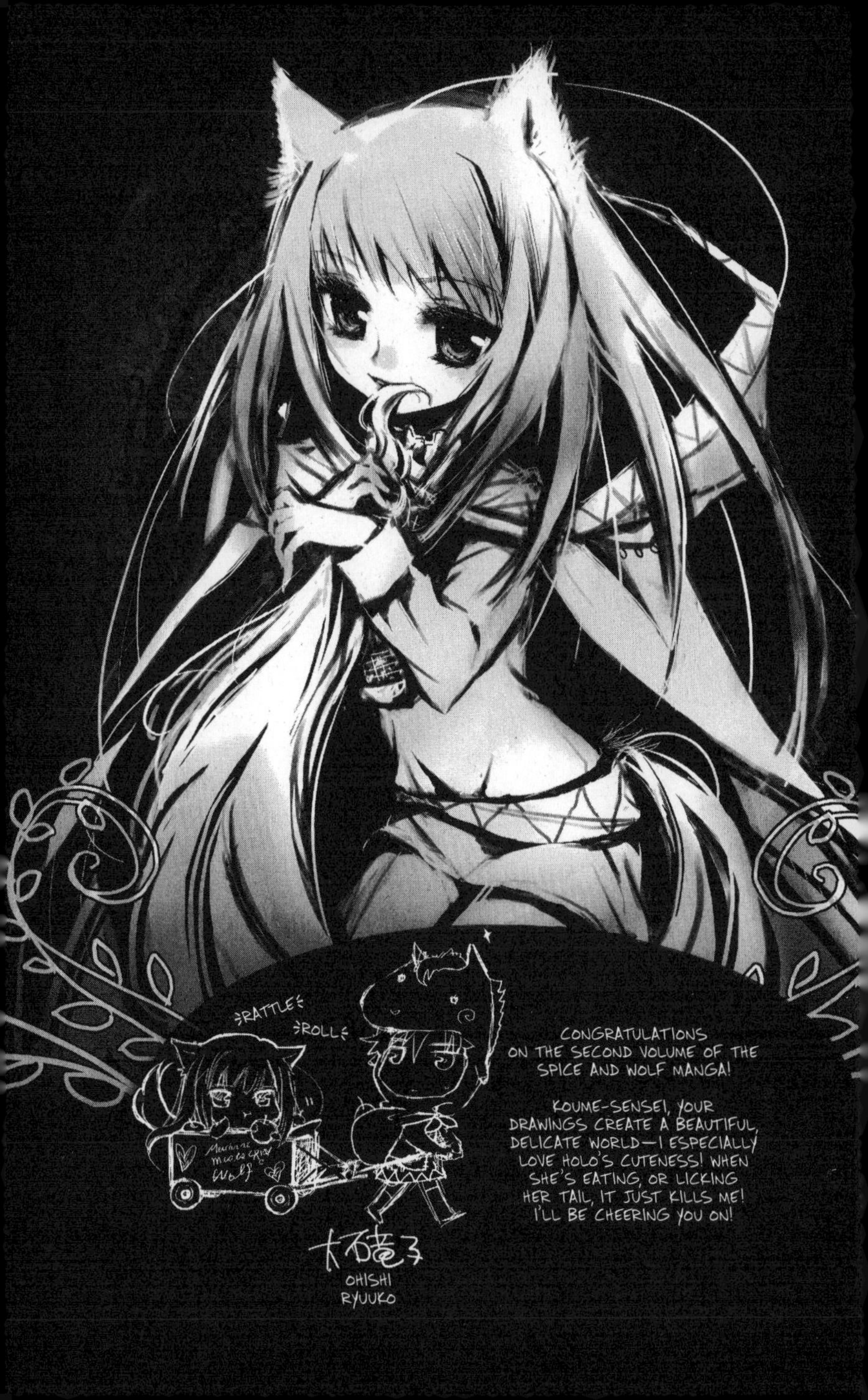

RATTLE
ROLL
CONGRATULATIONS ON THE SECOND VOLUME OF THE SPICE AND WOLF MANGA!
KOUME-SENSEI, YOUR DRAWINGS CREATE A BEAUTIFUL, DELICATE WORLD—I ESPECIALLY LOVE HOLO'S CUTENESS! WHEN SHE'S EATING, OR LICKING HER TAIL, IT JUST KILLS ME! I'LL BE CHEERING YOU ON!
大石竜子
OHISHI RYUUKO

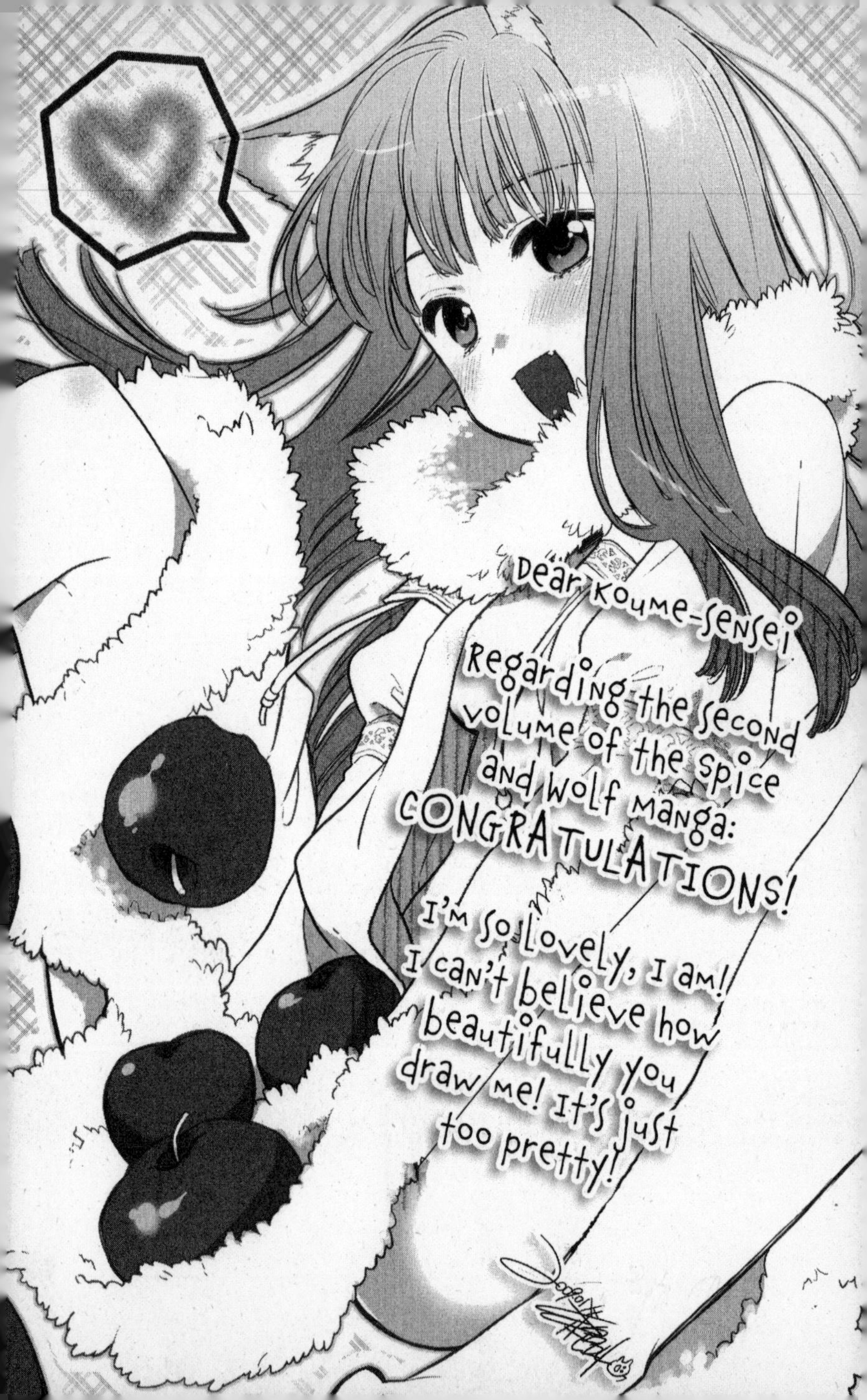
Dear Koume-sensei
Regarding the second volume of the Spice and Wolf manga:
CONGRATULATIONS!
I'm so lovely, I am! I can't believe how beautifully you draw me! It's just too pretty!

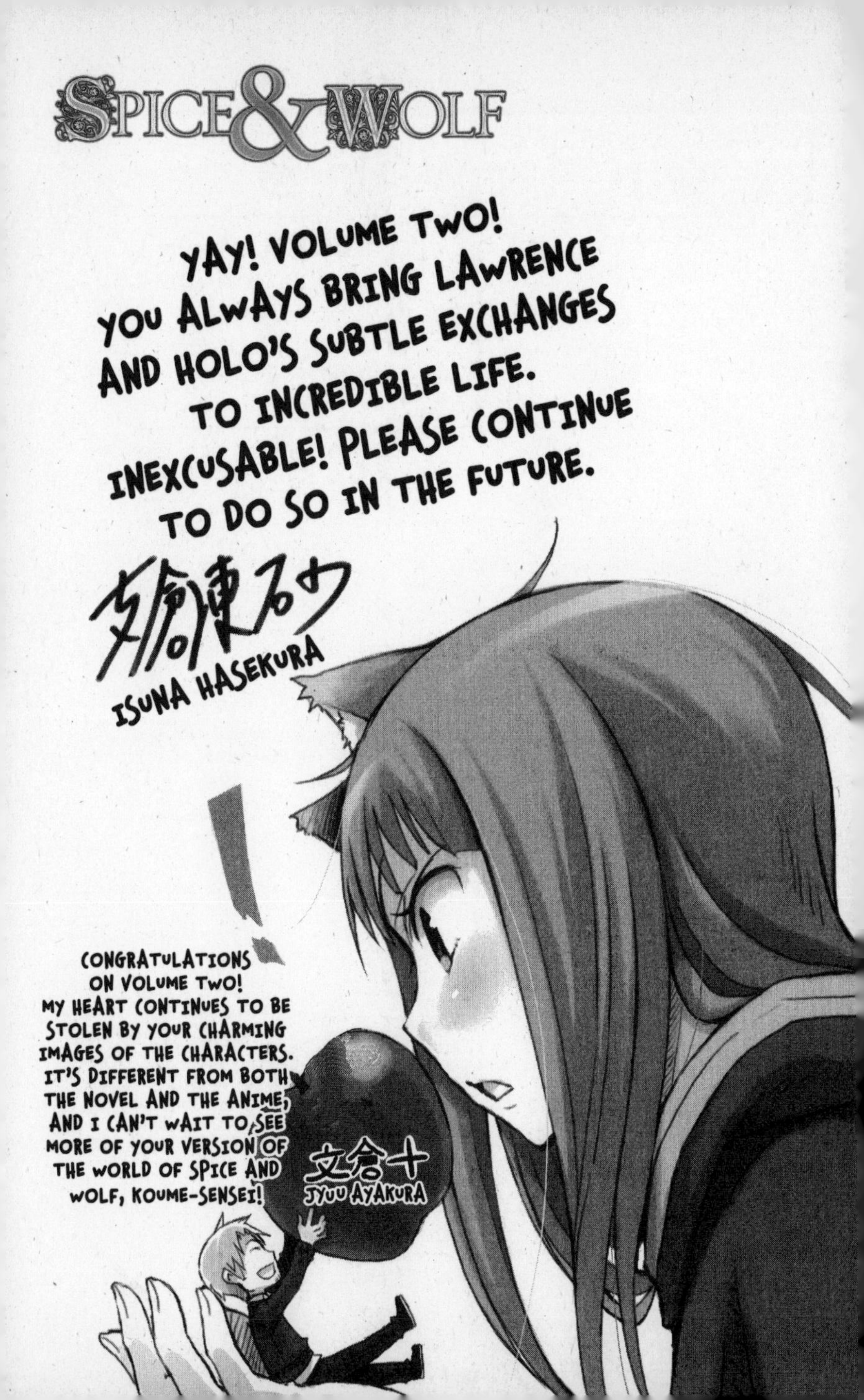
SPICE & WOLF
YAY! VOLUME TWO!
YOU ALWAYS BRING LAWRENCE AND HOLO'S SUBTLE EXCHANGES TO INCREDIBLE LIFE.
INEXCUSABLE! PLEASE CONTINUE TO DO SO IN THE FUTURE.
支倉凍砂
ISUNA HASEKURA
!
CONGRATULATIONS ON VOLUME TWO!
MY HEART CONTINUES TO BE STOLEN BY YOUR CHARMING IMAGES OF THE CHARACTERS. IT'S DIFFERENT FROM BOTH THE NOVEL AND THE ANIME, AND I CAN'T WAIT TO SEE MORE OF YOUR VERSION OF THE WORLD OF SPICE AND WOLF, KOUME-SENSEI!
文倉十
JYUU AYAKURA

SPICE & WOLF ❷

Isuna Hasekura
Keito Koume

Translation: Paul Starr

Lettering: Terri Delgado

OOKAMI TO KOUSHINRYO Vol. 2 © Isuna Hasekura / ASCII
MEDIA WORKS 2009 © Keito Koume 2009. All rights reserved. First
published in Japan in 2009 by ASCII MEDIA WORKS INC., Tokyo.
English translation rights in USA, Canada, and UK arranged with
ASCII MEDIA WORKS INC. through Tuttle-Mori Agency, Inc., Tokyo.

Translation © 2010 by Hachette Book Group

Yen Press
Hachette Book Group
237 Park Avenue, New York, NY 10017

www.HachetteBookGroup.com
www.YenPress.com

Yen Press is an imprint of Hachette Book Group, Inc. The Yen Press
name and logo are trademarks of Hachette Book Group, Inc.

First Yen Press Edition: July 2010

ISBN-13: 978-0-316-10232-2

10 9 8 7 6 5 4 3 2 1

BVG

Printed in the United States of America